Lecture Notes in Artificial Intelligence   4772

Edited by J. G. Carbonell and J. Siekmann

Subseries of Lecture Notes in Computer Science

Henri Prade   V.S. Subrahmanian (Eds.)

Scalable Uncertainty Management

First International Conference, SUM 2007
Washington, DC, USA, October 10-12, 2007
Proceedings

 Springer

Series Editors

Jaime G. Carbonell, Carnegie Mellon University, Pittsburgh, PA, USA
Jörg Siekmann, University of Saarland, Saarbrücken, Germany

Volume Editors

Henri Prade
Université Paul Sabatier
IRIT
118 route de Narbonne, 31062 Toulouse Cedex, France
E-mail: prade@irit.fr

V.S. Subrahmanian
University of Maryland
Department of Computer Science and UMIACS
AV Williams Building, College Park MD 20742, USA
E-mail: vs@cs.umd.edu

Library of Congress Control Number: 2007936370

CR Subject Classification (1998): I.2, F.4.1

LNCS Sublibrary: SL 7 – Artificial Intelligence

ISSN   0302-9743
ISBN-10   3-540-75407-5 Springer Berlin Heidelberg New York
ISBN-13   978-3-540-75407-7 Springer Berlin Heidelberg New York

Springer is a part of Springer Science+Business Media

springer.com

© Springer-Verlag Berlin Heidelberg 2007
Printed in Germany

Typesetting: Camera-ready by author, data conversion by Scientific Publishing Services, Chennai, India
Printed on acid-free paper   SPIN: 12168651   06/3180   5 4 3 2 1 0

Preface

Although there has been extensive work on the management of uncertainty, relatively little work has been done on efficient and scalable methods to manage the uncertainty that arises in real-world applications. While the artificial intelligence community has studied mathematical models of uncertainty and developed many useful applications, the database community has focused on building uncertainty tools directly into underlying database infrastructure.

The goal of the Scalable Uncertainty Management (SUM) conference is to take the first steps toward bringing together artificial intelligence researchers, database researchers, and practitioners to see how the best theoretical techniques can be made to scale up to the needs of large-scale applications.

SUM 2007 used a rigorous refereeing procedure to review all papers. Papers by the PC chairs were reviewed by a subcommittee unknown to the PC chairs. After this review process, we accepted a total of 20 papers which are presented in this volume.

October 2007

Henri Prade
V.S. Subrahmanian

Organization

SUM 2007 was organized by the University of Maryland Institute for Advanced Computer Studies (UMIACS), University of Marlyand College Park.

Executive Committee

Conference General Chair   Didier Dubois (Paul Sabatier University, France)

Program Chairs   Henri Prade (Paul Sabatier University, France)
V.S. Subrahmanian (University of Maryland, USA)

Publicity Chair   Andrea Pugliese (University of Calabria, Italy)

Program Committee

Chitta Baral (Arizona State University, USA)
Leo Bertossi (Carleton University, Canada)
Bir Bhanu (University of California-Riverside, USA)
Val Breazu-Tannen (University of Pennsylvania, USA)
Rama Chellappa (University of Maryland, USA)
Laurence Cholvy (ONERA, France)
Jan Chomicki (State University of NY-Buffalo, USA)
Amol Deshpande (University of Maryland, USA)
Guy De Tre (Ghent University, Belgium)
Luc de Raedt (K.U. Leuven, Belgium)
Michael Dekhtyar (Tver State University, Russia)
Debabrata Dey (University of Washington - Seattle, USA)
Juergen Dix (Tech. University Clausthal, Germany)
Thomas Eiter (Tech. University of Vienna, Austria)
Ronald Fagin (IBM Almaden, USA)
Andrew Frank (Tech. University of Vienna, Austria)
Lise Getoor (University of Maryland, USA)
John Grant (Towson University, USA)
Eyke Huellermeier (University of Magdeburg, Germany)
Edward Hung (Hong Kong Polytechnic University)
Anthony Hunter (University College London, UK)
Michael Kifer (State University of New York - Stonybrook, USA)
Sarit Kraus (Bar-Ilan University Israel)
Mounia Lalmas (Queen Mary University London, UK)
Weiru Liu (Queen's University Belfast, UK)
Laks V.S. Lakshmanan (University of British Columbia, Canada)

Thomas Lukasiewicz (University of Rome "La Sapienza", Italy)
Serafin Moral (University of Granada, Spain)
Nicola Leone (University of Calabria, Italy)
Raymond Ng (University of British Columbia, Canada)
Mads Nygaard (Norwegian University of Science and Tech., Norway)
Simon Parsons (City University of New York)
Gabriella Pasi (University of Milan, Italy)
Antonio Picariello (University of Naples, Italy)
Mike Pitarelli (State University of NY - Utica, USA)
Andrea Pugliese (University of Calabria, Italy)
Nick Roussopoulos (University of Maryland, USA)
Emad Saad (Abu Dhabi University, UAE)
Daniel Sanchez (University of Granada, Spain)
Maria-Luisa Sapino (University of Turin, Italy)
Yufei Tao (Chinese University of Hong Kong)
Nic Wilson (Cork Constraint Computation Center, Ireland)

Referees

Amol Deshpande	Gerardo Simari	Maria Luisa Sapino
Anthony Hunter	Gerhard Navratil	Massimo Ruffolo
Antonio Picariello	Guy De Tr	Michael Dekhtyar
Axel Polleres	Henri Prade	Michael Fink
Chitta Baral	Hui Wan	Mounia Lalmas
Daniel Sanchez	Jan Chomicki	Rama Chellappa
Debabrata Dey	John Grant	Ronald Fagin
Didier Dubois	Juergen Dix	Serafin Moral
Edward Hung	Laks V.S. Lakshmanan	Thomas Lukasiewicz
Emad Saad	Leopoldo Bertossi	Val Tannen
Eyke Huellermeier	Lise Getoor	V.S. Subrahmanian
Francesco Calimeri	Luigi Palopoli	Weiru Liu
Francesco Ricca	Mads Nygaard	
Gabriella Pasi	Mantas Simkus	

Sponsoring Institutions

This conference was supported in part by the University of Maryland Institute for Advanced Computer Studies

Table of Contents

Probabilistic Planning in Hybrid Probabilistic Logic Programs

Emad Saad

College of Computer Science and Information Technology
Abu Dhabi University
Abu Dhabi, UAE
emad.saad@adu.ac.ae

Abstract. In this paper, we present a new approach to probabilistic planning based on logic programming, by relating probabilistic planning to hybrid probabilistic logic programs with probabilistic answer set semantics [32]. We show that any probabilistic planning problem, $\mathcal{P}$, can be translated into a hybrid probabilistic logic program whose probabilistic answer sets correspond to trajectories in $\mathcal{P}$, with associated probabilities. We formally prove the correctness of our approach. Moreover, we show that the complexity of finding a plan for a probabilistic planning problem in our approach is NP-complete. In addition, we show that any probabilistic planning problem, $\mathcal{P}$, can be encoded as a classical logic program with answer set semantics, whose answer sets corresponds to valid trajectories in $\mathcal{P}$. We also show that probabilistic planning problems can be encoded as proportional satisfiability problems.

1 Introduction

An important limitation to classical planning, in general, and logic-based planning, in particular, is that it underlies strong and unrealistic assumptions which limits its applicability to many real-world domains [23]. Therefore, based on the success of the classical planning as propositional satisfiability (SAT planning) [15], a probabilistic planning approach has been presented in [22]. The probabilistic extension to SAT planning in [22] is developed by converting a probabilistic planning problem into a stochastic satisfiability problem and solving the stochastic satisfiability problem instead to generate plans. However, the problems with SAT planning in general are that [23] translating a planning problem as propositional satisfiability (SAT) problem causes an explosion in the size of the problem representation compared to the other planning approaches, which affects the performance of the planner. Moreover, encoding a planning problem as a SAT problem affects the planning problem structure which makes it not obvious to clearly understand the planning process. Consequently, this leads to a difficulty in using our knowledge and intuition about the planning process to construct search heuristics. Moreover, solving a probabilistic planning problem as a stochastic satisfiability problem is NP^{PP}-complete [23]. But, on the other hand, SAT planning has a number of advantages. These include that [23]

H. Prade and V.S. Subrahmanian (Eds.): SUM 2007, LNAI 4772, pp. 1–15, 2007.

SAT problem is a central widely studied problem in computer science, therefore, many techniques have been developed to solve the problem. The existence of many efficient solvers that solve the SAT problem.

Another successful logic based approach to classical planning is answer set planning [35]. In answer set planning, a planning problem, $\mathcal{P}$, is solved by translating $\mathcal{P}$ into a logic program with answer set semantics whose answer sets corresponds to trajectories in $\mathcal{P}$. It has been shown in [18] that the answer sets of a logic program are equivalent to the models of a corresponding SAT problem. Therefore, efficient SAT solvers are employed to find the answer sets of logic programs [18], and hence, they can be used to efficiently solve classical planning problems in answer set planning. An important limitation to answer set planning is that it considers only certain domains, which limits its applicability to many real-world domains. As pointed out in [34], the choice of logic programs with answer set semantics for planning underlies many desirable advantages over the other approaches, e.g., SAT planning. These include that logic programs with answer set semantics is non-monotonic and hence appropriate for knowledge representation and reasoning tasks. In addition, it is easier in logic programs with answer set semantics than SAT to represent the properties of actions.

A probabilistic extension to (normal) logic programs with answer set semantics has been presented in [32], by introducing the notion of Normal Hybrid Probabilistic Programs (NHPP). NHPP allows non-monotonic negation and inherits the advantages of (normal) logic programs. Two different semantics have been provided for NHPP namely; probabilistic answer set (stable probabilistic model) semantics and well-founded probabilistic model semantics. It was shown in [32] that the relationship between the probabilistic answer set semantics and the well-founded probabilistic model semantics *preserves* the relationship between the answer set semantics and the well-founded semantics for normal logic programs [10]. Moreover, the probabilistic answer set semantics and the well-founded probabilistic model semantics *naturally extend* the answer set semantics [11] and the well-founded semantics [10] of normal logic programs.

In this paper we relate probabilistic planning to Normal Hybrid Probabilistic Logic Programs with probabilistic answer set semantics introducing a novel logic based probabilistic planning approach that is a probabilistic extension to answer set planning to account for probabilistic domains.

The contributions of this paper are as follows. We show that any probabilistic planning problem, $\mathcal{P}$, can be translated into a program in NHPP whose probabilistic answer sets correspond to trajectories in $\mathcal{P}$, with associated probabilities. We formally prove the correctness of our approach. We show that the complexity of finding a plan for a probabilistic planning problem in our approach is NP-complete. In addition, we show that any probabilistic planning problem, $\mathcal{P}$, can be encoded as a classical normal logic program, Π, with answer set semantics, where the answer sets of Π correspond to valid trajectories in $\mathcal{P}$. However, plan evaluation in classical normal logic programs is not as intuitive as in NHPP. Moreover, we show that probabilistic planning problems can be encoded as SAT problems. The importance of that is probabilistic planning problems can be now solved as SAT problems instead of stochastic satisfiability problems. This development is the first work that relates probabilistic planning to a logic programming paradigm in general and to a probabilistic logic programming approach in particular.

2 Syntax and Semantics of NHPP

Now, we present the basic notions associated to the language of NHPP [6,32].

2.1 Probabilistic Strategies

Let $C[0,1]$ denotes the set of all closed intervals in $[0,1]$. In the context of NHPP, probabilities are assigned to primitive events (atoms) and compound events (conjunctions or disjunctions of atoms) as intervals in $C[0,1]$. Let $[a_1,b_1],[a_2,b_2] \in C[0,1]$. Then the *truth order* asserts that $[a_1,b_1] \leq_t [a_2,b_2]$ iff $a_1 \leq a_2$ and $b_1 \leq b_2$. The type of dependency among the primitive events within a compound event is described by *probabilistic strategies*, which are explicitly selected by the user. We call ρ, a pair of functions $\langle c, md \rangle$, a probabilistic strategy (p-strategy), where $c : C[0,1] \times C[0,1] \rightarrow C[0,1]$, the *probabilistic composition function*. Whereas, $md : C[0,1] \rightarrow C[0,1]$ is the *maximal interval function*. The maximal interval function md of a certain p-strategy returns an estimate of the probability range of a primitive event, A, from the probability range of a compound event that contains A. The composition function c returns the probability range of a conjunction (disjunction) of two events given the ranges of its constituents. For convenience, given a multiset of probability intervals $M = \{\!\{[a_1,b_1],\ldots,[a_n,b_n]\}\!\}$, we use cM to denote $c([a_1,b_1], c([a_2,b_2],\ldots,c([a_{n-1},b_{n-1}],[a_n,b_n]))\ldots)$. According to the type of combination among events, p-strategies are classified into *conjunctive* p-strategies and *disjunctive* p-strategies. Conjunctive (disjunctive) p-strategies are employed to compose events belonging to a conjunctive (disjunctive) formula (please see [6,31] for the formal definitions).

2.2 The Languages of NHPP

Let $\mathcal{L}$ be an arbitrary first-order language with finitely many predicate symbols, constants, function symbols, and infinitely many variables. In addition, let $S = S_{conj} \cup S_{disj}$ be an arbitrary set of p-strategies, where S_{conj} (S_{disj}) is the set of all conjunctive (disjunctive) p-strategies in S. The Herbrand base of $\mathcal{L}$ is denoted by $\mathcal{B}_\mathcal{L}$. An *annotation* denotes a probability interval. The building blocks of the language of NHPP are *hybrid basic formulae*. Let us consider a collection of atoms $A_1,\ldots,A_n$, a conjunctive p-strategy ρ, and a disjunctive p-strategy ρ'. Then $A_1 \wedge_\rho \ldots \wedge_\rho A_n$ and $A_1 \vee_{\rho'} \ldots \vee_{\rho'} A_n$ are called *hybrid basic formulae*. $bf_S(\mathcal{B}_\mathcal{L})$ is the set of all ground hybrid basic formulae formed using distinct atoms from $\mathcal{B}_\mathcal{L}$ and p-strategies from S, such that for any collection of equivalent hybrid basic formulae, $\mathsf{X} = \{A_1 *_\rho A_2 *_\rho \ldots *_\rho A_n,\ A_2 *_\rho A_1 *_\rho \ldots *_\rho A_n,\ldots\}$, where $* \in \{\wedge, \vee\}$, only one $A_{i_1} *_\rho A_{i_2} *_\rho \ldots *_\rho A_{i_n} \in \mathsf{X}$ is in $bf_S(\mathcal{B}_\mathcal{L})$.

Definition 1 (Rules). *A normal hybrid probabilistic rule (nh-rule) is an expression of the form*

$$A : \mu \leftarrow F_1 : \mu_1, \ldots, F_n : \mu_n, not\ (G_1 : \mu_{n+1}), \ldots, not\ (G_m : \mu_{n+m})$$

where A is an atom, $F_1, \ldots, F_n, G_1, \ldots, G_m$ are hybrid basic formulae, and μ, μ_i $(1 \leq i \leq m + n)$ are annotations.

The intuitive meaning of an nh-rule, in Definition 1, is that, if for each $F_i : \mu_i$, the probability interval of F_i is at least μ_i and for each *not* $(G_j : \mu_j)$, it is not *provable* that the probability interval of G_j is at least μ_j, then the probability interval of A is μ. A normal hybrid probabilistic program over S (*nh-program*) is a pair $P = \langle R, \tau \rangle$, where R is a finite set of nh-rules with p-strategies from S, and τ is a mapping $\tau : \mathcal{B}_{\mathcal{L}} \to S_{disj}$. The mapping τ associates to each atomic hybrid basic formula A a disjunctive p-strategy that will be employed to combine the probability intervals obtained from different rules having A in their heads. An nh-program is ground if no variables appear in any of its rules.

2.3   Probabilistic Answer Set Semantics

A probabilistic interpretation (p-interpretation) is a mapping $h : bf_S(\mathcal{B}_{\mathcal{L}}) \to C[0, 1]$.

Definition 2 (Probabilistic Satisfaction). *Let $P = \langle R, \tau \rangle$ be a ground nh-program, h be a p-interpretation, and r be*

$$A : \mu \leftarrow F_1 : \mu_1, \ldots, F_n : \mu_n, not\ (G_1 : \beta_1), \ldots, not\ (G_m : \beta_m) \in R.$$

Then

- *h satisfies $F_i : \mu_i$ (denoted by $h \models F_i : \mu_i$) iff $\mu_i \leq_t h(F_i)$.*
- *h satisfies not $(G_j : \beta_j)$ (denoted by $h \models not\ (G_j : \beta_j)$) iff $\beta_j \not\leq_t h(G_j)$.*
- *h satisfies Body $\equiv F_1 : \mu_1, \ldots, F_n : \mu_n, not\ (G_1 : \beta_1), \ldots, not\ (G_m : \beta_m)$ (denoted by $h \models Body$) iff $\forall (1 \leq i \leq n), h \models F_i : \mu_i$ and $\forall (1 \leq j \leq m), h \models not\ (G_j : \beta_j)$.*
- *h satisfies $A : \mu \leftarrow Body$ iff $h \models A : \mu$ or h does not satisfy Body.*
- *h satisfies P iff h satisfies every nh-rule in R and for every formula $F \in bf_S(\mathcal{B}_{\mathcal{L}})$, we have*
  - *If $F = A$ is atomic then*

    $$c_{\tau(A)}\{\!\!\{\mu | A : \mu \leftarrow Body \in R \text{ such that } h \models Body\}\!\!\} \leq_t h(A).$$

  - *If $F = A_1 *_\rho \ldots *_\rho A_n$ is not atomic then*

    $$c_\rho\{\!\!\{(h(A_1), \ldots, h(A_n)\}\!\!\} \leq_t h(F).$$

A probabilistic model of an nh-program P (*p-model*) is a p-interpretation of P that satisfies P. We say that h is a minimal p-model of P (w.r.t. $\leq_t$) if there is no other p-model h' of P such that $h' <_t h$.

Probabilistic answer set semantics is defined in two steps. First, we guess a p-model h for a certain nh-program P, then we define the notion of the probabilistic reduct of P with respect to h—which is an nh-program without non-monotonic negation. Second, we determine whether h is a probabilistic answer set for P or not by verifying whether h is the minimal (least) p-model of the probabilistic reduct of P w.r.t. h. It must be noted that every nh-program without non-monotonic negation has a unique minimal (least) p-model [31].

Definition 3 (Probabilistic Reduct). *Let $P = \langle R, \tau \rangle$ be a ground nh-program and h be a probabilistic interpretation. The probabilistic reduct P^h of P w.r.t. h is $P^h = \langle R^h, \tau \rangle$ where:*

$$R^h = \left\{ A : \mu \leftarrow F_1 : \mu_1, \ldots, F_n : \mu_n \left| \begin{array}{c} A : \mu \leftarrow F_1 : \mu_1, \ldots, F_n : \mu_n, \\ not\,(G_1 : \beta_1), \ldots, not\,(G_m : \beta_m) \in R\,and \\ \forall (1 \leq j \leq m),\ \beta_j \not\leq_t h(G_j) \end{array} \right. \right\}$$

The probabilistic reduct P^h is an nh-program without non-monotonic negation. For any $not\,(G_j : \beta_j)$ in the body of $r \in R$ with $\beta_j \not\leq_t h(G_j)$ is simply satisfied by h, and $not\,(G_j : \beta_j)$ is removed from the body of r. If $\beta_j \leq_t h(G_j)$ then the body of r is not satisfied and r is trivially ignored.

Definition 4 (Probabilistic Answer Set). *A probabilistic interpretation h is a probabilistic answer set of an nh-program P if h is the least p-model of P^h.*

3   Probabilistic Planning

In this section we review the basic definitions associated to probabilistic planning as described in [16]. As usual, a literal is an atom or the negation of an atom. A state is a finite set of distinct literals and an expression $\mathcal{E}$ is a conjunction of a set of literals. Intuitively, a state gives a complete description of the world at a certain time point. If a literal l belongs to a state s, then we say l is true in s, and l is false in s if $\neg l$ is in s. The truth of an expression $\mathcal{E}$ with respect to a state s is determined recursively over the propositional connectives as usual. Let s be a state and $\mathcal{E}$ be an expression. The probability of $\mathcal{E}$ w.r.t. s is given by $Pr(\mathcal{E}|s) = 1$ if $s \models \mathcal{E}$, otherwise, $Pr(\mathcal{E}|s) = 0$. An action, $ac(c_1, \ldots, c_n)$, is defined by a set of triples $\{\langle t^1, p^1, e^1 \rangle, \ldots, \langle t^n, p^n, e^n \rangle\}$, where ac is an n-ary action name and each c_i is a constant in $\mathcal{L}$ and for each $1 \leq i \leq n$,

- t^i is an expression called a precondition of an action $ac(c_1, \ldots, c_n)$ that corresponds to an effect e^i.
- p^i is the conditional probability that e^i is true given that t^i is true, where $0 \leq p^i \leq 1$.
- e^i is a set of literals called an effect of $ac(c_1, \ldots, c_n)$.

The set of all preconditions t^i must be exhaustive and mutually exclusive where $\forall\, i\ \sum_s p^i\, Pr(t^i|s) = 1,\ \forall\, i, j, s \qquad t^i \neq t^j \Rightarrow Pr(t^i \wedge t^j|s) = 0$. We use $ac^i(c_1, \ldots, c_n)$ to denote the triple $\langle t^i, p^i, e^i \rangle$. We write ac to denote an action name whenever it is clear from the context.

Definition 5. *Let s be a state, ac be an action, and ac^i be $\langle t^i, p^i, e^i \rangle$. Then, a probabilistic transition function Φ is a mapping from the set of all pairs (ac^i, s) into a set of states, where the state $\Phi(ac^i, s)$ resulting from executing ac in s is defined as:*

- $l \in \Phi(ac^i, s)$ *and* $\neg l \notin \Phi(ac^i, s)$ *if* $l \in e^i$ *and the precondition* t^i *of* ac^i *holds in s.*
- $\neg l \in \Phi(ac^i, s)$ *and* $l \notin \Phi(ac^i, s)$ *if* $\neg l \in e^i$ *and the precondition* t^i *of* ac^i *holds in s.*
- $l \in \Phi(ac^i, s)$ *iff* $l \in s$ *and* $\neg l \in \Phi(ac^i, s)$ *iff* $\neg l \in s$, *otherwise.*

Uncertainty in the initial states of the world is represented by a probability distribution over the possible world initial states. The probability distribution over states s' resulting from executing an action ac in a state s is given by $Pr(s'|s, ac) = p^i \cdot Pr(s)$ if $ac^i = \langle t^i, p^i, e^i \rangle \in ac, s \models t^i$, and $s' = \Phi(ac^i, s)$, otherwise, $Pr(s'|s, ac) = 0$.

Example 1. Consider the following robot planning task from [16]. A robotic arm is trying to grasp a block; the grasping operation is not always successful, especially when the robot's gripper is wet. The robot is able to hold a block (HB) with a probability 0.95 after executing the *pickup* action in the state of the world in which the gripper is dry (GD), and is unable to hold the block ($\neg HB$), after executing the *pickup* action in the same state of the world, with 0.05 probability. On the other hand, executing the *pickup* action in the state of the world in which the gripper is wet ($\neg GD$) yields HB with 0.5 probability and $\neg HB$ with 0.5 probability. Let us assume that, initially, the robot is not holding the block ($\neg HB$), and the gripper is dry (GD) with probability 0.7. Therefore, there are two possible initial states $s_1 = \{GD, \neg HB\}$ and $s_2 = \{\neg GD, \neg HB\}$, with the probability distribution $Pr(s_1) = 0.7$ and $Pr(s_2) = 0.3$.

Therefore, the *pickup* action is represented by the triples $pickup^1 = \langle GD, 0.95, \{HB\}\rangle, pickup^2 = \langle GD, 0.05, \{\neg HB\}\rangle, pickup^3 = \langle \neg GD, 0.5, \{HB\}\rangle, pickup^4 = \langle \neg GD, 0.5, \{\neg HB\}\rangle$. The probability distribution resulting from executing the *pickup* action in the initial states consists of four states where:

- $s_1' = \{GD, HB\} = \Phi(pickup^1, \{GD, \neg HB\})$, where $pickup^1 = \langle GD, 0.95, \{HB\}\rangle$ and $Pr(s_1'|s_1, pickup) = 0.95 \times Pr(s_1) = 0.95 \times 0.7 = 0.665$.
- $s_2' = \{GD, \neg HB\} = \Phi(pickup^2, \{GD, \neg HB\})$, where $pickup^2 = \langle GD, 0.05, \{\neg HB\}\rangle$ and $Pr(s_2'|s_1, pickup) = 0.05 \times Pr(s_1) = 0.05 \times 0.7 = 0.035$.
- $s_3' = \{\neg GD, HB\} = \Phi(pickup^3, \{\neg GD, \neg HB\})$, where $pickup^3 = \langle \neg GD, 0.5, \{HB\}\rangle$ and $Pr(s_3'|s_2, pickup) = 0.5 \times Pr(s_2) = 0.5 \times 0.3 = 0.15$.
- $s_4' = \{\neg GD, \neg HB\} = \Phi(pickup^4, \{\neg GD, \neg HB\})$, where $pickup^4 = \langle \neg GD, 0.5, \{\neg HB\}\rangle$ and $Pr(s_4'|s_2, pickup) = 0.5 \times Pr(s_2) = 0.5 \times 0.3 = 0.15$.

Let s be an initial state, $\tilde{s}_I$ be a random variable over the initial states, s' be a state, and $\langle ac_1, ac_2, \ldots, ac_n \rangle$ be a sequence of actions. The probability that s' holds after executing $\langle ac_1, ac_2, \ldots, ac_n \rangle$ in s is given by

$$Pr(s'|s, \langle ac_1, ac_2, \ldots, ac_n \rangle) = \sum_{s''} Pr(s''|s, ac_1) \, Pr(s'|s'', \langle ac_2, \ldots, ac_n \rangle),$$

where $Pr(s'|s, \langle \rangle) = 1$ if $s' = s$, otherwise, $Pr(s'|s, \langle \rangle) = 0$, where, $\langle \rangle$ is an empty sequence of actions. The probability that an expression $\mathcal{E}$ is true after executing $\langle ac_1, \ldots, ac_n \rangle$ in a state s is given by

$$Pr(\mathcal{E}|s, \langle ac_1, \ldots, ac_n \rangle) = \sum_{s'} Pr(s'|s, \langle ac_1, \ldots, ac_n \rangle) \, Pr(\mathcal{E}|s').$$

However, the probability that $\mathcal{E}$ is true after executing $\langle ac_1, \ldots, ac_n \rangle$ in the initial states $\tilde{s}_I$ is given by

$$Pr(\mathcal{E}|\tilde{s}_I, \langle ac_1, \ldots, ac_n \rangle) = \sum_{s} Pr(\mathcal{E}|s, \langle ac_1, \ldots, ac_n \rangle) \, Pr(\tilde{s}_I = s)$$

For example, to compute the probability that HB holds after performing the *pickup* action in the possible initial states s_1 and s_2, from Example 1, we consider all resulting states in which HB is satisfied. There are two states, s_1' and s_3', of the world in which the robot can hold the block after executing the action *pickup* in s_1 and s_2. Therefore, $Pr(HB|\tilde{s}_I, pickup) = Pr(s_1'|s_1, pickup)Pr(HB|s_1') + Pr(s_3'|s_2, pickup)Pr(HB|s_3') = 0.665 + 0.15 = 0.815$, since $Pr(HB|s_1') = Pr(HB|s_3') = 1$.

A probabilistic planning problem is a 4-tuple $\mathcal{P} = \langle \tilde{s}_I, \mathcal{G}, \mathcal{T}, \mathcal{A} \rangle$, where

- $\tilde{s}_I$ is a random variable over states that represents the initial agent knowledge about the world at the time of execution.
- $\mathcal{G}$ is an expression represents the goal to be satisfied.
- $\mathcal{T}$ is the probability threshold for the goal $\mathcal{G}$ to be achieved, where $0 \leq \mathcal{T} \leq 1$.
- $\mathcal{A}$ is a set of actions from which plans are formed.

We say that $\langle ac_1, \ldots, ac_n \rangle$ is plan for $\mathcal{P}$ iff each ac_i belongs to $\mathcal{A}$ and $Pr(\mathcal{G}|\tilde{s}_I, \langle ac_1, \ldots, ac_n \rangle) \geq \mathcal{T}$.

4   Probabilistic Answer Set Planning

Probabilistic answer set planning is a new approach to solve probabilistic planning problems using the probabilistic answer set semantics of NHPP. This is achieved by providing a translation from a probabilistic planning problem, $\mathcal{P}$, into an nh-program, $\Pi_{\mathcal{P}}$, in NHPP, where the nh-rules in $\Pi_{\mathcal{P}}$ encode (i) the initial probability distribution over states ($\tilde{s}_I$), (ii) the probabilistic transition function Φ (which causes a transition from a probability distribution over states to another probability distribution), (iii) the goal ($\mathcal{G}$), (iv) and the set of actions ($\mathcal{A}$) appear in $\mathcal{P}$. The probabilistic answer sets of $\Pi_{\mathcal{P}}$ correspond to valid trajectories in $\mathcal{P}$, with associated probabilities. The nh-program translation of a probabilistic planning problem is mainly adapted from [34]. We assume that the length of plans we are searching for is known, which is traditional in encoding planning problems. We use a special predicate $time(T)$, where T is a non-negative integer, to describe the time moment where the world in. In addition, we use the predicates (i) $holds(L, T)$ to represent the fact that a literal L holds at time moment T, (ii) $occ(AC, T)$ to describe that an action AC executes at time moment T, and (iii) $state(T)$ to represent a possible state of the world at time moment T. As customary in logic programming, we use lower case letters to represent constants and upper case letters to represent variables.

Let $\Pi_{\mathcal{P}} = \langle R, \tau \rangle$ be the nh-program translation of a probabilistic planning problem, $\mathcal{P} = \langle \tilde{s}_I, \mathcal{G}, \mathcal{T}, \mathcal{A} \rangle$, where τ is any arbitrary assignment of disjunctive p-strategies and R is the set of nh-rules described as follows.

- Each action of the form $ac = \{ac^1, \ldots, ac^n\} \in \mathcal{A}$ is represented in R by the set of facts

$$action(ac^i) : [1, 1] \leftarrow$$

In addition, literals that describe the states of the world are encoded in R by the nh-rules

$$literal(A) : [1, 1] \leftarrow atom(A) : [1, 1] \tag{1}$$
$$literal(\neg A) : [1, 1] \leftarrow atom(A) : [1, 1] \tag{2}$$

where $atom(A) : [1, 1]$ is a set of facts that describe the properties of the world. However, the following nh-rules specify that A and $\neg A$ are contrary literals.

$$contrary(A, \neg A) : [1, 1] \leftarrow atom(A) : [1, 1] \tag{3}$$
$$contrary(\neg A, A) : [1, 1] \leftarrow atom(A) : [1, 1] \tag{4}$$

- To encode the initial probability distribution over the possible initial states we proceed as follows. Let $s_{I_1}, s_{I_2}, \ldots, s_{I_n}$ be the set of possible initial states, where for each $1 \leq i \leq n$, $s_{I_i} = \{l_1^{I_i}, \ldots, l_m^{I_i}\}$, and the initial probability distribution, over these initial states, be $Pr(\tilde{s}_I = s_{I_i}) = [p_i, p_i]$. Moreover, let $s_I = s_{I_1} \cup s_{I_2} \cup \ldots \cup s_{I_n}$, $s'_I = s_{I_1} \cap s_{I_2} \cap \ldots \cap s_{I_n}$, and $\hat{s}_I = s_I - s'_I$. We denote $s''_I = \{l \mid l \in \hat{s}_I \vee \neg l \in \hat{s}_I\}$. Intuitively, for any literal l in $\hat{s}_I$, if l or $\neg l$ belongs to $\hat{s}_I$, then s''_I contains only l. Therefore, to generate the set of all possible initial states we have the following set of nh-rules. For each literal $l \in s'_I$, the fact

$$holds(l, 0) : [1, 1] \leftarrow \tag{5}$$

belongs to R. This fact asserts that the literal l holds at time moment 0. This set of facts represents the set of literals that hold in every possible initial state. In addition, for each literal $l \in s''_I$, the nh-rules

$$holds(l, 0) : [1, 1] \leftarrow not\ (holds(\neg l, 0) : [1, 1]) \tag{6}$$
$$holds(\neg l, 0) : [1, 1] \leftarrow not\ (holds(l, 0) : [1, 1]) \tag{7}$$

belong to R. The above nh-rules says that the literal l (similarly $\neg l$) holds at time moment 0, if $\neg l$ (similarly l) does not hold at the time moment 0. This set of nh-rules corresponds to the fact that, for any possible initial state, s_{I_i}, either l or $\neg l$ belongs to s_{I_i}. The initial probability distribution over the initial states is encoded in R as follows. For each possible initial state $s_{I_i} = \{l_1^{I_i}, \ldots, l_m^{I_i}\}$, the nh-rule

$$state(0) : [p_i, p_i] \leftarrow holds(l_1^{I_i}, 0) : [1, 1], \ldots, holds(l_m^{I_i}, 0) : [1, 1] \qquad (8)$$

belongs to R. The above nh-rule says that the probability of a state at time moment 0 (a possible initial state) is $[p_i, p_i]$ if the literals $l_{i_1}^{I}, \ldots, l_{i_m}^{I}$ holds at the time moment 0.

- For each action $ac = \{ac^1, \ldots, ac^n\}$, where $\forall$ $(1 \leq i \leq n)$, $ac^i = \langle t^i, p^i, e^i \rangle$, $t^i = l_1^{t^i} \wedge \ldots \wedge l_k^{t^i}$, and $e^i = \{l_1^{e^i}, \ldots, l_m^{e^i}\}$. Then, $\forall$ $(1 \leq j \leq m)$, $l_j^{e^i} \in e^i$, we have

$$holds(l_j^{e^i}, T + 1) : [1, 1] \leftarrow time(T) : [1, 1], occ(ac^i, T) : [1, 1],$$
$$holds(l_1^{t^i}, T) : [1, 1], \ldots, holds(l_k^{t^i}, T) : [1, 1] \qquad (9)$$

belongs to R. This nh-rule states that if the action ac occurs at time moment T and the literals $l_1^{t^i}, \ldots, l_k^{t^i}$ (the precondition t^i) hold at the same time moment, then the literal $l_j^{e^i}$ holds at the time moment $T + 1$.

- The following nh-rule encodes the frame axioms. For any literal L we have

$$holds(L, T + 1) : [1, 1] \leftarrow time(T) : [1, 1], holds(L, T) : [1, 1],$$
$$not\ (holds(L', T + 1) : [1, 1]), contrary(L, L') : [1, 1],$$
$$literal(L) : [1, 1], literal(L') : [1, 1] \qquad (10)$$

belongs to R. The above nh-rule states that if L holds at the time moment T and its contrary does not hold at the time moment $T + 1$, then L continues to hold at the time moment $T + 1$.

- In addition, we add the following nh-rule in R to encode the fact that a literal A and its negation $\neg A$ cannot hold at the same time.

$$inconsistent : [1, 1] \leftarrow not\ (inconsistent : [1, 1]), atom(A) : [1, 1],$$
$$time(T) : [1, 1], holds(A, T) : [1, 1], holds(\neg A, T) : [1, 1] \qquad (11)$$

where $inconsistent$ is a special literal that does not appear in $\mathcal{P}$.

- Action generation rules are represented in R by the following nh-rules.

$$occ(AC^i, T) : [1, 1] \leftarrow time(T) : [1, 1], action(AC^i) : [1, 1],$$
$$not\ (abocc(AC^i, T) : [1, 1]) \qquad (12)$$
$$abocc(AC^i, T) : [1, 1] \leftarrow time(T) : [1, 1], action(AC^i) : [1, 1],$$
$$action(AC^j) : [1, 1], occ(AC^j, T) : [1, 1], AC^i \neq AC^j \qquad (13)$$

The above two nh-rules generate action occurrences once at a time, where AC^i and AC^j are variables representing actions.

- Let $\mathcal{G} = g_1 \wedge \ldots \wedge g_m$ be a goal expression, then $\mathcal{G}$ is encoded in R as an nh-rule of the form

$$goal : [1,1] \leftarrow time(T) : [1,1], holds(g_1, T) : [1,1], \ldots, holds(g_m, T) : [1,1] \tag{14}$$

- Probability distribution over states is represented in R using the following nh-rules. For each action $ac = \{ac^1, \ldots, ac^n\}$, where $\forall (1 \le i \le n)$, $ac^i = \langle t^i, p^i, e^i \rangle$, $t^i = l_1^{t^i} \wedge \ldots \wedge l_k^{t^i}$, and $e^i = \{l_1^{e^i}, \ldots, l_m^{e^i}\}$, then, for each $ac^i \in ac$, we have

$$state(T+1) : [p^i * V, p^i * V] \leftarrow state(T) : [V,V], occ(ac^i, T) : [1,1],$$
$$time(T) : [1,1], holds(l_1^{t^i}, T) : [1,1], \ldots, holds(l_k^{t^i}, T) : [1,1],$$
$$holds(l_1^{e^i}, T+1) : [1,1], \ldots, holds(l_m^{e^i}, T+1) : [1,1] \tag{15}$$

where V is an annotation variable ranging over $[0,1]$ acts as a place holder. The above nh-rule says that the probability of a state at time moment $T+1$ is $[p^i * V, p^i * V]$ if the effect e^i of an action ac becomes true in the same state, after executing an action ac in a state of the world at time T, whose probability is $[V,V]$, in which the precondition t^i is true.

Example 2. The nh-program translation, $\Pi_{\mathcal{P}} = \langle R, \tau \rangle$, of the probabilistic planning problem $\mathcal{P} = \langle \tilde{s}_I, \mathcal{G}, \mathcal{T}, \mathcal{A} \rangle$ presented in Example 1 proceeds as follows, where τ is any arbitrary assignment of disjunctive p-strategies and R consists of the following nh-rules, in addition to the nh-rules (1), (2), (3),(4), (10), (11), (12), (13):

$$action(pickup^1) : [1,1] \leftarrow \qquad action(pickup^2) : [1,1] \leftarrow$$
$$action(pickup^3) : [1,1] \leftarrow \qquad action(pickup^4) : [1,1] \leftarrow$$

where $pickup$ is in $\mathcal{A}$. Properties of the world are described by the atoms gD (gripper dry) and hB (holding block), which are encoded in R by the nh-rules

$$atom(gD) : [1,1] \leftarrow \qquad atom(hB) : [1,1] \leftarrow$$

The set of possible initial states are encoded by the nh-rules:

$$holds(\neg hB, 0) : [1,1] \leftarrow$$
$$holds(gD, 0) : [1,1] \quad \leftarrow not\,(holds(\neg gD, 0) : [1,1])$$
$$holds(\neg gD, 0) : [1,1] \leftarrow not\,(holds(gD, 0) : [1,1])$$

The initial probability distribution over the possible initial states is encoded by the nh-rules

$$state(0) : [0.7, 0.7] \leftarrow holds(gD, 0) : [1,1], holds(\neg hB, 0) : [1,1]$$
$$state(0) : [0.3, 0.3] \leftarrow holds(\neg gD, 0) : [1,1], holds(\neg hB, 0) : [1,1]$$

Effects of the *pickup* action are encoded by the nh-rules

$$holds(hB, T+1) : [1,1] \leftarrow time(T) : [1,1], occ(pickup^1, T) : [1,1], holds(gD, T) : [1,1]$$
$$holds(\neg hB, T+1) : [1,1] \leftarrow time(T) : [1,1], occ(pickup^2, T) : [1,1], holds(gD, T) : [1,1]$$
$$holds(hB, T+1) : [1,1] \leftarrow time(T) : [1,1], occ(pickup^3, T) : [1,1], holds(\neg gD, T) : [1,1]$$
$$holds(\neg hB, T+1) : [1,1] \leftarrow time(T) : [1,1], occ(pickup^4, T) : [1,1], holds(\neg gD, T) : [1,1]$$

The goal is encoded by the nh-rule

$$goal : [1,1] \leftarrow holds(hB, T) : [1,1]$$

Probability distributions over states are encoded by

$$state(T+1) : [0.95 * V, 0.95 * V] \leftarrow time(T) : [1,1], occ(pickup^1, T) : [1,1], state(T) : [V, V],$$
$$holds(gD, T) : [1,1], holds(hB, T+1) : [1,1]$$
$$state(T+1) : [0.05 * V, 0.05 * V] \leftarrow time(T) : [1,1], occ(pickup^2, T) : [1,1], state(T) : [V, V],$$
$$holds(gD, T) : [1,1], holds(\neg hB, T+1) : [1,1]$$
$$state(T+1) : [0.5 * V, 0.5 * V] \leftarrow time(T) : [1,1], occ(pickup^3, T) : [1,1], state(T) : [V, V],$$
$$holds(\neg gD, T) : [1,1], holds(hB, T+1) : [1,1]$$
$$state(T+1) : [0.5 * V, 0.5 * V] \leftarrow time(T) : [1,1], occ(pickup^4, T) : [1,1], state(T) : [V, V],$$
$$holds(\neg gD, T) : [1,1], holds(\neg hB, T+1) : [1,1]$$

5 Correctness

In this section we prove the correctness of the probabilistic answer set planning. We show that the probabilistic answer sets of the nh-program translation of a probabilistic planning problem, $\mathcal{P}$, correspond to trajectories in $\mathcal{P}$, with associated probabilities. Moreover, we show that the complexity of finding a plan for $\mathcal{P}$ in probabilistic answer set planning is NP-complete. Let the domain of T be $\{0, \ldots, n\}$. Let $\mathcal{P} = \langle \tilde{s}_I, \mathcal{G}, \mathcal{T}, \mathcal{A} \rangle$ be a probabilistic planning problem, Φ be a probabilistic transition function associated with $\mathcal{P}$, s_0 is a possible initial state, and $ac_0, \ldots, ac_n$ be a collection of actions in $\mathcal{A}$. We say that $s_0 \; ac_0^{j_0} \; s_1 \ldots ac_n^{j_n} \; s_{n+1}$ is a trajectory in $\mathcal{P}$ if $s_{i+1} = \Phi(ac_i^{j_i}, s_i)$, where $\forall (0 \leq i \leq n)$, s_i is a state, ac_i is an action, and $ac_i^{j_i} = \langle t_i^{j_i}, p_i^{j_i}, e_i^{j_i} \rangle \in ac_i$. A trajectory $s_0 \; ac_0^{j_0} \; s_1 \ldots ac_n^{j_n} \; s_{n+1}$ in $\mathcal{P}$ is said to achieve an expression $\mathcal{G}$ if $s_{n+1} \models \mathcal{G}$. Moreover, let $\mathcal{R}_{\mathcal{G}}$ be the set of all trajectories $s_0 \; ac_0^{j_0} \; s_1 \ldots ac_n^{j_n} \; s_{n+1}$ in $\mathcal{P}$ that achieve $\mathcal{G}$. We say $\langle ac_0, \ldots, ac_n \rangle$ achieves $\mathcal{G}$ if $\mathcal{R}_{\mathcal{G}}$ is not empty.

Theorem 1. *Let* $\mathcal{P} = \langle \tilde{s}_I, \mathcal{G}, \mathcal{T}, \mathcal{A} \rangle$ *be a probabilistic planning problem and* $\mathcal{G} = g_1 \wedge \ldots \wedge g_m$. *Then,* $\mathcal{G}$ *is achievable from* $\mathcal{P}$ *iff* $\mathcal{G}'(t) \equiv holds(g_1, t) : [1,1], \ldots, holds(g_m, t) : [1,1]$ *is true (satisfied) in some probabilistic answer set of* $\Pi_{\mathcal{P}}$, *for some* $0 \leq t \leq n$.

Theorem 1 says that any probabilistic planning problem, $\mathcal{P}$, can be translated into an nh-program, $\Pi_{\mathcal{P}}$, such that a trajectory in, $\mathcal{P}$, that achieves the goal $\mathcal{G}$ is equivalent to a probabilistic answer set h of $\Pi_{\mathcal{P}}$ that satisfies a related goal $\mathcal{G}'$. Probability of a state s_t at time moment t is captured in a probabilistic answer set h of $\Pi_{\mathcal{P}}$ by $h(state(t))$.

Lemma 1. *Let* h *be a probabilistic answer set of* $\Pi_{\mathcal{P}}$ *and* $\langle ac_0, \ldots, ac_n \rangle$ *(possibly empty) be a plan for* $\mathcal{P}$. *Then,*

$$\sum_{h \models \mathcal{G}'(n+1)} h(state(n+1)) = [\, Pr(\mathcal{G}|\tilde{s}_I, \langle ac_0, \ldots, ac_n \rangle),\ Pr(\mathcal{G}|\tilde{s}_I, \langle ac_0, \ldots, ac_n \rangle)\,]$$

where $\mathcal{G} = g_1 \wedge \ldots \wedge g_m$ *and* $\mathcal{G}'(n+1) \equiv holds(g_1, n+1) : [1,1], \ldots, holds(g_m, n+1) : [1,1]$.

Lemma 1 shows that the probability that a goal $\mathcal{G}$ is true after executing a sequence of actions $\langle ac_0, \ldots, ac_n \rangle$ in the possible initial states $\tilde{s}_I$ is equivalent to the summation of the probability intervals $h(state(n+1))$ over the probabilistic answer sets h of $\Pi_{\mathcal{P}}$ that satisfy a related goal $\mathcal{G}'(n+1)$. The following theorem follows directly from Lemma 1.

Theorem 2. *Let* h *be a probabilistic answer set of* $\Pi_{\mathcal{P}}$ *and* $\langle ac_0, \ldots, ac_n \rangle$ *(possibly empty) be a plan for* $\mathcal{P}$. *Then,* $Pr(\mathcal{G}|\tilde{s}_I, \langle ac_0, \ldots, ac_n \rangle) \geq \mathcal{T}$ *iff*

$$\sum_{h \models \mathcal{G}'(n+1)} h(state(n+1)) \geq [\mathcal{T}, \mathcal{T}].$$

Probabilistic answer set planning produces totally ordered plans using flat representation of the probabilistic planning domains. A totally ordered plan is a finite sequence of actions that must be executed in order, however, flat representation of probabilistic planning domains is the explicit enumeration of world states [20]. Hence, Theorem 4 follows directly from Theorem 3.

Theorem 3 ([20]). *The plan existence problem for totally ordered plans in flat representation of probabilistic planning domains is NP-complete.*

Theorem 4. *The plan existence problem in probabilistic answer set planning is NP-complete.*

6   Probabilistic Planning Using Answer Sets

In this section we show that probabilistic planning problems can be encoded as classical normal logic programs with classical answer set semantics. Excluding nh-rules (8) and (15) from the nh-program translation, $\Pi_{\mathcal{P}}$, of a probabilistic planning problem, $\mathcal{P}$, yields an nh-program, denoted by $\Pi_{\mathcal{P}}^{normal}$, with only annotations of the form $[1,1]$. As shown in [32], the syntax and semantics of this class of nh-programs is equivalent to classical normal logic programs with answer set semantics.

Theorem 5. *Let* $\Pi_{\mathcal{P}}^{normal}$ *be the* normal logic program *resulting from* $\Pi_{\mathcal{P}}$ *after deleting the nh-rules (8) and (15). Then, a trajectory* $s_0\, ac_0^{j_0}\, s_1 \ldots ac_n^{j_n}\, s_{n+1}$ *in* $\mathcal{P}$ *achieves* $\mathcal{G} = g_1 \wedge \ldots \wedge g_m$ *iff* $\mathcal{G}'(n+1) \equiv holds(g_1, n+1) : [1,1], \ldots, holds(g_m, n+1) : [1,1]$ *is true in some answer set of* $\Pi_{\mathcal{P}}^{normal}$.

Theorem 5 shows that classical normal logic programs with answer set semantics can be used to solve probabilistic planning problems in two steps. The first step is to translate a probabilistic planning problem, $\mathcal{P}$, into a classical normal logic program whose answer sets corresponds to valid trajectories in $\mathcal{P}$. From the answer sets of the normal logic program translation of $\mathcal{P}$, we can determine the trajectories $\mathcal{R}_{\mathcal{G}}$ in $\mathcal{P}$ that achieve the goal $\mathcal{G}$. The second step is to calculate the probability that the goal is satisfied by

$$\sum_{s_0\ ac_0^{j_0}\ s_1...ac_n^{j_n}\ s_{n+1}\in\mathcal{R}_{\mathcal{G}}} Pr(s_0)\ \prod_{i=0}^{n} p_i^{j_i}.$$

Now, we show that any probabilistic planning problem can be encoded as a SAT problem. Hence, state-of-the-art SAT solvers can be used to solve probabilistic planning problems. In [18], it has been shown that any normal logic program, Π, can be translated into a SAT problem, $\mathcal{S}$, where the models of $\mathcal{S}$ are equivalent to the answer sets of Π. Hence, the normal logic program encoding of a probabilistic planning problem $\mathcal{P}$ can be translated into an equivalent SAT problem, where the models of $\mathcal{S}$ correspond to valid trajectories in $\mathcal{P}$.

Proposition 1. *Let $\mathcal{P}$ be a probabilistic planning problem and $\Pi_{\mathcal{P}}^{normal}$ be a normal logic program translation of $\mathcal{P}$. The models of the SAT problem encoding of $\Pi_{\mathcal{P}}^{normal}$ are equivalent to valid trajectories in $\mathcal{P}$.*

However, in encoding probabilistic planning problems in normal logic programs, (i) explicit representation of probabilities, (ii) explicit assignment of probabilities to states, (iii) and the direct propagation of probabilities through states, rely on an external mechanism to normal logic programs syntax and semantics and not on normal logic programs syntax and semantics themselves. These issues can be overcome naturally by encoding probabilistic planning problems in NHPP. The idea of a two step solution for probabilistic reasoning tasks using the answer sets of logic programs is not new. A similar idea has been used in [2] for reasoning with causal Bayes nets.

7   Conclusions and Related Work

We presented probabilistic answer set planning, a new probabilistic planning approach, by relating probabilistic planning to NHPP. Probabilistic answer set planning is built upon classical answer set planning to account for probabilistic domains. The translation from a probabilistic planning problem into an NHPP program mainly relies on a similar translation from classical planning problems into normal logic problems described in [34]. Probabilistic planning approaches can be classified into two main categories of approaches; probabilistic extension to classical planning approaches and decision-theoretic approaches. Decision-theoretic planning approaches search for a plan that has a maximum expected utility (see [3] for detailed survey on decision-theoretic planning), however, in addition to our approach is declarative, probabilistic answer set planning is searching for a plan that has maximum probability value of success.

   Probabilistic planning approaches that are extensions to classical planning approaches include probabilistic extensions to partial order planning, planning as propositional satisfiability, and heuristic based planning. In [16] a probabilistic partial order planning approach is presented. Moreover, [16] is extended in [8] to generate contingent plans for probabilistic domains. Although, we use the same probabilistic planning problems characterization presented in [16], our approach is different, since our approach is a logic based. Based on planning as satisfiability approach [15] for deterministic domains, a probabilistic planning approach has been developed, in [22], for probabilistic domains. A probabilistic planning problem in [22] is solved by converting a probabilistic planning problem into a stochastic satisfiability problem and solving the stochastic satisfiability problem instead. Our approach is similar in spirit to [22] in the sense that both approaches are logic based approaches. However, solving stochastic satisfiability problem is NP^{PP}-complete, but, probabilistic answer set planning is NP-complete. The probabilistic planning approach in [5] is based on another classical planning approach (heuristic based planner) [4]. Unlike [4], [5] produces probabilistic contingent plans. Similar to [5,8], [23] produces probabilistic contingent plans. However, [23] employs a different approach. Similar to [22], [23] is based on planning as satisfiability approach (logic based approach). In [23], the search for probabilistic contingent plans is achieved by solving a corresponding stochastic satisfiability problem compiled from a probabilistic contingent planning problem.

References

1. Baral, C.: Knowledge representation, reasoning, and declarative problem solving. Cambridge University Press, Cambridge (2003)
2. Baral, C., Gelfond, M., Rushton, N.: Probabilistic reasoning with answer sets. In: Logic Programming and Non-monotonic Reasoning. Springer, Heidelberg (2004)
3. Boutilier, C., Dean, T., Hanks, S.: Decision-theoretic planning: structural assumptions and computational leverage. Journal of AI Research 11, 1–94 (1999)
4. Blum, A., Furst, M.: Fast planning through planning graph analysis. Artificial Intelligence 90(1-2), 297–298 (1997)
5. Blum, A., Langford, J.: Probabilistic planning in the Graphplan framework. In: Proc. of the 5th European Conference on Planning (1999)
6. Dekhtyar, A., Subrahmanian, V.S.: Hybrid probabilistic program. Journal of Logic Programming 43(3), 187–250 (2000)
7. Dekhtyar, M., Dekhtyar, A., Subrahmanian, V.S.: Hybrid probabilistic programs: algorithms and complexity. In: Proc. of UAI Conference, pp. 160–169 (1999)
8. Draper, D., Hanks, S., Weld, D.: Probabilistic planning with information gathering and contingent execution. In: Proc. of the 2nd International Conference on Artificial Intelligence Planning Systems, pp. 31–37 (1994)
9. Eiter, T., et al.: Declarative problem solving in dlv. In: Logic Based Artificial Intelligence (2000)
10. Van Gelder, A., Ross, K.A., Schlipf, J.S.: The well-founded semantics for general logic programs. Journal of ACM 38(3), 620–650 (1991)
11. Gelfond, M., Lifschitz, V.: The stable model semantics for logic programming. In: ICSLP. MIT Press, Cambridge (1988)
12. Gelfond, M., Lifschitz, V.: Classical negation in logic programs and disjunctive databases. New Generation Computing 9(3-4), 363–385 (1991)

13. Gelfond, M., Lifschitz, V.: Representing action and change by logic programs. Journal of Logic Programming 17, 301–321 (1993)
14. Giunchiglia, E., Lierler, Y., Maratea, M.: Answer set programming based on propositional satisfiability. Journal of Automated Reasoning 36(4), 345–377 (2006)
15. Kautz, H., Selman, B.: Pushing the envelope: planning, propositional logic, and stochastic search. In: Proc. of 13th National Conference on Artificial Intelligence (1996)
16. Kushmerick, N., Hanks, S., Weld, D.: An algorithm for probabilistic planning. Artificial Intelligence 76(1-2), 239–286 (1995)
17. Lifschitz, V.: Answer set planning. In: Proceedings of ICLP (1999)
18. Lin, F., Zhao, Y.: ASSAT: Computing answer sets of a logic program by SAT solvers. Artificial Intelligence 157(1-2), 115–137 (2004)
19. Lukasiewicz, T.: Probabilistic logic programming. In: 13th European Conference on Artificial Intelligence, pp. 388–392 (1998)
20. Littman, M., Goldsmith, J., Mundhenk, M.: The computational complexity of probabilistic planning. Journal of Artificial Intelligence Research 9, 1–36 (1998)
21. Littman, M., Majercik, S.: Large-scale planning under uncertainty: A survey. In: NASA Workshop on Planning and Scheduling in Space (1997)
22. Majercik, S., Littman, M.: MAXPLAN: A new approach to probabilistic planning. In: Proc. of the 4th International Conference on Artificial Intelligence Planning, pp. 86–93 (1998)
23. Majercik, S., Littman, M.: Contingent planning under uncertainty via stochastic satisfiability. Artificial Intelligence 147(1–2), 119–162 (2003)
24. Ng, R.T., Subrahmanian, V.S.: Probabilistic logic programming. Information & Computation 101(2) (1992)
25. Ng, R.T., Subrahmanian, V.S.: Stable semantics for probabilistic deductive databases. Information & Computation 110(1) (1994)
26. Niemela, I., Simons, P.: Efficient implementation of the well-founded and stable model semantics. In: Joint International Conference and Symposium on Logic Programming, pp. 289–303 (1996)
27. Poole, D.: The Independent choice logic for modelling multiple agents under uncertainty. Artificial Intelligence 94(1-2), 7–56 (1997)
28. Saad, E.: Incomplete knowlege in hybrid probabilistic logic programs. In: Fisher, M., van der Hoek, W., Konev, B., Lisitsa, A. (eds.) JELIA 2006. LNCS (LNAI), vol. 4160, Springer, Heidelberg (2006)
29. Saad, E.: Towards the computation of the stable probabilistic model semantics. In: Freksa, C., Kohlhase, M., Schill, K. (eds.) KI 2006. LNCS (LNAI), vol. 4314, Springer, Heidelberg (2007)
30. Saad, E.: A logical approach to qualitative and quantitative reasoning. In: 9th European Conference on Symbolic and Quantitative Approaches to Reasoning with Uncertainty (ECSQARU'07) (2007)
31. Saad, E., Pontelli, E.: Towards a more practical hybrid probabilistic logic programming framework. Practical Aspects of Declarative Languages (2005)
32. Saad, E., Pontelli, E.: Hybrid probabilistic logic programs with non-monotonic negation. In: International Conference of Logic Programming, Springer, Heidelberg (2005)
33. Saad, E., Pontelli, E.: A new approach to hybrid probabilistic logic programs. Annals of Mathematics and Artificial Intelligence Journal 48(3-4), 187–243 (2006)
34. Son, T., Baral, C., Nam, T., McIlraith, S.: Domain-dependent knowledge in answer set planning. ACM Transactions on Computational Logic 7(4), 613–657 (2006)
35. Subrahmanian, V.S., Zaniolo, C.: Relating stable models and AI planning domains. In: International Conference of Logic Programming, pp. 233–247 (1995)

Top-k Retrieval in Description Logic Programs Under Vagueness for the Semantic Web

Thomas Lukasiewicz[1,2] and Umberto Straccia[3]

[1] DIS, Sapienza Università di Roma, Via Ariosto 25, I-00185 Roma, Italy
lukasiewicz@dis.uniroma1.it
[2] Institut für Informationssysteme, Technische Universität Wien,
Favoritenstraße 9-11, A-1040 Wien, Austria
lukasiewicz@kr.tuwien.ac.at
[3] ISTI-CNR, Via G. Moruzzi 1, I-56124 Pisa, Italy
straccia@isti.cnr.it

Abstract. Description logics (DLs) and logic programs (LPs) are important representation languages for the Semantic Web. In this paper, we address an emerging problem in such languages, namely, the problem of evaluating ranked top-k queries. Specifically, we show how to compute the top-k answers in a data-complexity tractable combination of DLs and LPs under vagueness.

1 Introduction

Description logics (DLs) and logic programs (LPs) are important representation languages for the Semantic Web. In this paper, we address an emerging issue, namely, the problem of evaluating ranked top-k queries in a combination of such languages under vagueness. Under the classical semantics, an answer to a query is a set of tuples that satisfy a query. The information need of a user, however, very often involves so-called *vague predicates*. For instance, in a logic-based e-commerce process, we may ask "find a car costing *around* $15000" (see [12]); or in ontology-mediated access to multimedia information, we may ask "find images *about* cars, which are *similar* to a given one" (see, e.g., [11,19]). Unlike the classical case, tuples now satisfy these queries to a degree (usually in $[0, 1]$). Therefore, a major problem is that now an answer is a set of tuples *ranked* according to their degree. This poses a new challenge when we have to deal with a huge amount of facts. Indeed, virtually every tuple may satisfy a query with a non-zero degree, and thus has to be ranked. Of course, computing all these degrees, ranking them, and then selecting the top-k ones is likely not feasible in practice.

In this work, we address the top-k retrieval problem for a data complexity tractable combination of DLs and LPs under a many-valued semantics. In our language, at the extensional level, each fact may have a truth value, while at the intensional level many-valued DL axioms and LP rules describe the application domain.

2 Preliminaries

The truth space that we consider here is the finite set $[0, 1]_m = \{\frac{0}{m}, \frac{1}{m}, \ldots, \frac{m-1}{m}, \frac{m}{m}\}$ (for a natural number $m > 0$), which is pretty common in fuzzy logic. Throughout the

H. Prade and V.S. Subrahmanian (Eds.): SUM 2007, LNAI 4772, pp. 16–30, 2007.

ID	MODEL	TYPE	PRICE	KM	COLOR	AIRBAG	INTERIOR TYPE	AIR COND	ENGINE FUEL
455	MAZDA 3	Sedan	12500	10000	Red	0	VelvetSeats	1	Gasoline
34	ALFA 156	Sedan	12000	15000	Black	1	LeatherSeats	0	Diesel
1812	FORD FOCUS	StationVagon	11000	16000	Gray	1	LeatherSeats	1	Gasoline

Fig. 1. The car table

ID	HOTEL	PRICE Single	PRICE Double	DISTANCE	s
1	Verdi	100	120	5Min	0.75
2	Puccini	120	135	10Min	0.5
3	Rossini	80	90	15Min	0.25

Fig. 2. The hotel table

paper, we assume $m = 100$ in the examples with usual decimal rounding (e.g., 0.375 becomes 0.38, while 0.374 becomes 0.37).

A *knowledge base* $\mathcal{K}$ consists of a *facts component* $\mathcal{F}$, a *DL component* $\mathcal{O}$, and an *LP component* $\mathcal{P}$, which are all three defined below.

Facts Component. $\mathcal{F}$ is a finite set of expressions of the form

$$\langle R(c_1, \ldots, c_n), s \rangle \, ,$$

where R is an n-ary relation, every c_i is a constant, and s is a degree of truth (or simply *score*) in $[0,1]_m$. For each R, we represent the facts $\langle R(c_1, \ldots, c_n), s \rangle$ in $\mathcal{F}$ by means of a relational $n + 1$-ary table T_R, containing the records $\langle c_1, \ldots, c_n, s \rangle$. We assume that there cannot be two records $\langle c_1, \ldots, c_n, s_1 \rangle$ and $\langle c_1, \ldots, c_n, s_2 \rangle$ in T_R with $s_1 \neq s_2$ (if there are, then we remove the one with the lower score). Each table is sorted in descending order with respect to the scores. For ease, we may omit the score component and in such cases the value 1 is assumed.

Example 1 ([12]). Suppose we have a car selling site, and we would like to buy a car. The cars belong to the relation *CarTable* shown in Fig. 1. Here, the score is implicitly assumed to be 1 in each record. For instance, the first record corresponds to the fact

$$\langle CarTable(455, MAZDA3, Sedan, 12500, 10000, Red, 0, VelvetSeats, 1, Gasoline), 1 \rangle \, .$$

Example 2 ([15,20]). Suppose we have information about hotels and their degree of closeness to the city center, computed from the walking distance according to some pre-defined function, and we would like to find a cheap hotel close to the city center. The hotels belong to the relation *CloseHotelTable* shown in Fig. 2. The column s indicates the degree of closeness. For instance, the first record corresponds to the fact

$$\langle CloseHotelTable(1, Verdi, 100, 120, 5Min), 0.75 \rangle \, .$$

Semantically, an *interpretation* $\mathcal{I} = \langle \Delta, \cdot^{\mathcal{I}} \rangle$ consists of a *fixed infinite domain* Δ and an *interpretation function* $\cdot^{\mathcal{I}}$ that maps every n-ary relation R to a partial function $R^{\mathcal{I}} \colon \Delta^n \to [0,1]_m$ and every constant to an element of Δ such that $a^{\mathcal{I}} \neq b^{\mathcal{I}}$ if $a \neq b$ (unique name assumption). We assume to have one object for each constant, denoting exactly that object. In other words, we have standard names, and we do not distinguish

$Cars \sqsubseteq Vehicles$	$LeatherSeats \sqsubseteq Seats$
$Trucks \sqsubseteq Vehicles$	$VelvetSeats \sqsubseteq Seats$
$Vans \sqsubseteq Vehicles$	$MidSizeCars \sqsubseteq PassengerCars$
$LuxuryCars \sqsubseteq Cars$	$SportyCars \sqsubseteq PassengerCars$
$PassengerCars \sqsubseteq Cars$	$CompactCars \sqsubseteq PassengerCars$
$\exists 1 : CarTable \sqsubseteq Cars$	$Vehicles \sqsubseteq \exists 1 : hasMaker$
$Sedan \sqsubseteq Cars$	$Vehicles \sqsubseteq \exists 1 : hasPrice$
$StationWagon \sqsubseteq Cars$	$\exists 1 : hasPrice \sqsubseteq Vehicles$
$\exists 9 : CarTable \sqsubseteq Seats$	$\exists 1 : hasMaker \sqsubseteq Vehicles$
$Mazda \sqsubseteq CarMake$	$\exists 2 : hasMaker \sqsubseteq CarMaker$
$AlfaRomeo \sqsubseteq CarMake$	$Cars \sqsubseteq \exists 1 : hasKm$
$Ford \sqsubseteq CarMake$	$\exists 2 : hasFuel \sqsubseteq FuelType$

Fig. 3. A car selling ontology

between the alphabets of constants and the objects in Δ. Note that, since $R^{\mathcal{I}}$ may be a partial function, some tuples may not have a score. Alternatively, we may assume $R^{\mathcal{I}}$ to be a total function. We use the former formulation to distinguish the case where a tuple c may be retrieved, even though the score is 0, from the case where a tuple is not retrieved, since it does not satisfy the query. In particular, if a tuple does not belong to an extensional relation, then its score is assumed to be undefined, while if $R^{\mathcal{I}}$ is total, then the score of this tuple would be 0.

An interpretation $\mathcal{I}$ is a *model* of (or *satisfies*) a fact $\langle R(c_1, \ldots, c_n), s \rangle$, denoted $\mathcal{I} \models \langle R(c_1, \ldots, c_n), s \rangle$, iff $R^{\mathcal{I}}(c_1, \ldots, c_n) \geqslant s$ whenever $R^{\mathcal{I}}(c_1, \ldots, c_n)$ is defined.

DL Component. $\mathcal{O}$ is a finite set of *axioms* having the form

$$C_1 \sqcap \ldots \sqcap C_l \sqsubseteq C$$

(called *concept inclusion*), where all C_i and C are concept expressions. Informally, $C_1 \sqcap \ldots \sqcap C_l \sqsubseteq C$ says that if c is an instance of C_i to degree s_i, then c is an instance of C to degree at least $\min(s_1, \ldots, s_l)$. A concept expression is either an atomic concept A or of the form $\exists i : R$, where R is an n-ary relation and $i \in \{1, \ldots, n\}$. Informally, $\exists i : R$ is the projection of R on the i-th column. These concepts are inspired by the description logic *DLR-Lite* [2], a LogSpace data complexity family of DL languages, but still with good representation capabilities.

We recall that despite the simplicity of its language, the DL component is able to capture the main notions (though not all, obviously) to represent structured knowledge. In particular, the axioms allow us to specify *subsumption*, concept A_1 is subsumed by concept A_2, using $A_1 \sqsubseteq A_2$; *typing*, using $\exists i : R \sqsubseteq A$ (the i-th column of R is of type A); and *participation constraints*, using $A \sqsubseteq \exists i : R$ (all instance of A occur in the projection of R on the i-th column).

Example 3. Consider again Example 1. An excerpt of the domain ontology is described in Fig. 3 and partially encodes the web directory behind the car selling site www.autos.com. For instance, the axiom

$$Vehicles \sqsubseteq \exists 1 : hasPrice$$

dictates that each vehicle has a price.

Semantically, an interpretation $\mathcal{I} = \langle \Delta, \cdot^{\mathcal{I}} \rangle$ maps every atom A to a partial function $A^{\mathcal{I}} \colon \Delta \to [0,1]_m$. In the following, c denotes an n-tuple of constants, and $c[i]$ denotes the i-th component of c. Then, $\cdot^{\mathcal{I}}$ has to satisfy, for all $c \in \Delta$:

$$(\exists i \colon R)^{\mathcal{I}}(c) = \sup_{c' \in \Delta^n,\, c'[i]=c,\ R^{\mathcal{I}}(c') \text{ is defined}} R^{\mathcal{I}}(c') \,.$$

Then, $\mathcal{I} \models C_1 \sqcap \ldots \sqcap C_l \sqsubseteq C$ iff, for all $c \in \Delta$, $\min(C_1^{\mathcal{I}}(c), \ldots, C_l^{\mathcal{I}}(c)) \leqslant C^{\mathcal{I}}(c)$ whenever all $C_i^{\mathcal{I}}(c)$ are defined.

LP Component. $\mathcal{P}$ is a finite set of *vague rules* of the form (an example of a rule is shown in Example 4 below.)

$$R(\boldsymbol{x}) \leftarrow \exists \boldsymbol{y}.f(R_1(\boldsymbol{z}_1), \ldots, R_l(\boldsymbol{z}_l), p_1(\boldsymbol{z}_1'), \ldots, p_h(\boldsymbol{z}_h')) \,,$$

where

1. R is an n-ary relation, every R_i is an n_i-ary relation,
2. $\boldsymbol{x}$ are the *distinguished variables*;
3. $\boldsymbol{y}$ are existentially quantified variables called the *non-distinguished variables*;
4. $\boldsymbol{z}_i, \boldsymbol{z}_j'$ are tuples of constants or variables in $\boldsymbol{x}$ or $\boldsymbol{y}$;
5. p_j is an n_j-ary *fuzzy predicate* assigning to each n_j-ary tuple c_j a score $p_j(c_j) \in [0,1]_m$. Such predicates are called *expensive predicates* in [3] as the score is not pre-computed off-line, but is computed on query execution. We require that an n-ary fuzzy predicate p is *safe*, that is, there is not an m-ary fuzzy predicate p' such that $m < n$ and $p = p'$. Informally, all parameters are needed in the definition of p;
6. f is a *scoring* function $f \colon ([0,1]_m)^{l+h} \to [0,1]_m$, which combines the scores of the l relations $R_i(c_i')$ and the n fuzzy predicates $p_j(c_j'')$ into an overall *score* to be assigned to the rule head $R(c)$. We assume that f is *monotone*, that is, for each $v, v' \in ([0,1]_m)^{l+h}$ such that $v \leqslant v'$, it holds $f(v) \leqslant f(v')$, where $(v_1, \ldots, v_{l+h}) \leqslant (v_1', \ldots, v_{l+h}')$ iff $v_i \leqslant v_i'$ for all i. We also assume that the computational cost of f and all fuzzy predicates p_i is bounded by a constant.

We call $R(\boldsymbol{x})$ the *head* and $\exists \boldsymbol{y}.f(R_1(\boldsymbol{z}_1), \ldots, R_l(\boldsymbol{z}_l), p_1(\boldsymbol{z}_1'), \ldots, p_h(\boldsymbol{z}_h'))$ the *body* of the rule. We assume that relations occurring in $\mathcal{O}$ may appear in rules in $\mathcal{P}$ and that relations occurring in $\mathcal{F}$ do not occur in the head of rules and axioms (so, we do not allow that the fact relations occurring in $\mathcal{F}$ can be redefined by $\mathcal{P}$ or $\mathcal{O}$). As usual in deductive databases, the relations in $\mathcal{F}$ are called *extensional* relations, while the others are *intensional* relations.

Example 4. Consider again Example 2. The following rule may be used to retrieve a cheap single room in a hotel close to the city center:

$$q(x_1, x_2) \leftarrow CloseHotelTable(x_1, x_2, x_3, x_4, x_5) \cdot cheap(x_3) \,,$$

where

$$cheap(price) = \max\left(0, 1 - \frac{price}{250}\right).$$

In the rule, *cheap* is a fuzzy predicate that computes the degree of cheapness of a given price. The overall score to be assigned to the retrieved hotels $\langle c_1, c_2 \rangle$ is computed as the product (which is here the scoring function) of the degree of the closeness of a hotel (that is, the score of $CloseHotelTable(c_1, c_2, c_3, c_4, c_5)$) and the degree of cheapness of it ($cheap(c_3)$). Clearly, the product is a monotone score combination function. We will see that the instances of $q(x_1, x_2)$ together with their score will be

ID	HOTEL	s
1	Verdi	0.45
2	Puccini	0.26
3	Rossini	0.17 .

Semantically, an interpretation $\mathcal{I}$ is a *model* of a rule r of the form $R(x) \leftarrow \exists y.\phi(x, y)$, where $\phi(x, y) = \exists y.f(R_1(z_1), \ldots, R_l(z_l), p_1(z_1'), \ldots, p_h(z_h'))$, denoted $\mathcal{I} \models r$, iff for all $c \in \Delta^n$ such that $R^{\mathcal{I}}(c)$ is defined, the following holds (where $\phi^{\mathcal{I}}(c, c')$ is obtained from $\phi(c, c')$ by replacing every R_i by $R_i^{\mathcal{I}}$ and every constant c by $c^{\mathcal{I}}$):

$$R^{\mathcal{I}}(c) \geqslant \sup_{c' \in \Delta \times \cdots \times \Delta, \ \phi^{\mathcal{I}}(c, c') \text{ is defined}} \phi^{\mathcal{I}}(c, c') .$$

We say $\mathcal{I}$ is a *model* of a knowledge base $\mathcal{K}$, denoted $\mathcal{I} \models \mathcal{K}$, iff $\mathcal{I}$ is a model of each expression $E \in \mathcal{F} \cup \mathcal{O} \cup \mathcal{P}$. We say $\mathcal{K}$ entails $R(c)$ to degree s, denoted $\mathcal{K} \models \langle R(c), s \rangle$, iff for each model $\mathcal{I}$ of $\mathcal{K}$, it is true that $R^{\mathcal{I}}(c) \geqslant s$ whenever $R^{\mathcal{I}}(c)$ is defined. The *greatest lower bound* of $R(c)$ relative to $\mathcal{K}$ is $glb(\mathcal{K}, R(c)) = \sup\{s \mid \mathcal{K} \models \langle R(c), s \rangle\}$.

Example 5. The table in Example 4 reports the greatest lower bound of the instances of $q(x_1, x_2)$. In particular, $glb(\mathcal{K}, q(1, Verdi)) = 0.45$.

Example 6. Consider again Example 3. Now, suppose that in buying a car, preferably we would like to pay around \$12000 and the car should have less than 15000 km. Of course, our constraints on price and kilometers are not crisp as we may still accept to some degree, e.g., a car's cost of \$12200 and with 16000 km. Hence, these constraints are rather *vague*. We model this by means of so-called left-shoulder functions (see Fig. 4 for some typical fuzzy membership functions), which is a well known fuzzy membership function in fuzzy set theory. We may model the vague constraint on the cost with $ls(x; 10000, 14000)$ dictating that we are definitely satisfied if the price is less than \$10000, but can pay up to \$14000 to a lesser degree of satisfaction. Similarly, we may model the vague constraint on the kilometers with $ls(x; 13000, 17000)$.[1] We also set some preference (weights) on these two vague constraints, say the weight 0.7 to the price constraint and 0.3 to the kilometers constraint, indicating that we give more priority to the price rather than to the car's kilometers. The rules encoding the above conditions are represented in Fig. 5. Rule (1) in Fig. 5 encodes the preference on the price. Here, $ls(p; 10000, 14000)$ is the function that given a price p returns the degree of truth provided by the left-shoulder function $ls(\cdot; 10000, 14000)$ evaluated on the input p. Similarly, for rule (2). Rule (3) encodes the combination of the preferences by taking into account the weight given to each preference. The table below reports the instances of $Buy(x, p, k)$ together with their greatest lower bound.

---

[1] Recall that in our setting, all fuzzy membership functions provide a truth value in $[0, 1]_m$.

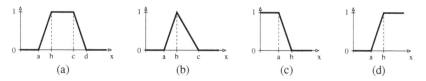

Fig. 4. (a) Trapezoidal function $trz(x; a, b, c, d)$, (b) triangular function $tri(x; a, b, c)$, (c) left shoulder function $ls(x; a, b)$, and (d) right shoulder function $rs(x; a, b)$

$$Pref1(x,p) \leftarrow min(Cars(x), hasPrice(x,p), ls(p; 10000, 14000)) ; \quad (1)$$
$$Pref2(x,k) \leftarrow min(Cars(x), hasKM(x,k), ls(k; 13000, 17000)) ; \quad (2)$$
$$Buy(x,p,k) \leftarrow 0.7 \cdot Pref1(x,p) + 0.3 \cdot Pref2(x,k) . \quad (3)$$

Fig. 5. The car buying rules

ID	PRICE	KM	s
455	12500	10000	0.56
34	12000	15000	0.50
1812	11000	16000	0.60 .

The basic inference problem that we are interested in here is the top-k retrieval problem, which is formulated as follows.

Top-k Retrieval. Given a knowledge base $\mathcal{K}$, retrieve k tuples $\langle c, s \rangle$ that instantiate the query relation R with maximal scores (if k such tuples exist), and rank them in decreasing order relative to the score s, denoted

$$ans_k(\mathcal{K}, R) = Top_k\{\langle c, s \rangle \mid s = glb(\mathcal{K}, R(c))\} .$$

Example 7. It can be verified that the answer to the top-2 problem for Example 6 is

ID	PRICE	KM	s
1812	11000	16000	0.60
455	12500	10000	0.56 .

Whereas for Example 5 the answer to the top-2 problem is

ID	HOTEL	s
1	Verdi	0.45
2	Puccini	0.26 .

3   Top-k Query Answering for Deterministic KBs

We next provide a top-down top-k query answering algorithm.

We say that $\mathcal{K}$ is *deterministic* if for each relation symbol R there is at most one axiom or rule in $\mathcal{K}$ having R in its head. Given $\mathcal{K}$, we first note that we can remove the $\mathcal{O}$

component by transforming axioms into rules. Indeed, can rewrite $C_1 \sqcap \ldots \sqcap C_l \sqsubseteq C$ as $\sigma_C \leftarrow \min(\sigma_{C_1}, \ldots, \sigma_{C_l})$, where

$$\sigma_C = \begin{cases} A(x) & \text{if } C = A \\ R(x_1, \ldots, x_{i-1}, x, x_{i+1}, \ldots, x_n) & \text{if } C = \exists i{:}R \,, \end{cases}$$

and A is an atomic concept name. So, without loss of generality, we assume that $\mathcal{O}$ is empty. Obviously, we may also use a more expressive $\mathcal{O}$ component in which we consider axioms of the form $f(C_1, \ldots, C_l) \sqsubseteq C$ instead, where f is a score combination function. The translation (and so semantics) would be $\sigma_C \leftarrow f(\sigma_{C_1}, \ldots, \sigma_{C_l})$.

Concerning the computation of the top-k answers, of course, we always have the possibility to compute all answers, to rank them afterwards, and to select the top-k ones only. However, this requires computing the scores of all answers. We would like to avoid this in cases in which the extensional database is large and potentially too many tuples would satisfy the query.

A distinguishing feature of our query answering procedure is that we do not determine all answers, but collect, during the computation, answers incrementally together and we can stop as soon as we have gathered k answers above a computed threshold.

Overall, we build a procedure on top of current technology for top-k retrieval in databases, specifically on RankSQL [9]. In the database we store the facts and new derived facts and use RankSQL to retrieve incrementally new tuples. On top of it, we have a reasoning module, which deals with the rules of the KB.

The presentation of our algorithm proceeds as follows. We first present a top-k answering procedure for deterministic KBs. Then we address the more general case of non-deterministic KBs as well. In the following, given an intensional relation Q, we denote by r_Q the set of all rules $r : Q(x) \leftarrow \phi \in \mathcal{P}$ (that is, the set of all rules r in $\mathcal{P}$ having Q in their head). Given $r : Q(x) \leftarrow \phi \in \mathcal{P}$, we denote by $s(Q, r)$ the set of all *sons* of Q relative to r (that is, the set of all intensional relation symbols occurring in ϕ). We denote by $p(Q)$ the set of all *parents* of Q, that is, the set $p(Q) = \{R_i : Q \in s(R_i, r)\}$ (that is, the set of all relation symbols directly depending on Q).

The procedure *TopAnswers* is detailed in Fig. 6. We assume that facts are stored into database tables, as specified in the facts component description. We also use some auxiliary functions and data structures: (i) for each intensional relation P, $rankedList(P)$ is a database relation containing the current top-ranked instances of P together with their score. For each P, the tuples $\langle c, s \rangle$ in $rankedList(P)$ are ranked in decreasing order with respect to the score s. We do not allow $\langle c, s \rangle$ and $\langle c, s' \rangle$ to occur in $rankedList(P)$ with $s \neq s'$ (if so, then we remove the tuple with the lower score); (ii) the variable dg collects the relation symbols that the query relation Q depends on[2]; (iii) the array variable exp traces the rule bodies that have been "expanded" (the relation symbols occurring in the rule body are put into the active list); (iv) the variable in keeps track of the relation symbols that have been put into the active list so far due to an expansion (to avoid, to put the same relation symbol multiple times in the active list due to rule body expansion); (v) δ is a threshold with the property that if we have retrieved k tuples for Q

---

[2] Given a rule, the relation in the head *directly depends on* the relations in the body. *Depends on* is the transitive closure of the relation "directly depends on" with respect to a set of rules.

Procedure $TopAnswers(\mathcal{K}, Q, k)$
Input: KB $\mathcal{K}$, intensional query relation symbol Q, $k \geqslant 1$;
Output: Mapping $rankedList$ such that $rankedList(Q)$ contains top-k answers of Q
Init: $\delta = 1$, **for all** rules $r : P(\boldsymbol{x}) \leftarrow \phi$ in $\mathcal{P}$ **do**
               if P intensional **then** $rankedList(P) = \emptyset$;
               if P extensional **then** $rankedList(P) = T_P$ **endfor**
1. **loop**
2. $Active := \{Q\}$, $dg := \{Q\}$, $in := \emptyset$,
               for all rules $r : P(\boldsymbol{x}) \leftarrow \phi$ **do** $exp(P, r) = false$;
3.   **while** $Active \neq \emptyset$ **do**
4.   **select** $P \in A$ where $r : P(\boldsymbol{x}) \leftarrow \phi$, $Active := Active \setminus \{P\}$, $dg := dg \cup s(P, r)$;
5. $\langle t, s \rangle := getNextTuple(P, r)$
6.   **if** $\langle t, s \rangle \neq NULL$ **then** insert $\langle t, s \rangle$ into $rankedList(P)$,
               $Active := Active \cup (p(P) \cap dg)$;
7.   **if not** $exp(P, r)$ **then** $exp(P, r) = true$,
               $Active := Active \cup (s(P, r) \setminus in)$, $in := in \cup s(p, r)$;
    endwhile
8.   Update threshold δ;
9. **until** $rankedList(Q)$ does contain k top-ranked tuples with score above δ
             or $rL' = rankedList$;
10. **return** top-k ranked tuples in $rankedList(Q)$;

Procedure $getNextTuple(P, r)$
Input: intensional relation symbol P and rule $r: P(\boldsymbol{x}) \leftarrow \exists \boldsymbol{y}. f(R_1(\boldsymbol{z}_1), \ldots, R_n(\boldsymbol{z}_l)) \in \mathcal{P}$;
Output: Next tuple satisfying the body of the r together with the score
  loop
1.   Generate next new instance tuple $\langle t, s \rangle$ of P,
             using tuples in $rankedList(R_i)$ and RankSQL
2.   **if** there is no $\langle t, s' \rangle \in rankedList(P, r)$ with $s \leqslant s'$ **then** exit loop
  until no new valid join tuple can be generated
3. **return** $\langle t, s \rangle$ if it exists **else return** $NULL$

Fig. 6. The top-k query answering procedure

with the score above δ, then we can stop, as it is guaranteed that any new tuple being an instance of Q has a score below δ. The threshold δ is determined by the RankSQL system and is described in more detail in [3,6].

Overall, the procedure works as follows. Assume, we are interested in determining the top-k answers of $Q(\boldsymbol{x})$. We start with putting the relation symbol Q in the *active* list of relation symbols $Active$. At each iteration step, we select a new relation symbol P from the queue $Active$ and get a new tuple ($getNexTuple(P, r)$) satisfying the rule body r whose head contains P with respect to the answers gathered so far. If the evaluation leads to a new answer for P ($\langle t, s \rangle \neq NULL$), we update the current answer set $rankedList(P)$ and add all relations P_j directly depending on p to the queue $Active$. At some point, the active list will become empty and we have actually found correct answers of $Q(\boldsymbol{x})$. A threshold will be used to determine when we can stop retrieving tuples. Indeed, the threshold determines when any newly retrieved tuple for Q scores lower than the current top-k, and thus cannot modify the top-k ranking (step 9). So, step 1 loops until we do not have k answers above the threshold, or two successive loops do not modify the current set of answers (step 9). Step 2 initializes the active list of relations. Step 3 loops until no relation symbol has to be processed anymore. In step 4, we select a relation symbol to be processed. In step 5, we retrieve the next answer for P. If a new answer has been retrieved (step 6, $\langle t, s \rangle \neq NULL$), then we update the current answer set $rankedList(P)$ and add all relations P_j that directly depend on P to the queue $Active$. In step 7, we put once all intensional relation symbols appearing in the rule body of P in the active list for further processing.

Finally, the $getNextTuple$ procedure's (see Fig. 6) main purpose is, given a relation symbol P and a rule $r : P(x) \leftarrow \phi$, to get back the next tuple (and its score) satisfying the conditions of the rule r. It essentially converts r into a RankSQL query to be submitted to the database engine (the translation is pretty standard) and returns the next top ranked unseen tuple.

Example 8. For instance, consider

$$Buy(x, p, k) \leftarrow 0.7 \cdot Pref1(x, p) + 0.3 \cdot Pref2(x, k)$$

as described in Example 6. Step 2 of the $getNextTuple$ procedure can be implemented as the RankSQL query

SELECT	p1.id, p1.price, p2.km
FROM	rankedList(Pref1) p1, rankedList(Pref2) p2
WHERE	p1.id = p2.id AND (exclude already processed tuples for rule r)
ORDER BY	0.7*p1.s + 0.3*p2.s
NEXT	1

The NEXT k statement allows incrementally to access to the next k tuples of the query (see the iMPro algorithm in [3]). We also use the condition "exclude already processed tuples for rule r" to guarantee that we do not join tuples twice for the rule r. This can be implemented using additional flags in $rankedList(Pref_i)$. Afterwards, we can proceed with the other steps of the $getNextTuple$ procedure.

For more details on RankSQL, the interested reader may refer to [9,8]. Using Rank-SQL [9] has a further advantage as it directly provides us the threshold δ (see [3,6]) to be used to stop the computation.

Example 9. Assume that we have the following query rule

$$Q(x) \leftarrow \min(R_1(x, y), R_2(y, z)),$$

where Q is the query relation, and R_1 and R_2 are extensional relations with tables as described in Fig. 7, left side. A top-2 retrieval computation is reported in Fig. 7, right side. In this case, the threshold δ is computed as (see [6])

$$\delta_1 = t_1^{\perp}.score \cdot t_2^{\top}.score$$
$$\delta_2 = t_1^{\top}.score \cdot t_2^{\perp}.score$$
$$\delta = \max(\delta_1, \delta_2),$$

ID	R_1	R_2
1	a b 1.0	m h 0.95
2	c d 0.9	m j 0.85
3	e f 0.8	f k 0.75
4	l m 0.7	m n 0.65
5	o p 0.6	p q 0.55
⋮	⋮ ⋮ ⋮	⋮ ⋮ ⋮

			TopAnswers		
It.	Active	P	Δ_r	rankedList(P)	δ
1.	Q	Q	$\langle e,k,0.75\rangle$	$\langle e,k,0.75\rangle$	0.8
2.	Q	Q	$\langle l,h,0.7\rangle$	$\langle e,k,0.75\rangle, \langle l,h,0.7\rangle$	0.75
3.	Q	Q	$\langle l,j,0.7\rangle$	$\langle e,k,0.75\rangle, \langle l,h,0.7\rangle, \langle l,j,0.7\rangle$	0.75
4.	Q	Q	$\langle l,n,0.65\rangle$	$\langle e,k,0.75\rangle, \langle l,h,0.7\rangle,$ $\langle l,j,0.7\rangle, \langle l,n,0.65\rangle$	0.7

Fig. 7. Facts and computation of Example 9

			TopAnswers		
It.	Active	P	Δ_r	rankedList(P)	δ
1.	Q	Q	$\langle 1, Verdi, 0.45\rangle$	$\langle 1, Verdi, 0.45\rangle$	–
2.	Q	Q	$\langle 2, Puccini, 0.26\rangle$	$\langle 1, Verdi, 0.45\rangle, \langle 2, Puccini, 0.26\rangle$	0.25

Fig. 8. Facts and computation of Example 10

where $t_i^{\perp}$ is the last tuple seen in R_i, while $t_i^{\top}$ is the top ranked one in R_i. With $t_i.score$ we indicate the tuple's score.

The first call of $getNextTuple(Q)$ finds the tuple $\langle e, k, 0.75\rangle$. In the second call, we get $\langle l, h, 0.7\rangle$. In the third call, we get $\langle l, j, 0.7\rangle$. Finally, in the fourth call, we retrieve $\langle l, n, 0.65\rangle$. As now $rankedList(Q)$ contains two answers not smaller than the threshold 0.7, RankSQL will stop in providing new tuples in the $getNextTuple$ procedure, and we return $\{\langle e, k, 0.75\rangle, \langle l, h, 0.7\rangle\}$. Note that no additional retrieved answer may have a score above 0.7. Indeed, the next one would be $\langle o, q, 0.55\rangle$. Hence, in this case, not all tuples are processed.

Example 10. Consider Example 4 and the query

$$q(x_1, x_2) \leftarrow CloseHotelTable(x_1, x_2, x_3, x_4, x_5) \cdot cheap(x_3) \ .$$

The top-2 computation is shown in Fig. 8. After the second iteration, RankSQL stops (see [3]) in providing new tuples in the $getNextTuple$ as we have already two tuples for q above the threshold, and RankSQL also knows that any successively retrieved tuple have a score below $0.25 \cdot 1.0 = 0.25$ (1.0 is assumed as the highest possible score for the degree of cheapness of the price for the single room in hotel Rossini). Of course, in the worst case, RankSQL has to sequentially scan the whole table as we may not know in advance how the fuzzy predicate *cheap* evaluates on the tuples. In fact, the tuple with the lowest degree of closeness may end up with the highest degree of cheapness.

Let us briefly discuss the computational complexity. Let $\mathcal{K}$ be a KB. As we have seen, the $\mathcal{O}$ component can be translated into $\mathcal{P}$, and thus $\mathcal{O} = \emptyset$ can be assumed. Let D_Q be the set of relation symbols that *depend* on the query relation symbol Q. Of course, only relation symbols in D_Q may appear in *Active*. Let $ground(\mathcal{F} \cup \mathcal{P})$ denote the grounding of the logic program $\mathcal{F} \cup \mathcal{P}$. For a rule r_i of the form $R_i(\boldsymbol{x}) \leftarrow \exists \boldsymbol{y}.\phi_i(\boldsymbol{x}, \boldsymbol{y})$, let k_i be the arity of the body of the rule r, and let k be the maximal arity for all rules in $\mathcal{P}$. Let p_i be of arity n_i, and let n be the maximal arity of relation symbols. Therefore, the number of ground instances of this rule is bounded by $|HU|^{k_i}$, and thus is bounded by $|HU|^k$, where HU is the Herbrand universe of $\mathcal{F} \cup \mathcal{P}$. Similarly, the number of ground instance of R_i is bounded by $|HU|^{n_i}$, and thus is bounded by $|HU|^n$. Let c_i be the cost of evaluating the score of the rule body of r_i.

Now, observe that any tuple's score is increasing as it enters in *rankedList*. Hence, the truth of any ground instance of relation symbol R_i is increasing as R_i enters in the *Active* list (step 6), except it enters due to step 7, which may happen one time only. Therefore, each R_i will appear in *Active* at most $O(|HU|^{n_i} \cdot m + 1)$ times,[3] as a relation symbol is only re-entered into *Active* if a ground instance of $R_i(\boldsymbol{x})$ evaluates to an increased value, plus the additional entry due to step 7. As a consequence, the worst-case complexity is

$$O(\sum_{R_i \in D_Q} c_i \cdot (|HU|^{n_i} \cdot m + 1)) \, .$$

If for ease we assume that the cost c_i is $O(1)$ and that m is a fixed parameter (that is, a constant), then we get a worst-case complexity of

$$O(|ground(\mathcal{F} \cup \mathcal{P})|) \, ,$$

and so *TopAnswer* is exponential with respect to $|\mathcal{F} \cup \mathcal{P}|$ (combined complexity), but polynomial in $|\mathcal{F}|$ (data complexity), and so is as for classical Datalog. The complexity result is not surprising as we resemble a top-down query answering procedure for Datalog. We have the following termination and correctness result (termination is guaranteed by the finiteness of $[0, 1]_m$ and the monotonicity of the score combination functions).

Theorem 1. *Let $\mathcal{K}$ be a deterministic KB, and let Q be a query. Then, TopAnswers($\mathcal{K}$, Q, k) terminates with TopAnswers($\mathcal{K}, Q, k) = ans_k(\mathcal{K}, Q)$.*

4   Top-k Query Answering for General KBs

Our top-k retrieval algorithm is based on the fact that whenever we find k tuples with score above the threshold we can stop. Unfortunately, if R is in the head of more than one rule, this is no longer true, and we have to modify slightly the computation of the threshold. Note that since interpretations involve partial functions, e.g., $R(x) \leftarrow R_1(x)$ and $R(x) \leftarrow R_2(x)$ are not the same as $Q(x) \leftarrow \max(R_1(x), R_2(x))$ (in the latter case, x has to belong to both R_1 and R_2, while in the former case, it suffices that x belongs either to R_1 or to R_2).[4]

To accommodate the case where not always $|r_R| \leqslant 1$, we have to make the following modifications to the *TopAnswer* procedure as shown in Fig. 9. Essentially, we process all rules related to a selected relation symbol P (step 4.1), and the threshold is updated according to step 8, where each δ_r, for $r \in r_Q$, is the threshold determined by RankSQL

---

[3] We recall that m is the parameter in $[0, 1]_m$.

[4] If for an application we may live with $Q(x) \leftarrow \max(R_1(x), R_2(x))$, then this guarantees that we may restrict our attention to deterministic KBs.

Procedure $TopAnswersGen(\mathcal{K}, Q, k)$
Input: KB $\mathcal{K}$, intensional query relation Q, $k \geqslant 1$;
Output: Mapping $rankedList$ such that $rankedList(Q)$ contains top-k answers of Q
Init: $\delta = 1$, $\forall r \in r_Q.\delta_r = 1$, **for all** rules $r : P(\boldsymbol{x}) \leftarrow \phi$ in $\mathcal{P}$ **do**
              if P intensional **then** $rankedList(P) = \emptyset$;
              if P extensional **then** $rankedList(P) = T_P$ **endfor**
1. **loop**
2. $Active := \{Q\}$, $dg := \{Q\}$, $in := \emptyset$,
                    for all rules $r : P(\boldsymbol{x}) \leftarrow \phi$ **do** $exp(P, r) = false$;
3.   **while** $Active \neq \emptyset$ **do**
4.   **select** $P \in A$, $Active := Active \setminus \{P\}$;
4.1   **for all** $r : P(\boldsymbol{x}) \leftarrow \phi \in \mathcal{P}$, $dg := dg \cup s(P, r)$;
5. $\langle t, s \rangle := getNextTuple(P, r)$
6.   **if** $\langle t, s \rangle \neq NULL$ **then** insert $\langle t, s \rangle$ into $rankedList(P)$,
                          $Active := Active \cup (p(P) \cap dg)$;
7.   **if not** $exp(P, r)$ **then** $exp(P, r) = true$,
                          $Active := Active \cup (s(P, r) \setminus in)$, $in := in \cup s(p, r)$;
              endfor
          endwhile
8.   Update threshold as $\delta = \max_{r \in r_Q} \delta_r$;
9. **until** $rankedList(Q)$ does contain k top-ranked tuples with score above δ
                    or $rL' = rankedList$;
10. **return** top-k ranked tuples in $rankedList(Q)$;

Fig. 9. The top-k query answering procedure for general KBs

as for the deterministic case. Here, we have to use max, since a tuple instantiating the query relation Q may be derived for *some* of the rules in r_Q. The following example illustrates the basic principle behind the $TopAnswersGen$ procedure.

Example 11. Consider the rules

$$r_1 : Q(x) \leftarrow R_1(x) \ ;$$
$$r_2 : Q(x) \leftarrow P(x) \ ;$$
$$r_3 : P(x) \leftarrow R_2(x)$$

and facts in Fig. 10, left side. The top-2 computation is shown in Fig. 10, right side. After step 5, we can stop, since we already have two answers with a score above the threshold 0.4, and we do not need to continue anymore. Note that any successively retrieved answer, e.g., $\langle e, 0.3 \rangle$ has a score below the threshold 0.4.

The complexity is as for the deterministic case, and we have the following termination and correctness result.

Theorem 2. *Let $\mathcal{K}$ be a general KB, and let Q be a query. Then, $TopAnswersGen(\mathcal{K}, Q, k)$ terminates with $TopAnswersGen(\mathcal{K}, Q, k) = ans_k(\mathcal{K}, Q)$.*

R_1		R_2		*TopAnswers*							
				It.	Active	P	Δ_r	rankedList(P)	δ	δ_{r_1}	δ_{r_2}
ID	s	ID	s	1.	Q	Q	$\langle a,0.5\rangle$	$\langle a,0.5\rangle$	1.0	0.5	1.0
a	0.5	c	0.7	2.	P	P	$\langle c,0.7\rangle$	$\langle c,0.7\rangle$	–	–	–
b	0.4	d	0.2	3.	Q	Q	$\langle b,0.4\rangle$	$\langle a,0.5\rangle, \langle b,0.4\rangle$	1.0	0.4	1.0
e	0.3	g	0.1		Q	Q	$\langle c,0.7\rangle$	$\langle c,0.7\rangle, \langle a,0.5\rangle, \langle b,0.4\rangle$	0.7	0.4	0.7
f	0.1	h	0.05	4.	P	P	$\langle d,0.2\rangle$	$\langle c,0.7\rangle, \langle d,0.2\rangle$	–	–	–
				5.	Q	Q	$\langle d,0.2\rangle$	$\langle c,0.7\rangle, \langle a,0.5\rangle, \langle b,0.4\rangle, \langle d,0.2\rangle$	0.4	0.4	0.2

Fig. 10. Facts and computation of Example 11

5   Related Work

While there are many works addressing the top-k problem for vague queries in databases (cf. [1,3,5,4,6,7,9,8,10]), little is known for the corresponding problem in knowledge representation and reasoning. For instance, [21] considers non-recursive fuzzy logic programs in which the score combination function is a function of the score of the atoms in the body only (no expensive fuzzy predicates are allowed). The work [16] considers non-recursive fuzzy logic programs as well, though the score combination function may consider expensive fuzzy predicates. However, a score combination function is allowed in the query rule only. We point out that in the case of non-recursive rules and/or axioms, we may rely on a query rewriting mechanism, which, given an initial query, rewrites it, using rules and/or axioms of the KB, into a set of new queries until no new query rule can be derived (this phase may require exponential time relative to the size of the KB). The obtained queries may then be submitted directly to a top-k retrieval database engine. The answers to each query are then merged using the disjunctive threshold algorithm given in [16]. The works [17,15] address the top-k retrieval problem for the description logic *DL-Lite* only, though recursion is allowed among the axioms. Again, the score combination function may consider expensive fuzzy predicates. However, a score combination function is allowed in the query only. The work [19] shows an application of top-k retrieval to the case of multimedia information retrieval by relying on a fuzzy variant of *DLR-Lite*. Finally, [18] addresses the top-k retrieval for general (recursive) fuzzy LPs, though no expensive fuzzy predicates are allowed. Closest to our work is clearly [18]. In fact, our work extends [18] by allowing expensive fuzzy predicates, which have the effect that the threshold mechanism designed in [18] does not work anymore. Furthermore, in this paper, we made an effort to plug-in current top-k database technology, while [18] does not and provides an ad-hoc solution. Though we have not yet performed experimental evaluations, we hope that this choice, beside allowing a more expressive language, will provide better efficiency.

6   Summary and Outlook

The top-k retrieval problem is an important problem in logic-based languages for the Semantic Web. We have addressed this issue for a combination of a fuzzy DL and LP.

An implementation of our algorithm is under development, by relying on RankSQL. Other main topics for future work include: (i) Can we apply similar ideas to more expressive DLs and/or non-monotonic LPs? (ii) How can we approach the top-k problem under a probabilistic setting, or more generally under uncertainty, possibly relying on emerging top-k retrieval systems for uncertain database management [13,14]?

Acknowledgments. Thomas Lukasiewicz is supported by the German Research Foundation (DFG) under the Heisenberg Programme. We thank the reviewers for their constructive and useful comments, which helped to improve this work.

References

1. Bruno, N., Chaudhuri, S., Gravano, L.: Top-k selection queries over relational databases: Mapping strategies and performance evaluation. ACM TODS 27(2), 153–187 (2002)
2. Calvanese, D., De Giacomo, G., Lembo, D., Lenzerini, M., Rosati, R.: Data complexity of query answering in description logics. In: Proc. KR-2006, pp. 260–270 (2006)
3. Chang, K.C.-C., Hwang, S.-W.: Minimal probing: Supporting expensive predicates for top-k queries. In: Proc. SIGMOD-2002, pp. 346–357 (2002)
4. Fagin, R.: Combining fuzzy information: An overview. SIGMOD Rec. 31(2), 109–118 (2002)
5. Fagin, R., Lotem, A., Naor, M.: Optimal aggregation algorithms for middleware. In: Proc. PODS-2001 (2001)
6. Ilyas, I.F., Aref, W.G., Elmagarmid, A.K.: Supporting top-k join queries in relational databases. In: Aberer, K., Koubarakis, M., Kalogeraki, V. (eds.) DBISP2P 2003. LNCS, vol. 2944, pp. 754–765. Springer, Heidelberg (2004)
7. Ilyas, I.F., Aref, W.G., Elmagarmid, A.K., Elmongui, H.G., Shah, R., Vitter, J.S.: Adaptive rank-aware query optimization in relational databases. ACM TODS 31(4), 1257–1304 (2006)
8. Li, C., Chang, K.C.-C., Ilyas, I.F.: Supporting ad-hoc ranking aggregates. In: Proc. SIGMOD-2006, pp. 61–72 (2006)
9. Li, C., Chang, K.C.-C., Ilyas, I.F., Song, S.: RankSQL: Query algebra and optimization for relational top-k queries. In: Proc. SIGMOD-2005, pp. 131–142 (2005)
10. Marian, A., Bruno, N., Gravano, L.: Evaluating top-k queries over web-accessible databases. ACM TODS 29(2), 319–362 (2004)
11. Meghini, C., Sebastiani, F., Straccia, U.: A model of multimedia information retrieval. J. ACM 48(5), 909–970 (2001)
12. Ragone, A., Straccia, U., Di Noia, T., Di Sciascio, E., Donini, F.M.: Vague knowledge bases for matchmaking in P2P e-marketplaces. In: Proc. ESWC-2007, pp. 414–428 (2007)
13. Ré, C., Dalvi, N., Suciu, D.: Efficient top-k query evaluation on probabilistic data. In: Proc. ICDE-2007, pp. 886–895 (2007)
14. Soliman, M.A., Ilyas, I.F., Chang, K.C.: Top-k query processing in uncertain databases. In: Proc. ICDE-2007, pp. 896–905 (2007)
15. Straccia, U.: Answering vague queries in fuzzy *DL-Lite*. In: Proc. IPMU-2006, pp. 2238–2245 (2006)
16. Straccia, U.: Towards top-k query answering in deductive databases. In: Proc. SMC-2006, pp. 4873–4879 (2006)
17. Straccia, U.: Towards top-k query answering in description logics: The case of DL-Lite. In: Fisher, M., van der Hoek, W., Konev, B., Lisitsa, A. (eds.) JELIA 2006. LNCS (LNAI), vol. 4160, pp. 439–451. Springer, Heidelberg (2006)

18. Straccia, U.: Towards vague query answering in logic programming for logic-based information retrieval. In: Proc. IFSA-2007, pp. 125–134 (2007)
19. Straccia, U., Visco, G.: DLMedia: An ontology mediated multimedia information retrieval system. In: Proc. DL-2007 (2007)
20. Vojtáš, P.: Fuzzy logic programming. Fuzzy Sets and Systems 124, 361–370 (2001)
21. Vojtáš, P.: Fuzzy logic aggregation for semantic web search for the best (top-k) answer. In: Sanchez, E. (ed.) Fuzzy Logic and the Semantic Web. Capturing Intelligence, ch. 17, pp. 341–359. Elsevier, Amsterdam (2006)

A Fuzzy Set-Based Approach to Temporal Databases

J. Campaña[1], M.C. Garrido[2], N. Marín[1], and O. Pons[1,*]

[1] Dept. Computer Science and A.I.,
University of Granada, 18071 - Granada, Spain
{jesuscg,nicm,opc}@decsai.ugr.es
[2] Junta de Andalucía
cglupi@gmail.com

Abstract. The primary aim of temporal databases is to offer a common framework to those DB applications that need to store or handle different types of temporal data from a variety of sources since they allow the concept of time to be unified from the point of view of meaning, representation and manipulation. Although at first sight the incorporation of time into a DB might appear to be a direct and even simple task, it is, however, quite complex because not only must new structures and specific operators be included but the semantics of classical manipulation sentences (insert, update or delete) must be changed when temporal data are present. In addition, temporal information is not always as precise as desired since it is affected by imprecision due to the use of natural language or to the nature of the source. In this paper, we deal with the problem of the update and query operations when time is expressed by means of a fuzzy interval of dates. Throughout the text, we will see how the delete and insert operations are particular cases of the update process and will therefore be implicitly presented in the paper.

Keywords: Fuzzy Data, Temporal Database, Fuzzy Interval.

1   Introduction

Temporal databases (TDB), in the broadest sense, offer a common framework for all database applications that involve certain temporal aspects when organizing data. These databases allow the time concept to be unified in terms of the representation, the semantics and the manipulation.

Although there is nothing new about database (DB) applications involving temporal data and they have in fact been developed since relational databases were first used, application programmers were responsible for designing, representing, programming and managing the necessary temporal concepts.

One of the first formalizations of the concept of granularity in the time domain can be seen in [Clif88], but the approach to this problem from the DB and the temporal reasoning points of view came later and was first studied in depth in

---

* Corresponding author.

H. Prade and V.S. Subrahmanian (Eds.): SUM 2007, LNAI 4772, pp. 31–44, 2007.
© Springer-Verlag Berlin Heidelberg 2007

1990. In this sense, the papers by Duncan [Dun98], Goralwalla [Gora98] and Bettini [Bett98a] are very relevant because of the introduction of the concept of calendar and the extension of the granularity definition.

Up until now, most work (both theoretical and practical) carried out on this topic has used the relational DB model as a starting point (since it is the most complete and consolidated model) with the results based on the extension of the table schemata [Tans93], the range of operators to be used [Elma90] and on the addition of specific integrity constraints related to the new data types [Snod95] [Etzi98] [Bett00].

There are other interesting proposals about the architecture of a system that supports the time concept, as can be seen in [Bett98b]. In line with the theoretical results obtained, much effort has therefore been devoted to achieving a temporal language either as an extension of SQL [Sard90] [Snod98] or of Quel [Snod87].

Other approaches to temporal databases deal with the problem of imperfect temporal data in the sense that we do not know exactly when an event happened but we have approximate information about it. In [Dyre98] this problem is tackled from the probability theory point of view by assigning a probability distribution to the set of possible instants. The authors call this interpretation valid-time indeterminacy. The main inconvenience of this proposal is that in many cases it is very difficult (or even impossible) for the user to give the underlying mass function that associates a probability to every chronon. More over, if the user does not provide the mass function, the method proposed is useless and some important information provided by the user is wasted. This problem is also dealt with in [Chou05] by attaching a probability distribution to every chronon.

On the other hand, certain authors working in the area of soft computing have opted to study temporal data affected by imprecision from the possibility theory point of view, which is more flexible and better represents users' appreciations. In the case of relational databases (as in our case), Kurutach's paper [Kuru98] presents a preliminary study of this topic with a formal representation of fuzzy-temporal data and various query-related operators. Nevertheless, crucial operations such as insert, update and delete (which have strong constraints) are not addressed.

A significant survey of papers relating to spatio-temporal databases can be found in [Calu04]. More specifically in [Dragi04] and [Bord04] the fuzzy sets theory is used to perform temporal interpolation in a GIS object-oriented database. In [Tre97] the problem of fuzzy time is also addressed in an object-oriented environment, something which is beyond the scope of this paper.

In summary, there are a wide range of interesting proposals on this topic but there are still many important problems to be solved, such as the ones being tackled in this paper.

The paper is organized as follows. The second section explores the preliminary concepts and includes a brief summary of temporal databases, fuzzy sets and fuzzy database operators. Section 3 introduces our particular way of representing and interpreting fuzzy time. Section 4 examines the manipulation of fuzzy temporal data focusing on the *update* operator since *delete* and *insert* are particular cases of it. In order to complete the DML, Section 5 describes different types of queries on a fuzzy TDB and explains how to compute a final fulfillment degree for the selected tuples. Finally, Section 6 presents some of our conclusions and indicates some missing points for future lines of research.

2   Preliminaries

In this section we will introduce some previous concepts on classical temporal databases, give a brief explanation of fuzzy numbers, and summarize the main operators of the Fuzzy SQL language, since these topics form the basis of this paper.

2.1   Temporal Databases

TDB provide suitable data types and operators for handling time. In terms of the TDB, time is an application-based ordered sequence of points of the same granularity; in other words, one of several measurement units will be used depending on requirements: a second, a day, a week, etc..

From the point of view of the real world, there are basically two ways to associate concepts to a fact:

1. *Punctual facts*: a fact is related to a single time mark that depends on the granularity and provides information about the time when it happened (e.g. birthdays, the date of purchase, an academic year, etc.).
2. *Time periods*: a fact is related to a period represented by a starting and an ending instant and so the duration (or valid time) of the fact is implicit (e.g. [admission date, discharge date], [contract start date, contract end date], etc.).

The time dimension may appear with many semantics according to the problem to be represented. In many situations, time periods are used to express the validity of the data representing a fact. This way of interpreting time is called **valid time**.

In a TDB, however, in addition to the valid time, another interesting use of the time dimension is to reflect the instant when the fact was stored (this may be calculated using the system time) and is called the **transaction time**. Certain applications only use one of the two dimensions while others use both. When this is the case, the TDB is called a bitemporal database. In order to take one or both interpretations into account, table schemata in the TDB must be extended with specific attributes, as shown in Figure 1 for Tables EMP (employees) and DPT (departments).

When only the valid time interpretation is used, the schema must be extended in order to include the attributes VST (Valid Start Time) and VET (Valid End Time), and a valid time relation (VTR) is obtained.

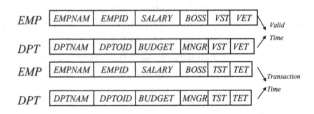

Fig. 1. Schema extensions in a temporal database

When only the transaction time interpretation is used, the schema must be extended in order to include the attributes TST (Transaction Start Time) and TET (Transaction End Time), and a transactional time relation (TTR) is obtained. If both interpretations are necessary at the same time, then all the previously mentioned attributes must be included in the schema. In the following sections of this paper, we will focus on the valid time approach since we are dealing with imprecise data and system timestamps are always precise.

Following on with our example of the time relation EMP, each tuple represents a version of the available information about an employee, and every version is valid only when used in its time interval [VST,VET]. The current version (also called the valid tuple) takes the special *undefined* value in the attribute VET since the interval is still open. In the Table 1 an instance of EMP is shown.

Table 1. Instance of EMP valid-time relation

EMPNAM	EMPID	SALARY	BOSS	EXPERTISE	VST	VET
GRANT	1245	1500	9877	TRAINEE	15-06-1997	31-05-1998
GRANT	1245	1800	9877	JUNIOR	01-06-1998	Undefined
REDFORD	9877	1200	4588	TRAINEE	20-08-1994	31-01-1996
REDFORD	9877	1500	4588	JUNIOR	01-02-1996	31-03-1997
REDFORD	9877	2200	9989	SENIOR	01-04-1997	Undefined
BROWN	1278	2800	4588	JUNIOR	01-05-2005	10-08-2008
STREEP	6579	4000	9877	TRAINEE	15-06-1997	Undefined

At first sight, the inclusion of time features in a DB seems to be easy and direct, but extending schemata with these new attributes has many complex consequences, such as:

- In a VTR, the old primary key is not unique. The new primary key is the result of combining the previous value for the key and one of the valid time attributes, VST or VET. In the case of Table EMP, the primary key is not EMPID (employee's code) but EMPID+VST or EMPID+VET.
- There is only one valid tuple for each entity at a given time. Every operation must be strictly controlled so that the valid time periods of the same entity do not overlap.
- Internal implementation of common operations is completely different from those implemented in a non-temporal database. For instance, when an UPDATE is required, the current version of the tuple is closed and a new version

of it is created with the modified data. In this case, the user is responsible for giving the valid time; when closing the active version, the value of the attribute VET is updated with the previous grain to the value of the VST of the new version. In a similar way, the DELETE operation is carried out by closing the active version (i.e. updating the value of the attribute VET) whereas the INSERT operation involves creating a new tuple, the valid one.

However, it is not always possible for the user to give an exact but an imprecise starting/ending point for a fact validity period. In this case, the fuzzy set theory is a very suitable tool for not missing such information since fuzzy time values can be represented and managed.

This paper explores the fuzzy representation of time together with the UP-DATE and the SELECT operations when the time is expressed in fuzzy terms. It should be noted that the study of the UPDATE operation also includes the DELETE and the INSERT operations as particular cases; therefore, the results obtained can be extrapolated to the whole data manipulation language.

2.2 Fuzzy Numbers

A fuzzy value is a fuzzy representation of the real value of a property (attribute) when it is not precisely known.

In this paper, following Goguen's Fuzzification Principle [Gogu67], we will call every fuzzy set of the real line a *fuzzy quantity*. A *fuzzy number* is a particular case of a fuzzy quantity with the following properties:

Definition 1
The fuzzy quantity A with membership function $\mu_A(x)$ is a **fuzzy number** [Dubo85a] if:

1. $\forall \alpha \in [0,1]$, $A_\alpha = \{x \in R \mid \mu_A(x) \geq \alpha\}$ (α-cuts of A) is a convex set.
2. $\mu_A(x)$ is an upper-semicontinuous function.
3. The support set of A, defined as $Supp(A) = \{x \in R \mid \mu_A(x) > 0\}$, is a bounded set of R, where R is the set of real numbers.

We will use $\tilde{R}$ to denote the set of fuzzy numbers, and $h(A)$ to denote the height of the fuzzy number A. For the sake of simplicity, we will use capital letters at the beginning of the alphabet to represent fuzzy numbers.

The interval $[a_\alpha, b_\alpha]$ is called the α-cut of A. Therefore, fuzzy numbers are fuzzy quantities with α-cuts which are closed and bounded intervals: $A_\alpha = [a_\alpha, b_\alpha]$ with $\alpha \in (0,1]$.

If there is at least one point x verifying $\mu_A(x) = 1$ we say that A is a *normalized* fuzzy number.

A trapezoidal shape is sometimes used to represent fuzzy values. This representation is very useful as the fuzzy number is completely characterized by four parameters (m_1, m_2, a, b) and the height $h(A)$ when the fuzzy value is not normalized (as shown in Figure 2). We will use *modal set* to denote all the values

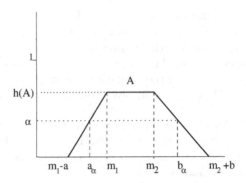

Fig. 2. Trapezoidal fuzzy number

in the interval $[m_1, m_2]$, i.e. the set $\{x \in Supp(A) \mid \forall\, y \in R,\ \mu_A(x) \geq \mu_A(y)\}$. The values a and b are called left and right *spreads*, respectively.

In our approach, we will use trapezoidal and normalized fuzzy values interpreted as possibility distributions on the domain of the dates.

2.3   FSQL (Fuzzy SQL)

The FSQL language [Gali98] [Gali06] extends the SQL language in order to express flexible queries. Due to its complex format, we only show here a brief summary with the main extensions to the `select` command.

- **Linguistic Labels:** These labels will be preceded by the symbol \$ to distinguish them easily and have associated a trapezoidal possibility distribution. So, for example, we can define the labels \$Short, \$Normal, \$Tall, ... on the `Height` attribute.
- **Fuzzy Comparators:** Besides the typical comparators (=, >...), FSQL includes the fuzzy comparators shown in table 2. Like in SQL, fuzzy comparators compare one column with one constant or two columns of the same type.

  Possibility comparators are less restrictive than necessity comparators are. For example, `NFEQ` uses the following equation:

$$\Theta^{\text{NFEQ}}(\widetilde{p}, \widetilde{p'}) = \inf_{d \in U} \max\left(1 - \mu_{\widetilde{p}}(d), \mu_{\widetilde{p'}}(d)\right) \tag{1}$$

Table 2. Fuzzy Comparators for FSQL (Fuzzy SQL)

Comparator for:		Semantics
Possibility	Necessity	
FEQ	NFEQ	Fuzzy EQual (Possibly/Necessarily Equal)
FGT	NFGT	Fuzzy Greater Than
FGEQ	NFGEQ	Fuzzy Greater or Equal
FLT	NFLT	Fuzzy Less Than
FLEQ	NFLEQ	Fuzzy Less or Equal
MGT	NMGT	Much Greater Than
MLT	NMLT	Much Less Than

– **Fulfilment thresholds** (γ): For each simple condition a fulfilment threshold may be established (default is 1) with the format:

<condition> THOLD γ

indicating that the condition must be satisfied with minimum degree $\gamma \in [0, 1]$ to be considered. The reserved word THOLD is optional and may be substituted by a traditional crisp comparator ($=, \leq ...$).

Example 1. Find the people that are necessarily taller than label $Tall (in minimum degree 0.8):

SELECT * FROM Person WHERE Height NFGT $Tall THOLD 0.8

– **Function** CDEG(<attribute>): It shows a column with the fulfilment degree of the condition imposed on a specific attribute. If logic operators appear, the calculation of this compatibility degree is carried out as table 3 shows. We use the minimum T-norm and the maximum T-conorm, but the user may change these values by modifying a view (FSQL_NOTANDOR). In this view the user can set the function to be used for every logic operator (NOT, AND, OR). Obviously, that function must be implemented in the FSQL Server or by the user himself.

Table 3. Default CDEG computation with logic operators

<Condition>	CDEG(<Condition>)
<cond1> AND <cond2>	min(CDEG(<cond1>),CDEG(<cond2>))
<cond1> OR <cond2>	max(CDEG(<cond1>),CDEG(<cond2>))
NOT <cond1>	1 - CDEG(<cond1>)

– **Fuzzy Constants:** We can use the fuzzy constants detailed in table 4.

Table 4. Fuzzy constants that may be used in FSQL queries

F. Constant	Significance
UNKNOWN	Unknown value but the attribute is applicable.
UNDEFINED	The attribute is not applicable or it is meaningless.
NULL	Total ignorance: We know nothing about it.
$[a,b,c,d]	Fuzzy trapezoid ($a \leq b \leq c \leq d$).
$label	Linguistic Label: It may be a trapezoid or a scalar.
[n,m]	Interval "Between n and m" (a=b=n and c=d=m).
#n	Fuzzy value "Approximately n" (b=c=n and n–a=d–n=margin).

3   Fuzzy Time Representation

In the introduction to this paper, we saw that in classical TDB, valid time is managed thanks to the extension of the tables schemata by adding two new attributes - the valid start time (VST) and the valid end time (VET) - to determine the fact period of validity expressed by a tuple.

In this paper we will consider that the information provided by the VST and VET attributes is fuzzy in that we are not completely sure about when the current values of the tuple began to be valid. For example, in our case, we cannot say when an employee was promoted from the junior to the senior category.

A more immediate solution to this problem is to soften the VST and the VET in such a way that they may contain a fuzzy date (for a day granularity) represented by means of a fuzzy number and interpreted as a possibility distribution. This means that if we use the parametrical representation for fuzzy numbers, we need to store four values for the VST and four values for the VET, as shown in Figure 3. Since the meaning of the attributes VST and VET is the period of time during which the values of a tuple are possibly valid, it is more convenient to summarize the information given by the two fuzzy attributes in a fuzzy interval. This situation can be represented by the trapezoidal fuzzy set shown in Figure 4 which incorporates the semantics of our problem. Let us call this attribute the *fuzzy validity period* (FVP).

As this figure shows, the right side of the interval (VET) is set to the maximum value of the date domain (31/12/2050 in our example) in order to specify that the associated tuple is currently valid, while the left side of the interval is the part that reflects the imprecision about the starting time point of the interval or VST.

EMPNAM	EMPID	SALARY	BOSS	EXPERTISE	VST	VET
GRANT	1245	1500	9877	TRAINEE	~15-06-1997	~ 31-05-1998
GRANT	1245	1500	9877	JUNIOR	~01-06-1998	~undefined

(01-06-1998,01-06-1998,2,2) (31-12-2050,31-12-2050,0,0)

Fig. 3. Sample tuple with fuzzy VST and VET

The advantage of this representation is that both periods of time and fuzzy dates can be represented in an unified way. Let us consider a parametrical representation such as (m,m,a,b) which represents a central time point with some imprecision on both sides, and this is interpreted as a fuzzy date.

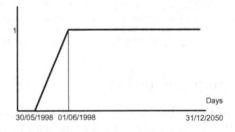

Days

30/05/1998 01/06/1998   31/12/2050

Fig. 4. Fuzzy Period of Time for a Valid Tuple

In [Medi94] a generalized fuzzy DB model is presented which supports this representation for fuzzy data and the corresponding implementation in a classical relational DB system (Oracle).

4   Update Operation with Fuzzy Periods of Time

As we explained in the introduction, information is never deleted in a TDB when an update operation is carried out. The process is to leave the old version of the data in the DB and to add the new version with any suitable modifications made, closing the old one and setting as the valid end time the immediately previous granule to the valid start time of the inserted tuple. It should be noted that closing the old version of a tuple is a *deletion* operation in the TDB environment whereas adding a new version corresponds to an *insert* operation.

One key point that arises when the time period considered is fuzzy is that we cannot identify the time point immediately prior to a given one for a concrete granularity since there are many values with different possibility degrees. Computing this value is very important for the update operation since we need to close the old version for the new one to be valid.

Definition 2
Let us use $\mu_O(x)$ to denote the membership function associated to the fuzzy interval of the *old* version of the tuple to be updated and $\mu_N(x)$ the membership function associated to the new fuzzy interval. Then, the membership function of the fuzzy interval $(\mu'_O(x))$ that serves to *close* the validity time of the old one is (see Figure 5):

$$\mu'_O(x) = \begin{cases} \mu_O(x) & \forall x \mid \mu_N(x) = 0 \\ 1 - \mu_N(x) & \forall x \mid \mu_N(x) > 0 \end{cases}$$

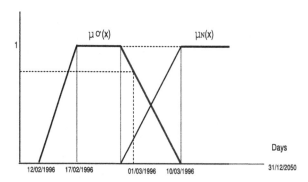

Fig. 5. Fuzzy value O' that closes a version of a tuple with new valid time N

We will use *closing interval* to denote all the values $x \in D$ such that $0 < \mu_N(x) < 1$ and $0 < \mu'_O(x) < 1$.

It can be seen how in the closing interval of the domain D, the greater the possibility of belonging to the new interval, the smaller the possibility of belonging to the old one, which makes sense since the interval is finishing for the old valid time but starting for the new valid time. It is obvious that the non-overlapping condition required for the crisp TDB is no longer valid, but the function used to close the old version guarantees that the overlapping degree will never reach value 1 for the sake of consistency (it is not possible for two versions to be valid with possibility degree 1).

5 Querying the Fuzzy TDB

Once we are able to represent fuzzy periods of valid time, queries about a crisp/fuzzy date or period to the valid time relations can be solved computing the corresponding fulfillment degree between the time we are querying about (QT) and the database valid time (FVP). In the next section we explain the most representative types of queries. In order to illustrate all the cases, let us consider the fuzzy TDB instance represented in Table 5.

Table 5.

EMPNAM	EMPID	SALARY	BOSS	EXPERTISE	FVP
GRANT	1245	1500	9877	TRAINEE	(15/06/1997, 31/05/1998, 2,2)
GRANT	1245	1800	9877	JUNIOR	(02/06/1998, 31/12/2050,2,0)
REDFORD	9877	1200	4588	TRAINEE	(20/08/1994, 31/01/1996, 2,3)
REDFORD	9877	1500	4588	JUNIOR	(03/02/1996, 31/03/1997,3,4)
REDFORD	9877	2200	9989	SENIOR	(04/04/1997, 31/12/2050,4,0)
BROWN	1278	2800	4588	JUNIOR	(01/05/1996,10/08/97,0,0)
STREEP	6579	4000	9877	TRAINEE	(15/06/1997,31/12/2050,0,0)
NEWMAN	5546	2300	9877	SENIOR	(18/06/1997,29/04/1998,8,10)

5.1 Queries About a Precise Date

In this case, QT is a date d and the system must find the tuples whose FVP includes d in the support set, that is, those tuples for which the membership of this date to the fuzzy period is greater than 0. Once found, the fulfillment degree of the resulting tuple will be computed as:

$$\mu_{FVP}(d)$$

It should be noted that this degree will be 1 when the date d belongs to the modal set of the fuzzy interval.

As explained before, it may happen that not only one but two versions of the same tuple have a validity period that includes d in the support set. This is the case when the mentioned date belongs to the closing interval of two consecutive periods. In this case, the answer will be the tuple whose validity time best fits the query date.

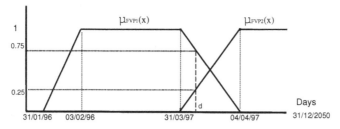

Fig. 6. Membership degrees when date d belongs to the closing interval of two tuples

Example 2. One example of this type of query is *Find the expertise level of employee number 9877 on 1st April 1997.* This situation can be graphically seen in figure 6 and the formal expression of this query using FSQL syntax is:

```
fsql> SELECT empnam,expertise,CDEG(fvp) FROM employees
      WHERE empid=9877 AND
      fvp FEQ TO_DATE('01/04/1997') THOLD 0.0;
```

EMPNAM	EXPERTISE	FVP	CDEG(FVP)
REDFORD	JUNIOR	(03-02-1996, 31-03-1997,3,4)	0.75
REDFORD	SENIOR	(04-04-1997, 31/12/2050,4,0)	0.25

5.2   Queries About a Fuzzy or Crisp Period of Time

In this case, QT is another fuzzy interval of dates and the system should find the tuples whose FVP includes QT and compute to what degree this inclusion is fulfilled. This situation can be modelled by means of the implication:

$$QT \longrightarrow FVP$$

If we assume that the implication function $I(QT(d), FVP(d))$ used is the material implication, then the fulfillment degree of this fuzzy inclusion will be:

$$N(FVP|QT) = min_{x \in D} I(\mu_{QT}(x), \mu_{FVP}(x))$$

$$N(FVP|QT) = min_{x \in D}\{(1 - \mu_{QT}(x)) \oplus \mu_{FVP}(x)\}$$

If the t-conorm considered is the *maximum*, the resulting measure is a *necessity*. Note that this measure includes the classical sets inclusion as a particular case.

If more than one version of a tuple give a positive result for the inclusion degree, then the best answer will be the one with the highest degree.

Example 3. One example of this type of query is *Find the boss of employee number 9877 by the beginning of April 1997* (01/04/97,04/04/97,0,2). The formal expression of this query using FSQL syntax is:

```
fsql> SELECT e.empnam, e.expertise, e.boss, CDEG(e.fvp)
      FROM employees WHERE e.empid=9877 AND
      $['01/04/1997','05/04/1997',0,2] NFEQ fvp THOLD 0.0;

      EMPNAM      EXPERTISE   BOSS    CDEG(FVP)
      ----------------------------------------
      REDFORD     SENIOR      9989    0,25
```

where NFEQ (necessity-based fuzzy equal) computes to what degree the left side fuzzy set is included in the right side one using the expression given above.

5.3 Simultaneous Events

The problem now is to compute to what degree two events are simultaneous. This operation is very useful since *joins* are based on it. The simultaneity degree or temporal equality between two periods of time can be carried out computing the degree to which both fuzzy/crisp sets -FVP_1 and FVP_2- are mutually included one in the other, that is, we should compute:

$$\otimes\{N(FVP_1/FVP_2), N(FVP_2/FVP_1)\}$$

as the final value for the fuzzy equality degree between the two fuzzy sets where $\otimes$ stands for a T-norm (*minimum* is our case).

Example 4. A query of this type could be *Find employees with the boss 9877 during the same period of time*. The formal expression of this query using FSQL syntax is:

```
fsql> SELECT e.empnam,f.empnam,CDEG(*)
      FROM employees e, employees f WHERE e.boss=9877
      AND f.boss=9877 AND e.empid<>f.empid AND (f.fvp NFEQ e.fvp) >0
      and (e.fvp NFEQ f.fvp) >0

      E.EMPNAM   F.EMPNAM   CDEG(*)
      ---------------------------
      GRANT      NEWMAN     0,4
```

where CDEG(*) computes the minimum of the fulfillment degrees obtained.

6   Conclusions and Future Work

In this paper we have shown the advantages of representing imprecise temporal data with a fuzzy parametrical representation. On this temporal data, we have explained how an update operation can be carried out by taking into account that no deletion is possible when temporal information is stored. As a result of this operation, a modification to the old version of the tuple is needed by changing some of the parameters that define it. As a consequence of our approach, the queries return a set of tuples together with a fulfillment degree when a query is made on these fuzzy temporal data. The paper also analyzes the different types of queries that can be made on these data. We are currently analyzing the behavior of other linguistic operators (after, before, short time, long time ago, etc.) and considering a wider range of temporal data. We are also studying the problem of primary keys in the presence of fuzzy intervals instead of VST and VET attributes and trying to find out new indexing techniques that take the new primary keys into account.

Acknowledgments. This paper has been partially supported by research project TIC-1570.

References

[Bett98a]   Bettini, C., Wang, X., Jajodia, S.: A general framework for time granularities and its application to temporal reasoning. Annals of Mathematics and Artificial Intelligence 22, 29–58 (1998)

[Bett98b]   Bettini, C., Wang, X., Jajodia, S.: An architecture to inter-operability in temporal databases. En Temporal Databases, 36–55 (1998)

[Bord04]   Bordogna, G., Chiesa, S.: Representing and Querying Imperfect Spatio-Temporal Information in an Object-Oriented Framework. In: de Caluwe, R., de Tré, G., Bordogna, G. (eds.) Spatio-Temporal Databases Flexible Querying and Reasoning (2004) ISBN: 978-3-540-22214-9

[Calu04]   de Caluwe, R., de Tr, G., Bordogna, G. (eds.): Spatio-Temporal Databases Flexible Querying and Reasoning (2004) ISBN: 978-3-540-22214-9

[Chou05]   Chountas, P., Petrounias, I.: Modeling and Representation of Uncertain Temporal Information. Requirements Eng. 5, 144–156 (2005)

[Clif88]   Clifford, J., Rao, A.: A simple general structure for temporal domains. In: Proc. de IFIP Working Conference on Temporal Aspects in Information Systems, pp. 17–28. Elservier, Amsterdam (1988)

[Dragi04]   Dragizevic, S.: Fuzzy Sets for the representation of the spatial and temporal dimensions in GIS databases. In: de Caluwe, R., de Tr, G., Bordogna, G. (eds.) Spatio-Temporal Databases Flexible Querying and Reasoning (2004) ISBN: 978-3-540-22214-9

[Dyre98]   Dyresson, C.E., Snodgrass, R.T.: Supporting Valid-Time Indeterminacy. ACM Trans. on Database Systems 23(1), 1–57 (1998)

[Dubo85]   Dubois, D., Prade, H.: Fuzzy Numbers. An Overview. In: Bezdek (ed.) The Analysis of Fuzzy Information. CRS Press, Boca Raton (1985)

[Dun98]   Duncan, D.E.: Calendar: Humanity's Epci Struggle to Determine a True and Accurate Year. Avon books Inc., New York (1998)

[Elma90]   Elmarsi, R., Wuu, G.T.: A Temporal Model and Query Language for ER Databases (1990)

[Etzi98]   Etzion, O., Jajodia, S., Sripada, S. (eds.): Temporal Databases: Research and Practice. LNCS, vol. 1399. Springer, Heidelberg (1998)

[Gali98]   Galindo, J., Medina, J.M., Pons, O., Cubero, J.C.: A Server for Fuzzy SQL Queries. In: Andreasen, T., Christiansen, H., Larsen, H.L. (eds.) FQAS 1998. LNCS (LNAI), vol. 1495, pp. 164–174. Springer, Heidelberg (1998)

[Gali06]   Galindo, J., Urrutia, A., Piattini, M.: Fuzzy Databases: Modeling, Design and Implementation. Idea Group Publishing, Hershey, USA (2006)

[Gogu67]   Goguen, J.A.: L-Fuzzy Sets. Journ. of Math. Anal. and Applications 18, 145–174 (1967)

[Gora98]   Goralwalla, I.A., Leontiev, Y., Ozsu, M.T., Szafron, D., Combi, C.: Temporal Granularity for Unanchored Temporal Data. In: Proc. de ACM Conference on Information and Acnowledge Management, pp. 414–423. ACM Press, New York (1998)

[Jens01]   Jensen, C.S., Lomet, D.B.: Transaction timestamping in temporal databases. In: Proc. of 17th VLDB conference (2001)

[Kuru98]   Kurutach, W.: Handling Fuzziness in Temporal Databases. In: Proc. of IEEE Int. Conf. on Systems, Man and Cybernetics, vol. 3, pp. 2762–2767 (1998)

[Medi94]   Medina, J.M., Pons, O., Vila, M.A.: GEFRED: A Generalized Model of Fuzzy Relational Databases. Information Sciences 76, 87–109 (1994)

[Medi95]   Medina, J.M., Cubero, J.C., Pons, O., Vila, M.A.: Towards the Implementation of a Generalized Fuzzy Relational Database Model. Fuzzy Sets and Systems 75, 273–289 (1995)

[Sard90]   Sarda, N.L.: Extensions to SQL for historical databases. IEEE Transactions on Knowledge and Data Engineering 2, 220–230 (1990)

[Snod87]   Snodgrass, R.T.: The temporal Query language TQuel. ACM Transactions on Database Systems 12, 247–298 (1987)

[Snod95]   Snodgrass, R.T., Ahn, I., Ariav, G., Batory, D.S., et al. (eds.): The TSQL2 temporal query language. Kluwer Academic Publishers, Dordrecht (1995)

[Snod98]   Snodgrass, R.T., Bohlen, M.H., Jensen, C.S., Steiner, A.: Transitioning Temporal Support in TSQL2 to SQL3. In: Etzion, O., Jajodia, S., Sripada, S. (eds.) Temporal Databases: Research and Practice. LNCS, vol. 1399, pp. 150–194. Springer, Heidelberg (1998)

[Tans93]   Tansel, A., Clifford, J., Gadia, S.: Temporal Databases: Theory, Design and Implementation. Bejamin Cummings (1993)

[Torp99]   Torp, K., Jensen, C.S., Snodgrass, R.T.: Effective Timestamping in Databases. VLDB Journal 8, 267–288 (1999)

[Tre97]   Van der Cruyssen, B., de Caluwe, R., de Tre, G.: A Theoretical Time Model for Dealing with Crisp and Fuzzy Time. In: Proceeings of NAFIPS (1997)

[TSQL2a]   Snodgrass, R.: Temporal Support in Standard SQL. In: Intelligent Database Programming and Design (1998)

[TSQL2b]   Snodgrass, R. (ed.): The TSQL2 Temporal Query Language. Kluwer Academic Publishers, Dordrecht (1995)

Finding Most Probable Worlds
of Probabilistic Logic Programs

Samir Khuller, Vanina Martinez, Dana Nau,
Gerardo Simari, Amy Sliva, and V.S. Subrahmanian*

University of Maryland College Park, College Park, MD 20742, USA
{samir,mvm,nau,gisimari,asliva,vs}@cs.umd.edu

Abstract. Probabilistic logic programs have primarily studied the problem of entailment of probabilistic atoms. However, there are some interesting applications where we are interested in finding a possible world that is most probable. Our first result shows that the problem of computing such "maximally probable worlds" (MPW) is intractable. We subsequently show that we can often greatly reduce the size of the linear program used in past work (by Ng and Subrahmanian) and yet solve the problem exactly. However, the intractability results still make computational efficiency quite impossible. We therefore also develop several heuristics to solve the MPW problem and report extensive experimental results on the accuracy and efficiency of such heuristics.

1 Introduction

Probabilistic logic programs (PLPs) [1] have been proposed as a paradigm for probabilistic logical reasoning with no independence assumptions. PLPs used a possible worlds model based on prior work by [2], [3], and [4] to induce a set of probability distributions on a space of possible worlds. Past work on PLPs [5,1] focuses on the entailment problem of checking if a PLP entails that the probability of a given formula lies in a given probability interval.

However, we have recently been developing several applications for cultural adversarial reasoning [6] where PLPs and their variants are used to build a model of the behavior of certain socio-cultural-economic groups in different parts of the world.[1] Such PLPs contain rules that state things like "There is a 50 to 70% probability that group g will take action(s) a when condition C holds." In such applications, the problem of interest is that of finding the most probable action (or sets of actions) that the group being modeled might do. This corresponds precisely to the problem of finding a "most probable world" that is the focus of this paper.

In Section 2 of this paper, we recall the syntax and semantics of such programs [5,1]. We state the *most probable world* (MPW) problem by immediately using the linear programming methods of [5,1] - these methods are exponential because the linear

---

* Authors listed in alphabetical order; the authors were funded in part by grant N6133906C0149, ARO grant DAAD190310202, AFOSR grants FA95500610405 and FA95500510298, and NSF grants 0540216 and IIS0412812.

[1] Our group has thus far built models of the Afridi tribe in Pakistan, Hezbollah in the Middle East, and the various stakeholders in the Afghan drug economy.

H. Prade and V.S. Subrahmanian (Eds.): SUM 2007, LNAI 4772, pp. 45–59, 2007.

programs are exponential in the number of ground atoms in the language. Then, in Section 4, we present the *Head Oriented Processing (HOP)* approach where a (usually) smaller linear program is introduced. We show that using HOP, we can often find a much faster solution to the MPW problem. We define a variant of HOP called Semi-HOP that has slightly different computational properties, but is still guaranteed to find the most probable world. Thus, we have three exact algorithms to find the most probable world.

Subsequently, in Section 5, we develop a heuristic that can be applied in conjunction with the *Naive*, HOP, and SemiHOP algorithms. The basic idea is that rather than examining all worlds, only some fixed number of worlds is explored using a linear program that is reduced in size. Section 6 describes a prototype implementation of our APLP framework and includes a set of experiments to assess combinations of exact algorithm and the heuristic. We assess both the efficiency of our algorithms, as well as the accuracy of the solutions they produce.

2   Overview of Action Probabilistic Logic Programs

Action probabilistic logic programs (APLPs) are an immediate and obvious variant of the probabilistic logic programs introduced in [5,1]. We assume the existence of a logical alphabet that consists of a finite set $\mathcal{L}_{cons}$ of constant symbols, a finite set $\mathcal{L}_{pred}$ of predicate symbols (each with an associated arity) and an infinite set $\mathcal{V}$ of variable symbols. Function symbols are not allowed in our language. Terms and atoms are defined in the usual way [7]. We assume that a subset $\mathcal{L}_{act}$ of $\mathcal{L}_{pred}$ are designated as *action symbols* - these are symbols that denote some action. Thus, an atom $p(t_1, \ldots, t_n)$, where $p \in \mathcal{L}_{act}$, is an *action atom*. Every (resp. action) atom is a (resp. action) wff. If F, G are (resp. action) wffs, then $(F \wedge G), (F \vee G)$ and $\neg G$ are all wffs (resp. action wffs).

Definition 1. *If F is a wff (resp. action wff) and $\mu = [\alpha, \beta] \subseteq [0, 1]$, then $F : \mu$ is called a p-annotated (resp. ap-annotated—short for "action probabilistic" annotated) wff. μ is called the p-annotation (resp. ap-annotation) of F.*

Without loss of generality, throughout this paper we will assume that F is in conjunctive normal form (i.e. it is written as a conjunction of disjunctions).

Definition 2 (ap-rules). *If F is an action formula, $A_1, A_2, \ldots, A_m$ are action atoms, $B_1, \ldots, B_n$ are non-action atoms, and $\mu, \mu_1, \ldots, \mu_m$ are ap-annotations, then $F : \mu \leftarrow A_1 : \mu_1 \wedge A_2 : \mu_2 \wedge \ldots \wedge A_m : \mu_m \wedge B_1 \wedge \ldots B_m$ is called an ap-rule. If this rule is named c, then $Head(c)$ denotes $F : \mu$; $Body^{act}(c)$ denotes $A_1 : \mu_1 \wedge A_2 : \mu_2 \wedge \ldots \wedge A_m : \mu_m$ and $Body^{state}(c)$ denotes $B_1 \wedge \ldots B_n$.*

Intuitively, the above ap-rule says that an unnamed entity (e.g. a group g, a person p etc.) *will take action F with probability in the range μ if $B_1, \ldots, B_n$ are true in the current state (we will define this term shortly) and if the unnamed entity will take each action A_i with a probability in the interval μ_i for $1 \leq i \leq n$.*

Definition 3 (ap-program). *An action probabilistic logic program (ap-program for short) is a finite set of ap-rules.*

1. *kidnap:* $[0.35, 0.45]$ ← *interOrganizationConflicts.*
2. *kidnap:* $[0.60, 0.68]$ ← *notDemocratic* ∧ *internalConflicts.*
3. *armed_attacks:* $[0.42, 0.53]$ ← *typeLeadership(strongSingle)* ∧ *orgPopularity(moderate).*
4. *armed_attacks:* $[0.93, 1.0]$ ← *statusMilitaryWing(standing).*

Fig. 1. Four simple rules for modeling the behavior of a group in certain situations

Figure 1 shows a small rule base consisting of some rules we have derived automatically about Hezbollah using behavioral data in [8]. The behavioral data in [8] has tracked over 200 terrorist groups for about 20 years from 1980 to 2004. For each year, values have been gathered for about 300 measurable variables for each group in the sample. These variables include tendency to commit assassinations and armed attacks, as well as background information about the type of leadership, whether the group is involved in cross border violence, etc. Our automatic derivation of these rules was based on a data mining algorithm we have separately developed [9]. We show 4 rules we have extracted for the group Hezbollah in Figure 1. For example, the third rule says that when Hezbollah has a strong, single leader and its popularity is moderate, its propensity to conduct armed attacks has been 42 to 53%. However, when it has had a standing military, its propensity to conduct armed attacks is 93 to 100%.

Definition 4 (world/state). *A* world *is any set of ground action atoms. A* state *is any finite set of ground non-action atoms.*

Note that both worlds and states are just ordinary Herbrand interpretations. As such, it is clear what it means for a state to satisfy $Body^{state}$.

Definition 5. *Let Π be an ap-program and s a state. The* reduction of Π *w.r.t. s, denoted by Π_s is $\{F : \mu \leftarrow Body^{act} \mid s$ satisfies $Body^{state}$ and $F : \mu \leftarrow Body^{act} \land Body^{state}$ is a ground instance of a rule in $\Pi\}$.*

Note that Π_s never has any non-action atoms in it.

Key differences. The key differences between action probabilistic LPs (APLPs) and the programs of [5,1] are that APLPs have a bipartite structure (action atoms and state atoms) and they allow arbitrary formulas (including ones with negation) in rule heads ([5,1] do not). They can easily be extended to include variable annotations and annotation terms as in [5]. Likewise, as in [5], they can be easily extended to allow complex formulas rather than just atoms in rule bodies. Due to space restrictions, we do not do either of these in the paper. *However, the most important difference between our paper and [5,1] is that this paper focuses on finding most probable worlds, while those papers focus on entailment, which is a fundamentally different problem.*

   Throughout this paper, we will assume that there is a fixed state s. Hence, once we are given Π and s, Π_s is fixed. We can associate a fixpoint operator T_{Π_s} with Π, s which maps sets of ground ap-annotated wffs to sets of ground ap-annotated wffs as follows.

Definition 6. *Suppose X is a set of ground annotated action atoms. We first define an intermediate operator $U_{\Pi_s}(X)$ as follows. $U_{\Pi_s}(X) = \{F : \mu \mid F : \mu \leftarrow A_1 :$*

$\mu_1 \wedge \cdots \wedge A_m : \mu_m$ is a ground instance of a rule in Π_s and for all $1 \leq j \leq m$, there is an $A_j : \eta_j \in X$ such that $\eta_j \subseteq \mu_j\}$.

Intuitively, $U_{\Pi_s}(X)$ contains the heads of all rules in Π_s whose bodies are deemed to be "true" if the action atoms in X are true. However, $U_{\Pi_s}(X)$ may not contain all ground action atoms. This could be because such atoms don't occur in the head of a rule - $U_{\Pi_s}(X)$ never contains any action wff that is not in a rule head.

In order to assign a probability interval to each ground action atom, we use the same procedure followed in [5]. We use $U_{\Pi_s}(X)$ to set up a linear program $CONS_U(\Pi, s, X)$ as follows. For each world w_i, let p_i be a variable denoting the probability of w_i being the "real world". As each w_i is just a Herbrand interpretation, the notion of satisfaction of an action formula F by a world w, denoted by $w \mapsto F$, is defined in the usual way.

1. If $F : [\ell, u] \in U_{\Pi_s}(X)$, then $\ell \leq \Sigma_{w_i \mapsto F}\, p_i \leq u$ is in $CONS_U(\Pi, s, X)$.
2. $\Sigma_{w_i} p_i = 1$ is in $CONS_U(\Pi, s, X)$.

We refer to these as constraints of type (1) and (2), respectively. To find the lower (resp. upper) probability of a ground action atom A, we merely minimize (resp. maximize) $\Sigma_{w_i \mapsto A} p_i$ subject to the above constraints. We also do the same w.r.t. each formula F that occurs in $U_{\Pi_s}(X)$ — this is because this minimization and maximization may sharpen the bounds of F. Let $\ell(F)$ and $u(F)$ denote the results of these minimizations and maximizations, respectively. Our operator $T_{\Pi_s}(X)$ is then defined as follows.

Definition 7. *Suppose Π is an APLP, s is a state, and X is a set of ground ap-wffs. Our operator $T_{\Pi_s}(X)$ is then defined to be $\{F : [\ell(F), u(F)] \mid (\exists \mu)\, F : \mu \in U_{\Pi_s}(X)\} \cup \{A : [\ell(A), u(A)] \mid A \text{ is a ground action atom }\}$.*

Thus, $T_{\Pi_s}(X)$ works in two phases. It first takes each formula $F : \mu$ that occurs in $U_{\Pi_s}(X)$ and finds $F : [\ell(F), u(F)]$ and puts this in the result. Once all such $F : [\ell(F), u(F)]$'s have been put in the result, it tries to infer the probability bounds of all ground action atoms A from these $F : [\ell(F), u(F)]$'s.

Given two sets X_1, X_2 of ap-wffs, we say that $X_1 \leq X_2$ iff for each $F_1 : \mu_1 \in X_1$, there is an $F_1 : \mu_2 \in X_2$ such that $\mu_2 \subseteq \mu_1$. Intuitively, $X_1 \leq X_2$ may be read as "X_1 is less precise than X_2." The following straightforward variation of similar results in [5] shows that

Proposition 1. *1. T_{Π_s} is monotonic w.r.t. the $\leq$ ordering.*
2. T_{Π_s} has a least fixpoint, denoted $T_{\Pi_s}^{\omega}$.

3 Maximally Probable Worlds

We are now ready to introduce the problem of finding the most probable world. As explained through our Hezbollah example, we may be interested in knowing what actions Hezbollah might take in a given situation.

Definition 8 (lower/upper probability of a world). *Suppose Π is an ap-program and s is a state. The lower probability, $\mathsf{low}(w_i)$ of a world w_i is defined as: $\mathsf{low}(w_i) = \text{minimize } p_i$ subject to $\mathsf{CONS}_U(\Pi, s, T_{\Pi_s}^{\omega})$. The upper probability, $up(w_i)$ of world w_i is defined as $up(w_i) = \text{maximize } p_i$ subject to $\mathsf{CONS}_U(\Pi, s, T_{\Pi_s}^{\omega})$.*

Thus, the low probability of a world w_i is the lowest probability that that world can have in any solution to the linear program. Similarly, the upper probability for the same world represents the highest probability that that world can have. It is important to note that for any world w, we cannot *exactly* determine a point probability for w. This observation is true even if all rules in Π have a point probability in the head because our framework does not make any simplifying assumptions (e.g. independence) about the probability that certain things will happen.

We now present two simple results that state that checking if the low (resp. up) probability of a world exceeds a given bound (called the BOUNDED-LOW and BOUNDED-UP problems respectively) is intractable. The hardness results, in both cases, are by reduction from the problem of checking consistency of a generalized probabilistic logic program. The problem is in the class EXPTIME.

Proposition 2 (BOUNDED LOW COMPLEXITY). *Given an ap-program Π, a state s, a world w, and a probability threshold p_{th}, deciding if $low(w) > p_{th}$ is NP-hard.*

Proposition 3 (BOUNDED UP COMPLEXITY). *Given an ap-program Π, a state s, a world w_i, and a probability threshold p_{th}, deciding if $up(w) < p_{th}$ is NP-hard.*

The MPW Problem. The *most probable world* problem (MPW for short) is the problem where, given an APLP Π and a state s as input, we are required to find a world w_i where $low(w_i)$ is maximal. [2]

A Naive Algorithm. A *naive* algorithm to find the most probable world would be:

1. Compute $T_{\Pi_s}^\omega$; $Best = NIL$; $Bestval = 0$;
2. For each world w_i,
   (a) Compute $low(w_i)$ by minimizing p_i subject to the set $\mathsf{CONS}_U(\Pi, s, T_{\Pi_s}^\omega)$ of constraints.
   (b) If $low(w_i) > Bestval$ then set $Best = w_i$ and $Bestval = low(w_i)$;
3. If $Best = NIL$ then return any world whatsoever, else return $Best$.

The Naive algorithm does a brute force search after computing $T_{\Pi_s}^\omega$. It finds the low probability for each world and chooses the best one. Clearly, we can use it to solve the MPW-Up problem by replacing the minimization in Step 2(a) by a maximization.

There are two key problems with the naive algorithm. The first problem is that in Step (1), computing $T_{\Pi_s}^\omega$ is very difficult. When some syntactic restrictions are imposed, this problem can be solved without linear programming at all as in the case when Π is a probabilistic logic program (or p-program as defined in [1]) where all heads are atomic.

The second problem is that in Step 2(a), the number of (linear program) variables in $\mathsf{CONS}_U(\Pi, s, T_{\Pi_s}^\omega)$ is exponential in the number of ground atoms. When this number is, say 20, this means that the linear program contains over a million variables. However, when the number is say 30 or 40 or more, this number is inordinately large. This paper focuses primarily on improving Step 2(a).

---

[2] A similar **MPW-Up Problem** can also be defined. The *most probable world-up* problem (MPW-Up) is given an APLP Π and a state s as input, and tries to find a world w_i where $up(w_i)$ is maximal. Due to space constraints, we only address the MPW problem.

4   HOP: Head-Oriented Processing

We can do better than the naive algorithm. Given a world w, state s, and an ap-program Π, let $Sat(w) = \{F \mid c$ is a ground instance of a rule in Π_s and $Head(c) = F : \mu$ and $w \mapsto F\}$. Intuitively, $Sat(w)$ is the set of heads of rules in Π_s (without probability annotations) whose bodies are satisfied by w.

Definition 9. *Suppose Π is an APLP, s is a state, and w_1, w_2 are two worlds. We say that w_1 and w_2 are equivalent, denoted $w_1 \sim w_2$, iff $Sat(w_1) = Sat(w_2)$.*

In other words, we say that two worlds are considered equivalent iff the two worlds satisfy the formulas in the heads of exactly the same rules in Π_s. It is easy to see that $\sim$ is an equivalence relation. We use $[w_i]$ to denote the $\sim$-equivalence class to which a world w_i belongs. The intuition for the HOP algorithm is given in Example 1.

Example 1. Consider the set $\mathrm{CONS}_U(\Pi, s, T_{\Pi_s}^\omega)$ of constraints. For example, consider a situation where $\mathrm{CONS}_U(\Pi, s, T_{\Pi_s}^\omega)$ contains just the three constraints below:

$$0.7 \leq p_2 + p_3 + p_5 + p_6 + p_7 + p_8 \leq 1 \tag{1}$$

$$0.2 \leq p_5 + p_7 + p_8 \leq 0.6 \tag{2}$$

$$p_1 + p_2 + p_3 + p_4 + p_5 + p_6 + p_7 + p_8 = 1 \tag{3}$$

In this case, each time one of the variables p_5, p_7, or p_8 occur in a constraint, the other two also occur. Thus, we can replace these by one variable (let's call it y for now). In other words, suppose $y = p_5 + p_7 + p_8$. Thus, the above constraints can be replaced by the simpler set

$$0.7 \leq p_2 + p_3 + p_6 + y \leq 1$$

$$0.2 \leq y \leq 0.6$$

$$p_1 + p_2 + p_3 + p_4 + p_6 + y = 1$$

The process in the above example leads to a reduction in the size of $\mathrm{CONS}_U(\Pi, s, T_{\Pi_s}^\omega)$. Moreover, suppose we minimize y subject to the above constraints. In this case, the minimal value is 0.2. As $y = p_5 + p_7 + p_8$, it is immediately obvious that the low probability of any of the p_i's is 0. Note that we can also group p_2, p_3, and p_6 together in the same manner.

We build on top of this intuition. The key insight here is that for any $\sim$-equivalence class $[w_i]$, the entire summation $\Sigma_{w_j \in [w_i]} p_j$ either appears *in its entirety* in each constraint of type (1) in $\mathrm{CONS}_U(\Pi, s, T_{\Pi_s}^\omega)$ or does not appear at all (i.e. none of the p_j variables associated with worlds w_j in $[w_i]$ appear in any constraint of type (1) in $\mathrm{CONS}_U(\Pi, s, T_{\Pi_s}^\omega)$). This is what the next result states.

Proposition 4. *Suppose Π is an ap-program, s is a state, and $[w_i]$ is a $\sim$-equivalence class. Then for each constraint of the form*

$$\ell \leq \Sigma_{w_r \mapsto F}\, p_r \leq u \tag{4}$$

in $\mathrm{CONS}_U(\Pi, s, T_{\Pi_s}^\omega)$, either every variable in the summation $\Sigma_{w_j \in [w_i]} p_j$ appears in the summation in (4) above or no variable in the summation $\Sigma_{w_j \in [w_i]} p_j$ appears in the summation in (4).

Example 2. Here is a toy example of this situation. Suppose Π_s consists of the two very simple rules:

$$(a \lor b \lor c \lor d) : [0.1, 0.5] \leftarrow .$$
$$(a \land e) : [0.2, 0.5] \leftarrow .$$

Assuming our language contains only the predicate symbols a, b, c, d, e, there are 32 possible worlds. However, what the preceding proposition tells us is that we can group the worlds into four categories. Those that satisfy both the above head formulas (ignoring the probabilities), those that satisfy the first but not the second head formula, those that satisfy the second but not the first head formula, and those that satisfy neither. This is shown graphically in Figure 2, in which p_i is the variable in the linear program corresponding to world w_i. For simplicity, we numbered the worlds according to the binary representation of the set of atoms. For instance, world $\{a, c, d, e\}$ is represented in binary as 10111, and is thus w_{23}. Note that only three variables appear in the new linear constraints; this is because it is not possible to satisfy $\neg(a \lor b \lor c \lor d \lor e)$ and $(a \land e)$ at once.

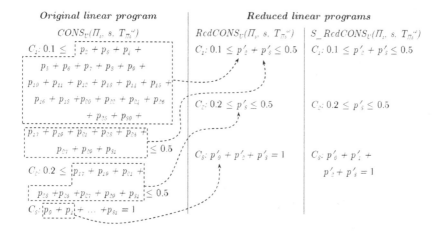

Fig. 2. Reducing $\text{CONS}_U(\Pi, s, T^\omega_{\Pi_s})$ by grouping variables. The new LPs are called $\text{RedCONS}_U(\Pi, s, T^\omega_{\Pi_s})$ and $\text{S\_RedCONS}_U(\Pi, s, T^\omega_{\Pi_s})$, as presented in Definition 10 and 12.

Effectively, what we have done is to modify the number of variables in the linear program from $2^{card(\mathcal{L}_{act})}$ to $2^{card(\Pi_s)}$ - a saving that can be significant in some cases (though not always!). The number of constraints in the linear program stays the same. Formally speaking, we define a *reduced set of constraints* as follows.

Definition 10 ($\text{RedCONS}_U(\Pi, s, T^\omega_{\Pi_s})$). *For each equivalence class $[w_i]$, RedCONS_U $(\Pi, s, T^\omega_{\Pi_s})$ uses a variable p'_i to denote the summation of the probability of each of the worlds in $[w_i]$. For each ap-wff $F : [\ell, u]$ in $T^\omega_{\Pi_s}$, $\text{RedCONS}_U(\Pi, s, T^\omega_{\Pi_s})$ contains the constraint:*

$$\ell \leq \Sigma_{[w_i] \mapsto F} p'_i \leq u.$$

Here, $[w_i] \mapsto F$ means that some world in $[w_i]$ satisfies F. In addition, RedCONS$_U$
$(\Pi, s, T_{\Pi_s}^{\omega})$ *contains the constraint*

$$\Sigma_{[w_i]} p_i' = 1.$$

When reasoning about RedCONS$_U(\Pi, s, T_{\Pi_s}^{\omega})$, we can do even better than mentioned
above. The result below states that in order to find the most probable world, we only
need to look at the equivalence classes that are of cardinality 1.

Theorem 1. *Suppose Π is an ap-program, s is a state, and w_i is a world. If
$card([w_i]) > 1$, then $low(w_i) = 0$.*

Going back to Example 1, we can conclude that $low(w_5) = low(w_7) = low(w_8) = 0$.
As a consequence of this result, we can suggest the Head Oriented Processing (HOP)
algorithm which works as follows. Before presenting HOP, we present some simple
notation. Let $FixedWff(\Pi, s) = \{F \mid F : \mu \in U_{\Pi_s}(T_{\Pi_s}^{\omega})\}$. Given a set $X \subseteq FixedWff$
(Π, s), we define $Formula(X, \Pi, s)$ to be

$$\bigwedge_{G \in X} G \wedge \bigwedge_{G' \in FixedWff(\Pi,s)-X} \neg G'.$$

Here, $Formula(X, \Pi, s)$ is the formula which says that X consists of all and only those
formulas in $FixedWff(\Pi, s)$ that are true. Given two sets $X_1, X_2 \subseteq FixedWff(\Pi, s)$,
we say that $X_1 \approx X_2$ iff $Formula(X_1, \Pi, s)$ and $Formula(X_2, \Pi, s)$ are logically
equivalent.

HOP Algorithm.

1. Compute $T_{\Pi_s}^{\omega}$. $bestval = 0$; $best = NIL$.
2. Let $[X_1], \dots, [X_n]$ be the $\sim$-equivalence classes defined above for Π, s.
3. For each equivalence class $[X_i]$ do:
   (a) If there is exactly one interpretation that satisfies $Formula(X_i, \Pi, s)$ then:
       i. **Minimize p_i' subject to** RedCONS$_U(\Pi, s, T_{\Pi_s}^{\omega})$ where $[w_i]$ is the set of
          worlds satisfying exactly those heads in X_i. Let Val be the value returned.
       ii. If $Val > best$, then $\{best = w_i; bestval = Val\}$.
4. If $bestval = 0$ then return any world whatsoever otherwise return $best$.

Theorem 2 (correctness of HOP). *Algorithm HOP is correct, i.e. it is guaranteed to
return a world whose low probability is greater than or equal to that of any other world.*

Step $3(a)$ of the HOP algorithm is known as the **UNIQUE-SAT** problem—it can be
easily implemented via a SAT solver as follows.

1. If $\bigwedge_{F \in X} F \wedge \bigwedge_{G \in \bar{X}} \neg G$ is satisfiable (using a SAT solver that finds a satisfying
   world w) then
   (a) If $\bigwedge_{F \in X} F \wedge \bigwedge_{G \in \bar{X}} \neg G \wedge (\bigvee_{a \in w} \neg a \vee \bigvee_{a' \in \bar{w}} a')$ is satisfiable (using a
       SAT solver) then return "two or more" (two or more satisfying worlds exist)
       else return "exactly one"
2. else return "none."

The following example shows how the HOP algorithm would work on the program from Example 2.

Example 3. Consider the program from Example 2, and suppose $X = \{(a \vee b \vee c \vee d \vee e), (a \wedge e)\}$. In Step $(3a)$, the algorithm will find that $\{a, d, e\}$ is a model of $(a \vee b \vee c \vee d \vee e) \wedge (a \wedge e)$; afterwards, it will find $\{a, c, e\}$ to be a model of $(a \vee b \vee c \vee d \vee e) \wedge (a \wedge e) \wedge ((\neg a \vee \neg d \vee \neg e) \vee (b \vee c))$. Thus, X has more than one model and the algorithm will not consider any of the worlds in the equivalence class induced by X as a possible solution, which avoids solving the linear program for those worlds.

The complexity of HOP is also exponential. However, HOP can sometimes be preferable to the Naive algorithm. The number of variables in $\mathrm{RedCONS}_U(\Pi, s, T_{\Pi_s}^\omega)$ is $2^{card(T_{\Pi_s}^\omega)}$, which is much smaller than the number of variables in $\mathrm{CONS}_U(\Pi, s, T_{\Pi_s}^\omega)$ when the number of ground rules whose bodies are satisfied by state s is smaller than the number of ground atoms. The checks required to find all the equivalence classes $[X_i]$ take time proportional to $2^{2*card(T_{\Pi_s}^\omega)}$. Lastly, HOP avoids solving the reduced linear program for all the non-singleton equivalence classes (for instance, in Example 3, the algorithm avoids solving the LP three times). This last saving, however, comes at the price of solving SAT twice for each equivalence class and the time required to find the $[X_i]$'s.

A variant of the HOP algorithm, which we call the SemiHOP algorithm, tries to avoid computing the full equivalence classes. The SemiHOP algorithm omits finding pairs of sets that represent the same equivalence class, and therefore does not need to compute the checks for logical equivalence of every possible pair, a computation which can be very expensive.

Proposition 5. *Suppose Π is an APLP, s is a state, and X is a subset of FixedWff (Π, s). Then there exists a world w_i such that $\{w \mid w \mapsto Formula(X, \Pi, s)\} \subseteq [w_i]$.*

We now define the concept of a sub-partition.

Definition 11. *A* sub-partition *of the set of worlds of Π w.r.t. s is a partition $W_1, \ldots, W_k$ where:*

1. *$\bigcup_{i=1}^k W_i$ is the entire set of worlds.*
2. *For each W_i, there is an equivalence class $[w_i]$ such that $W_i \subseteq [w_i]$.*

The following result - which follows immediately from the preceding proposition - says that we can generate a subpartition by looking at all subsets of FixedWff (Π, s).

Proposition 6. *Suppose Π is an APLP, s is a state, and $\{X_1, \ldots, X_k\}$ is the power set of FixedWff (Π, s). Then the partition $W_1, \ldots, W_k$ where $W_i = \{w \mid w \mapsto Formula (X_i, \Pi, s)\}$ is a sub-partition of the set of worlds of Π w.r.t. s.*

The intuition behind the SemiHOP algorithm is best presented by going back to constraints 1 and 2 given in Example 1. Obviously, we would like to collapse all three variables p_5, p_7, p_8 into one variable y. However, if we were to just collapse p_7, p_8 into a single variable y', we would still reduce the size of the constraints (through the elimination of one variable), though the reduction would not be maximal. The SemiHOP algorithm allows us to use subsets of equivalence classes instead of full equivalence classes. We first define a *semi-reduced set of constraints* as follows.

Definition 12 (S_RedCONS$_U(\Pi, s, T^{\omega}_{\Pi_s})$). *Let $W_1, \ldots, W_k$ be a subpartition of the set of worlds for Π and s. For each W_i, S_RedCONS$_U(\Pi, s, T^{\omega}_{\Pi_s})$ uses a variable $p^{\star}_i$ to denote the summation of the probability of each of the worlds in W_i. For each ap-wff $F : [\ell, u]$ in $T^{\omega}_{\Pi_s}$, RedCONS$_U(\Pi, s, T^{\omega}_{\Pi_s})$ contains the constraint:*

$$\ell \leq \Sigma_{W_i \mapsto F} p^{\star}_i \leq u.$$

Here, $W_i \mapsto F$ implies that some world in W_i satisfies F. In addition, S_RedCONS$_U$ $(\Pi, s, T^{\omega}_{\Pi_s})$ contains the constraint

$$\Sigma_{W_i} p^{\star}_i = 1.$$

Example 4. Returning to Example 1, S_RedCONS$_U(\Pi, s, T^{\omega}_{\Pi_s})$ could contain the following constraints: $0.7 \leq p_2 + p_3 + p_5 + p_6 + y' \leq 1$, $0.2 \leq p_5 + y' \leq 0.6$, and $p_1 + p_2 + p_3 + p_4 + p_5 + p_6 + y' = 1$ where $y' = p_7 + p_8$.

SemiHOP Algorithm.

1. Compute $T^{\omega}_{\Pi_s}$.
2. $bestval = 0; best = NIL$.
3. For each set $X \subseteq FixedWff(\Pi, s)$ do:
   (a) If there is exactly one interpretation that satisfies $Formula(X, \Pi, s)$ then:
      i. **Minimize $p^{\star}_i$ subject to** S_RedCONS$_U(\Pi, s, T^{\omega}_{\Pi_s})$ where W_i is a subpartition of the set of worlds of Π w.r.t. s. Let Val be the value returned.
      ii. If $Val > best$, then $\{best = w_i; bestval = Val\}$.
4. If $bestval = 0$ then return any world whatsoever otherwise return $best$.

Theorem 3 (correctness of SemiHOP). *Algorithm SemiHOP is correct, i.e. it is guaranteed to return a world whose low probability is greater than or equal to that of any other world.*

The key advantage of SemiHOP over HOP is that we do not need to construct the set $[w_i]$ of worlds, i.e. we do not need to find the equivalence classes $[w_i]$. This is a potentially big saving because there are 2^n possible worlds (where n is the number of ground action atoms) and finding the equivalence classes can be expensive. This advantage comes with a drawback - the size of the set S_RedCONS$_U(\Pi, s, T^{\omega}_{\Pi_s})$ can be a bit bigger than the size of the set RedCONS$_U(\Pi, s, T^{\omega}_{\Pi_s})$.

5   Heuristic Methods for Finding a Maximally Probable World

In the preceding sections, we have developed three sets of constraints associated, respectively, with the naive algorithm, HOP, and SemiHOP. In all cases, the set of constraint variables can be enormous, even though HOP and SemiHOP try to reduce the number of variables. In this section, we develop a heuristic algorithm to reduce the number of variables even further. To see how the algorithm works, let $\mathcal{C}$ be the set of constraints generated by either Naive, HOP, or SemiHOP. The constraints have one of the forms

$$\ell \leq q_1 + \cdots + q_r \leq u \tag{5}$$

$$q_1 + \cdots + q_m = 1. \tag{6}$$

Suppose we make an *a priori* commitment to only look at some set S_k of k variables from the linear program. In this case, we could eliminate variables not in S_k from any summation in (5). Thus, we might weaken (5) and (6) above to

$$\ell \leq \Sigma_{\{q_1,\ldots,q_r\} \cap S_k} q_i \leq u \tag{7}$$

$$\Sigma_{\{q_1,\ldots,q_m\} \cap S_k} q_i \leq 1. \tag{8}$$

Let C' be the modification of the constraints in C derived in this way. It is immediately apparent that as all the lower bounds are set to ℓ, a solution to C' may or may not exist. Rather than weakening the lower bound from ℓ to 0 (which would guarantee a solution), we wondered how "close" to ℓ one can get while still having a solvable system of equations.

As a consequence, our *binary heuristic* works as follows by *only modifying lower bounds* of such constraints. We start with C' and see if it is solvable by itself. If so, we minimize each variable in S_k subject to C' and return the variable (and value) with the highest value. If not, we try to decrease the lower bounds of one or more constraints in C' as follows. Suppose c^* is one such constraint of the form

$$\ell^* \leq \Sigma_{q_i \in S_k} q_i \leq u$$

Furthermore, suppose this constraint was derived from a constraint of the type shown in Equation (5). In this case, we try to replace ℓ^* by $\frac{\ell^*}{2}$. If this yields a solvable set of equations, we try to replace $\frac{\ell^*}{2}$ by $\frac{3 \times \ell^*}{4}$ - if the resulting system of equations is unsolvable, we try to replace it with $\frac{5 \times \ell^*}{8}$ and so forth. Effectively, we try to keep the lower bounds of constraints as close to those in C as possible, while still being solvable when terms not in S_k are eliminated from the summations in Equation (5). We will call this the *binary heuristic* due to the fact that it resembles a binary search.

Once we have completed this process of modifying the lower bounds of constraints in C' (let the resulting system of constraints be called $C^{\bullet}$) we minimize each and every variable in S_k subject to the constraints in $C^{\bullet}$. The variable with the highest minimal value is returned (together with its value).

Example 5. Suppose we have the same set $CONS_U(\Pi, s, T_{\Pi_s}^{\omega})$ as in Example 1. If we now choose the set of four variables $S_k = \{p_2, p_4, p_6, p_8\}$, C' contains the following constraints:

$$0.7 \leq p_2 + p_6 + p_8 \leq 1$$
$$0.2 \leq p_8 \leq 0.6$$
$$p_2 + p_4 + p_6 + p_8 \leq 1$$

If the algorithm starts by considering the first constraint in C' it replaces it with $0.35 \leq p_2 + p_6 + p_8 \leq 1$, which yields an unsolvable set of constraints. The lower bound gets succesively replaced by 0.525, 0.4375, and 0.39375, which finally yields a solvable system. At this point, the algorithm decides to accept this value as the lower bound for the constraint. The same process is also carried out for the other constraint.

6   Implementation and Experiments

We have implemented four of the algorithms described in this paper—the naive, HOP, SemiHOP, and the binary heuristic algorithms—using approximately 6,000 lines of Java code. The binary heuristic algorithm was applied to each of the ($CONS_U$ ($\Pi, s, T_{\Pi_s}^\omega$), RedCONS$_U(\Pi, s, T_{\Pi_s}^\omega)$, and S_RedCONS$_U(\Pi, s, T_{\Pi_s}^\omega)$) constraint sets; we refer to these approximations as the naive$_{bin}$, HOP$_{bin}$, and SemiHOP$_{bin}$ algorithms respectively. Our experiments were performed on a Linux computing cluster comprised of 16 dual-core, dual-processor nodes with 8GB RAM. The linear constraints were solved using the QSopt linear programming solver library, and the logical formula manipulation code from the COBA belief revision system and SAT4J satisfaction library were used in the implementation of the HOP and SemiHOP algorithms.

For each experiment, we held the number of rules constant at 10 and did the following: (i) we generated a new ap-program and sent it to each of the three algorithms, (ii) varied the number of worlds from 32 to 16,384, performing at least 4 runs for each value and recording the average time taken by each algorithm, and (iii) we also measured the quality of the SemiHOP and all algorithms that use the binary heuristic by calculating the average distance from the solution found by the exact algorithm. Due to the immense time complexity of the HOP algorithm, we do not directly compare its performance to the naive algorithm or SemiHOP. In the results below we use the metric $ruledensity = \frac{\mathcal{L}_{act}}{card(T_{\Pi_s}^\omega)}$ to represent the size of the ap-program; this allows for the comparison of the naive, HOP and SemiHOP algorithms as the number of worlds increases.

Running time. Figure 3 shows the running times for each of the naive, SemiHOP, naive$_{binary}$, and SemiHOP$_{binary}$ algorithms for increasing number of worlds. As expected, the binary search approximation algorithm is superior to the exact algorithms in terms of computation time, when applied to both the naive and SemiHOP contstraint sets. With a sample size of 25%, naive$_{binary}$ and SemiHOP$_{binary}$ take only about 132.6 seconds and 58.19 seconds for instances with 1,024 worlds, whereas the naive algorithm requires almost 4 hours (13,636.23 seconds). This result demonstrates that the naive algorithm is more or less useless and takes prohibitive amounts of time, even for small instances. Similarly, the checks for logical equivalence required to obtain each $[w_i]$ for HOP cause the algorithm to consistently require an exorbitant amount of time; for instances with only 128 worlds, HOP takes 58,064.74 seconds, which is much greater even than the naive algorithm for 1,024 worlds. Even when using the binary heuristic to further reduce the number of variables, HOP$_{bin}$ still requires a prohibitively large amount of time.

At low rule densities, SemiHOP runs slower than the naive algorithm; with 10 rules, SemiHOP uses 18.75 seconds and 122.44 seconds for 128 worlds, while the naive algorithm only requires 1.79 seconds and 19.99 seconds respectively. However, SemiHOP vastly outperforms naive for problems with higher densities—358.3 seconds versus 13,636.23 seconds for 1,024 worlds—which more accurately reflect real-world problems in which the number of possible worlds is far greater than the number of ap-rules. Because the SemiHOP algorithm uses subpartions rather than unique

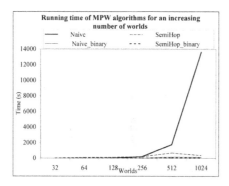

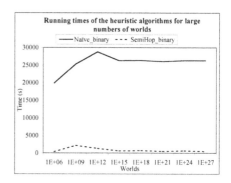

Fig. 3. Running time of the algorithms for increasing number of worlds

Fig. 4. Running time of naive$_{bin}$ and Semi-HOP$_{bin}$ for large number of worlds

equivalence classes in the $\mathsf{RedCONS}_U(\Pi, seconds, T^{\omega}_{\Pi_s})$ constraints, the algorithm overhead is much lower than that of the HOP algorithm, and thus yields a more efficient running time.

The reduction in the size of $\mathcal{C}'$ afforded by the binary heuristic algorithm allows us to apply the naive and SemiHOP algorithms to much larger ap-programs. In Figure 4, we examine the running times of the naive$_{bin}$ and SemiHOP$_{bin}$ algorithms for large numbers of worlds (up to about 1.23794×10^{27} possible worlds) with a sample size for the binary heuristic of 2%; this is to ensure that the reduced linear program is indeed tractable. SemiHOP$_{binary}$ consistently takes less time than naive$_{binary}$, though both algorithms still perform rather well. For 1.23794×10^{27} possible worlds, naive$_{binary}$ takes on average 26,325.1 seconds while SemiHOP$_{binary}$ requires only 458.07 seconds. This difference occurs because, $|\mathsf{S\_RedCONS}_U(\Pi, s, T^{\omega}_{\Pi_s})| < |\mathsf{CONS}_U(\Pi, s, T^{\omega}_{\Pi_s})|$ that is the heuristic algorithm is further reducing an already smaller constraint set. In addition, because SemiHOP only solves the linear constraint problem when there is exactly one satisfying interpretation for a subpartition, it performs fewer computations overall. Figure 5 contains additional experiments running SemiHOP$_{binary}$ on very large ap-programs (from 1,000 to 100,000 ground atoms). Even for such a large number of worlds, the running time is only around 300 seconds for a 2% sample rate.

Quality of solution. Figure 6 compares the accuracy of the probability found for the most probable world by SemiHOP, naive$_{binary}$, and SemiHOP$_{binary}$ to the solution obtained by the naive algorithm, averaged over at least 4 runs for each number of worlds. The results are given as a percentage of the solution returned by the naive algorithm, and are only reported in cases where both algorithms found a solution. The SemiHOP and SemiHOP$_{binary}$ algorithms demonstrate near perfect accuracy; this is significant because in the SemiHOP$_{binary}$ algorithm, the binary heuristic was only sampling 25% of the possible subpartitions. However, in many of these cases, both the naive and the SemiHOP algorithms found most probable worlds with a probability of zero. The most probable world found by the naive$_{binary}$ algorithm can be between 75% and 100% as likely as those given by the regular naive algorithm; however, the naive$_{binary}$ algorithm also was often unable to find a solution.

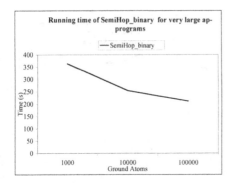

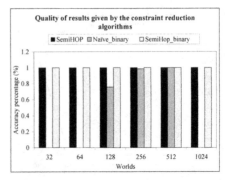

Fig. 5. Running time of the SemiHOP$_{binary}$ algorithm for very large numbers of possible worlds

Fig. 6. Quality of the solutions produced by SemiHOP, naive$_{bin}$, and SemiHOP$_{bin}$ as compared to Naive

7   Conclusions and Related Work

Probabilistic logic programming was introduced in [5,1] and later studied by several authors [10,11,12,13]. This work was preceded by earlier—non-probabilistic—papers on quantitative logic programming of which [14] is an example. [10] presents a model theory, fixpoint theory, and proof procedure for conditional probabilistic logic programming. [11] combines probabilistic LP with maximum entropy. [15] presents a conditional semantics for probabilistic LPs where each rule is interpreted as specifying the conditional probability of the rule head, given the body. [12] develops a semantics for logic programs in which different general axiomatic methods are given to compute probabilities of conjunctions and disjunctions, and [13] presents an approach to a similar problem. gp-programs were implemented by [16], based on the DisLOG system [17].

However, all works to date on probabilistic logic programming have addressed the problem of checking whether a given formula of the form $F : [L, U]$ is entailed by a probabilistic logic program. This usually boils down to finding out if all interpretations that satisfy the PLP assign a probability between L and U to F.

Our work builds on top of the gp-program paradigm [5]. Our framework modifies gp-programs in three ways: (i) we do not allow non-action predicates to occur in rule heads, while gp-programs do, (ii) we allow arbitrary formulas to occur in rule heads, whereas gp-programs only allow the so-called "basic formulas" to appear in rule heads. (iii) Most importantly, of all, we solve the problem of finding the most probable model whereas [5] solve the problem of entailment.

This is justified because in certain classes of applications, a p-program describes probabilities on possible worlds, and we are interested in finding that world which has the highest probability. Such an example could be a market model of bidding in a specialized auction, such as an electricity auction, which contains rules specifying what actions a potential competitor might take in a given situation. Here, the organization coming up with the model might want to know the most likely scenarios (worlds) that they have to face. We have been working on an economic application about what may occur in a given market when certain actions such as "reduce price of fruit by 10%" are taken (e.g., by increasing supply). Of course, this can be viewed as an entailment problem (take the conjunction of positive atoms in a world, conjoin that with the conjunction of negative atoms in that world, solve a linear program for each world, and choose the best one). This corresponds to the naive (exact) solution in this paper which is easily shown to not work at all once the amount of worlds exceeds a small number. What we do in this paper is provide algorithms to find the world that has the maximal probability, and to our knowledge, we are the first to do this. We further provide two approximation algorithms that have been experimentally shown to produce solutions within about 10-15% of the optimal solution in a small fraction of the time required to find the best solution.

References

1. Ng, R.T., Subrahmanian, V.S.: Probabilistic logic programming. Information and Computation 101(2), 150–201 (1992)
2. Hailperin, T.: Probability logic. Notre Dame Journal of Formal Logic 25 (3), 198–212 (1984)
3. Fagin, R., Halpern, J.Y., Megiddo, N.: A logic for reasoning about probabilities. Information and Computation 87(1/2), 78–128 (1990)
4. Nilsson, N.: Probabilistic logic. Artificial Intelligence 28, 71–87 (1986)
5. Ng, R.T., Subrahmanian, V.S.: A semantic framework for supporting subjective and conditional probabilities in deductive databases. In: Furukawa, K. (ed.) Proc. of the 8th Int. Conf. on Logic Programming, pp. 565–580. The MIT Press, Cambridge (1991)
6. Subrahmanian, V., Albanese, M., Martinez, V., Reforgiato, D., Simari, G.I., Sliva, A., Udrea, O., Wilkenfeld, J.: CARA: A Cultural Adversarial Reasoning Architecture. IEEE Intelligent Systems 22(2), 12–16 (2007)
7. Lloyd, J.W.: Foundations of Logic Programming, 2nd edn. Springer, Heidelberg (1987)
8. Wilkenfeld, J., Asal, V., Johnson, C., Pate, A., Michael, M.: The use of violence by ethnopolitical organizations in the middle east. Technical report, National Consortium for the Study of Terrorism and Responses to Terrorism (2007)
9. Ernst, J., Martinez, V., Simari, G.I., Sliva, A.: Mining rules about behaviors of terror groups. In preparation for submission to a conference (2007)
10. Ngo, L., Haddawy, P.: Probabilistic logic programming and bayesian networks. In: Asian Computing Science Conf., pp. 286–300 (1995)
11. Lukasiewicz, T., Kern-Isberner, G.: Probabilistic logic programming under maximum entropy. In: Hunter, A., Parsons, S. (eds.) ECSQARU 1999. LNCS (LNAI), vol. 1638, Springer, Heidelberg (1999)
12. Lakshmanan, L.V.S., Shiri, N.: A parametric approach to deductive databases with uncertainty. IEEE Trans. on Knowledge and Data Engineering 13(4), 554–570 (2001)
13. Dekhtyar, A., Subrahmanian, V.S.: Hybrid probabilistic programs. In: Int. Conf. on Logic Programming, pp. 391–405 (1997)
14. van Emden, M.: Quantitative deduction and its fixpoint theory. Journal of Logic Programming 4, 37–53 (1986)
15. Lukasiewicz, T.: Probabilistic logic programming. In: European Conference on Artificial Intelligence, pp. 388–392 (1998)
16. Pillo, A.: Implementation and investigation of probabilistic reasoning in deductive databases. Diploma Thesis, University of Wuerzburg (1998)
17. Seipel, D., Thöne, H.: DISLOG - A system for reasoning in disjunctive deductive databases. In: DAISD 1994, pp. 325–343 (1994)

Managing Uncertainty in Schema Matcher Ensembles

Anan Marie and Avigdor Gal

Technion – Israel Institute of Technology
{sananm@cs,avigal@ie}.technion.ac.il

Abstract. Schema matching is the task of matching between concepts describing the meaning of data in various heterogeneous, distributed data sources. With many heuristics to choose from, several tools have enabled the use of schema matcher ensembles, combining principles by which different schema matchers judge the similarity between concepts. In this work, we investigate means of estimating the uncertainty involved in schema matching and harnessing it to improve an ensemble outcome. We propose a model for schema matching, based on simple probabilistic principles. We then propose the use of machine learning in determining the best mapping and discuss its pros and cons. Finally, we provide a thorough empirical analysis, using both real-world and synthetic data, to test the proposed technique. We conclude that the proposed heuristic performs well, given an accurate modeling of uncertainty in matcher decision making.

1 Introduction

Schema matching is the task of matching between concepts describing the meaning of data in various heterogeneous, distributed data sources. It is recognized to be one of the basic operations required by the process of data and schema integration [21], and thus has a great impact on its outcome.

Research into schema matching has been going on for more than 25 years now (see surveys such as [25] and various online lists, *e.g.*, OntologyMatching,[1]) first as part of a broader effort of schema integration and then as a standalone research. Due to its cognitive complexity, schema matching has been traditionally considered to be AI-complete, performed by human experts [15]. The move from manual to semi-automatic schema matching has been justified in the literature using arguments of scalability (especially for matching between large schemata [14]) and by the need to speed-up the matching process. Researchers also argue for moving to fully-automatic (that is, unsupervised) schema matching in settings where a human expert is absent from the decision process. In particular, such situations characterize numerous emerging applications triggered by the vision of the Semantic Web and machine-understandable Web resources [26]. In these applications, schema matching is no longer a preliminary task to the data integration effort, but rather ad-hoc and incremental.

---

[1] http://www.ontologymatching.org/

H. Prade and V.S. Subrahmanian (Eds.): SUM 2007, LNAI 4772, pp. 60–73, 2007.

The AI-complete nature of the problem dictates that semi-automatic and automatic algorithms for schema matching will be of heuristic nature at best. Over the years, a significant body of work was devoted to the identification of *schema matchers*, heuristics for schema matching. Examples of algorithmic tools providing means for schema matching include COMA [6] and OntoBuilder [13], to name but a couple. The main objective of schema matchers is to provide schema mappings that will be effective from the user point of view, yet computationally efficient (or at least not disastrously expensive). Such research has evolved in different research communities, including databases, information retrieval, information sciences, data semantics, and others.

Although these tools comprise a significant step towards fulfilling the vision of automated schema matching, it has become obvious that the consumer of schema matchers must accept a degree of imperfection in their performance [4, 12]. A prime reason for this is the enormous ambiguity and heterogeneity of data description concepts: It is unrealistic to expect a single schema matcher to identify the correct mapping for any possible concept in a set. This argument has also been validated empirically [12]. Another (and probably no less crucial) reason is that "the syntactic representation of schemas and data do not completely convey the semantics of different databases" [22]; *i.e.*, the description of a concept in a schema can be semantically misleading. [2] went even further, arguing philosophically that even if two schemata fully agree on the semantics and the language is rich enough, schemata may still not convey the same meaning, due to some hidden semantics, beyond the scope of the schemata. Therefore, [18] argues that "[w]hen no accurate mapping exists, the issue becomes choosing the *best* mapping from the viable ones."

Choosing a heuristic that can stand up to this challenge is far from being trivial. The number of schema matchers is continuously growing, and this diversity by itself complicates the choice of the most appropriate tool for a given application domain. In fact, due to effectively unlimited heterogeneity and ambiguity of data description, it seems unavoidable that optimal mappings for many pairs of schemata will be considered as "best mappings" by none of the existing schema matchers. Striving to increase robustness in the face of the biases and shortcomings of individual matchers, several tools have enabled the use of *schema matcher ensembles*,[2] combining principles by which different schema matchers judge the similarity between concepts. The idea is appealing since an ensemble of complementary matchers can potentially compensate for the weaknesses of each other. Indeed, several studies report on encouraging results when using schema matcher ensembles (*e.g.*, see [6, 19, 8]).

In this work, we investigate means of estimating the uncertainty involved in schema matching and harnessing it to improve an ensemble outcome. We propose a model for schema matching, based on simple probabilistic principles. We then propose the use of machine learning in determining the best mapping and discuss its pros and cons. Finally, we provide a thorough empirical analysis, using both real-world and synthetic data, to test the proposed technique.

---

[2] The term *ensemble* is borrowed from [14, 8].

The specific contribution of this work are as follows:

- On a conceptual level, we provide a new model for schema matching, explaining the process uncertainty using simple probabilistic terms.
- We propose a new schema matching heuristic for combining existing schema matchers. The heuristic utilizes a naïve Bayes classifier, a known machine learning technique. While naïve Bayes classifiers were introduced before in the schema matching research, this technique was never applied to schema matcher ensembles.
- We present a thorough empirical analysis of the model and the heuristic, using a large data set of 230 real-world schemata as well as synthetic data. Our comparative analysis shows that the proposed heuristic performs well, given an accurate modeling of uncertainty in matcher decision making.

The rest of the paper is organized as follows. Section 2 presents the schema matching model. Section 3 introduces the new heuristic, followed by a comparative empirical analysis in Section 4. We conclude with an overview of related work (Section 5) and future research directions (Section 6).

2   Model

Let *schema* $S = \{A_1, A_2, ..., A_n\}$ be a finite set of some *attributes*. We set no particular limitations on the notion of schema attributes; attributes can be both simple and compound, compound attributes should not necessarily be disjoint, *etc.* For any schemata pair S and S', let $\mathcal{S} = S \times S'$ be the set of all possible *attribute mappings* between S and S'. Let $M(S, S')$ be an $n \times n'$ *similarity matrix* over $\mathcal{S}$, where $M_{i,j}$ represents a degree of similarity between the i-th attribute of S and the j-th attribute of S'. The majority of works in the schema matching literature define $M_{i,j}$ to be a real number in $(0, 1)$. $M(S, S')$ is a *binary similarity matrix* if for all $1 \leq i \leq n$ and $1 \leq j \leq n'$, $M_{i,j} \in \{0, 1\}$.

Schema matchers are instantiations of the schema matching process. Schema matchers differ in the way they encode the application semantics into M. Some matchers (*e.g.*, [27]) assume similar attributes are more likely to have similar names. Other matchers (*e.g.*, [19]) assume similar attributes share similar domains. Others yet (*e.g.*, [3]) take instance similarity as an indication to attribute similarity.

Let Σ be a set of possible schema mappings, where a schema mapping $\sigma \in \Sigma$ is a set of attribute mappings, $\sigma \subseteq \mathcal{S}$. Definition 1 defines the output of a schema matching process in terms of matrix satisfiability.

Definition 1 (Matrix Satisfaction). *Let $M(S, S')$ be an $n \times n'$ similarity matrix over $\mathcal{S}$ and let σ be a set of schema mappings. A schema mapping $\sigma \in \Sigma$ is said to satisfy $M(S, S')$ (denoted $\sigma \models M(S, S')$) if $\left(A_i, A'_j\right) \in \sigma \rightarrow M_{i,j} > 0$. $\sigma \in \Sigma$ is said to maximally satisfy $M(S, S')$ if $\sigma \models M(S, S')$ and for each $\sigma' \in \Sigma$ such that $\sigma' \models M(S, S')$, $\sigma' \subset \sigma$.*

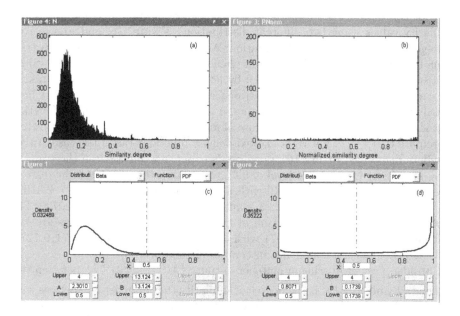

Fig. 1. Illustration of Matcher Behavior

We can therefore define the output of a schema matching process to be a similarity matrix $M(S, S')$ and derive the output schema mapping to be $\sigma \in \Sigma$ that maximally satisfies $M(S, S')$. Handling constraints such as $1 : 1$ cardinality constraints can be done by matrix manipulation, a topic which is beyond the scope of this paper.

When encoding the application semantic in a similarity matrix, a matcher would be inclined to put a value of 0 for each pair it conceives not to match, and a similarity measure higher than 0 (and probably closer to 1) for those attribute matches that are conceived to be correct. This tendency, however, is masked by "noise," whose sources are rooted in missing and uncertain information. Therefore, instead of expecting a binary similarity matrix, with a 0 score for all incorrect attribute mappings and a unit score for all correct attribute mappings, we would expect the values in a similarity matrix to form two probability distributions over $[0, 1]$, one for incorrect attribute mappings (with higher density around 0), and another for correct mappings.

Figure 1 provides an empirical validation for our hypothesis, based on more than 106,000 attribute mappings of 115 ontology pairs.[3] Figure 1(a) shows a distribution with a higher density around 0 that represents the similarity values that were assigned to incorrect attribute mappings by an OntoBuilder algorithm dubbed *Precedence* [13]. Figure 1(b) reflects a set of normalized similarity values of correct attribute mappings. Normalization was achieved by dividing all similarity values in a matrix by the highest value in that matrix. Figure 1 illustrates

---

[3] Detailed description of the data set we have used is given in Section 4.2.

that for this data set our hypothesis indeed stands and matchers indeed choose similarity values using two different distributions. Figure 1(c) and Figure 1(d) were generated using a beta distribution. According to [24]: "[t]he beta distribution can be used to model a random phenomenon whose set of possible values is in some finite interval $[c, d]$—which by letting c denote the origin and taking $d - c$ as a unit measurement can be transformed into the interval $[0, 1]$." A beta distribution has two tuning parameters, a and b. To receive a density function that is skewed to the left (as in the case of false attribute mappings, Figure 1(c)) we require that $b > a$. For right skewed density functions (as in the case of true attribute mappings, Figure 1(d)) one needs to set $a > b$. Based on the training data, and using a confidence level of 95% ($\alpha = 0.05$), the a value of the distribution of incorrect values is 2.3010 with a confidence interval of $[2.2827, 2.3192]$. We also have $b = 13.1242$ with a confidence interval $[13.0413, 13.2072]$. The confidence levels of the distribution of the correct attribute mappings are less concentrated. We have $a = 0.6071$ with a confidence interval of $[0.4871, 0.7270]$ and $b = 0.1739$ with a confidence interval of $[0.1680, 0.1798]$.

Consider a set of m schema matcher outputs $\{M^{(1)}, \ldots, M^{(m)}\}$ between two schemata S and S'. $M_{i,j}^{(l)}$ is the degree of similarity that matcher l associates with mapping the i-th attribute of S to the j-th attribute of S'. A *schema matching ensemble* is a set of schema matchers. An ensemble aggregates the similarities assigned by individual matchers to reason about the resulting aggregated ranking of alternative mappings. Such an aggregation can be modeled in various ways, one of which is presented next.

3   Naïve Bayes Heuristic

In this section we present a new heuristic for schema matching, using our schema matching model, presented in Section 2. Recall that the values in a similarity matrix are assumed to form two probability distributions over $[0, 1]$, one for incorrect attribute mappings and another for correct mappings (see Figure 1). The *naïve Bayes* heuristic attempts, given a similarity degree, to use Bayes theorem to classify an attribute mapping to one of the two groups. The naïve Bayes method is a simple probabilistic classifier that applies Bayes theorem under a strong (naïve) independence assumptions.

Given an attribute mapping (A_i, A_j) and an ensemble of matchers' output $\{M^{(1)}, M^{(2)}, ..., M^{(m)}\}$, a feature vector of (A_i, A_j) is defined to be $\left\langle M_{i,j}^{(1)}, M_{i,j}^{(2)}, ..., M_{i,j}^{(m)} \right\rangle$, where $M_{i,j}^{(l)}$ is the (i, j) similarity value of $M^{(l)}$. Let $\mathcal{F}$ be an m dimension feature space. We would like to predict the most likely target value ($v = +1$ or $v = -1$), based on the observed data sample. $+1$ stands for a correct mapping while -1 stands for an incorrect mapping. Formally, our target function is

$$f_c : \mathcal{F} \rightarrow \{+1, -1\} \tag{1}$$

The Bayesian approach to classifying a new instance (attribute mapping in our case) is to assign the most probable target value, v_{MAP}, given the attribute values $\left\langle M_{i,j}^{(1)}, M_{i,j}^{(2)}, ..., M_{i,j}^{(m)} \right\rangle$ that describe the instance:

$$v_{MAP} = argmax_{v_j \in \{+1,-1\}} P\left\{ v_j | M_{i,j}^{(1)}, M_{i,j}^{(2)}, ..., M_{i,j}^{(m)} \right\} \tag{2}$$

Eq. 2, together with Bayes theorem and under the simplifying assumption that the similarity values are conditionally independent given the target value, is used to specify the target value output of the naïve Bayes classifier v_{NB} to be:

$$v_{NB} = argmax_{v_j \in \{+1,-1\}} P\{v_j\} \prod_{l=1}^{m} P\left\{ M_{i,j}^{(l)} | v_j \right\} \tag{3}$$

$P\{v_j\}$ is estimated by counting the frequency with which each target value $v_j \in \{+1,-1\}$ occurs in the training dataset. $P\left\{ M_{i,j}^{(l)} | v_j \right\}$, the probability to observe a mapping with similarity degree equal to $M_{i,j}^{(l)}$ given that the mapping is correct/incorrect is taken from the estimated distribution of correct and incorrect mappings, as suggested in Section 2.

Example 1. To illustrate the naïve Bayes heuristic, consider a naïve Bayes classifier with two matchers (a bivariate instance space). Each mapping is represented by a vector of length 2, consisting of the similarity values of the Precedence and Graph matchers. Figure 1 provides an illustration of the two Precedence matcher distributions used by the classifier and Table 1 (Section 4.2) provides the tuning parameters for the distributions. The number of training negative mappings is $N_{neg} = 104387$ and the number of positive training mappings is $N_{pos} = 1706$. Consider a new mapping pair with a similarity value vector $\overrightarrow{\mu} = \langle \mu_{prec}, \mu_{graph} \rangle = \langle 0.5, 0.6 \rangle$ and assume that the maximum values in the *Precedence* and *Graph* similarity matrices are $max_{\mu}^{prec} = 0.6$ and $max_{\mu}^{graph} = 0.8$, respectively. The probability of the mapping to be negative, given the vector of similarity measures $\overrightarrow{\mu} = \langle 0.5, 0.6 \rangle$ is

$$P(neg|\overrightarrow{\mu}) = \frac{N_{neg}}{N_{neg} + N_{pos}} \cdot P_{\alpha_{neg}^{prec}, \beta_{neg}^{prec}}(\mu_{prec}) \cdot P_{\alpha_{neg}^{graph}, \beta_{neg}^{graph}}(\mu_{graph}) \tag{4}$$

$$= \frac{104387}{104387 + 1706} \cdot 0.0097 \cdot 0.0034 = 3.2449e - 005 \tag{5}$$

where $P_{\alpha_{neg}^{prec}, \beta_{neg}^{prec}}$ and $P_{\alpha_{neg}^{graph}, \beta_{neg}^{graph}}$ are the density functions of the beta distributions of the *Precedence* and *Graph* matchers, respectively. To evaluate the probability of the given mapping to be positive, one needs to first normalize the values in $\overrightarrow{\mu}$ yielding a vector $\overrightarrow{\mu}' = \langle \mu'_{prec}, \mu'_{graph} \rangle = \langle \frac{0.5}{0.6}, \frac{0.6}{0.8} \rangle$, followed by calculating $\frac{N_{pos}}{N_{neg}+N_{pos}} \cdot P_{\alpha_{pos}^{prec}, \beta_{pos}^{prec}}(\mu'_{prec}) \cdot P_{\alpha_{pos}^{graph}, \beta_{pos}^{graph}}(\mu'_{graph})$, yielding $P(pos|\langle 0.83, 0.75 \rangle) = 0.0057$. Therefore, the naïve Bayes heuristic will determine this mapping to be positive.

The time complexity of the *naïve Bayes* heuristic is $O(n^2)$, since each entry in the matrix requires a constant number of computations. As a final comment, it is worth noting that the naïve Bayes heuristic no longer guarantees, in an by itself, a 1 : 1 cardinality constraint. To enforce this requirements, a constraint enforcer [16], such as an algorithm for solving Maximum Weight Bipartite Graph problem, should be applied to the resulting binary matrix of the heuristic.

4   Experiments

We now present an empirical evaluation of our heuristic. We report in details on our experimental setup (Section 4.1), the data that was used (Section 4.2), and the evaluation methodology (Section 4.3). We then present in Section 4.4 the experiment results and provide an empirical analysis of these results.

4.1   Experiment Setup

In our experiments we have used three matchers, briefly discussed below. Detailed description of these matchers can be found in [13]:

Term: Term matching compare attribute names to identify syntactically similar terms. To achieve better performance, terms are preprocessed using several techniques originating in IR research. Term matching is based on either complete word or string comparison.

Composition: A composite term is composed of other terms (either atomic or composite). Composition can be translated into a hierarchy. Similarity is determined based on the similarity of their neighbors.

Precedence: In any interactive process, the order in which data are provided may be important. In particular, data given at an earlier stage may restrict the availability of options for a later entry. When matching two terms, we consider each of them to be a pivot within its own schema, thus partitioning the graph into subgraphs of all preceding terms and all succeeding terms. By comparing preceding subgraphs and succeeding subgraphs, we determine the confidence strength of the pivot terms.

The *naïve Bayes* heuristic uses each of the three matchers as input to its feature vector. The *Naïve Bayes* heuristic was implemented using Java 2 JDK version 1.5.0_09 environment, using an API to access OntoBuilder's matchers and get the output matrices.

We have also experimented with each of the three matchers and a weighted linear combination of them into a combined matcher. This combination also included a fourth matcher, called Value, which uses the domain of attributes as evidence to their similarity. The combined matcher is clearly dependent on the other matchers and therefore violates the *naïve Bayes* heuristic assumption. The experiments were run on a laptop with Intel Centrino Pentium m, 1.50GHz CPU, 760MB of RAM Windows XP Home edition OS.

4.2   Data

For our experiments, we have selected 230 Web forms from different domains, such as dating and matchmaking, job hunting, Web mail, hotel reservation, news, and cosmetics. We extracted each Web form ontology (containing the schema and composition and precedence ontological relationships) using OntoBuilder. We have matched the Web forms in pairs (115 pairs), where pairs were taken from the same domain, and generated the exact mapping for each pair.[4] The ontologies vary in size and the proportion of number of attribute pairs in the exact mapping relative to the target ontology. Another dimension is the size difference between matched ontologies.

We ran the four matchers and generated 460 matrices. For each such matrix, we have applied an algorithm for solving Maximum Weight Bipartite Graph problem, to generate a 1 : 1 schema mapping, as a baseline comparison.

Table 1. Beta parameters

Matcher	α_{pos}	β_{pos}	α_{neg}	β_{neg}
Term	0.2430	0.0831	0.2951	4.6765
Graph	0.4655	0.1466	0.8360	9.1653
Precedence	0.6071	0.1739	2.3010	13.1242
Combined	0.6406	0.2040	2.6452	16.3139

In addition, we have generated 100 synthetic schema pairs. For each pair S and S' we have uniformly selected its schema sizes from the range $[30, 60]$. As an exact mapping we selected a set of n mapping pairs, where n takes one of three possible values, $n_1 = \min(|S|, |S'|)$, $n_2 = 0.5n_1$, and $n_3 = 2n_1$. For n_1 we have enforced a 1 : 1 cardinality constraint. n_2 represents a situation in which not all attributes can be mapped and n_3 represents a matching that is not of 1 : 1 cardinality. Then, using the beta distributions learned from the training data for each of the four matchers we have created, for each schema pair, four synthetic matrices, one per a matcher using a beta generator class *cern.jet.random.Beta* distributed with *colt.jar* jar file. The entries of a matrix use $(\alpha_{pos}, \beta_{pos})$ and $(\alpha_{neg}, \beta_{neg})$ parameters (See Table 1) for the beta distribution of the positive mapping measures and the negative mapping measures, respectively.

4.3   Evaluation Methodology

We use two main evaluation metrics, namely Precision and Recall. Precision is computed as the ratio of correct element mappings, with respect to some exact mapping, out of the total number of element mappings suggested by the heuristic. Recall is computed as the ratio of correct element mappings, out of the total number of element mappings in the exact mapping. Both Recall and Precision are measured on a $[0, 1]$ scale. An optimal schema matching results in both Precision and Recall equal to 1. Lower precision means more false positives, while lower recall suggests more false negatives. To extend Precision and Recall to the case of non 1 : 1 mappings, we have adopted a correctness criteria according

---

[4] All ontologies and exact mappings are available for download from the OntoBuilder Web site, http://ie.technion.ac.il/OntoBuilder).

to which any attribute pair that belongs to the exact mapping is considered to be correct, even if the complex mapping is not fully captured. This method aims at compensating the matchers for the 1 : 1 cardinality enforcement.

It is worth noting that our test was conducted on a wide range of real-world schemata. Such a real world challenge was tried at the 2006 OAEI ontology matching evaluation [10] with average performance of 39.25% Precision, 40.40% Recall, and 39.82% F-Measure.[5]

4.4   Results and Analysis

We are now ready to present our results and empirical analysis. We present a comparative analysis of the proposed heuristic with existing heuristics, using the full data set. We then analyze two obstacles in successfully using the heuristic and describe two additional experiments, aimed at evaluating the impact of each such obstacle on the heuristic performance.

Comparative Performance Analysis. In our first experiment we provide a comparative analysis of the performance of the naïve Bayes heuristic with four heuristics that enforce a mapping cardinality of 1 : 1. Figure 2 illustrates the results. The x axis represents the four different data sets, with Precision on the y axis in Figure 2(left) and Recall in Figure 2(right).

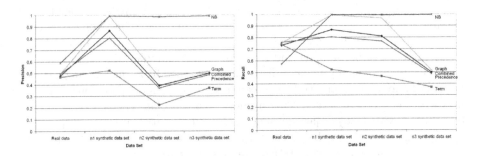

Fig. 2. Comparative Performance Analysis

In terms of Precision, the naïve Bayes heuristic outperforms all other heuristics. For the real data set, this improvement in Precision comes at the cost of Recall. This disadvantage disappears in the simulated data, where the naïve Bayes heuristic dominates other heuristics, even for the simulated data with n_1, where the 1 : 1 cardinality constraint holds (although not enforced for the proposed heuristic). For this case, the Graph heuristic comes in very close behind.

Two main reasons may explain this behavior. First, the naïve assumption of independence does not hold in our case, since OntoBuilder heuristics are all heavily based on syntactic comparisons. Second, it is possible that the training data set, based on which the beta distributions are determined, does not serve

---

[5] See http://keg.cs.tsinghua.edu.cn/project/RiMOM/oaei2006/main.html for details.

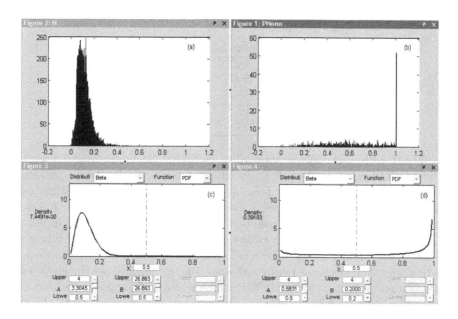

Fig. 3. Illustration of Matcher Behavior after Outlier Elimination

as a good estimator for the matchers decision making. We shall now investigate these hypotheses in more depth.

Cleaning the Data. In this experiment we have eliminated from the real-world data set some of the matrices that have a high percentage of outliers. In statistics, an outlier is an observation that is numerically distant from the rest of the data. Outliers in our matrices involve correct attribute mappings with very low similarity measures and incorrect attribute mappings with relatively high similarity measures. To compute (either positive or negative) outliers, we define $Q1$ and $Q3$ to be first and third quartiles, respectively, over all the similarity measures of the positive (negative) mappings, and IQR to be the interquartile range $Q3 - Q1$. An outlier is a mapping that its similarity measure $\mu < Q1 - 1.5 \cdot IQR$ or $\mu > Q3 + 1.5 \cdot IQR$. We have ranked all the Combined heuristic matrices in a decreasing order of outlier numbers and chose the top 51 schema pairs (153 matrices), based on which we have regenerated the beta distributions for all heuristics. Figure 3 presents the beta distribution of the Preference heuristic for the new data set. Compared with Figure 1, we see that the distribution of normalized values of correct attribute mappings remain stable. The distribution of incorrect attribute mappings is tighter here, yielding lower variance. As a result, we expect less false negatives and increasing Recall. The confidence levels of the new distributions reveal a slightly different story. Again, we are looking at a confidence level of $\alpha = 0.05$. For the incorrect attribute mappings we have $a = 3.3045$ with a confidence interval of $[3.2680, 3.3409]$ and $b = 26.8633$ with a confidence interval of $[26.5499, 27.1768]$. For correct attribute mappings,

Table 2. Change of Precision and Recall between Data Sets

Matcher	Change in Precision	Change in Recall
Term	−8.13%	−5.97%
Graph	−8.97%	−8.88%
Precedence	−7.15%	−6.37%
Combined	−8.76%	−9.06%
NB	−4.28%	1.93%

$a = 0.5831$ with a confidence interval of $[0.4076, 0.7586]$ and $b = 0.2$ with a confidence interval of $[0.191, 0.209]$. For all parameters, we observe an increased confidence interval, suggesting a possibly higher rate in probability estimation.

Table 2 summarizes the changes in Precision and Recall between the full data set and the reduced one. The results show that indeed Recall was increased for the naïve Bayes heuristic. It comes at the cost of Precision, indicating an increase in the number of false positives in parallel. A somewhat surprising result was that all other matchers performed worse on the reduced set. In any event, these changes were not extremely big, which leads us to hypothesize that the naïve Bayes heuristic performance in both data sets was impaired by the invalid assumption of matcher independence.

Simulating Matcher Independence. To test the performance of the naïve Bayes heuristic in a setting of matcher independence, we have used the synthetic matrices. In this synthetic data sets, while all values in each matrix were generated using the same distribution, a specific attribute pair is assigned a value by a matcher independently of other matchers.

A comparison of the performance of the naïve Bayes heuristic with the same three heuristics we have used before are given in Figure 2 above. We observe that Precision improves for all matchers, when using the synthetic data and keeping the 1 : 1 cardinality constraints. This is most likely due to the way the matrices are generated. The amount of improvement depends on the beta distribution parameters of each matcher. For example, the Term matcher has a weaker distinction between correct and incorrect mappings, yielding less accurate prediction. This may also explain the reduced Recall for the Term matcher, while all other matchers increase their Recall measure.

The naïve Bayes heuristic dominates the other matchers for all synthetic data, indicating that indeed the matcher independence assumption serves as an obstacle to better performance. Another interesting observation involves the ability of the naïve Bayes heuristic to manage non 1 : 1 mappings. The other four matchers show a sharp decline in Precision for n_2, since about half of their attribute mappings are bound to be incorrect. For n_3 we see an increase in Precision, since the range of possibilities of mapping correctly has significantly increased. For Recall, we see deterioration with the n_3 data set, due to the inability of these matchers to choose attributes that violate the 1 : 1 cardinality constraint. We note that the naïve Bayes heuristic maintains an almost perfect Precision and

Recall for all three synthetic data sets, which means, among other things, that the specific method for measuring Precision and Recall for the n_2 and n_3 data sets could not affect the true effectiveness of the heuristic.

5   Related Work

In this section we focus on two specific aspects that are most relevant to this work, namely uncertainty management in schema matching and the use of machine learning in schema matching.

5.1   Uncertainty Management

Attempts to provide clear semantics to schema matching involves model theory for schema mappings [1, 18, 2]. In [1] mappings were represented using schema morphisms in categories. Roughly speaking, a category is a collection of schemata and their inter-schema mappings, represented as a morphisms. A morphism can be composed in an associative manner. Morphisms are designed so that they preserve integrity constraints among schemata. The work in [18] provides explicit semantics to mappings, using models and satisfiability. [2] provides a formal model of schema matching for topic hierarchies, rooted directed trees, where a node has a "meaning," generated using some ontology. A schema matcher (schema matching method in the authors own terminology) is a function from a mapping to a boolean variable. The limitations in this line of models, with respect to uncertainty modeling was presented in [18, 2] and discussed in Section 1.

The research described in [12] proposes a model that represents uncertainty (as a measure of imprecision) in the matching process outcome. In [11], building on the results of [12], the current "best mapping" approach was extended into one that considers top-K mappings as an uncertainty management tool. In this work, we propose a model for estimating the level of uncertainty in matcher decision making and offer a heuristic to harness uncertainty and improve on existing matching methods.

5.2   Machine Learning and Schema Matching

Machine learning has been used for schema matching in several works. Autoplex [3], LSD [7], and iMAP [5] use a naïve Bayes classifier to learn attribute mappings probabilities using instance training set. SEMINT [17] use neural networks to identify attribute mappings. APFEL [9] determine heuristic weights in an ensemble and threshold levels using various machine learning techniques, namely decision trees in general and C4.5 in particular, neural networks, and support vector machines. C4.5 was also used in [28], using WordNet relationships as features. sPLMap [23] use naïve Bayes, kNN, and KL-distance as content-based classifiers. All these works applied machine learning directly to the schemata, while our approach is to apply it to the similarity matrix outcome.

6   Conclusions

In this work we have presented a heuristic for schema matching, based on a probabilistic model of matchers and a well-known machine learning classifier. We have empirically analyzed the properties of the naïve Bayes heuristic using both real world and synthetic data. Our empirical analysis shows that the proposed heuristic performs well, given an accurate modeling of uncertainty in matcher decision making. We have also discussed the current limitations of the heuristic, and in particular its naïve assumption regarding matcher independence. Therefore, future research involves fine tuning the similarity measure distribution estimation. We will also look into more advanced methods (*e.g.*, discriminant analysis [20]) that do away with the independence assumption of the naïve Bayes classifier.

References

[1] Alagic, S., Bernstein, P.: A model theory for generic schema management. In: Ghelli, G., Grahne, G. (eds.) DBPL 2001. LNCS, vol. 2397, pp. 228–246. Springer, Heidelberg (2002)

[2] Benerecetti, M., Bouquet, P., Zanobini, S.: Soundness of schema matching methods. In: Gómez-Pérez, A., Euzenat, J. (eds.) ESWC 2005. LNCS, vol. 3532, pp. 211–225. Springer, Heidelberg (2005)

[3] Berlin, J., Motro, A.: Autoplex: Automated discovery of content for virtual databases. In: Batini, C., Giunchiglia, F., Giorgini, P., Mecella, M. (eds.) CoopIS 2001. LNCS, vol. 2172, pp. 108–122. Springer, Heidelberg (2001)

[4] Cudré-Mauroux, P., et al.: Viewpoints on emergent semantics. Journal on Data Semantics 6, 1–27 (2006)

[5] Dhamankar, R., Lee, Y., Doan, A., Halevy, A., Domingos, P.: imap: Discovering complex mappings between database schemas. In: Proceedings of the ACM-SIGMOD conference on Management of Data (SIGMOD), pp. 383–394. ACM Press, New York (2004)

[6] Do, H., Rahm, E.: COMA - a system for flexible combination of schema matching approaches. In: Proceedings of the International conference on Very Large Data Bases (VLDB), pp. 610–621 (2002)

[7] Doan, A., Domingos, P., Halevy, A.: Reconciling schemas of disparate data sources: A machine-learning approach. In: Aref, W.G. (ed.) Proceedings of the ACM-SIGMOD conference on Management of Data (SIGMOD), Santa Barbara, California, pp. 509–520. ACM Press, New York (2001)

[8] Domshlak, C., Gal, A., Roitman, H.: Rank aggregation for automatic schema matching. IEEE Transactions on Knowledge and Data Engineering (TKDE) 19(4), 538–553 (2007)

[9] Ehrig, M., Staab, S., Sure, Y.: Bootstrapping ontology alignment methods with apfel. In: Gil, Y., Motta, E., Benjamins, V.R., Musen, M.A. (eds.) ISWC 2005. LNCS, vol. 3729, pp. 186–200. Springer, Heidelberg (2005)

[10] Euzenat, J., Mochol, M., Svab, O., Svatek, V., Shvaiko, P., Stuckenschmidt, H., van Hage, W., Yatskevich, M.: Introduction to the ontology alignment evaluation 2006. In: Cruz, I., Decker, S., Allemang, D., Preist, C., Schwabe, D., Mika, P., Uschold, M., Aroyo, L. (eds.) ISWC 2006. LNCS, vol. 4273, Springer, Heidelberg (2006)

[11] Gal, A.: Managing uncertainty in schema matching with top-k schema mappings. Journal of Data Semantics 6, 90–114 (2006)

[12] Gal, A., Anaby-Tavor, A., Trombetta, A., Montesi, D.: A framework for modeling and evaluating automatic semantic reconciliation. VLDB Journal 14(1), 50–67 (2005)

[13] Gal, A., Modica, G., Jamil, H., Eyal, A.: Automatic ontology matching using application semantics. AI Magazine 26(1), 21–32 (2005)

[14] He, B., Chang, K.-C.: Making holistic schema matching robust: an ensemble approach. In: Proceedings of the Eleventh ACM SIGKDD International Conference on Knowledge Discovery and Data Mining, Chicago, Illinois, USA, August 21-24, 2005, pp. 429–438 (2005)

[15] Hull, R.: Managing semantic heterogeneity in databases: A theoretical perspective. In: Proceedings of the ACM SIGACT-SIGMOD-SIGART Symposium on Principles of Database Systems (PODS), pp. 51–61. ACM Press, New York (1997)

[16] Lee, Y., Sayyadian, M., Doan, A., Rosenthal, A.: eTuner: tuning schema matching software using synthetic scenarios. VLDB Journal 16(1), 97–122 (2007)

[17] Li, W.-S., Clifton, C.: SEMINT: A tool for identifying attribute correspondences in heterogeneous databases using neural networks. Data & Knowledge Engineering 33(1), 49–84 (2000)

[18] Madhavan, J., Bernstein, P., Domingos, P., Halevy, A.: Representing and reasoning about mappings between domain models. In: Proceedings of the Eighteenth National Conference on Artificial Intelligence and Fourteenth Conference on Innovative Applications of Artificial Intelligence (AAAI/IAAI), pp. 80–86 (2002)

[19] Madhavan, J., Bernstein, P., Rahm, E.: Generic schema matching with Cupid. In: Proceedings of the International conference on Very Large Data Bases (VLDB), Rome, Italy, pp. 49–58 (September 2001)

[20] Marcoulides, G., Hershberger, S.: Multivariate Statistical Methods. Lawrence Erlbaum Associates, Mahwah (1997)

[21] Melnik, S.: Generic Model Management: Concepts and Algorithms. Springer, Heidelberg (2004)

[22] Miller, R., Haas, L., Hernández, M.: Schema mapping as query discovery. In: Abbadi, A.E., Brodie, M., Chakravarthy, S., Dayal, U., Kamel, N., Schlageter, G., Whang, K.-Y. (eds.) Proceedings of the International conference on Very Large Data Bases (VLDB), pp. 77–88. Morgan Kaufmann, San Francisco (2000)

[23] Nottelmann, H., Straccia, U.: Information retrieval and machine learning for probabilistic schema matching. Information Processing and Management 43(3), 552–576 (2007)

[24] Ross, S.: A First Course in Probability, 5th edn. Prentice-Hall, Englewood Cliffs (1997)

[25] Shvaiko, P., Euzenat, J.: A survey of schema-based matching approaches. Journal of Data Semantics 4, 146–171 (2005)

[26] Srivastava, B., Koehler, J.: Web service composition - Current solutions and open problems. In: Workshop on Planning for Web Services (ICAPS-03), Trento, Italy (2003)

[27] Su, W., Wang, J., Lochovsky, F.: Aholistic schema matching for web query interfaces. In: Grust, T., Höpfner, H., Illarramendi, A., Jablonski, S., Mesiti, M., Müller, S., Patranjan, P.-L., Sattler, K.-U., Spiliopoulou, M., Wijsen, J. (eds.) EDBT 2006. LNCS, vol. 4254, pp. 77–94. Springer, Heidelberg (2006)

[28] Xu, L., Embley, D.: A composite approach to automating direct and indirect schema mappings. Information Systems 31(8), 697–886 (2006)

The Consistency Extractor System: Querying Inconsistent Databases Using Answer Set Programs

Monica Caniupan[1] and Leopoldo Bertossi[2]

[1] Universidad del Bio-Bio
Departamento de Sistemas de Informacion Concepcion, Chile
mcaniupa@ubiobio.cl
[2] Carleton University, School of Computer Science
Ottawa, Canada
bertossi@scs.carleton.ca

Abstract. We present the *Consistency Extractor System* (*ConsEx*) that uses *answer set programming* to compute consistent answers to first-order queries posed to relational databases that may be inconsistent wrt their integrity constraints. Among other features, *ConsEx* implements a *magic sets* technique to evaluate queries via disjunctive logic programs with stable model semantics that specify the repair of the original database. We describe the methodology and the system; and also present some experimental results.

1 Introduction

For several reasons, databases may become inconsistent wrt certain integrity constraints (ICs) they are supposed to satisfy [1, 6]. However, in most of the cases only a small portion of the database violates the ICs, and the inconsistent database can still be queried and give us useful and correct information. In order to characterize this correct data, the notion of *consistent answer* to a query was introduced in [1], along with a mechanism for computing those answers.

Intuitively, an answer to a query Q in a relational database instance D is *consistent* wrt a set IC of ICs if it is an answer to Q in every repair of D, where a repair of D is an instance over the same schema that satisfies IC and is obtained from D by deleting or inserting a minimal set -under set inclusion- of whole database tuples. More precisely, if a database instance is conceived as a finite set of ground atoms, then for a repair D' of D wrt IC it holds: (a) D' satisfies IC, denoted $D' \models IC$, and (b) the symmetric difference $D \triangle D'$ is minimal under set inclusion [1].

The algorithm for consistent query answering (CQA) in [1] is based on a first-order query rewriting of the original query. The new query is posed to the original database, and the usual answers are the consistent answers to the original query. This algorithm has limitations wrt the class of ICs and queries it can handle. CQA based on first-order query rewriting was later extended [17, 22, 27], but it is still limited in its applicability (cf. Section 6), which is explained by the intrinsic data complexity of CQA (cf. [6, 7] for surveys in this direction).

In several papers [2, 25, 3, 4, 20, 9, 10], database repairs have been specified as the stable models of disjunctive logic programs with stable model semantics [23] (aka.

H. Prade and V.S. Subrahmanian (Eds.): SUM 2007, LNAI 4772, pp. 74–88, 2007.

answer set programs). It turns out that the data complexity of query evaluation from disjunctive logic programs with stable model semantics [19] matches the data complexity of CQA. In this line, the approach in [10] is the most general and also the more realistic, in the sense that it takes into consideration possible occurrences of null values and the way they are used in real database practice, and these null values are also used to restore consistency wrt referential ICs.

In *ConsEx* we implement, use and optimize the repair logic programs introduced in [10]. In consequence, *ConsEx* can be used for CQA wrt arbitrary universal ICs, acyclic sets of referential ICs, and NOT-NULL constraints. The queries supported are Datalog queries with negation, which goes beyond first-order queries. Consistent answers to queries can be computed by evaluating queries against the repair programs, e.g. using the *DLV* system, that implements the stable model semantics of disjunctive logic programs [28].

The *ConsEx* system implements the most general methodology for CQA wrt the class of ICs and queries that can be handled. To achieve this goal, *ConsEx* computes and optimizes the logic programs that specify database repairs or represent queries. These programs are internally passed as inputs to *DLV*, which evaluates them. All this is done in interaction with IBM DB2 relational DBMS. *ConsEx* can be applied to relational databases containing NULL, and all the first-order ICs and (non-aggregate) queries used in database practice and beyond.

Using logic programs for CQA in a straightforward manner may not be the most efficient alternative. As shown in [12], a more efficient way to go is to apply the so-called *magic sets* (MS) techniques, that transform the combination of the query program and the repair program into a new program that, essentially, contains a subset of the original rules in the repair program, those that are relevant to evaluate the query.

Classically, MS optimizes the bottom-up processing of queries in deductive (Datalog) databases by simulating a top-down, query-directed evaluation [5, 15]. More recently, the MS techniques have been extended to logic programs with stable models semantics [21, 24, 18, 26]. In [12] it was shown how to adopt and adapt those techniques to our repair programs, resulting in a sound and complete MS methodology for the repair programs with program constraints. In Section 3, we briefly describe this particular MS methodology, which is the one implemented in the *ConsEx* system. In Section 5, we show that the use of MS in the evaluation of queries improves considerably the execution time of queries.

In this paper we describe both the methodologies implemented in *ConsEx* (more details about them can be found in [12]), and the features, functionalities, and performance of this system (again, more details and proofs of results can be found in [13]).

2   Preliminaries

We consider a relational database schema $\Sigma = (\mathcal{U}, \mathcal{R}, \mathcal{B})$, where $\mathcal{U}$ is the possibly infinite database domain with $null \in \mathcal{U}$, $\mathcal{R}$ is a fixed set of database predicates, each of them with a finite, and ordered set of attributes, and $\mathcal{B}$ is a fixed set of built-in predicates, like comparison predicates, e.g. $\{<, >, =, \neq\}$. There is a predicate $IsNull(\cdot)$, and $IsNull(c)$ is true iff c is *null*. Instances for a schema Σ are finite collections D of ground atoms of the form $R(c_1, ..., c_n)$, called *database tuples*, where $R \in \mathcal{R}$, and $(c_1, ..., c_n)$ is a *tuple* of constants, i.e. elements of $\mathcal{U}$. The extensions for built-in predicates are fixed, and possibly infinite in every database instance. There is also a fixed set IC of integrity constraints, that are sentences in the first-order language $\mathcal{L}(\Sigma)$ determined by Σ. They are expected to be satisfied by any instance for Σ, but they may not.

A *universal integrity constraint* is a sentence in $\mathcal{L}(\Sigma)$ that is logically equivalent to a sentence of the form [10]: $\forall \bar{x}(\bigwedge_{i=1}^{m} P_i(\bar{x}_i) \rightarrow \bigvee_{j=1}^{n} Q_j(\bar{y}_j) \vee \varphi)$, where $P_i, Q_j \in \mathcal{R}$, $\bar{x} = \bigcup_{i=1}^{m} \bar{x}_i$, $\bar{y}_j \subseteq \bar{x}$, and $m \geq 1$. Here φ is a formula containing only disjunctions of built-in atoms from $\mathcal{B}$ whose variables appear in the antecedent of the implication. We will assume that there exists a propositional atom **false** $\in \mathcal{B}$ that is always false in the database. Domain constants different from *null* may appear in a UIC. A *referential integrity constraint* (RIC) is a sentence of the form:[1] $\forall \bar{x}(P(\bar{x}) \rightarrow \exists \bar{z}\, Q(\bar{y}, \bar{z}))$, where $\bar{y} \subseteq \bar{x}$ and $P, Q \in \mathcal{R}$. A *NOT NULL*-constraint (NNC) is a denial constraint of the form: $\bar{\forall}\bar{x}(P(\bar{x}) \wedge IsNull(x_i) \rightarrow \textbf{false})$, where $x_i \in \bar{x}$ is in the position of the attribute that cannot take null values.

Notice that our RICs contain at most one database atom in the consequent. E.g. tuple-generating joins in the consequent are excluded, and this is due to the fact that RICs will be repaired using null values (for the existential variables), whose participation in joins is problematic. It would be easy to adapt our methodology in order to include that kind of joins as long as they are repaired using other values in the domain. However, this latter alternative opens the ground for undecidability of CQA [11], which is avoided in [10] by using null values to restore consistency.

Based on the repair semantics and the logic programs introduced in [10], CQA as implemented in *ConsEx* works for *RIC-acyclic* sets of universal, referential, and NNCs. In this case, there is a one-to-one correspondence between the stable models of the repair program and the database repairs [10]. That a set of ICs is RIC-acyclic essentially means that there are no cycles involving RICs (cf. [12, 10] for details). For example, $IC = \{\forall x(S(x) \rightarrow Q(x)), \forall x(Q(x) \rightarrow S(x)), \forall x(Q(x) \rightarrow \exists y T(x, y))\}$ is RIC-acyclic, whereas $IC' = IC \cup \{\forall xy(T(x, y) \rightarrow Q(y))\}$ is not, because there is a cycle involving the RIC $\forall x(Q(x) \rightarrow \exists y T(x, y))$. In the following, we will assume that IC is a fixed, finite and RIC-acyclic set of UICs, RICs and NNCs. A database instance D is said to be *consistent* if it satisfies IC. Otherwise, it is *inconsistent* wrt IC.

In particular, RICs are repaired by tuple deletions or tuple insertion with null values. Notice that introducing null values to restore consistency makes it necessary to modify the repair semantics introduced in [1], which does not consider RICs or null values. This is needed in order to give priority to null values over arbitrary domain constants when restoring consistency wrt RICs. It becomes necessary to modify accordingly the notion of minimality associated to repair as shown in the following example (cf. [10] for details).

Example 1. The database instance $D = \{P(a, null), P(b, c), R(a, b)\}$ is inconsistent wrt IC: $\forall\, xy\, (P(x, y) \rightarrow \exists z R(x, z))$. There are two repairs: $D_1 = \{P(a, null),$ $P(b, c),\, R(a, b),\, R(b, null)\}$, with $\Delta(D, D_1) = \{R(b, null)\}$, and $D_2 = \{P(a, null),$

---

[1] For simplification purposes, we assume that the existential variables appear in the last attributes of Q, but they may appear anywhere else in Q.

$R(a, b)\}$, with $\Delta(D, D_2) = \{P(b, c)\}$. For every $d \in \mathcal{U} \setminus \{null\}$, the instance $D_3 = \{P(a, null), P(b, c), R(a, b), R(b, d)\}$ is not a repair, because it is not minimal.   □

Database repairs can be specified as stable models of disjunctive logic programs. The repair programs introduced in [10] build on the repair programs first introduced in [3] for universal ICs. They use annotation constants to indicate the atoms that may become true or false in the repairs in order to satisfy the ICs. Each atom of the form $P(\bar{a})$ (except for those that refer to the extensional database) receives one of the annotation constants. In $P_-(\bar{a}, \mathbf{t_a})$, the annotation $\mathbf{t_a}$ means that the atom is advised to made true (i.e. inserted into the database). Similarly, $\mathbf{f_a}$ indicates that the atom should be made false (deleted).[2] For each IC, a disjunctive rule is constructed in such a way that the body of the rule captures the violation condition for the IC; and the head describes the alternatives for restoring consistency, by deleting or inserting the participating tuples (cf. rules 2. and 3. in Example 2).

Annotation $\mathbf{t^*}$ indicates that the atom is true or becomes true in the program. It is introduced in order to keep repairing the database if there are interacting ICs; and e.g. the insertion of a tuple may generate a new IC violation. Finally, atoms with constant $\mathbf{t^{**}}$ are those that become true in the repairs. They are use to read off the database atoms in the repairs. All this is illustrated in the following example (cf. [10] for the general form of the repair programs).

Example 2. Consider the database schema $\Sigma = \{S(ID, NAME), R(ID, NAME), T(ID, DEPTO), W(ID, DEPTO, SINCE)\}$, the instance $D = \{S(a, c), S(b, c), R(b, c), T(a, null), W(null, b, c)\}$, and $IC = \{\forall xy(S(x, y) \rightarrow R(x, y)), \forall xy(T(x, y) \rightarrow \exists z W(x, y, z)), \forall xyz(W(x, y, z) \wedge IsNull(x) \rightarrow \textbf{false})\}$. The repair program $\Pi(D, IC)$ contains the following rules:

1. $S(a, c).\quad S(b, c).\quad R(b, c).\quad T(a, null).\quad W(null, b, c).$
2. $S_-(x, y, \mathbf{f_a}) \vee R_-(x, y, \mathbf{t_a}) \leftarrow S_-(x, y, \mathbf{t^*}), R_-(x, y, \mathbf{f_a}), x \neq null, y \neq null.$
    $S_-(x, y, \mathbf{f_a}) \vee R_-(x, y, \mathbf{t_a}) \leftarrow S_-(x, y, \mathbf{t^*}), \ not\ R(x, y), x \neq null, y \neq null.$
3. $T_-(x, y, \mathbf{f_a}) \vee W_-(x, y, null, \mathbf{t_a}) \leftarrow T_-(x, y, \mathbf{t^*}), \ not\ aux(x, y), x \neq null, y \neq null.$
        $aux(x, y) \leftarrow W_-(x, y, z, \mathbf{t^*}), \ not\ W_-(x, y, z, \mathbf{f_a}), x \neq null, y \neq null, z \neq null.$
4. $W_-(x, y, z, \mathbf{f_a}) \leftarrow W_-(x, y, z, \mathbf{t^*}), x = null.$
5. $S_-(x, y, \mathbf{t^*}) \leftarrow S(x, y).$
    $S_-(x, y, \mathbf{t^*}) \leftarrow S_-(x, y, \mathbf{t_a}).$
6. $S_-(x, y, \mathbf{t^{**}}) \leftarrow S_-(x, y, \mathbf{t^*}), \ not\ S_-(x, y, \mathbf{f_a}).$

$\left.\begin{array}{c}\ \\ \ \\ \ \end{array}\right\}$ (Similarly for R, T and W)

7. $\leftarrow W_-(x, y, z, \mathbf{t_a}), W_-(x, y, z, \mathbf{f_a}).$

The rules in 2. establish how to repair the database wrt the first IC: by making $S(x, y)$ false or $R(x, y)$ true. Conditions of the form $x \neq null$ in the bodies are used to capture occurrences of null values in relevant attributes [10]. The rules in 3. specify the form of restoring consistency wrt the RIC: by deleting $T(x, y)$ or inserting $W(x, y, null)$. Here, only the variables in the antecedent of the RIC cannot take null values. Rule 4. indicates how to restore consistency wrt the NNC: by eliminating $W(x, y, z)$. Finally, the

---

[2] In order to distinguish a predicate P that may receive annotations in an extra argument from the same predicate in the extensional database, that does not contain annotations, the former is replaced by P_-.

program constraint 7. filters out possible *non-coherent* stable models of the program, those that have an W-atom annotated with both $\mathbf{t_a}$ and $\mathbf{f_a}$.[3] Relevant program constraints can be efficiently generated by using a *dependency graph* [12], which captures the relationship between predicates in the ICs (cf. Section 4).

The program has two stable models:[4] $\mathcal{M}_1 = \{\underline{S}(a, c, \mathbf{t}^*), \underline{S}(b, c, \mathbf{t}^*), R(b, c, \mathbf{t}^*), \underline{T}(a, null, \mathbf{t}^*), W\_(null, b, c, \mathbf{t}^*), W\_(null, b, c, \mathbf{f_a}), R(a, c, \mathbf{t_a}), \underline{S}(a, c, \mathbf{t}^{**}), \underline{S}(b, c, \mathbf{t}^{**}), R(b, c, \mathbf{t}^{**}), \underline{R(a, c, \mathbf{t}^*)}, R(a, c, \mathbf{t}^{**}), \underline{T}(a, null, \mathbf{t}^{**})\}$, $\mathcal{M}_2 = \{\underline{S}(a, c, \mathbf{t}^*), \underline{S}(b, c, \mathbf{t}^*), R(b, c, \mathbf{t}^*), \underline{T}(a, null, \mathbf{t}^*), W\_(null, b, c, \mathbf{t}^*), W\_(null, b, c, \mathbf{f_a}), \underline{S}(a, c, \mathbf{f_a}), \underline{S}(b, c, \mathbf{t}^{**}), R(b, c, \mathbf{t}^{**}), \underline{T}(a, null, \mathbf{t}^{**})\}$. Thus, consistency is recovered, according to $\mathcal{M}_1$ by inserting atom $R(a, c)$ and deleting atom $W(null, b, c)$; or, according to $\mathcal{M}_2$ by deleting atoms $\{S(a, c), W(null, b, c)\}$. Two repairs can be obtained by concentrating on the underlined atoms in the stable models: $\{S(a, c), S(b, c), R(b, c), R(a, c), T(a, null)\}$ and $\{S(b, c), R(b, c), T(a, null)\}$, as expected. □

As established in [4, 10], repair programs are a correct specification of database repairs wrt *RIC-acyclic* sets of UICs, RICs, and NNCs.

To compute consistent answers to a query $\mathcal{Q}$, the query is expressed (or simply given) as a logic program, e.g. as non-recursive Datalog program with weak negation and built-ins if $\mathcal{Q}$ is first-order [29]. In this program the positive literals of the form $P(\bar{s})$, with P an extensional predicate, are replaced by $P\_(\bar{s}, \mathbf{t}^{**})$, and negative literals of the form *not* $P(\bar{s})$ by *not* $P\_(\bar{s}, \mathbf{t}^{**})$. We obtain a query program $\Pi(\mathcal{Q})$, that is "run" together with the repair program $\Pi(D, IC)$. In this way, CQA becomes a form of *cautious* or *skeptical* reasoning under the stable models semantics. Notice that for a fixed set of ICs, the same repair program can be used with every instance (compatible with the schema) and with every query we want to answer consistently, so it can be generated once, and *ConsEx* will store it.

For the repair program in Example 2, the Datalog query $\mathcal{Q} : Ans(x) \leftarrow S(b, x)$, becomes the program $\Pi(\mathcal{Q})$ consisting of the rule $Ans(x) \leftarrow \underline{S}(b, x, \mathbf{t}^{**})$. The combined program $\Pi(D, IC, \mathcal{Q}) := \Pi(D, IC) \cup \Pi(\mathcal{Q})$ has two stable models, both of them containing the atom $Ans(c)$. Therefore, the consistent answer to $\mathcal{Q}$ is (c).

3   Magic Sets for Repair Programs

The magic set (MS) techniques for logic programs with stable model semantics take as an input a logic program -a repair program in our case- and a query expressed as a logic program that has to be evaluated against the repair program. The output is a new logic program, the *magic program*, with its own stable models, that can be used to answer the original query more efficiently. As shown in [12], the stable models of the magic program are relevant in the sense that they contain extensions for the predicates that are relevant to compute the query. Also, they are only partially computed, i.e. each of them can be extended to a stable model of the original program (ignoring the "magic" predicates introduced in the magic program). This happens because the

---

[3] For the program in this example, given the logical relationship between the ICs, this phenomenon could happen only for predicate W, as analyzed in [12].

[4] In this paper, stable models are displayed without program facts.

magic program contains special auxiliary rules, the magic rules, that guide the course of query evaluation, avoiding unnecessary instantiation of rules and, as a consequence, achieving a faster computation of stable models. In this way, we may obtain less and smaller stable models. The stable models of the magic program are expected to provide the same answers to the original query as the models of the program used as input to MS.

The magic sets techniques for logic programs with stable model semantics introduced in [21], for the non-disjunctive case but possibly unstratified negation, and in [24] (improved in [18]), with disjunction but stratified negation, are sound and complete, i.e. they compute all and only correct answers for the query. In [26] a sound but incomplete methodology is presented for disjunctive programs with program constraints of the form $\leftarrow C(\bar{x})$, where $C(\bar{x})$ is a conjunction of literals (i.e. positive or negated atoms). The effect of these programs constraints is to discard models of the rest of the program that make true the existential closure of $C(\bar{x})$.

Our repair programs are disjunctive, contain non-stratified negation, and have program constraints; the latter with only positive intensional literals in their bodies. In consequence, none of the MS techniques mentioned above could be directly applied to optimize our repair programs. However, as shown in [12] (cf. also [13] for details), the following sound and complete MS methodology can be applied to repair programs (with program constraints): First, the program constraints are removed from the repair program. Next, a combination of the MS techniques in [18, 21] is applied to the resulting program. The disjunction is handled as in [18], and negation as in [21]. This combination works for repair programs because in them, roughly speaking, negation does not occur in odd cycles. For this kind of programs, soundness and completeness of MS can be obtained from results in [18, 21].[5] Finally, the program constraints are put back into the *magic program* obtained in the previous step, enforcing the magic program to have only coherent models.

The MS techniques currently implemented in *DLV* cannot be applied to disjunctive programs with program constraints. On the other side, when the program does not contain program constraints, *DLV* applies MS internally, without giving access to the magic program. As a consequence, the application of MS with *DLV* to repair programs (with program constraints) is not straightforward. *ConsEx*, that uses *DLV* for evaluation of logic programs, solves this problems as follows: First, *ConsEx* produces a magic program for the combination of the query and repair programs (as briefly mentioned above) without considering the program constraints. Next, the original program constraints are added to the magic program. Finally, this expanded magic program is given to *DLV* for evaluation, as any other logic program. This is the MS methodology implemented in the *ConsEx* system, which is correct for repair programs. An example below shows this process in detail.

The MS technique sequentially performs three well defined steps: *adornment, generation and modification*, which will be illustrated using Example 2 with the query program $Ans(x) \leftarrow S(b, x, \mathbf{t}^{\star\star})$.

---

[5] Personal communication from Wolfgang Faber. Actually, this combination is the MS technique implemented in *DLV*. Correctness is guaranteed for disjunctive programs with unstratified negation appearing in even cycles, which is what we need.

The *adornment* step produces a new, *adorned* program, in which each intensional (defined) predicate P takes the form P^A, where A is a string of letters b, f, for *bound* and *free*, resp., whose length is equal to the arity of P. Starting from the query, adornments are created and propagated. First $\Pi(\mathcal{Q}) : Ans(x) \leftarrow S\_(b, x, \mathbf{t}^{\star\star})$ becomes: $Ans^f(x) \leftarrow S\_^{bfb}(b, x, \mathbf{t}^{\star\star})$, meaning that the first and third arguments of $S\_$ are bound, and the second is a free variable. Annotation constants are always bound.

The adorned predicate $S\_^{bfb}$ is used to propagate bindings (adornments) onto the rules defining predicate S, i.e. rules in 2., 5., and 6. As an illustration, the rules in 5. become $S\_^{bfb}(x, y, \mathbf{t}^\star) \leftarrow S(x, y)$ and $S\_^{bfb}(x, y, \mathbf{t}^\star) \leftarrow S\_^{bfb}(x, y, \mathbf{t_a})$, resp. Extensional (base) predicates, e.g. S appearing as $S(x, y)$ in the first adorned rule, only bind variables and do not receive any annotation. Moreover, the adorned predicate $S\_^{bfb}$ propagates adornments over the disjunctive rules in 2. The adornments are propagated over the literals in the body of the rule, and to the head literal $R\_(x, y, \mathbf{t_a})$. Therefore, this rule becomes:[6] $S\_^{bfb}(x, y, \mathbf{f_a}) \vee R\_^{bfb}(x, y, \mathbf{t_a}), \leftarrow S\_^{bfb}(x, y, \mathbf{t}^\star), R\_^{bfb}(x, y, \mathbf{f_a})$. Now, the new adorned predicate $R\_^{bfb}$ also has to be processed, producing adornments on rules defining predicate R. The output of this step is an *adorned program* that contains only adorned rules.

The iterative process of passing bindings is called *sideways information passing strategies* (SIPS) [5]. There may be different SIPS strategies, but any SIP strategy has to ensure that all of the body and head atoms are processed. We follow the strategy adopted in [18], which is implemented in *DLV*. According to it, only extensional predicates bind new variables, i.e. variables that do not carry a binding already. As an illustration, suppose we have the adorned predicate P^{fbf} and the rule $P(x, y, z) \vee T(x, y) \leftarrow R(z), M(x, z)$, where R is a extensional predicate. The adorned rule is $P^{fbf}(x, y, z) \vee T^{fb}(x, y) \leftarrow R(z), M^{fb}(x, z)$. Notice that variable z is free according to the adorned predicate P^{fbf}. However, the extensional atom $R(z)$ binds this variable, and propagates this binding to $M(x, z)$, where z becomes *bound*, producing the adorned predicate M^{fb}.

The next step is the *generation of magic rules*; those that will direct the computation of the stable models of the rewritten program obtained in the previous step. For each adorned atom P^A in the body of an adorned non-disjunctive rule, a magic rule is generated as follows: (a) The head of the magic rule becomes the magic version of P^A, i.e. $magic\_P^A$, from which all the variables labelled with f in A are deleted. (b) The literals in the body of the magic rule become the magic version of the adorned rule head, followed by the literals (if any) that produced bindings on atom P^A. For example, for the adorned literal $S\_^{bfb}(x, y, \mathbf{t_a})$ in the body of the adorned rule $S\_^{bfb}(x, y, \mathbf{t}^\star) \leftarrow S\_^{bfb}(x, y, \mathbf{t_a})$, the magic rule is $magic\_S\_^{bfb}(x, \mathbf{t_a}) \leftarrow magic\_S\_^{bfb}(x, \mathbf{t}^\star)$. For disjunctive adorned rules, first, intermediate non-disjunctive rules are generated by moving, one at a time, head atoms into the bodies of rules. Next, magic rules are generated as described for non-disjunctive rules. For example, for the rule $S\_^{bfb}(x, y, \mathbf{f_a}) \vee R\_^{bfb}(x, y, \mathbf{t_a}) \leftarrow S\_^{bfb}(x, y, \mathbf{t}^\star), R\_^{bfb}(x, y, \mathbf{f_a})$, we have two non-disjunctive rules: (a) $S\_^{bfb}(x, y, \mathbf{f_a}) \leftarrow R\_^{bfb}(x, y, \mathbf{t_a}), S\_^{bfb}(x, y, \mathbf{t}^\star), R\_^{bfb}(x, y, \mathbf{f_a})$; and (b) $R\_^{bfb}(x, y, \mathbf{t_a}) \leftarrow S\_^{bfb}(x, y, \mathbf{f_a}), S\_^{bfb}(x, y, \mathbf{t}^\star), R\_^{bfb}(x, y, \mathbf{f_a})$. There are three magic rules for rule

---

[6] For simplification purposes, conditions of the form $x \neq null$ are omitted from the disjunctive rules.

(a): $magic\_R_-^{bfb}(x, \mathbf{t_a}) \leftarrow magic\_S_-^{bfb}(x, \mathbf{f_a})$; $magic\_S_-^{bfb}(x, \mathbf{t^*}) \leftarrow magic\_S_-^{bfb}(x, \mathbf{f_a})$; and $magic\_R_-^{bfb}(x, \mathbf{f_a}) \leftarrow magic\_S_-^{bfb}(x, \mathbf{f_a})$.

At this step also the *magic seed atom* is generated. This corresponds to the magic version of the Ans predicate from the adorned query rule, e.g. for rule $Ans^f(x) \leftarrow S_-^{bfb}(x, y, \mathbf{t^{**}})$, the magic seed atom is $magic\_Ans^f$.

The last phase is the *modification step*, where magic atoms constructed in the generation stage are included in the body of adorned rules. Thus, for each adorned rule, the magic version of its head is inserted into the body. For instance, the magic versions of the head atoms in rule $S_-^{bfb}(x, y, \mathbf{f_a}) \vee R_-^{bfb}(x, y, \mathbf{t_a}) \leftarrow S_-^{bfb}(x, y, \mathbf{t^*}), R_-^{bfb}(x, y, \mathbf{f_a})$, are $magic\_S_-^{bfb}(x, \mathbf{f_a})$ and $magic\_R_-^{bfb}(x, \mathbf{t_a})$, resp., which are inserted into the body of the adorned rule, generating the modified rule $S_-^{bfb}(x, y, \mathbf{f_a}) \vee R_-^{bfb}(x, y, \mathbf{t_a}) \leftarrow magic\_S_-^{bfb}(x, \mathbf{f_a}), magic\_R_-^{bfb}(x, \mathbf{t_a}), S_-^{bfb}(x, y, \mathbf{t^*}), R_-^{bfb}(x, y, \mathbf{f_a})$. From the modified rules the rest of the adornments are now deleted. Thus, the previous modified rule becomes $S_-(x, y, \mathbf{f_a}) \vee R_-(x, y, \mathbf{t_a}) \leftarrow magic\_S_-^{bfb}(x, \mathbf{f_a}), magic\_R_-^{bfb}(x, \mathbf{t_a}), S_-(x, y, \mathbf{t^*}), R_-(x, y, \mathbf{f_a})$.

The final, rewritten, magic program consists of the magic and modified rules, the *magic seed atom*, and the facts of the original program. In our case, it also contains the set of original program constraints that were not touched during the application of MS. Since in the MS program only magic atoms have adornments, the program constraints can be added as they come to the program. The program $\mathcal{MS}(\Pi)$ below is the magic program for the program Π consisting of the query program $Ans(x) \leftarrow S_-(b, x, \mathbf{t^{**}})$ plus the repair program in Example 2.

Program $\mathcal{MS}(\Pi)$: $magic\_Ans^f$.

$magic\_S_-^{bfb}(b, \mathbf{t^{**}}) \leftarrow magic\_Ans^f$.
$magic\_S_-^{bfb}(x, \mathbf{t_a}) \leftarrow magic\_S_-^{bfb}(x, \mathbf{t^*})$.
$magic\_S_-^{bfb}(x, \mathbf{t^*}) \leftarrow magic\_S_-^{bfb}(x, \mathbf{t^{**}})$.
$magic\_S_-^{bfb}(x, \mathbf{f_a}) \leftarrow magic\_S_-^{bfb}(x, \mathbf{t^{**}})$.
$magic\_R_-^{bfb}(x, \mathbf{t_a}) \leftarrow magic\_S_-^{bfb}(x, \mathbf{f_a})$.
$magic\_S_-^{bfb}(x, \mathbf{t^*}) \leftarrow magic\_S_-^{bfb}(x, \mathbf{f_a})$.
$magic\_R_-^{bfb}(x, \mathbf{f_a}) \leftarrow magic\_S_-^{bfb}(x, \mathbf{f_a})$.

$magic\_S_-^{bfb}(x, \mathbf{f_a}) \leftarrow magic\_R_-^{bfb}(x, \mathbf{t_a})$.
$magic\_S_-^{bfb}(x, \mathbf{t^*}) \leftarrow magic\_R_-^{bfb}(x, \mathbf{t_a})$.
$magic\_R_-^{bfb}(x, \mathbf{f_a}) \leftarrow magic\_R_-^{bfb}(x, \mathbf{t_a})$.
$magic\_R_-^{bfb}(x, \mathbf{t_a}) \leftarrow magic\_R_-^{bfb}(x, \mathbf{t^*})$.
$magic\_R_-^{bfb}(x, \mathbf{t^*}) \leftarrow magic\_R_-^{bfb}(x, \mathbf{t^{**}})$.
$magic\_R_-^{bfb}(x, \mathbf{f_a}) \leftarrow magic\_R_-^{bfb}(x, \mathbf{t^{**}})$.
$Ans(x) \leftarrow magic\_Ans^f, S_-(b, x, \mathbf{t^{**}})$.

$S_-(x, y, \mathbf{f_a}) \vee R_-(x, y, \mathbf{t_a}) \leftarrow magic\_S_-^{bfb}(x, \mathbf{f_a}), magic\_R_-^{bfb}(x, \mathbf{t_a}), S_-(x, y, \mathbf{t^*}), R_-(x, y, \mathbf{f_a})$.
$S_-(x, y, \mathbf{f_a}) \vee R_-(x, y, \mathbf{t_a}) \leftarrow magic\_S_-^{bfb}(x, \mathbf{f_a}), magic\_R_-^{bfb}(x, \mathbf{t_a}), S_-(x, y, \mathbf{t^*}), not\ R(x, y)$.
$S_-(x, y, \mathbf{t^*}) \leftarrow magic\_S_-^{bfb}(x, \mathbf{t^*}), S_-(x, y, \mathbf{t_a})$. $S_-(x, y, \mathbf{t^*}) \leftarrow magic\_S_-^{bfb}(x, \mathbf{t^*}), S(x, y)$.
$R_-(x, y, \mathbf{t^*}) \leftarrow magic\_R_-^{bfb}(x, \mathbf{t^*}), R_-(x, y, \mathbf{t_a})$. $R_-(x, y, \mathbf{t^*}) \leftarrow magic\_R_-^{bfb}(x, \mathbf{t^*}), R(x, y)$.
$S_-(x, y, \mathbf{t^{**}}) \leftarrow magic\_S_-^{bfb}(x, \mathbf{t^{**}}), S_-(x, y, \mathbf{t^*}), not\ S_-(x, y, \mathbf{f_a})$.
$R_-(x, y, \mathbf{t^{**}}) \leftarrow magic\_R_-^{bfb}(x, \mathbf{t^{**}}), R_-(x, y, \mathbf{t^*}), not\ R(x, y, \mathbf{f_a})$.
$\leftarrow W_-(x, y, z, \mathbf{t_a}), W_-(x, y, z, \mathbf{f_a})$.

Notice that $\mathcal{MS}(\Pi)$ contains rules related to predicates S, R, but no rules for predicates T, W, which are not relevant to the query. Therefore the program constraint will be trivially satisfied. Program $\mathcal{MS}(\Pi)$ (with the same facts of the original repair program) has only one stable model: $\mathcal{M} = \{S_-(b, c, \mathbf{t^*}), S_-(b, c, \mathbf{t^{**}}), Ans(c)\}$ (displayed here without the magic atoms), which indicates through its Ans predicate that (c) is the consistent answer to the original query, as expected. We can see that the magic program has only those models that are relevant to compute the query answers. Furthermore,

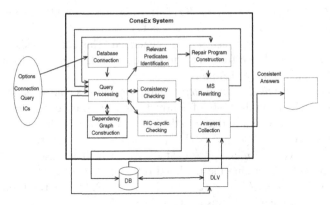

Fig. 1. *ConsEx* Architecture

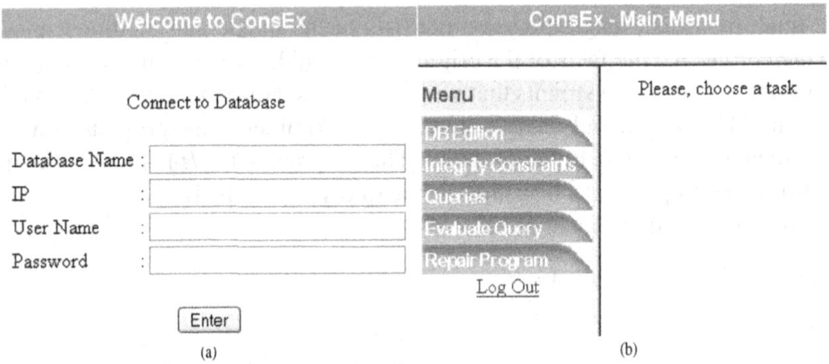

Fig. 2. *ConsEx*: Database Connection and Main Menu

these are partially computed, i.e. they can be extended to stable models of the program $\Pi(D, IC, Q)$. More precisely, except for the magic atoms, model $\mathcal{M}$ is contained in every model of the original repair program $\Pi(D, IC, Q)$ (cf. Section 2).[7]

4   System Description

In Figure 1, that describes the general architecture of *ConsEx*, the *Database Connection* module receives the database parameters (database name, user and password) and connects to the database instance. We show in Figure 2 (a) the connection screen; and in Figure 2 (b), the main menu, obtained after connecting to the database.

The *Query Processing* module receives the query and ICs; and coordinates the tasks needed to compute consistent answers. First, it checks queries for syntactic correctness. Currently in *ConsEx*, first-order queries can be written as logic programs in (rather standard) *DLV* notation, or as queries in SQL. The former correspond to non-recursive

---

[7] In [13] it has been shown that the magic program, and the original repair program are *query equivalent* under both brave and cautious reasoning.

Datalog queries with weak negation and built-ins, which includes first-order queries. SQL queries may have disjunction (i.e. UNION), built-in literals in the WHERE clause, but neither negation nor recursion, i.e. unions of conjunctive queries with built-ins.

After a query passes the syntax check, the query program is generated. For *DLV* queries, the query program is obtained by inserting the annotation $t^{\star\star}$ into the literals in the bodies of the rules of the query that do not have a definition in the query program (but are defined in the repair program). For SQL queries, the query program is obtained by first translating queries into equivalent Datalog programs, and then by adding the annotation $t^{\star\star}$ to the program rules as for the *DLV* queries.

Given a query, there might be ICs that are not related to the query. More precisely, their satisfaction or not by the given instance (and the corresponding portion of the repairs in the second case) does not influence the (standard or consistent) answers to the query. In order to capture the relevant ICs, the *Relevant Predicates Identification* module analyzes the interaction between the predicates in the query and those in the ICs by means of a *dependency graph* [12], which is generated by the *Dependency Graph Construction* module. We can use our running example to describe this feature and other system's components.

The dependency graph $\mathcal{G}(IC)$ for the ICs in Example 2 contains as nodes the predicates S, R, T, W, and the edges $(S, R), (T, W)$. Then, for the query $Ans(x) \leftarrow S(b, x)$ the relevant predicates are S and R, because they are in the same component as the predicate S that appears in the query. Thus, the relevant IC to check is $\forall xy(S(x, y) \rightarrow R(x, y))$, which contains the relevant predicates (cf. [12] for more details).

Next, *ConsEx* checks if the database is consistent wrt the ICs that are relevant to the query. This check is performed by the *Consistency Checking* module, which generates an SQL query for each relevant IC, to check its satisfaction. For example, for the relevant IC $\forall xy(S(x, y) \rightarrow R(x, y))$ identified before, *ConsEx* generates the SQL query: SELECT * FROM S WHERE (NOT EXISTS (SELECT * FROM R WHERE R.ID = S.ID AND R.NAME = S.NAME) AND ID IS NOT NULL AND NAME IS NOT NULL), asking for violating tuples.

If the answer is empty, *ConsEx* proceeds to evaluate the given query directly on the original database instance, i.e. without computing repairs. For example, if the query is $\mathcal{Q}: Ans(x) \leftarrow S(b, x)$, the SQL query "SELECT NAME FROM S WHERE ID='b'", is generated by *ConsEx* and posed to D. However, in Example 2 we do have $\{(a, c)\}$ as the non-empty set of violations of the relevant IC. In consequence, the database is inconsistent, and, in order to consistently answer the query $\mathcal{Q}$, the repair program has to be generated.

The *RIC-acyclic Checking* module uses the dependency graph to check if set of ICs is *RIC*-acyclic. If it is, the generation of programs is avoided, and a warning message is sent to the user. Otherwise, the *Repair Program Construction* module generates the repair program, which is constructed "on the fly", that is, all the annotations that appear in it are generated by the system, and the database is not affected. The facts of the program are not imported from the database into *ConsEx*. Instead, suitable sentences to import data are included into the repair program, as facilitated and understood by *DLV*.

The repair program may contain, for each extensional predicate P, the import sentence $\#import(dbName, dbUser, dbPass, $ "SELECT * FROM P", P), retrieving the tuples from relation P that will become the facts for predicate P in the program. As a result, when the program is evaluated by *DLV*, the database facts will be imported directly into the reasoning system. These data import sentences are required at this stage only if *ConsEx* will run the original repair program without any magic sets optimization, which is an option given by the system.

The *MS Rewriting* module generates the magic version of a program. It includes at the end appropriate database import sentences, which are generated by a static inspection of the magic program. This requires identifying first, in the rule bodies, the extensional database atoms (they have no annotation constants). Next, for each of these extensional atoms, it is checked if the magic atoms will have the effect of bounding their variables during the program evaluation. That is, it is checked if the constants appearing in the query will be pushed down to the program before query evaluation. For example, in the magic program $\mathcal{MS}(\Pi)$ for the query $Ans(x) \leftarrow S(b,x)$ shown in Section 3, the following rules contain database atoms: (a) $S_-(x,y,\mathbf{t}^\star) \leftarrow magic\_S_-^{bfb}(x,\mathbf{t}^\star), S(x,y)$; and (b) $R_-(x,y,\mathbf{t}^\star) \leftarrow magic\_R_-^{bfb}(x,\mathbf{t}^\star), R(x,y)$. In (a), the variable x in the extensional atom $S(x,y)$ will be bound during the evaluation due to the magic atom $magic\_S_-^{bfb}(x,\mathbf{t}^\star)$ appearing in the same body. This magic atom is defined in the magic program by the rule $magic\_S_-^{bfb}(x,\mathbf{t}^\star) \leftarrow magic\_S_-^{bfb}(x,\mathbf{t}^{\star\star})$, where atom $magic\_S_-^{bfb}(x,\mathbf{t}^{\star\star})$ is defined in its turn by the rule $magic\_S_-^{bfb}(b,\mathbf{t}^{\star\star}) \leftarrow magic\_Ans^f$. Since $magic\_Ans^f$ is always true in an MS program, $magic\_S_-^{bfb}(b,\mathbf{t}^{\star\star})$ will be true with the variable x in $S(x,y)$ eventually taking value b. As a consequence, the SQL query in the import sentence for predicate S will be: "SELECT * FROM S WHERE ID = 'b'". A similar static analysis can be done for rule (b), generating an import sentence for relation R. The generated import sentences will retrieve into *DLV* only the corresponding subsets of the relations in the database.

The resulting magic program is evaluated in *DLV*, that is automatically called by *ConsEx*, and the query answers are returned to the *Answer Collection* module, which formats the answers and returns them to the user as the consistent answers.

5   Experimental Evaluation

Several experiments on computation of consistent answers to queries were run with *ConsEx*. In particular, it was possible to quantify the gain in execution time when using magic sets instead of the direct evaluation of the repair programs. The experiments were run on an Intel Pentium 4 PC, processor of 3.00 Ghz, 512 MB of RAM, and with Linux distribution UBUNTU 6.0. The database instance was stored in the IBM DB2 Universal Database Server Edition, version 8.2 for Linux. All the programs were run in the version of *DLV* for Linux released on Jan 12, 2006.

We considered a database schema with eight relations, and a set of ICs composed of two primary key constraints, and three RICs. In order to analyze scalability of CQA trough logic programs, we considered two databases instances D_1, and D_2, with 3200 and 6400 stored tuples, resp. The number N of inconsistent tuples, i.e. participating in an IC violation varied between 20 and 400.[8]

---

[8] The files containing the database schema, ICs, the queries, and the instances used in the experiments are available in http://www.face.ubiobio.cl/~mcaniupa/ConsEx

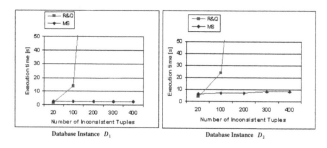

Fig. 3. Running Time for the Conjunctive Query with Free Variables

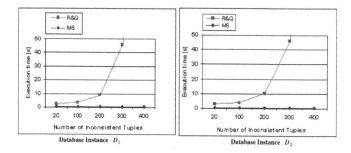

Fig. 4. Running Time for the Partially-Ground Conjunctive Query with Free Variables

Here, we report the execution time for two conjunctive queries, in both instances. The first query is of the form, $Ans(\bar{x}) \leftarrow P(\bar{y}), R(\bar{z})$, with $\bar{x} \subseteq \bar{y} \cup \bar{z}$, with free variables (an open query), joins ($\bar{y} \cap \bar{z} \neq \emptyset$), and no constants. The second query contains joins and is also partially-ground, like the query used in Section 3. Both queries fall in the class of *Tree*-queries for which CQA is tractable under key constraints [22]. However, since we are also considering RICs, which are repaired by inserting tuples with null values, it is not possible to use the polynomial time algorithm for CQA presented in [22]. Even more, it is not clear that the tractability result in [22] carries over to the queries and ICs used in our experiments.

In the charts, $R\&Q$ indicates the straightforward evaluation of the repair program combined with the query program, whereas its magic sets optimization is indicated with *MS*. Figure 3 shows the running time for the first query in the two instances. We can see that MS is faster than the straightforward evaluation. For $N = 200$ (in both database instances), the MS methodology returns answers in less than ten seconds, while the straightforward evaluation returns answers after one minute. Moreover, the execution time of the MS methodology is almost invariant wrt percentage of inconsistency. Despite the absence of constants in the query, MS still offers a substantial improvement because the magic program essentially keeps only the rules and relations that are relevant to the query, which reduces the ground instantiation of the program by *DLV*.

Figure 4 shows the execution time for the second, partially-ground query in both database instances. Again, MS computes answers much faster than the straightforward evaluation. In this case, MS has an even better performance due to the occurrence of constants in the query, which the magic rules push down to the database relations. This causes less tuples to be imported into *DLV*, and the ground instantiation of the magic program is reduced (wrt the original program).

Furthermore, MS shows an excellent scalability. For instance, MS computes answers to queries from database instances D_1 and D_2 in less than ten seconds, even with a database D_2 that contains twice as many tuples as D_1.

6   Conclusions

We have seen that the *ConsEx* system computes database repairs and consistent answers to first-order queries (and beyond) by evaluation of logic programs with stable model semantics that specify both the repairs and the query. In order to make query answering more efficient in practice, *ConsEx* implements sound and complete magic set techniques for disjunctive repair programs with program constraints [12]. Moreover, *ConsEx* takes advantage of the smooth interaction between the logic programming environment and the database management systems (DBMS), as enabled by *DLV*. In this way, it is possible to exploit capabilities of the DBMS, such as storing and indexing. Furthermore, bringing the whole database into *DLV*, to compute repairs and consistent answers, is quite inefficient. In our case, it is possible to keep the instance in the database, while only the relevant data is imported into the logic programming system.

The methodology for CQA based on repair logic programs is general enough to cover all the queries and ICs found in database practice (and more). On the other side, we know that CQA has a high intrinsic data complexity [16, 7]. The excellent performance exhibited by the magic sets techniques makes us think that CQA is viable and can be used in practical cases. Most likely real databases do not contain such a high percentage of inconsistent data as those used in our experiments.

Implementations of other systems for CQA have been reported before. The *Queca* system [14] implements the query rewriting methodology presented in [1], and can be used with universal ICs with at most two database atoms (plus built-ins) and projection-free conjunctive queries. The system *Hippo* [17] implements first-order query rewriting based on graph-theoretic methods. It works for denial constraints and inclusion dependencies under a tuple deletion repair semantics, and projection-free conjunctive queries. The system *ConQuer* [22] implements CQA for key constraints and a non-trivial class of conjunctive queries with projections. Comparisons in terms of performance between *ConsEx* and these more specialized and optimized systems, for the specific classes of ICs and queries they can handle, still have to be made.

In *ConsEx*, consistency checking of databases with SQL null values and repairs that appeal to SQL null values both follow the precise and general semantics introduced in [10]. However, when queries are answered in *ConsEx*, the query answer semantics is the usual logic programming semantics that treats nulls as any other constant. A semantics for query answering in the presence of SQL nulls that is compatible with the IC satisfaction and repair semantics used in *ConsEx* is proposed in [8]. Its implementation in *ConsEx* is left for future work. We also leave for future work the extension of CQA to broader classes of queries, in particular, to aggregate queries by means of logic programs as done in [13].

Acknowledgements. Research supported by an NSERC Discovery Grant, and the University of Bio-Bio (UBB-Chile) (Grant DIUBB 076215 4/R). L. Bertossi is Faculty Fellow of IBM Center for Advanced Studies (Toronto Lab.). We are grateful to Claudio Gutiérrez and Pedro Campos, both from UBB, for their help with the implementation of algorithms and the interface of *ConsEx*. Conversations with Wolfgang Faber and Nicola Leone are very much appreciated.

References

[1] Arenas, M., Bertossi, L., Chomicki, J.: Consistent Query Answers in Inconsistent Databases. In: Proc. ACM Symposium on Principles of Database Systems (PODS 99), pp. 68–79. ACM Press, New York (1999)

[2] Arenas, M., Bertossi, L., Chomicki, L.: Answer Sets for Consistent Query Answering in Inconsistent Databases. Theory and Practice of Logic Programming 3(4-5), 393–424 (2003)

[3] Barcelo, P., Bertossi, L.: Logic Programs for Querying Inconsistent Databases. In: Dahl, V., Wadler, P. (eds.) PADL 2003. LNCS, vol. 2562, pp. 208–222. Springer, Heidelberg (2002)

[4] Barcelo, P., Bertossi, L., Bravo, L.: Characterizing and Computing Semantically Correct Answers from Databases with Annotated Logic and Answer Sets. In: Bertossi, L., Katona, G.O.H., Schewe, K.-D., Thalheim, B. (eds.) Semantics in Databases. LNCS, vol. 2582, pp. 1–27. Springer, Heidelberg (2003)

[5] Bancilhon, F., Maier, D., Sagiv, Y., Ullman, J.: Magic Sets and Other Strange Ways to Implement Logic Programs (extended abstract). In: PODS 1986, pp. 1–15. ACM Press, New York (1986)

[6] Bertossi, L., Chomicki, J.: Query Answering in Inconsistent Databases. In: Logics for Emerging Applications of Databases, pp. 43–83. Springer, Heidelberg (2003)

[7] Bertossi, L.: Consistent Query Answering in Databases. ACM Sigmod Record 35(2), 68–76 (2006)

[8] Bravo, L.: Handling Inconsistency in Databases and Data Integration Systems. PhD. Thesis, Carleton University, Department of Computer Science (2007), http://homepages.inf.ed.ac.uk/lbravo/Publications.htm

[9] Bravo, L., Bertossi, L.: Consistent Query Answering under Inclusion Dependencies. In: CASCON 2004, pp. 202–216 (2004)

[10] Bravo, L., Bertossi, L.: Semantically Correct Query Answers in the Presence of Null Values. In: Grust, T., Höpfner, H., Illarramendi, A., Jablonski, S., Mesiti, M., Müller, S., Patranjan, P.-L., Sattler, K.-U., Spiliopoulou, M., Wijsen, J. (eds.) EDBT 2006. LNCS, vol. 4254, pp. 33–47. Springer, Heidelberg (2006)

[11] Cali, A., Lembo, D., Rosati, R.: On the Decidability and Complexity of Query Answering over Inconsistent and Incomplete Databases. In: PODS 2003, pp. 260–271. ACM Press, New York (2003)

[12] Caniupan, M., Bertossi, L.: Optimizing Repair Programs for Consistent Query Answering. In: SCCC 2005, pp. 3–12. IEEE Computer Society Press, Los Alamitos (2005)

[13] Caniupan, M.: Optimizing and Implementing Repair Programs for Consistent Query Answering in Databases. PhD. Thesis, Carleton University, Department of Computer Science (2007), http://www.face.ubiobio.cl/~mcaniupa/publications.htm

[14] Celle, A., Bertossi, L.: Querying Inconsistent Databases: Algorithms and Implementation. In: Palamidessi, C., Moniz Pereira, L., Lloyd, J.W., Dahl, V., Furbach, U., Kerber, M., Lau, K.-K., Sagiv, Y., Stuckey, P.J. (eds.) CL 2000. LNCS (LNAI), vol. 1861, pp. 942–956. Springer, Heidelberg (2000)

[15] Ceri, S., Gottlob, G., Tanca, L.: Logic Programming and Databases. Springer, Heidelberg (1990)

[16] Chomicki, J., Marcinkowski, J.: On the Computational Complexity of Minimal-Change Integrity Maintenance in Relational Databases. In: Bertossi, L., Hunter, A., Schaub, T. (eds.) Inconsistency Tolerance. LNCS, vol. 3300, pp. 119–150. Springer, Heidelberg (2005)

[17] Chomicki, J., Marcinkowski, J., Staworko, S.: Computing Consistent Query Answers using Conflict Hypergraphs. In: CIKM 2004, pp. 417–426. ACM Press, New York (2004)

[18] Cumbo, C., Faber, W., Greco, G., Leone, N.: Enhancing the Magic-Set Method for Disjunctive Datalog Programs. In: Demoen, B., Lifschitz, V. (eds.) ICLP 2004. LNCS, vol. 3132, pp. 371–385. Springer, Heidelberg (2004)

[19] Dantsin, E., Eiter, T., Gottlob, G., Voronkov, A.: Complexity and Expressive Power of Logic Programming. ACM Computing Surveys 33(3), 374–425 (2001)

[20] Eiter, T., Fink, M., Greco, G., Lembo, D.: Efficient Evaluation of Logic Programs for Querying Data Integration Systems. In: Palamidessi, C. (ed.) ICLP 2003. LNCS, vol. 2916, pp. 163–177. Springer, Heidelberg (2003)

[21] Faber, W., Greco, G., Leone, N.: Magic Sets and their Application to Data Integration. Journal of Computer and System Sciences 73(4), 584–609 (2007)

[22] Fuxman, A., Fazli, E., Miller, R.J.: ConQuer: Efficient Management of Inconsistent Databases. In: SIGMOD 2005, pp. 155–166. ACM Press, New York (2005)

[23] Gelfond, M., Lifschitz, V.: Classical Negation in Logic Programs and Disjunctive Databases. New Generation Computing 9, 365–385 (1991)

[24] Greco, S.: Binding Propagation Techniques for the Optimization of Bound Disjunctive Queries. IEEE Transac. on Knowledge and Data Eng. 15(2), 368–385 (2003)

[25] Greco, G., Greco, S., Zumpano, E.: A Logical Framework for Querying and Repairing Inconsistent Databases. IEEE Transactions on Knowledge and Data Eng. 15(6), 1389–1408 (2003)

[26] Greco, G., Greco, S., Trubtsyna, I., Zumpano, E.: Optimization of Bound Disjunctive Queries with Constraints. Theory and Practice of Logic Programming 5(6), 713–745 (2005)

[27] Lembo, D., Rosati, R., Ruzzi, M.: On the First-Order Reducibility of Unions of Conjunctive Queries over Inconsistent Databases. In: Grust, T., Höpfner, H., Illarramendi, A., Jablonski, S., Mesiti, M., Müller, S., Patranjan, P.-L., Sattler, K.-U., Spiliopoulou, M., Wijsen, J. (eds.) EDBT 2006. LNCS, vol. 4254, pp. 358–374. Springer, Heidelberg (2006)

[28] Leone, N., Pfeifer, G., Faber, W., Eiter, T., Gottlob, G., Perri, S., Scarcello, F.: The DLV System for Knowledge Representation and Reasoning. ACM Transactions on Computational Logic 7(3), 499–562 (2006)

[29] Lloyd, J.W.: Foundations of Logic Programming, 2nd edn. Springer, Heidelberg (1987)

Incomplete Statistical Information Fusion and Its Application to Clinical Trials Data

Jianbing Ma[1], Weiru Liu[1], and Anthony Hunter[2]

[1] School of Electronics, Electrical Engineering and Computer Science,
Queen's University Belfast, Belfast BT7 1NN, UK
{jma03,w.liu}@qub.ac.uk
[2] Department of Computer Science, University College London,
Gower Street, London WC1E 6BT, UK
a.hunter@cs.ucl.ac.uk

Abstract. In medical clinical trials, overall trial results are highlighted in the *abstracts* of papers/reports. These results are summaries of underlying statistical analysis where most of the time normal distributions are assumed in the analysis. It is common for clinicians to focus on the information in the abstracts in order to review or integrate several clinical trial results that address the same or similar medical question(s). Therefore, developing techniques to merge results from clinical trials based on information in the abstracts is useful and important. In reality information in an abstract can either provide sufficient details about a normal distribution or just partial information about a distribution. In this paper, we first propose approaches to constructing normal distributions from both complete and incomplete statistical information in the abstracts. We then provide methods to merge these normal distributions (or sampling distributions). Following this, we investigate the conditions under which two normal distributions can be merged. Finally, we design an algorithm to sequence the merging of trials results to ensure that the most reliable trials are considered first.

Keywords: Normal distribution, Merging statistical data, Consistency analysis.

1 Introduction

Clinical trials are widely used to test new drugs or to compare the effect of different drugs [10]. Overall trial results are summarized in *abstracts* of papers/reports that report the trial details. Given that there is a huge number of trials available and details of reports are very time consuming to read and understand, clinicians, medical practiceners and general users mainly make use of this highly summaritive information in the abstracts to obtain an overall impression about drugs of interest. For example, many clinical trials have been carried out to investigate the intraocular pressure-lowering efficacy of drugs, such as travoprost, bimatoprost, and latanoprost, [2,4,9,11,13,14,15,16,18]. When an overview or survey of a collection of clinical trials is required, a *merged or integrated* result is desirable.

When the full details about the statistics used in the trials are available, merging the results from these trials is usually a matter of systematic use of established techniques

H. Prade and V.S. Subrahmanian (Eds.): SUM 2007, LNAI 4772, pp. 89–103, 2007.

from statistics. However, in reality, it is impossible to read all the details about each trial. Most of the time, information in abstracts is most useful for the following reasons. First, it is common that a person reads the abstract of a paper before reading the full paper/report when deciding if the trial is relevant. Second, with more and more information available on the Web, obtaining an abstract is much easier and most of the time it is free while getting a full paper can be more difficult and expensive (one may need to pay a fee). Third, in the field of clinical trials, abstracts often provide sufficient information about trial analysis for a clinician to update their knowledge (such as about the pros and cons of a particular treatment). Therefore, we concentrate here on developing techniques to merging information solely provided in the abstracts.

As a convention, clinical trials usually use normal distributions to record trial results. So it is a natural idea to merge normal distributions to a single one as the integrated result. There is a classical method to merge normal distributions [3]. However, when using this method to merge two identical normal distributions, the merged result is a different normal distribution which is counterintuitive, since we would expect the merged result to be the same as the original distribution. Some other methods have been proposed to integrate probability distributions ([3,12,19]) or to learn the integrated probability distributions ([6,8]). But these methods generally do not lead to a normal distribution as a result, so they are not suitable for our purposes. Furthermore, in some abstracts about clinical trials, information about underlying statistics can be incomplete, e.g., the standard deviations are not given. To deal with this, we need to make use of some background knowledge in order to construct an adequate normal distribution to facilitate merging.

In this paper, we first propose approaches to constructing normal distributions from both complete and incomplete statistical information in the abstracts. We then provide methods to merge normal distributions. We also study how to measure if two normal distributions are in conflict (or consistent), in order to decide if they should be merged. To sequence a merging of multiple trials data, we introduce the notion of reliability to sort the merging sequence. An algorithm is designed to merge trials results based on both reliabilities of trials and consistencies among trials.

The remainder of this paper is organized as follows. Section 2 provides some preliminary knowledge about normal distributions and introduces the notion of degrees of consistency of normal distributions. Section 3 introduces categories of statistical information commonly found in abstracts and how they are related to normal distributions. Section 4 contains our merging methods for merging complete and incomplete statistical information. In Section 5, we give a definition for measuring conflict among normal distributions and how this is used to decide if a merging shall take place. Section 6 investigates how a collection of clinical trials results should be sequenced for merging and an algorithm is designed to implement this. Finally, in Section 7, we conclude the paper.

2   Preliminaries

We start with some basic concepts about normal distributions. We then define the notion of conflict (or consistency) of two normal distributions.

Definition 1. *A random variable X with mean value μ and variance σ^2 is **normally distributed** if its **probability density function** (pdf for short) f is defined as follows:*

$$f(x) = \frac{1}{\sqrt{2\pi}\sigma} exp(-\frac{(x-\mu)^2}{2\sigma^2})$$

In statistics, a normal distribution associated with a random variable is denoted as $X \sim N(\mu, \sigma^2)$. For the convenience of further calculations in the rest of the paper, we use notation $X \sim N(\mu, \sigma)$ instead of $X \sim N(\mu, \sigma^2)$ for a normal distribution of variable X. That is, we use a standard deviation rather than a variance because this will greatly simplify mathematical equations in Section 4.

A normal distribution with $X \sim N(0,1)$ is called a **standard normal distribution**. Any normal distribution $N(\mu, \sigma)$ can be standardized by letting a random variable $Z = \frac{X-\mu}{\sigma}$, then $Z \sim N(0,1)$ is a standard normal distribution. For $N(0,1)$, the standard normal distribution table in statistics [20] provides sufficient information for further calculations of probabilities, such as the probability of an interval that the variable falls in.

In statistics, random samples of individuals are often used as the representatives of the entire group of individuals (often denoted as a population) to estimate the values of some parameters of the population. The mean of variable X of the samples, when the sample size is reasonably large, follows a normal distribution. The **standard error of the mean** (SEM for short), which is the standard deviation of the sample mean, is given by SEM $= \frac{\sigma}{\sqrt{n}}$, where σ is the standard deviation of X of the population and n is the number of samples chosen from the population. We can write $\bar{X} \sim N(\mu, \text{SEM})$. When σ is unknown, the standard deviation s of the samples is often used to replace σ.

To help define the degree of consistency of normal distributions, we introduce the following well-known result.

Let v_1 and v_2 be two vectors. The angle between two vectors can be computed as follows:

$$cos(v_1, v_2) = \frac{< v_1, v_2 >}{\| v_1 \|_2 \| v_2 \|_2}$$

where $< v_1, v_2 >$ is the inner product of the vectors and $\| v \|_2$ is the L_2 norm.

Definition 2. *Let two normal distributions have $f_1(.)$ and $f_2(.)$ as their pdfs respectively. The **degree of consistency** of the two normal distributions, denoted as $c(f_1, f_2)$ is defined as follows:*

$$c(f_1, f_2) = \frac{< f_1, f_2 >}{\| f_1 \|_2 \| f_2 \|_2}$$

where $< f_1, f_2 >$ is the inner product given by:

$$< f_1, f_2 >= \int_{-\infty}^{+\infty} f_1(x) f_2(x) dx$$

and $\| f \|_2$ is the L_2 norm given by:

$$\| f \|_2 = \int_{-\infty}^{+\infty} f^2(x) dx$$

The degree of consistency $c(f_1, f_2)$ defined above is in $(0,1]$. When f_1 and f_2 are identical normal distributions, $c(f_1, f_2) = 1$, while $c(f_1, f_2) \to 0$ when $\| \mu_1 - \mu_2 \| \to \infty$. Value $c(f_1, f_2)$ increases along with the *closeness* of f_1 and f_2.

3   Statistical Information in Abstracts

In abstracts of papers about clinical trials, information about underlying statistics can be summarized into the following four categories.

- Category I: A normal distribution can be identified when both μ and σ are given.
- Category II: A normal distribution can be identified when only μ is given.
- Category III: A normal distribution can be constructed when a confidence interval is given.
- Category IV: A normal distribution can be constructed if at least two sentences, each of which gives a probability value of the variable in a particular range, are available in the abstract.

After looking through a large collection of abstracts of clinical trials on IOP reductions using different drugs, we believe that the above four categories cover a significant proportion of statistical information in abstracts [2,4,9,11,13,14,15,16,18]. In this paper, we concentrate on how to model and merge these four types of information.

For each category of statistical information, we try to interpret it in terms of a normal distribution. We use X to denote the random variable implied in the context of each sentence.

For the first category, a normal distribution is explicitly give, for example, sentence "Mean IOP reduction at 6 months was -9.3+/-2.9 mmHg in the travoprost group" can be interpreted as follows

$$X \sim N(-9.3, 2.9)$$

For the second category, a normal distribution can be defined with a missing standard deviation. For instance, sentence "There was at least 90% power to detect a mean IOP change from baseline of 2.9 mmHg" can be interpreted as

$$X \sim N(2.9, \sigma)$$

where σ is unknown. To make use of this information, we need to draw on background knowledge about the interval that σ lies. From our investigation, this information can be obtained either through a clinician or from some text books on this specific topic. Therefore, we can assume that this background knowledge is available and can be used during merging.

For the third category of information, a confidence interval $[a, b]$ is given. It is then possible to convert this confidence interval into a normal distribution as follows

$$\mu = \frac{a + b}{2}, \qquad \sigma = \frac{b - a}{2k}$$

As a convention, the presented analysis of clinical trials results usually use the 95% confidence interval. In this case, we have $k = 1.96$. However, if a given confidence interval is not the usual 95% confidence interval (say, it uses the p-confidence interval), it is possible to use the standardization of the normal distribution as $P(Z \in [-k, k]) = p$. Then value k can be found by looking up the standard normal distribution table.

For example, from sentence "Bimatoprost provided mean IOP reductions from baseline that ranged from 6.8 mmHg to 7.8 mmHg (27% to 31%)", it is possible to get a normal distribution $N(\mu, \sigma)$ with full information.

For the fourth category of information, a sentence like "By month 3, 85% of participants in the bimatoprost group had a mean IOP reduction of at least 20%" can be used to define a probability of the variable in a particular range, such as

$$P(X \geq 0.2b) = 0.85$$

where b is the baseline IOP value.

It is possible to generalize this expression to $P(X \geq x) = p$ and then further to

$$P(\frac{X - \mu}{\sigma} \geq \frac{x - \mu}{\sigma}) = p$$

using the standardization technique.

By looking up the standard normal distribution table, it is possible to determine the value for $(x - \mu)/\sigma$. Similarly, if another sentence is given in the abstract with another range for X, then another equation $(x' - \mu)/\sigma = y'$ can be obtained, therefore, the values of μ and σ can be calculated. In a situation where only one of such sentence is given but μ is provided, a normal distribution can still be constructed. Otherwise, it would be difficult to use this piece of information. From our analysis of abstracts, it seems that it is very rare that only one of these sentences is given, usually, two or more such descriptions are available.

To summarize, from our case study, usually we can get normal distributions from all the four type of information we normally find in abstracts.

4   Merging Normal Distributions

In this section, we discuss how to merge two normal distributions when either full information or partial information about them is available.

4.1   Normal Distributions with Full Information

Let the normal distributions associated with two random variables X_1 and X_2 be as following

$$X_1 \sim N(\mu_1, \sigma_1), \qquad X_2 \sim N(\mu_2, \sigma_2)$$

We want to merge them into a new normal distribution with random variable X as $X \sim N(\mu, \sigma)$. An intuitive idea for merging is to let the merged μ *divide* the two distributions equally. Since in general $\sigma_1 \neq \sigma_2$, we cannot simply let $\mu = \frac{\mu_1 + \mu_2}{2}$. We define the following criterion that μ should satisfy

$$P(X_1 \leq \mu) + P(X_2 \leq \mu) = P(X_1 \geq \mu) + P(X_2 \geq \mu). \tag{1}$$

Indeed, the above equation ensures that the merged μ divides the two distributions equally.

Proposition 1. *Assume we have $X_1 \sim N(\mu_1, \sigma_1)$, $X_2 \sim N(\mu_2, \sigma_2)$, and let μ be the merged result that satisfies (1), then we have*

$$\mu = \frac{\mu_1 \sigma_2 + \mu_2 \sigma_1}{\sigma_1 + \sigma_2}$$

The proof of this and other subsequent propositions are given in the Appendix.

It is easy to see that if $\sigma_1 = \sigma_2$, then $\mu = \frac{\mu_1 + \mu_2}{2}$. In particular, if two normal distributions are the same, then the merged μ should not be changed, which is exactly what we want.

From Proposition 1, we notice that the coefficients of μ_1 (also X_1) and μ_2 (X_2) in calculating μ are $\frac{\sigma_2}{\sigma_1 + \sigma_2}$ and $\frac{\sigma_1}{\sigma_1 + \sigma_2}$, respectively. So when calculating σ, we still use these two coefficients for X_1 and X_2 and the variance σ^2 should satisfy

$$\sigma^2 = \frac{\sigma_2}{\sigma_1 + \sigma_2} \int_{-\infty}^{+\infty} f_1(X_1)(x - \mu)^2 dx + \frac{\sigma_1}{\sigma_1 + \sigma_2} \int_{-\infty}^{+\infty} f_2(X_2)(x - \mu)^2 dx \quad (2)$$

where $f_1(X_1)$ and $f_2(X_2)$ are the pdfs for X_1 and X_2 respectively.

Proposition 2. *Assume we have $X_1 \sim N(\mu_1, \sigma_1)$, $X_2 \sim N(\mu_2, \sigma_2)$, and let variance σ^2 be the merged result that satisfies (2), then we have*

$$\sigma = \sqrt{\sigma_1 \sigma_2 \left(1 + \frac{(\mu_1 - \mu_2)^2}{(\sigma_1 + \sigma_2)^2}\right)}$$

It is easy to check that such a σ satisfies the following properties.

Proposition 3. *Assume we have $X_1 \sim N(\mu_1, \sigma_1)$, $X_2 \sim N(\mu_2, \sigma_2)$, and the merged result of these two distributions is $X \sim N(\mu, \sigma)$, then*

1. *If $\mu_1 = \mu_2$ and $\sigma_1 = \sigma_2$, then $\sigma = \sigma_1 = \sigma_2$.*
2. *If $\sigma_1 = \sigma_2$, but $\mu_1 \neq \mu_2$, then $\sigma > \sigma_1 = \sigma_2$.*
3. *If $\sigma_1 \neq \sigma_2$, but $\mu_1 = \mu_2$, then $\min(\sigma_1.\sigma_2) \leq \sigma \leq \max(\sigma_1, \sigma_2)$.*

Proof: The proof is straightforward and omitted.

Unfortunately, it does not satisfy the associative property.

Example 1. *The following two normal distributions are constructed from [15,16]. In [15], the baseline IOP (Intraocular Pressure) in the latanoprost 0.005% group is (Mean(SD)) 24.1(2.9) mm Hg. We use X_{NM} to denote the normal distribution of the baseline IOP in the latanoprost 0.005% group, so we get $X_{NM} \sim N(24.1, 2.9)$. Similarly, in [[16]], the corresponding baseline IOP is 23.8(1.7) mm Hg, so we get $X_{PY} \sim N(23.8, 1.7)$.*

Based on Propositions 1 and 2, we get

$$\mu = \frac{24.1 * 1.7 + 23.8 * 2.9}{1.7 + 2.9} = 23.9 \qquad \sigma = \sqrt{1.7 * 2.9 * \left(1 + \frac{(24.1 - 23.9)^2)}{(1.7 + 2.9)^2}\right)} = 2.2$$

So the merged normal distribution is $X_{NMPY} \sim N(23.9, 2.2)$ and it is closer to X_{PY} than to X_{NM}. This is natural because X_{PY} with a smaller standard deviation means that this normal distribution is more accurate and most of the values will be closer to its mean value. Therefore, the merged result has a mean value that is closer to this distribution.

There is another well known method for merging two normal distributions [3] which gives

$$\mu = \frac{\mu_1 \sigma_2^2 + \mu_2 \sigma_1^2}{\sigma_1^2 + \sigma_2^2} \qquad \sigma = \sqrt{\frac{\sigma_1^2 \sigma_2^2}{\sigma_1^2 + \sigma_2^2}} \tag{3}$$

The above two equations come from the mathematical result of the distribution of $X_1 + X_2$. A drawback of this equation is that when the two original normal distributions are the same, the merged σ is different from the original one. This is not intuitively what we want to get from a merging. Therefore, we start from the assumption that the mean value μ should divide the two normal distributions equivalently that is how we have obtained the different equations from above to calculate μ and σ.

4.2   A Special Case Considering the Sample Mean

Now we consider situations where variable X denotes the mean of the samples. From $SEM = \frac{\sigma}{\sqrt{n}}$, we get $n = \frac{\sigma^2}{SEM^2}$. Let X_1 be the mean of m_1 variables whose standard deviation is σ_1 and X_2 be the mean value of m_2 variables whose standard deviation is σ_2. Provided that m_1 and m_2 are reasonably large, X_1 and X_2 both follow a normal distribution as

$$X_1 \sim N(\mu_1, SEM_1), \qquad X_2 \sim N(\mu_1, SEM_2)$$

respectively. When we consider merging two clinical trials results, we need to assume that the populations of the two samples are similar (or even the same), therefore, it is reasonable to assume that $\sigma_1 = \sigma_2$. Under this assumption, we have the following merging result

Proposition 4. *Let $X_1 \sim N(\mu_1, SEM_1)$ and $X_2 \sim N(\mu_1, SEM_2)$, then for the merged normal distribution, we have*

$$\mu = \frac{\mu_1 * SEM_2^2 + \mu_2 * SEM_1^2}{SEM_1^2 + SEM_2^2}$$

Proposition 5. *Let $X_1 \sim N(\mu_1, SEM_1)$ and $X_2 \sim N(\mu_1, SEM_2)$, then for the merged normal distribution, we have*

$$SEM = \sqrt{\frac{SEM_1^2 * SEM_2^2}{SEM_1^2 + SEM_2^2}}$$

Although the above merging results happen to be similar to the pair of equations in (3), we need to point out that they are used in different circumstances. Unlike equations in (3) which solve the sum of two normal distributions, Propositions 4 and 5 deal with the merging of the sample means and with the assumption that the standard deviations of the populations of the two samples are equivalent.

Here if the two normal distributions are the same, the SEM^2 will be a half of the original one. This satisfies the property that the variation of the mean is in counter proportion to the sample size, so when the sample size is doubled (after merging), SEM^2 is halved. It is also easy to prove that the above merging method has the associative property.

Example 2. *The mean IOP reduction is a variable which is the mean of the distribution of samples. When the sample size is reasonably large, it follows a normal distribution. In [16], the mean IOP reduction of the travoprost 0.004% group at the end of three months is $X_{PY} \sim N(9.4, 3.1)$, while in [11], the corresponding mean IOP reduction at the end of three months with the same drug is $X_{HS} \sim N(8.7, 3.8)$.*

Based on Proposition 4 and Proposition 5, we get:

$$\mu = \frac{9.4 * 3.8^2 + 8.7 * 3.1^2}{3.8^2 + 3.1^2} = 9.1 \quad SEM = \sqrt{\frac{3.8^2 * 3.1^2}{3.8^2 + 3.1^2}} = 2.4$$

So the merged normal distribution is $X_{PYHS} \sim N(9.1, 2.4)$. We can see that the merged SEM is significantly smaller than the original ones, because SEM decreases when a sample size increases.

4.3   Normal Distributions with Missing Standard Deviations

We consider situations where one of the two standard deviations (or standard errors of the mean) in two normal distributions is missing. As we have observed, in medical domains there is usually an interval that contains σ or SEM. For example, in the clinical trials, σ for baseline IOP is usually in [1.5, 4.0] mm Hg. We can then use the interval for merging. Without loss of generality, we assume that σ_2 (or the SEM_2) is unknown, but it is in an interval.

Proposition 6. *Let $X_1 \sim N(\mu_1, \sigma_1)$ and $X_2 \sim N(\mu_2, \sigma_2)$ be two normal distributions where μ_1, σ_1, μ_2 are given but σ_2 is in interval $[a, b]$. Then the merged μ based on Proposition 1 is as follows*

If $\mu_1 > \mu_2$, then $\mu \in [\frac{\mu_1 a + \mu_2 \sigma_1}{\sigma_1 + a}, \frac{\mu_1 b + \mu_2 \sigma_1}{\sigma_1 + b}]$
If $\mu_1 = \mu_2$, then $\mu = \mu_1$
If $\mu_1 < \mu_2$, then $\mu \in [\frac{\mu_1 b + \mu_2 \sigma_1}{\sigma_1 + b}, \frac{\mu_1 a + \mu_2 \sigma_1}{\sigma_1 + a}]$

Proposition 7. *Let $X_1 \sim N(\mu_1, \sigma_1)$ and $X_2 \sim N(\mu_2, \sigma_2)$ be two normal distributions where μ_1, σ_1, μ_2 are given but σ_2 is in interval $[a, b]$. Then the merged σ based on Proposition 2 is as follows*

If $\mu_1 = \mu_2$, or $b \leq \sigma_1 + \frac{8\sigma_1^3}{(\mu_1 - \mu_2)^2}$, then $\sigma \in [\sqrt{\sigma_1 a(1 + \frac{(\mu_1 - \mu_2)^2}{(\sigma_1 + a)^2})}, \sqrt{\sigma_1 b(1 + \frac{(\mu_1 - \mu_2)^2}{(\sigma_1 + b)^2})}]$
If $\mu_1 \neq \mu_2$ and $a \geq \sigma_1 + \frac{(\sigma_1 + b)^3}{(\mu_1 - \mu_2)^2}$, then $\sigma \in [\sqrt{\sigma_1 b(1 + \frac{(\mu_1 - \mu_2)^2}{(\sigma_1 + b)^2})}, \sqrt{\sigma_1 a(1 + \frac{(\mu_1 - \mu_2)^2}{(\sigma_1 + a)^2})}]$

Proposition 8. *Let $X_1 \sim N(\mu_1, SEM_1)$ and $X_2 \sim N(\mu_2, SEM_2)$ be two normal distributions where μ_1, SEM_1, μ_2 are known but SEM_2 is in interval $[a, b]$. Then the merged μ based on Proposition 4 is as follows*

If $\mu_1 > \mu_2$, then $\mu \in [\frac{\mu_1 a^2 + \mu_2 SEM_1^2}{SEM_1^2 + a^2}, \frac{\mu_1 b^2 + \mu_2 SEM_1^2}{SEM_1^2 + b^2}]$
If $\mu_1 = \mu_2$, then $\mu = \mu_1$
If $\mu_1 < \mu_2$, then $\mu \in [\frac{\mu_1 b^2 + \mu_2 SEM_1^2}{SEM_1^2 + b^2}, \frac{\mu_1 a^2 + \mu_2 SEM_1^2}{SEM_1^2 + a^2}]$

Proposition 9. *Let $X_1 \sim N(\mu_1, SEM_1)$ and $X_2 \sim N(\mu_2, SEM_2)$ be two normal distributions where μ_1, SEM_1, μ_2 are known but SEM_2 is in interval $[a, b]$. Then the merged SEM based on Proposition 5 is as follows*

$$SEM \in [\sqrt{\frac{SEM_1^2 + a^2}{SEM_1^2 a^2}}, \sqrt{\frac{SEM_1^2 + b^2}{SEM_1^2 b^2}}]$$

In situations where both standard deviations (or the SEMs) are missing, the only method we can use is to let the merged $\mu = \frac{\mu_1 + \mu_2}{2}$ and leave the new σ (or the SEM) still in the interval $[a, b]$.

5   Consistency Analysis of Two Normal Distributions

Merging should take place when two normal distributions refer to the trials that have been undertaken in similar conditions. More specifically, we shall consider the following conditions. First, both trials should be for the same variable (e.g, both for the mean IOP reduction), for the same drug used (e.g, both for travoprost 0.004%), and for the same duration (e.g, both for 12-months). Second, they should be under a similar trial design (e.g, both are cross-over designs) and with similar participants (e.g, the average age should be approximately equivalent). Third, the two distributions from two trials should not be contradict with each other, that is, we need to define a kind of measure to judge how consistent (or conflicting) the two distributions are and give a threshold to indicate whether two distributions can be merged.

Proposition 10. *Let f_1 and f_2 be the pdfs for $X_1 \sim N(\mu_1, \sigma_1)$ and $X_2 \sim N(\mu_2, \sigma_2)$ respectively, then the degree of consistency of X_1 and X_2 based on Definition 2 is*

$$c(f_1, f_2) = \sqrt{\frac{2\sigma_1 \sigma_2}{\sigma_1^2 + \sigma_2^2}} exp(-\frac{(\mu_1 - \mu_2)^2}{2(\sigma_1^2 + \sigma_2^2)})$$

Definition 3. *Let $X_1 \sim N(\mu_1, \sigma_1)$ and $X_2 \sim N(\mu_2, \sigma_2)$ be two normal distributions with f_1 and f_2 as their pdfs respectively. They are consistent and can be merged if $c(f_1, f_2) \geq t$ holds where t is pre-defined threshold for consistency (such as 0.9).*

The degree of inconsistency (or conflict) can be defined as $1 - c(f_1, f_2)$. The threshold is application dependent and can be tuned to suit a particular application.

When variables X_1 and X_2 denote the means of samples, the above proposition still holds except that we should replace σs with SEMs. In a situation where a standard deviation is missing from one of the normal distributions, we assume the two given normal distributions share similar conditions, so we simply let the missing standard deviation be equal to the existing one. Then the above equation is reduced to:

$$c(f_1, f_2) = exp(-\frac{(\mu_1 - \mu_2)^2}{4\sigma_1^2})$$

When both of the standard deviations are not given, as discussed in Section 4, if we know that $\sigma \in [a, b]$, then we have

$$c(f_1, f_2) \in [exp(-\frac{(\mu_1 - \mu_2)^2}{4a^2}), exp(-\frac{(\mu_1 - \mu_2)^2}{4b^2})]$$

For this case if the given threshold t also falls within this interval, it would be hard to tell whether $t \geq c(f_1, f_2)$ holds. A simple method is to compare t with the middle value of the interval, if t is less than the middle value, a merge shall take place otherwise a merge may not be appropriate.

Example 3. *(Con't Example 1) For the two normal distributions in Example 1, we have $c(f_1, f_2) > 0.9$, so these two distributions can be merged.*

If we use the two normal distributions of the baseline IOP of the travoprost 0.004% group in [[11], data collected at 10am] and [16], we have $X_1 \sim N(28.0, 3.1)$, $X_2 \sim N(25.4, 3.0)$, which gives $c(f_1, f_2) < 0.9$, so we advise that these two distributions should not be merged. However, if t is changed to be 0.8, they can be merged. This example also reveals that in our definition of consistency between two normal distributions, the values of means from the distributions play more dominating roles than the standard deviations.

6 Sequencing the Merge of Multiple Trials Data

When there are more than two (potentially many) clinical trials data to be merged, the sequence of merging is very important because our merging methods of two normal distributions are not associative. For the four categories of information we summarized in Section 3, we can get a normal distributions with full information for three types and for the 2nd category, we get a distribution with a missing standard deviation. Since merging a full distribution with an incomplete distribution results in σ (or SEM) being in an interval, this result will make any subsequence merging more complicated. To address this issue, we merge full and incomplete distributions separately first and then merge the merged results from these two separate sequences.

To decide which trial should be the first data to consider, we consider reliabilities. Unlike the use of reliabilities in the form $\lambda_1 P_1 + \lambda_2 P_2$ where the λ_i, $i = 1, 2$ are used to denote the reliabilities of the sources [1,5,7,17], we use the reliability information to rank clinical trials data. Reliability information is usually provided separately as extra information, for clinical·trials, we do not have this information, so we take the number of samples used in a trial as a measure of reliability. That is, the larger the sample size, the more reliable the trial result.

Given a set of trials results that are modeled with incomplete distributions (σ is missing), we rank them based on their sample sizes as (we denote each trial result as μ) $\mu_1, \mu_2, \ldots, \mu_n$. Then the merging of these results are as follows. We first find all the μs that are consistent with μ_1 (the most reliable one) and calculate their average (including μ_1). The result is denoted as μ_1^1. We delete these entries from the above sequence, and we then repeat this procedure for the current most reliable μ in the remaining sequence, and so on. When the initial sequence is empty, we get a new set of μs: $\mu_1^1, \mu_2^1, \ldots, \mu_{n_1}^1$.

When $n_1 = n$, no merging has been taken. That is all trials data are inconsistent with each other. We return μ_1 as the merged result as it is the most reliable one. If $n_1 < n$, we repeat the above merging procedure for the new sequence $\mu_1^1, \mu_2^1, \ldots, \mu_{n_1}^1$.

This merging procedure is described in the following algorithm.

Algorithm Merge(μs)
Begin
  $\Psi_1 = \{< \mu_1, 1 >, < \mu_2, 2 >, \ldots, < \mu_n, n >\}, \Psi_2 = \{\}, m = n;$
  //Here $< \mu_i, i >$ means that μ_i is the ith most reliable one.
  while $n \neq 1$ **do**
    while $|\Psi_1| > 0$ **do**
      Let $< \mu_i, i >$ have the minimal i (or, the most reliable one) in Ψ_1, and let
      $S = \{< \mu_{i_1}, i_1 >, < \mu_{i_2}, i_2 >, \ldots, < \mu_{i_j}, i_j >\}$ containing all the elements
      in Ψ_1 where the $\mu_{i_k}, 1 \leq k \leq j$ are consistent with μ_i based on Def 3 (note that
      μ_i itself is in S), let $\mu_i' = (\sum_{k=1}^j \mu_{i_k})(|S|)$, and $\Psi_2 = \Psi_2 \cup \{< \mu_i', i >\}$.
      Let $\Psi_1 = \Psi_1 \setminus S$.
    End of while
    If $|\Psi_2| = m$, **Return** μ_1' in Ψ_2 as the result.
    Else Let $\Psi_1 = \Psi_2, m = |\Psi_2|$, and $\Psi_2 = \{\}$.
  End of while
Return μ_1 in the Ψ_1 which has the index 1.

This algorithm stops when no further merging is possible, either because all trials are in conflict or all the results have already been merged into one.

In terms of computational complexity, the number of consistency checks is $O(n^3)$, and the number of arithmetic calculation is $O(n)$. So the complexity of the algorithm is $O(n^3)$.

When we replace the set of trials results in the above algorithm with a set of complete normal distributions $N(\mu_1, \sigma_1), N(\mu_2, \sigma_2), \ldots, N(\mu_n, \sigma_n)$, this algorithm merges these full distributions except that the calculation of averages of μs should be replaced by the equations in Proposition 1 and Proposition 2.

Finally, we merge the results of these two separate sequences to obtain a final result.

7 Conclusion

In this paper, we investigated different types of statistical information implied in abstracts (of papers/reports) about clinical trials. We summarized four types of statistical information and three out of these four types would enable us to get a full normal distribution about a trial result. The 2nd category provides us with only incomplete distributions. Based on this, we developed methods to merge these types of information. We also defined how to measure the degree of consistency between two distributions. An algorithm was designed to sequence multiple merges.

There are a number of issues we will further look at. First, the threshold used in consistency checking would have an effect on the final result of merging, we will experiment with different threshold values to see how much effect they have. Second, the algorithm divides trials results based on whether a distribution is complete. There can be other sequences for merging which may be able to merge consistent results (currently in the two separate sequences) at an earlier stage. We will need to experiment on this to see what sequence provides the most suitable merging and what conditions are required. Third, we will consider some necessary background knowledge in order to select trials from a large collection of trials data in order to perform a merge.

Acknowledgement. This work is funded by the EPSRC projects with reference numbers: EP/D070864/1 and EP/D074282/1.

References

1. Boussion, N., Soulez, G., Guise De, J., Daronat, M., Qin, Z., Cloutie, G.: Geometrical accuracy and fusion of multimodal vascular images: a phantom study. Med. Phys. 31(6) (2004)
2. Chiselita, D., Antohi, I., Medvichi, R., Danielescu, C.: Comparative analysis of the efficacy and safety of latanoprost, travoprost and the fixed combination timolol-dorzolamide; a prospective, randomized, masked, cross-over design study. Oftalmologia 49(3), 39–45 (2005)
3. Catherine, M., Alison, C., Christophe, M., William, J.: Experimental issues of functional merging on probability density estimation. Artificial Neural Networks, Conference Publication No. 440 pp. 7–9 (1997)
4. Cantor, L.B., Hoop, J., Morgan, L., Wudunn, D., Catoira, Y.: Bimatoprost-Travoprost Study Group, Intraocular pressure-lowering efficacy of bimatoprost 0.03% and travoprost 0.004$ in patients with glaucoma or ocular hypertension. Br J Ophthalmol 90(11), 1370–1373 (2006)
5. Delmotte, F., Borne, P.: Modeling of reliability with possibility theory. IEEE Trans. SMC 28(1), 78–88 (1998)
6. DasGupta, S.: Learning mixtures of Gaussians. In: Proc. IEEE Foundations of Computer Science (1999)
7. Elouedi, Z., Mellouli, K., Smets, P.: Assessing sensor reliability for multisensor data fusion within the transferable belief model. IEEE Trans. on SMC-Part B 34(1), 782–787 (2004)
8. Freund, Y., Mansour, Y.: Estimating a mixture of two product distributions. In: Estimating a mixture of two product distributions, ACM Press, New York (1999)
9. Gracia-Feijo, J., Martinez-de-la-Casa, J.M., Castillo, A., Mendez, C., Fernandez-Vidal, A., Garcia-Sanchez, J.: Circadian IOP-lowering efficacy of travoprost 0.004$ ophthalmic solution compared to latanoprost 0.005%. Curr. Med. Res. Opin. 22(9), 1689–1697 (2006)
10. Greenhalgh, T.: How to Read a Paper: The Basics of Evidence-Based Medicine. BMJ Press (1997)
11. Howard, S., Silvia, O.N., Brian, E., John, S., Sushanta, M., Theresa, A., Michael, V.: The Safety and Efficacy of Travoprost 0.004%/Timolol 0.5% Fixed Combination Ophthalmic Solution. Ame J. Ophthalmology 140(1), 1–8 (2005)

12. Molina, C., Niranjan, M.: Pruning with replacement on limited resource allocating networks by F-projections. Neural Computation 8, 345–356 (1996)
13. Michael, T., David, W., Alan, L.: Projected impact of travoprost versus timolol and latanoprost on visual field deficit progression and costs among black glaucoma subjects. Trans. Am. Ophthalmol Soc. 100, 109–118 (2002)
14. Noecker, R.J., Earl, M.L., Mundorf, T.K., Silvestein, S.M., Phillips, M.P.: Comparing bimatoprost and travoprost in black Americans. Curr. Med. Res. Opin. 22(11), 2175–2180 (2006)
15. Nicola, C., Michele, V., Tiziana, T., Francesco, C., Carlo, S.: Effects of Travoprost Eye Drops on Intraocular Pressure and Pulsatile Ocular Blood Flow: A 180-Day, Randomized, Double-Masked Comparison with Latanoprost Eye Drops in Patients with Open-Angle Glaucoma. Curr. Ther. Res. 64(7), 389–400 (2003)
16. Parmarksiz, S., Yuksel, N., Karabas, V.L., Ozkan, B., Demirci, G., Caglar, Y.: A comparison of travoprost, latanoprost and the fixed combination of dorzolamide and timolol in patients with pseudoexfoliation glaucoma. Eur. J. Ophthalmol. 16(1), 73–80 (2006)
17. Rogova, G., Nimier, V.: Reliability in information fusion: literature survey. In: Proc. of Information Fusion, pp. 1158–1165 (2004)
18. Stefan, C., Nenciu, A., Malcea, C., Tebeanu, E.: Axial length of the ocular globe and hypotensive effect in glaucoma therapy with prostaglandin analogs. Oftalmologia 49(4), 47–50 (2005)
19. Arora, S., Kannan, R.: Learning mixtures of arbitrary Gaussians. In: STOC(STOC 2001), pp. 6–8 (2001)
20. Standard probability Table: http://onlinepubs.trb.org/onlinepubs/nchrp/cd-22/v2appendixc_files/image002.gif

Appendix

Proof of Proposition 1: From $P(X_1 \leq \mu) + P(X_2 \leq \mu) = P(X_1 \geq \mu) + P(X_2 \geq \mu)$ and $P(X_1 \leq \mu) + P(X_2 \leq \mu) + P(X_1 \geq \mu) + P(X_2 \geq \mu) = 2$, we get:

$$P(X_1 \leq \mu) + P(X_2 \leq \mu) = 1.$$

By using the standardization of the normal distributions, we get

$$P(\frac{X_1 - \mu_1}{\sigma_1} \leq \frac{\mu - \mu_1}{\sigma_1}) + P(\frac{X_2 - \mu_2}{\sigma_2} \leq \frac{\mu - \mu_2}{\sigma_2}) = 1.$$

So it is equivalent to say: $\frac{\mu - \mu_1}{\sigma_1} + \frac{\mu - \mu_2}{\sigma_2} = 0$. Therefore, we have

$$\mu = \frac{\mu_1 \sigma_2 + \mu_2 \sigma_1}{\sigma_1 + \sigma_2}$$

Proof of Prop 2: From $f(X) = \frac{\sigma_2}{\sigma_1 + \sigma_2} f_1(X_1) + \frac{\sigma_1}{\sigma_1 + \sigma_2} f_2(X_2)$, we get

$$DX = \frac{\sigma_2}{\sigma_1 + \sigma_2} D_1 X + \frac{\sigma_1}{\sigma_1 + \sigma_2} D_2 X$$

Now Let us compute $D_1 X$ first. Let $z = \frac{x - \mu_1}{\sigma_1}$,

$$
\begin{aligned}
D_1 X &= \int_{-\infty}^{+\infty} \frac{1}{\sqrt{2\pi}\sigma_1} exp(-\frac{(x - \mu_1)^2}{2\sigma_1^2})(x - \frac{\mu_1\sigma_2 + \mu_2\sigma_1}{\sigma_1 + \sigma_2})^2 dx \\
&= \int_{-\infty}^{+\infty} \frac{\sigma_1^2}{\sqrt{2\pi}} exp(-\frac{z^2}{2})(z + \frac{\mu_1 - \mu_2}{\sigma_1 + \sigma_2})^2 dz \\
&= \frac{\sigma_1^2}{\sqrt{2\pi}} (\int_{-\infty}^{+\infty} exp(-\frac{z^2}{2})z^2 dz + 2\frac{\mu_1 - \mu_2}{\sigma_1 + \sigma_2} \int_{-\infty}^{+\infty} exp(-\frac{z^2}{2}) z dz \\
&\quad + (\frac{\mu_1 - \mu_2}{\sigma_1 + \sigma_2})^2 \int_{-\infty}^{+\infty} exp(-\frac{z^2}{2}) dz) \\
&= \frac{\sigma_1^2}{\sqrt{2\pi}} (\sqrt{2\pi} + 0 + (\frac{\mu_1 - \mu_2}{\sigma_1 + \sigma_2})^2 \sqrt{2\pi}) \\
&= \sigma_1^2 (1 + (\frac{\mu_1 - \mu_2}{\sigma_1 + \sigma_2})^2)
\end{aligned}
$$

Similarly, we get $D_2 X = \sigma_2^2(1 + (\frac{\mu_1 - \mu_2}{\sigma_1 + \sigma_2})^2)$. So after some simple calculation, we have
$$
DX = \sigma_1\sigma_2(1 + (\frac{\mu_1 - \mu_2}{\sigma_1 + \sigma_2})^2), \sigma = \sqrt{DX} = \sqrt{\sigma_1\sigma_2(1 + (\frac{\mu_1 - \mu_2}{\sigma_1 + \sigma_2})^2)}
$$

Proof of Prop 4: $\mu = \frac{\mu_1 * m_1 + \mu_2 * m_2}{m_1 + m_2} = \frac{\mu_1 * \frac{\sigma^2}{SEM_1^2} + \mu_2 * \frac{\sigma^2}{SEM_2^2}}{\frac{\sigma^2}{SEM_1^2} + \frac{\sigma^2}{SEM_2^2}} = \frac{\mu_1 * SEM_2^2 + \mu_2 * SEM_1^2}{SEM_1^2 + SEM_2^2}$

Proof of Prop 5: $SEM = \frac{\sigma}{\sqrt{m_1 + m_2}} = \frac{\sigma}{\sqrt{\frac{\sigma^2}{SEM_1^2} + \frac{\sigma^2}{SEM_2^2}}} = \sqrt{\frac{SEM_1^2 * SEM_2^2}{SEM_1^2 + SEM_2^2}}$

Proof of Proposition 6: If $\mu_1 = \mu_2$, it is straightforward that $\mu = \mu_1$. The remaining part of the proposition is equivalent to prove that when $\mu_1 > \mu_2$, $\mu = \frac{\mu_1\sigma_2 + \mu_2\sigma_1}{\sigma_1 + \sigma_2}$, denoted as $g(\sigma_2)$, is an increasing function of σ_2, while when $\mu_1 < \mu_2$, a decreasing function. As the differential of $g(\sigma_2)$ is $g'(\sigma_2) = \frac{(\mu_1 - \mu_2)\sigma_1}{(\sigma_1 + \sigma_2)^2}$, the result is straightforward.

Proof of Proposition 7: Let $g(\sigma_2)$ denote $\sigma_1\sigma_2(1 + (\frac{\mu_1 - \mu_2}{\sigma_1 + \sigma_2})^2)$, then σ is an increasing or decreasing function of σ_2 is equivalent to say that $g(\sigma_2)$ is an increasing or decreasing function of σ_2. The differential of $g(\sigma_2)$ is $g'(\sigma_2) = \sigma_1(1 + (\frac{\mu_1 - \mu_2}{\sigma_1 + \sigma_2})^2) - 2\sigma_1\sigma_2\frac{(\mu_1 - \mu_2)^2}{(\sigma_1 + \sigma_2)^3}$.

It is obvious that if $\mu_1 = \mu_2$, $g'(\sigma_2) = \sigma_1 > 0$. If $\mu_1 \neq \mu_2$, the $+/-$ sign of $g'(\sigma_2)$ is equivalent to the $+/-$ sign of $\sigma_1(\sigma_1 + \sigma_2)^3 + \sigma_1(\sigma_1 + \sigma_2)(\mu_1 - \mu_2)^2 - 2\sigma_1\sigma_2(\mu_1 - \mu_2)^2$, and consequently equivalent to the $+/-$ sign of $(\sigma_1 + \sigma_2)^3 - (\sigma_2 - \sigma_1)(\mu_1 - \mu_2)^2$. When condition $b \leq \sigma_1 + \frac{8\sigma_1^3}{(\mu_1 - \mu_2)^2}$ holds, if $\sigma_2 < \sigma_1$, obviously the sign of $g'(\sigma_2)$ is $+$; moreover, if $\sigma_2 \geq \sigma_1$, then $(\sigma_2 - \sigma_1)(\mu_1 - \mu_2)^2 \leq (b - \sigma_1)(\mu_1 - \mu_2)^2 \leq 8\sigma_1^3 \leq (\sigma_1 + \sigma_2)^3$, the sign of $g'(\sigma_2)$ is still $+$.

When $\mu_1 \neq \mu_2$ and condition $a \geq \sigma_1 + \frac{(\sigma_1 + b)^3}{(\mu_1 - \mu_2)^2}$ holds, we have $(\sigma_2 - \sigma_1)(\mu_1 - \mu_2)^2 \geq (a - \sigma_1)(\mu_1 - \mu_2)^2 \geq (\sigma_1 + b)^3 \geq (\sigma_1 + \sigma_2)^3$, so the sign is $-$.

Proof of Proposition 8: The proof is similar to the proof the Proposition 6, except that

$$g'(SEM_2) = \frac{2(\mu_1 - \mu_2)SEM_1^2 SEM_2}{(SEM_1^2 + SEM_2^2)^2}$$

Proof of Proposition 9: Simply notice that $\frac{SEM_1^2 + SEM_2^2}{SEM_1^2 SEM_2^2}$ is an increasing function of SEM_2.

Proof of Proposition 10: It is easy to computer that

$$\| f_1 \|_2 = \sqrt{\frac{1}{2\sqrt{\pi}\sigma_1}}, \| f_2 \|_2 = \sqrt{\frac{1}{2\sqrt{\pi}\sigma_2}}$$

and

$$< f_1, f_2 > = \frac{\sqrt{a}\exp(-c)}{2\sqrt{\pi}\sigma_1\sigma_2},$$

where

$$a = \frac{2\sigma_1^2\sigma_2^2}{\sigma_1^2 + \sigma_2^2}, c = \frac{(\mu_1 - \mu_2)^2}{2(\sigma_1^2 + \sigma_2^2)}$$

Therefore

$$c(f_1, f_2) = \frac{< f_1, f_2 >}{\| f_1 \|_2 \| f_1 \|_2} = \sqrt{\frac{2\sigma_1\sigma_2}{\sigma_1^2 + \sigma_2^2}}\exp(-\frac{(\mu_1 - \mu_2)^2}{2(\sigma_1^2 + \sigma_2^2)})$$

Quality Measures in Uncertain Data Management

Ander de Keijzer and Maurice van Keulen

Faculty of EEMCS, University of Twente
POBox 217, 7500AE Enschede, The Netherlands
{a.dekeijzer,m.vankeulen}@utwente.nl

Abstract. Many applications deal with data that is uncertain. Some examples are applications dealing with sensor information, data integration applications and healthcare applications. Instead of these applications having to deal with the uncertainty, it should be the responsibility of the DBMS to manage all data including uncertain data. Several projects do research on this topic. In this paper, we introduce four measures to be used to assess and compare important characteristics of data and systems: uncertainty density, answer decisiveness and adapted precision and recall measures.

1 Introduction

Many applications somehow depend on uncertain data. Currently, most of these applications handle this uncertainty themselves, or just ignore the uncertainty associated with the data. Since the uncertainty is associated with the data, the database would be the logical system to store and handle this uncertainty.

In recent years, the interest in management of uncertain data has increased greatly. Several projects on the subject have been initiated. A few examples in the relational setting are Trio [7], MystiQ [3] and ORION [4] and in the semistructured setting PXML [5] and IMPrECISE [6].

Since the topic *management of uncertain data* is relatively new to the database area, there is currently in our opinion a lack of means to assess and compare important characteristics of data and systems.

The contribution of this paper is the introduction of four measures for uncertain data and data management systems: uncertainty density, answer decisiveness, and specifically adapted notions of precision and recall measures to assess answer quality. We have tried to define the measures in a generic way to enable comparison between relational and XML systems.

The paper is organized as follows. Section 2 gives a short introduction into uncertain data and uncertain data management. In this paper we will use our own system IMPrECISE as a reference system for uncertain XML data and Trio as a reference system for uncertain relational data. We subsequently introduce the four measures for uncertain data in Section 3. The experiments in Section 4 are geared towards evaluating the behavior of the measures to validate their usefulness. Sections 5 and 6 contain conclusions and directions for future research.

H. Prade and V.S. Subrahmanian (Eds.): SUM 2007, LNAI 4772, pp. 104–115, 2007.

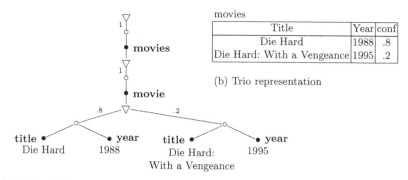

movies

Title	Year	conf
Die Hard	1988	.8
Die Hard: With a Vengeance	1995	.2

(b) Trio representation

(a) IMPrECISE representation

Fig. 1. Example movie database in IMPrECISE and Trio

2   Uncertain Data

Although all of the mentioned projects have their own unique details, they do have one aspect in common. In every project, the central theme is uncertain data. If we consider data to represent, or describe objects in the real world, then uncertain databases describe possible appearances of these objects.

As an example, we show a movie database with one movie that is the result of an integration between two different movie databases. Figure 1 shows this integrated database for two representative systems: IMPrECISE as a representative of an XML-based system (Figure 1(a)) and Trio as an representation of a relational system (Figure 1(b)). The databases show a movie database containing the title and year. Both databases hold information on one movie, but both the title and the year of the movie are uncertain. The title of the movie is either "Die Hard" or "Die Hard: With a Vengeance" and the year of the movie is either 1988 or 1995 respectively. Note that in Trio this single movie is captured in one *x-tuple* containing two alternative representations, or simply *alternatives*.

Another central concept in uncertain databases, is that of possible worlds. A possible world is a possible representation of the real world and is constructed by taking one possibility or alternative for each of the real world objects. In the previous example, there are 2 possible worlds, since only 1 real world object with 2 possible representations is captured in the database. Note that the alternatives for title and year are dependent here. Independent alternatives resulting in 4 possible worlds can of course also be represented in both systems. For the case where a real world object possibly doesn't exist, indicated by an empty possibility node in IMPrECISE or a question mark in Trio, this inexistence is also a possible appearance of the real world object when constructing the possible worlds.

Querying uncertain data results in uncertain answers. If probabilities are associated with the data, these are accessible in the query result as well. Query languages for uncertain data closely resemble query languages for *normal* data. In Trio the query language is called TriQL and is a superset of SQL. In

IMPrECISE the query language is a probabilistic version of XQuery. Although the syntax of the languages are (almost) equal to their normal counterparts, the semantics of course differs. Instead of returning answers to the questions, the system returns *possible answers*. The possible answers can be obtained by evaluating the query for each possible world. Of course this is the semantics behind query evaluation and in neither of the systems it is the actual execution plan.

2.1 IMPrECISE

We use the IMPrECISE system for the experiments in Section 4, so we give some more detail on this system here. The IMPrECISE system uses XML as a data model. The advantage of XML is that it more naturally and generically captures uncertainty. because it closely resembles a decision tree. The expressiveness is, because of the tree structure, high. We introduced two new kinds of nodes, probability nodes ($\bigtriangledown$) and possibility nodes ($\circ$). The root node is always a probability node, child nodes of probability nodes are possibility nodes, child nodes of possibility nodes are regular XML nodes and these, in turn, have probability nodes as child nodes.

Probability nodes indicate *choice points*. Sibling child nodes are mutually exclusive, which introduces possibilities. Each possibility has an associated probability. Probabilities of sibling possibility nodes sum up to at most 1. More details on this model can be found in [6].

IMPrECISE is developed as an XQuery module for the MonetDB/XQuery DBMS [2]. In this way, it demonstrates the power of this XML DBMS and the XQuery language as well.

3   Measures

The measures we introduce in this section can be used for all data models, as long as local possibilities or alternatives can be identified. In IMPrECISE probabilities are always local, because the probability associated with a possibility node expresses the likelihood of the subtree of that particular possibility node to hold the correct information about the real world. In Trio, probabilities are associated with alternatives, which indicate the likelihood of an alternative being correct in the real world. This type of probability is also local. The number of choice points in IMPrECISE is equal to the number of probability nodes, since at each of these nodes a choice for one of the possibility nodes has to be made. In Trio the choice points are determined by the number of *x-tuples* in the relation. For each x-tuple one alternative has to be chosen.

We first define some notation. Let N_{cp} be the number of choice points in the data (i.e., probability nodes in IMPrECISE), $N_{poss,cp}$ the number of possibilities or alternatives of choice point cp, and let P_{cp}^{max} be the probability of the most likely possibility of choice point cp.

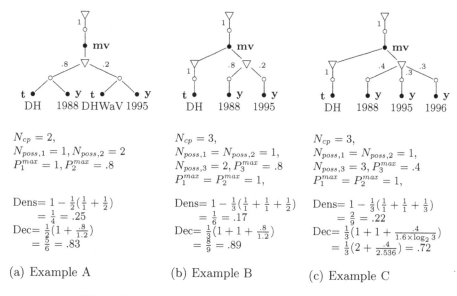

$N_{cp} = 2,$
$N_{poss,1} = 1, N_{poss,2} = 2$
$P_1^{max} = 1, P_2^{max} = .8$

Dens$= 1 - \frac{1}{2}(\frac{1}{1} + \frac{1}{2})$
$= \frac{1}{4} = .25$
Dec$= \frac{1}{2}(1 + \frac{.8}{1.2})$
$= \frac{5}{6} = .83$

(a) Example A

$N_{cp} = 3,$
$N_{poss,1} = N_{poss,2} = 1,$
$N_{poss,3} = 2, P_3^{max} = .8$
$P_1^{max} = P_2^{max} = 1,$

Dens$= 1 - \frac{1}{3}(\frac{1}{1} + \frac{1}{1} + \frac{1}{2})$
$= \frac{1}{6} = .17$
Dec$= \frac{1}{3}(1 + 1 + \frac{.8}{1.2})$
$= \frac{8}{9} = .89$

(b) Example B

$N_{cp} = 3,$
$N_{poss,1} = N_{poss,2} = 1,$
$N_{poss,3} = 3, P_3^{max} = .4$
$P_1^{max} = P_2^{max} = 1,$

Dens$= 1 - \frac{1}{3}(\frac{1}{1} + \frac{1}{1} + \frac{1}{3})$
$= \frac{2}{9} = .22$
Dec$= \frac{1}{3}(1 + 1 + \frac{.4}{1.6 \times \log_2 3})$
$= \frac{1}{3}(2 + \frac{.4}{2.536}) = .72$

(c) Example C

Fig. 2. Examples of uncertainty density and decisiveness

3.1   Uncertainty Density

An often used measure for the amount of uncertainty in a database is the number of possible worlds it represents. This measure, however, exaggerates the perceived amount of uncertainty, because it grows exponentially with linearly growing independent possibilities. Furthermore, we would like all measures to be numbers between 0 and 1. We therefore propose the *uncertainty density* as a measure for the amount of uncertainty in a database. It is based on the average number of alternatives per choice point:

$$\text{Dens} = 1 - \frac{1}{N_{cp}} \sum_{j=1}^{N_{cp}} \frac{1}{N_{poss,j}}$$

Dens is 0 for a databases that contains no uncertainty. Dens decreases if there is more certain data in the database for the same amount of uncertain data (compare Figures 2(a) and 2(b)). Dens rises if a choice point contains more alternatives (compare Figures 2(b) and 2(c)). If all choice points contain n alternatives, Dens is $(1 - \frac{1}{n})$, which approaches 1 with growing n. The uncertainty density is independent of the probabilities in the database. It can be used, for example, to relate query execution times to, because query execution times most probabily depend on the number of alternatives to consider.

3.2   Answer Decisiveness

Even if there is much uncertainty, if one possible world has a very high probability, then any query posed to this uncertain database will have one, easy to distinguish, most probable answer. We say that this database has a high *answer decisiveness*. In contrast, if there is much uncertainty and the probabilities are rather evenly distributed over the possible worlds, then possible answers to queries will be likely to have similar probabilities. We have defined the answer decisiveness as

$$Dec = \frac{1}{N_{cp}} \sum_{j=1}^{N_{cp}} \frac{P_j^{max}}{(2 - P_j^{max}) \times \log_2(max(2, N_{poss,j}))}$$

Dec is 1 for a database that contains no uncertainty, because each term in the sum becomes $\frac{1}{(2-1)\times\log_2 2} = 1$. If at each choice point j with two alternatives, there is one with a probability close to one (i.e., P_j^{max} is close 1), then all terms for j are also close to 1 and Dec is still almost 1. When P_j^{max} drops for some j, then Dec drops as well. Dec also drops when choice points occur with growing numbers of alternatives. This is accomplished by the $\log_2(max(2, N_{poss,j}))$ factor (compare Figures 2(b) and 2(c)). We have taken the logarithm to make it decrease gradually.

3.3   Answer Quality

Querying uncertain data results in answers containing uncertainty. Therefore, an answer is not correct or incorrect in the traditional sense of a database query. We need a more subtle notion of answer quality.

In the possible world approach, an uncertain answer represents a set of possible answers each with an associated probability. In Trio, it is possible to work with alternatives without probabilities, but these can be considered as equally likely, hence with uniformly distributed probabilities. The set of possible answers ranked according to probability has much in common with the result of an information retrieval query. We therefore base our answer quality measure on precision and recall [1]. We adapt these notions, however, by taking into account the probabilities of the possible answers. Correct answers with high probability are better than correct answers with a low probability. Analogously, incorrect answers with a high probability are worse than incorrect answers with a low probability.

XQuery answers are always sequences. The possible answers to an XQuery on an uncertain document, however, largely contain the same elements. Therefore, we construct an amalgamated answer by merging and ranking the elements of all possible answers. This can be accomplished in XQuery with the function in Figure 3. The effectiveness of this approach to querying a probabilistic database can be illustrated with an example. Suppose we query a probabilistic movie database asking for horror movies: `//movie[.//genre="Horror"]/title`. Even though the integrated document may contain thousands of possible worlds, the amalgamated answer is restricted to the available movie titles considered to be possibly belonging to a horror movie, which will be few in number.

```
declare function rank_results($pws as element(world)*)
    as element(answer)*
{
    for $v in distinct-values($pws/descendant::text())
    let $ws := $pws[./descendant::text()[.=$v]]
        ,$rank := sum($ws/@prob)
    order by $rank descending
    return <answer rank="{$rank}">{$v}</answer>
};
```

Fig. 3. XQuery function for ranking query results

Precision and recall are traditionally computed by looking at the presence of correct and incorrect answers. Let H be the set of correct answers to a query (as determined by a human), A the set of answers (the elements of the amalgamated query answer), and C the intersection of the two, i.e., the set of correct answers produced by the system (see Figure 4).

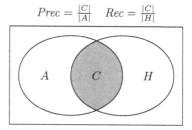

$$Prec = \frac{|C|}{|A|} \quad Rec = \frac{|C|}{|H|}$$

Fig. 4. Precision and recall

We adapt the precision and recall measures by taking into account the probabilities: An answer a is only present in the amount prescribed by its probability $P(a)$. This reasoning gives us the following definitions for precision and recall.

$$Prec = \frac{\sum_{a \in C} P(a)}{|C| + \sum_{a \in (A-C)} P(a)} \qquad Rec = \frac{\sum_{a \in C} P(a)}{|H|}$$

For example, say the answer to the query "Give me all horror movies" is "Jaws" and "Jaws 2". If the system returns this answer, but with a confidence of 90% for both movies, then precision and recall are both 90%. If, however, it also gives some other (incorrect) movie with a confidence of 20%, then precision drops to 82% and recall stays 90%.

4 Experiments

4.1 Set Up

The contributions of this paper are the uncertainty density, decisiveness, and answer quality measures. The purpose of the experiments hence is not to validate or compare systems or techniques, but an evaluation of the behavior of the measures to validate their usefulness.

As application of uncertainty in data, we selected data integration. In our research on IMPrECISE, we attempt to develop data management functionality for uncertain data to be used for this application area. When data sources contain data overlap, i.e., they contain data items referring to the same real world

name	repr.	#pws	#nodes
2x2	tree	16	469
4x4	tree	2,944	7,207
6x6	tree	33,856	25,201
6x9	tree	2,258,368	334,616
2x2 +rule	tree	4	328
4x4 +rule	tree	64	2,792
6x6 +rule	tree	256	8,328
6x9 +rule	tree	768	21,608
6x15 +rule	tree	3,456	87,960
2x2	dag	16	372
4x4	dag	2,944	1,189
6x6	dag	33,856	2,196
6x9	dag	2,258,368	13,208
2x2 +rule	dag	4	280
4x4 +rule	dag	64	761
6x6 +rule	dag	256	1,243
6x9 +rule	dag	768	1,954
6x15 +rule	dag	3,456	4,737

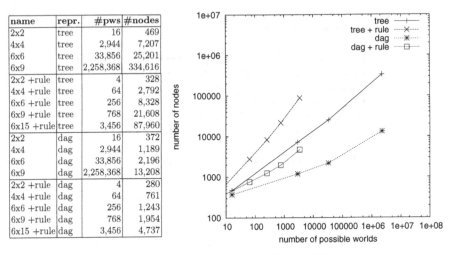

Fig. 5. Data sets (pws = possible worlds)

objects, they may conflict and it is not certain which of the sources holds the correct information. Moreover, without human involvement, it is usually not possible for a data integration system to establish with certainty which data items refer to the same real world objects. To allow for unattended data integration, it is imperative that the data integration system can handle this uncertainty and that the resulting (uncertain) integrated source can be used in a meaningful way.

The data set we selected concerns movie data: Data set 'IMDB' is obtained from the Internet Movie DataBase from which we converted title, year, genre and director data to XML. Data set 'Peggy' is obtained from an MPEG-7 data source of unknown but definitely independent origin. We selected those movies from these sources that create a lot confusion: sequels, documentaries, etc. of 'Jaws', 'Die Hard', and 'Mission Impossible'. Since the titles of these data items look alike, the data integration system often needs to consider the possibility of those data items referring to the same real-world objects, thus creating much uncertainty in the integration result. The integrated result is an XML document according to the aforementioned probabilistic tree technique [6].

To create integrated data sets of different sizes and different amounts of uncertainty, we integrated 2 with 2 movies selected from the sources, 4 with 4, 6 with 6, and 6 with 15 movies. We furthermore performed this integration with (indicated as '+rule') and without a specific additional rule that enables the integration system to much better distinguish data about different movies. This results in data sets with different characteristics. To be able to investigate uncertainty density, we additionally experiment with the data represented as tree as well as DAG. Although our implementation of the DAG representation does not produce the most optimally compact DAG yet, it suffices to experiment with its effect on uncertainty density. See Figure 5 for details of the data sets and an indication of the compactness of the representation.

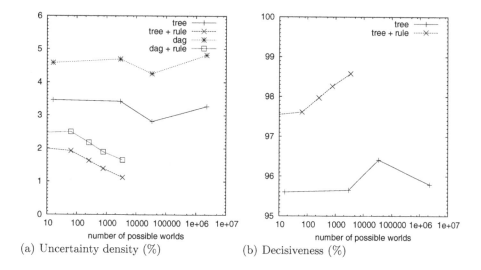

(a) Uncertainty density (%)   (b) Decisiveness (%)

Fig. 6. Uncertainty density and decisiveness

4.2 Uncertainty Density

Figure 6(a) shows the uncertainty density for our data sets. There is a number of things to observe.

- Density values are generally rather low. This is due to the fact that integration produces uncertain data with mostly choice points with only one alternative (certain data) and relatively few with two alternatives (uncertain data). For example, the '6x9 tree' case has 74191 choice points with one alternative and 5187 choice points with two alternatives.
- When comparing the lines for 'tree' with 'dag', and 'tree + rule' with 'dag + rule', we observe that the dag-versions have a considerable higher uncertainty density. This can be explained by the fact that the DAG representation shares common subtrees. Most commonality appears for certain data that occurs in all possible worlds. Hence, *relatively* more nodes are devoted to uncertainty in the DAG representation. The uncertainty density measure correctly exhibits this behavior.
- When comparing the lines for 'tree' with 'tree + rule', and 'dag' with 'dag + rule', we observe that the additional rule not only reduces the number of possible worlds, but also reduces the uncertainty density. The knowledge of the rule reduces uncertainty, but the amount of certain information stays the same. Therefore, it is logical that the uncertainty density goes down.
- The '+ rule' lines drop with growing database size, while the other two do not. Database growth in this experiment means additional movies in both data sources. The specific rule we used in this experiment helps the integration system to determine which pairs of data items from both sources cannot possibly refer to the same real world object. The density measure

correctly shows that the additional movies cause relatively more confusion without the rule than with it.

In general, we can say that important characteristics concerning the amount of uncertainty in the database can be assessed successfully with the uncertainty density measure. Moreover, it does not suffer from the disadvantage of exaggeration that the number of possible worlds has.

4.3   Answer Decisiveness

Figure 6(b) shows the answer decisiveness for our data sets. This experiment focuses on the tree representation only, because the answers produced by a query is independent of the representation, hence the answer decisiveness does not depend on the representation. There are a number of things to observe.

- Decisiveness values are generally rather high. This has the same reason as why density is generally low: there are mostly choice points with only one alternative and few with two alternative, hence in most cases it is easy to make a choice for an answer because there is only one to choose from.
- Similar patterns in the lines for decisiveness can be observed when comparing with uncertainty density. Both measures are related, because the more alternatives per choice point on average, the higher the uncertainty density, but also the lower the decisiveness. Decisiveness only starts to deviate from density if the associated probabilities ensure that it is easy to choose the most likely possible answer. The probability assignment logic in our system, however, is still in its infancy and is apparently not capable of giving good decisiveness despite high uncertainty density.

The relationship between the density and decisiveness measures is illustrated by Figure 7. The straight line marked 'uniform distribution' is drawn for the situation where the probabilities are always uniformly distributed and, for simplicity, where there are only choice points with at most two alternatives (which is the case for our test data and which makes the line straight). In this situation, uncertainty density fully determines answer decisiveness. The fact that the lines are not on the straight line shows that the probability assignment logic of our system has some impact on decisiveness despite the uncertainty den-

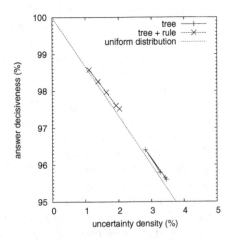

Fig. 7. Density vs. Decisiveness

sity, but the impact is (as expected) rather limited. We expect that an integration system with better probability assignment logic will produce points much higher

Table 1. Answer quality ('X' marks an incorrect answer)

(a) Query 1: `//movie[.//genre="Horror"]/title` (All horror movies)

Poll.	P(a)	Answer	Prec	Rec
2	79.4%	"Jaws"	79.4%	79.4%
	79.4%	"Jaws 2"		
5	77.4%	"Jaws"	69.5%	77.4%
	77.4%	"Jaws 2"		
	22.6% X	"Ma@ing of Steven Spielberg's 'Jaws', The"		
10	85.4%	"Jaws"	74.5%	85.4%
	85.4%	"Jaws 2"		
	29.2% X	"Ma@ing of Steven Spielberg's 'Jaws', The"		
20	85.4%	"Jaws"	74.5%	42.7%
	14.6% X	"Ma@ing of Steven Spielberg's 'Jaws', The"		

(b) Query 2: `//movie[./year="1995"]/title` (All movies produced in 1995)

Poll.	P(a)	Answer	Prec	Rec
2	100.0%	"Die Hard: With a Vengeance"	100.0%	100.0%
	100.0%	"Behind the Scenes: Die Hard - With a Vengeance"		
	100.0%	"Making of Steven Spielberg's 'Jaws', The"		
5	79.4%	"Die Hard: With a Vengeance"	56.3%	64.3%
	58.8%	"Behind the Scenes: Die Hard - With a Vengeance"		
	54.8%	"Making of Steven Spielberg's 'Jaws', The"		
	20.6% X	"Behind th@ Scenes: Die Hard - With a Vengeance"		
	11.3% X	"Ma@ing of Steven Spielberg's 'Jaws', The"		
	5.6% X	"Jaws"		
	5.6% X	"Jaws 2"		
10	85.4%	"Die Hard: With a Vengeance"	47.1%	56.3%
	41.7%	"Behind the Scenes: Die Hard - With a Vengeance"		
	41.7%	"Making of Steven Spielberg's 'Jaws', The"		
	21.9% X	"Behind th@ Scenes: Die Hard - With a Vengeance"		
	14.6% X	"Ma@ing of Steven Spielberg's 'Jaws', The"		
	7.3% X	"Jaws"		
	7.3% X	"Jaws 2"		
	7.3% X	"Die Hard 2"		
20	78.1%	"Die Hard: With a Vengeance"	52.6%	53.8%
	41.7%	"Behind the Scenes: Die Hard - With a Vengeance"		
	41.7%	"Making of Steven Spielberg's 'Jaws', The"		
	7.3% X	"Behind th@ Scenes: Die Hard - With a Vengeance"		

(c) Query 3: `//movie[./title="Jaws 2"]/year` (When has Jaws 2 been produced?)

Poll.	P(a)	Answer	Prec	Rec
2	69.1%	"1978"	62.6%	69.1%
	10.3% X	"1975"		
5	66.1%	"1978"	59.4%	66.1%
	5.6% X	"1975"		
	5.6% X	"1995"		
10	78.1%	"1978"	72.8%	78.1%
	7.3% X	"1995"		
20	78.1% X	"197@"	0.0%	0.0%
	7.3% X	"@995"		

in the graph. Most importantly, the decisiveness measure can be effectively used to measure the quality of the probability assignment logic.

4.4 Answer Quality

To obtain test data suitable for evaluating our answer quality measure, we took one of the data sources: an IMDB document with 9 movies. We made two copies of it, randomly polluted them by corrupting text nodes, and then integrated them. We made sure we didn't pollute the same text nodes, so 'the truth' is still available in the combined data of both sources and an ideal integration system would be able to reconstruct it. We furthermore took three queries and posed them to the data integration result of data sources with increasing pollution. A pollution of 2 means that 2 randomly chosen text nodes in both source have been corrupted by changing a randomly chosen character to '@'. This pollution not only affects the data integration, also in some of the answers we see these modified strings appear. Although they are seemingly almost correct, we classified these answers as incorrect.

Table 1 shows the answer quality measurements for the three queries. Even though our system produces the correct answers in most cases, the confidence scores the system produces are rather modest. This is due to the naive probability assignment explained earlier. Our adapted precision and recall measures effectively reflect this aspect of reduced answer quality. Missing answers (as in Query 1 / Pollution 20, and Query 3 / Pollution 20) is of course worse than just modest confidence scores; indeed radically lower recall is given to these cases.

5   Conclusions

In this paper we introduced several new measures for assessment and comparison of important characteristics of uncertain data and uncertain data management systems: uncertainty density, decisiveness, and modifications of two existing answer quality measures, precision and recall.

In contrast with the number of possible worlds as a measure for the amount of uncertainty present in the database, the uncertainty density measure doesn't exaggerate this uncertainty. The uncertainty density is based on the average number of alternatives per choice point, hence it also takes into account the amount of certain data.

The answer decisiveness is an indication how well in general a most likely answer can be distinguished among a set of possible answers. Even in the presence of much uncertainty, if one possible world has very high probability, then any query posed to this uncertain database will have one easily distinguishable most likely answer. The decisiveness is an indication of how well the confidence scores in the document were assigned. The ratio between decisiveness and density also shows this fact. The ratio can be used to evaluate how much the probabilities deviate from uniform distribution, i.e., how much the system tends to confidently give a high probability to one answer, hence aiding the user or application in selecting the most probable answer.

High decisiveness does of course not mean that the answers the system so adamantly claims to be the most probable ones, are indeed the correct answers. Therefore, we introduced adapted precision and recall measures to evaluate answer quality which takes into account the probabilities assigned to the answers.

6   Future Research

As a next step of this research, we plan to improve IMPrECISE and validate the improvements using the quality measures. For this purpose, a central component in the system which assigns the probabilities, called "The Oracle", has to be improved. "The Oracle" determines, at integration time, how likely it is that two elements refer to the same real world object. An improved "Oracle" will give a increased values for decisiveness, precision and recall.

The current DAG implementation does not produce the most compact representation of uncertain data possible. We have identified some patterns that can be used to improve the current implementation.

One of the reasons for inefficiency in querying at the moment, is confidence computation. In order to speed up this process we plan to investigate if provenance, or lineage as used in Trio is suitable for our model.

Another item on our agenda is to release IMPrECISE as a module of MonetDB/XQuery. Before we can do this, the probabilistic query functionality has to be extended and some operators and functions dealing with the confidences associated with possibility nodes, have to be made available.

References

1. Baeza-Yates, R., Ribeiro-Neto, B.: Modern Information Retrieval. Addison Wesley, Reading (1999)
2. Boncz, P.A., Grust, T., van Keulen, M., Manegold, S., Rittinger, J., Teubner, J.: MonetDB/XQuery: a fast XQuery processor powered by a relational engine. In: Proc. of SIGMOD, Chicago, IL, USA, pp. 479–490 (2006)
3. Boulos, J., Dalvi, N.N., Mandhani, B., Mathur, S., Re, C., Suciu, D.: MYSTIQ: a system for finding more answers by using probabilities. In: Proc. of SIGMOD, Baltimore, Maryland, USA, pp. 891–893 (2005)
4. Cheng, R., Singh, S., Prabhakar, S.: U-DBMS: A database system for managing constantly-evolving data. In: Proc. of VLDB, Trondheim, Norway, pp. 1271–1274 (2005)
5. Hung, E., Getoor, L., Subrahmanian, V.S.: PXML: A probabilistic semistructured data model and algebra. In: Proc. of ICDE, Bangalore, India, pp. 467–478 (2003)
6. van Keulen, M., de Keijzer, A., Alink, W.: A probabilistic xml approach to data integration. In: Proc. of ICDE, Tokyo, Japan, pp. 459–470 (2005)
7. Mutsuzaki, M., Theobald, M., de Keijzer, A., Widom, J., Agrawal, P., Benjelloun, O., Sarma, A.D., Murthy, R., Sugihara, T.: Trio-One: Layering uncertainty and lineage on a conventional DBMS. In: Proc. of CIDR, Monterey, USA, pp. 269–274 (2007)

Learning Different User Profile Annotated Rules for Fuzzy Preference Top-k Querying

A. Eckhardt, T. Horváth, and P. Vojtáš

Charles University, P. J. Šafárik University, Czech Academy of Science
Alan.Eckhardt@mff.cuni.cz, Tomas.Horvath@upjs.sk,
vojtas@cs.cas.cz

Abstract. Uncertainty querying of large data can be solved by providing top-k answers according to a user fuzzy ranking/scoring function. Usually different users have different fuzzy scoring function – a user preference model. Main goal of this paper is to assign a user a preference model automatically. To achieve this we decompose user's fuzzy ranking function to ordering of particular attributes and to a combination function. To solve the problem of automatic assignment of user model we design two algorithms, one for learning user preference on particular attribute and second for learning the combination function. Methods were integrated into a Fagin-like top-k querying system with some new heuristics and tested.

1 Introduction and Motivation

Huge amount of data accessible to different users with different preferences and context are a challenge for both uncertainty modeling and query optimization. We are addressing two problems – size of data represented in an uncertainty model and different user profiles. In this paper we use as a running example following data (in a real application this can be a sample for learning user preferences).

Table 1. Illustrative example

| Hotels properties | | | | Users evaluation | | | |
| | | | | User1 | | User 2 | |
Name	Distance	Price	Equipment	grade	num.	grade	num.
Apple	100 m	99 $	nothing	poor	1	poor	1
Danube	1300 m	120 $	tv	good	2	poor	1
Cherry	500 m	99 $	Internet	good	2	good	2
Iris	1100 m	35 $	internet, tv	excellent	3	excellent	3
Lemon	500 m	149 $	nothing	poor	1	excellent	3
Linden	1200 m	60 $	internet, tv	excellent	3	poor	1
Oak	500 m	149 $	internet, tv	good	2	excellent	3
Pear	500 m	99 $	tv	good	2	good	2
Poplar	100 m	99 $	internet, tv	good	2	poor	1
Rhine	500 m	99 $	nothing	poor	1	good	2
Rose	500 m	99 $	internet, tv	excellent	3	good	2
Spruce	300 m	40 $	internet	good	2	good	2
Themse	100 m	149 $	internet, tv	poor	1	poor	1
Tulip	800 m	45 $	internet, tv	excellent	3	good	2

H. Prade and V.S. Subrahmanian (Eds.): SUM 2007, LNAI 4772, pp. 116–130, 2007.

To illustrate our approach, imagine two users evaluating these hotels, using linguistic expressions (here also represented by natural number, later embedded into [0,1]). We want to create a general user model from these evaluations. This model will be used when performing top-k query on the database. Without this model, user has to state his/her preferences explicitly, which is often found annoying by most users.

We would like to have a solution with a formal model and practical usability. We look for the simplest solution which is still sufficient for user requirements. We suggest using some formalism with monotone rules. Nevertheless our data are usually not monotone, indeed projection of hotel evaluation to price and distance attributes in our example looks like

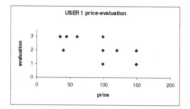 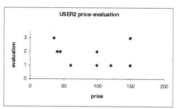

Fig. 1. Projections of attributes of objects to evaluation

Main contributions of this paper are

- a proposal of a method specifying attribute domain ordering in such a way, that user evaluation can be described by monotone rules according to these orderings which can be found in Section 3.1
- an inductive method for generalized annotated programs working on a fuzzy completion of data (hence able to find rules between attributes with different fuzzy/preference degrees) located in Sections 2.4 and 3.2
- efficient heuristics for finding top-k answers tested on an implementation and evaluated on experiments, studied in Section 4.1

First and second contribution are illustrated in following table.

Table 2. Rules corresponding to table 1

```
user_1_evaluation = excellent  IF distance >= 500 AND price <= 99 AND
equipment=tv AND equipment=internet

user_1_evaluation = good IF (distance >= 300 AND equipment=tv) OR
(price <= 120 AND equipment=internet)

user_2_evaluation = excellent  IF distance ∈ <300;1100> AND price ∈
<35;35> ∪ <149;149>

user_2_evaluation = good IF distance ∈ <300;1100>
```

Advantage of our method is that our rules can mix different fuzzy degrees in rule head and body (here hidden in generated domain ordering).

The task of creating rules of user preferences is for obtaining a global ordering of data. However, if the size of data is very large, we can not compute the user rating for every object. This deductive step is based on [5] which allows handling large data sets without the need to process every object separately. The typical query got from user will be of the form: "Show me the five most appealing hotels". We need only to find the best five hotels in database.

2 Models

We would like to base our solution in concordance with formal models and have our solution transferable to other domains and systems (this is not a proprietary solution for a specific domain nor a direct querying of a relational database).

2.1 Representation of Preferences and the Data Model

We work with the usual relational data model and would like to have model theoretic, proof theoretic and fixpoint semantics. Just for purpose of this paper we assume a set of attributes $A_1,...,A_n$ with attribute domains $D_1,...,D_n$ (e.g. A_1=distance, D_1=[100,1300]). The identificator is denoted by A with domain D (here A=Hotel, D={Apple, Danube,...}).

We work with user preferences being total (linear) orders here. Our position is that having partially ordered preferences (without contradictions, cycles) we can proceed with a linear extension of this (note that using the axiom of choice, any partial ordering can be extended to a linear one). We use finite subsets of the unit interval of real numbers [0, 1] for preference degrees.

For arbitrary set X, we use a fuzzy function f: $X \rightarrow [0, 1]$ as a representation of ordering $x <_f y$ iff $f(x) < f(y)$.

We assume we have extensional data in one table $R \subseteq D \times \prod D_i$ in which D attribute is a key (i.e. object attribute model where an object of interest is represented by uniquely assigned values, here $\prod$ denotes Cartesian product, indeces running through 1,...,n). For a tuple $(x, \mathbf{x}) \in R$, where $\mathbf{x} = (x_1, ..., x_n) \in \prod D_i$ this generates a mapping $data_R : D \rightarrow \prod D_i$.

Our model assumes that we have an evaluation of objects for each user u_j, which can be represented as a fuzzy function $f_A^{u_j} : D \rightarrow [0,1]$ with generated global ordering $<_{f_A^{u_j}}$ of domain D of classified attribute A generated by user (the ordering is sometimes written as $<_A^{u_j}$).

First step of our solution assumes (depending on user u_j) attribute domains D_i and orderings $<_{A_i}^{u_j}$ such that users evaluation, data mapping and induced @ are not contradictory and build a monotone mapping e such that following diagram #1 commutes (i.e. object with same properties are evaluated equally).

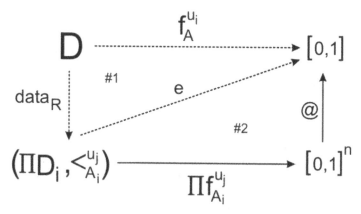

Fig. 2. Commutative diagram

Further we assume these orderings $<^{u_j}_{A_i}$ can be represented by fuzzy functions $f^{u_j}_{A_i}$. Let us note that these are very strong assumptions in general, in practice for finite domains and a finite subset of [0, 1], $f^{u_j}_{A_i}$ is often possible to find (subject to some decrease of precision of our method).

Finally, to complete the commutative diagram #2, we have to find a fuzzy aggregation function (an annotation function) @: $[0,1]^n \rightarrow [0,1]$ such that above diagram commutes.

This is an order theoretic content of our induction method. To have sound model and proof theoretic semantics we need some formal models.

2.2 Different Models of Logic Programming

In this paragraph, we describe two formal models of logic programming. We need them both, because first is more appropriate for deductive tasks and the second is more suitable for induction.

Fuzzy logic programming. In fuzzy (many valued) logic we refer to [9] and [13], we work with fuzzy logic in narrow sense, i.e. a truth functional many valued logic. In our example atoms can be predicate hotels_properties, or its decomposition to binary predicates hotel_distance, hotel_price, hotel_equipment and also user_1_evaluation (or also with propositionalization of these).

Note that truth functions of fuzzy conjunctions & and disjunctions ∨ are all fuzzy aggregation operators (so it suffices do deal with them). A fuzzy aggregation operator @ is an n-ary operation and has truth function @$^\bullet$, which is order preserving. Usually we assume that @$^\bullet$(0,...,0) = 0 and @$^\bullet$(1,...,1) = 1 hold, but sometimes we relax these.

Implications $\rightarrow_1, ..., \rightarrow_n$ have truth functions implicators $I_1 = \rightarrow_1^\bullet, ..., I_n = \rightarrow_n^\bullet$. Any formula built from atoms using aggregations is called a *body* $\boldsymbol{B} = @(B_1,... ,B_n)$. A *rule* of fuzzy logic programming (FLP) is a graded implication (H ← @(B₁,...,Bₙ).r), where H is an atom called *head*, @(B₁,...,Bₙ) is a body and r∈Q∩[0,1] is a rational number. Note that we do not have negation here (it is hidden in the choice of attribute domain ordering). A *fact* is a graded atom *(B.b)*. A finite set P of FLP rules and facts is said to be a *fuzzy logic program.*

Let $\mathcal{B}_L$ be the Herbrand base. A mapping f: $\mathcal{B}_L \rightarrow [0,1]$ is said to be a *fuzzy Herbrand interpretation*, f can be extended to $\hat{f}$ all formulas along the complexity of formula using the truth function of connectives. A graded formula $(\varphi.x)$ is *true in an interpretation* f

$$f \models_{FLP} \varphi.x \quad iff \quad \hat{f}(\varphi) \geq x.$$

A pair $(x;\theta)$ consisting of a real number $0 < x \leq 1$ and a substitution θ (substituting for some, not necessary all, domain variables) is a *correct answer* for a program P and a query "?-A" if for arbitrary interpretation f, which is a model of P, we have $f(\forall A\theta) \geq x$ (here $0 \forall A\theta$ denotes the denotes the universal quantification of remaining free variables in $A\theta$ (θ need not to bound all variables)).

In [13] the computational model uses conjunctors $C_1,...,C_n$ residual to implicators, $I_1, ..., I_n$, *fuzzy modus ponens* [9] .

$$\{(B.\ b), (H \leftarrow_I B.\ r)\} \models_{FLP} (H.\ C_i(b,r))$$

Our semantics is sound and approximately complete (see [13]). We have also fixpoint semantics based on Datalog production operator corresponding relational model was studied in [15].

In this paper the computational part of the deduction (querying) model will be based on some heuristics making the query answering more efficient and still preserving the semantics.

Generalized annotated programs. In [12] M. Kifer and V. S. Subrahmanian introduced generalized annotated logic programs (GAP). GAP unifies and generalizes various results and treatments of many valued logic programming.

The language of GAP also consists of qualitative and quantitative parts. The qualitative part is the usual language of predicate logic. The quantitative part of the language consists of annotation terms. If A is an atomic formula and α is an annotation term, then A:α is an *annotated atom*. If $\alpha \in [0, 1]$ then A:α is constant-annotated (or c-annotated). When α is an annotation variable, then A:α is said to be variable-annotated (or v-annotated).

If A:ρ is a possibly complex annotated atom and $B_1:\mu_1$, ..., $B_k:\mu_k$ are variable-annotated atoms, then A:$\rho(\mu_1, ..., \mu_k) \leftarrow B_1:\mu_1 \& ... \& B_k:\mu_k$ is an *annotated clause*.

Let us note, here we restrict to rules with atoms in the body of a rule have only variable annotations (to avoid problems with discontinuous restricted semantics). Only facts can have constant annotations.

Herbrand base B_L and interpretations f: $B_L \rightarrow [0,1]$ are same as in FLP. Suppose f: $B_L \rightarrow [0,1]$ is an interpretation, $\mu \in [0,1]$ and A is ground atom, then f $\models_{GAP}$ A:μ, i.e. f is a *model* of A:μ iff $f(A) \geq \mu$. The rest of satisfaction is defined similarly as in the two valued logic. Especially an annotated rule is true in the interpretation f

$$f \models_{GAP} A:\rho\ (\mu_1, ..., \mu_k) \leftarrow B_1:\mu_1 \& ... \& B_k:\mu_k$$

if for all assignments e of annotation variables we have

$$f(A) \geq_A \rho(e(\mu_1), ..., e(\mu_k)) \leftarrow f(B_1) \geq_{B1} e(\mu_1) \& ... \& f(B_k) \geq_{Bk} e(\mu_k)$$

Equivalence of FLP and GAP programs. In [13] we have introduced following transformations :

Assume C= A:$\rho \leftarrow B_1:\mu_1$ &... ...& $B_k:\mu_k$ is an annotated clause. Then flp(C) is the fuzzy rule A$\leftarrow \rho(B_1,...,B_k)$.1, here ρ is understood as an n-ary aggregator operator.

Assume D = A$\leftarrow_i$ @$(B_1,...,B_n)$.r is a fuzzy logic program rule. Then gap(D) is the annotated clause A:$C_i($@$(x_1,...,x_n),r) \leftarrow B_1:x_1,...,B_n:x_n$ (we abstract from technical details here, more in [13]).

In [13] the following is proved. Assume C is an annotated clause, D is a fuzzy logic program rule and f is a fuzzy Herbrand interpretation. Then

$$f \text{ is a model of C iff f is a model of flp(C),}$$
$$f \text{ is a model of D iff f is a model of gap(C)}$$

Transformations can be extended also to programs and in this case they have same computed answers (in substitutional semantics of [13]).

2.3 Induction

An extension of classical Inductive Logic Programming (ILP) [3] task to our many-valued Fuzzy Logic Programming model (FLP) is considered in our approach. We call this task Fuzzy Inductive Logic Programming (FILP) [10]. The most important requirement to FILP is that its formal model must be a generalization of the classical ones (as our many valued logic is a generalization of the classical one).

When *learning from entailment*, given is a set of examples E = P $\cup$ N, consisting of positive P and negative N examples (facts). Given is the background knowledge B (definite program). The task is to find a hypothesis H (definite clauses), such that the following conditions hold:

($\forall e \in$ P) H$\land$B $\models$ e *(crisp-completeness of H)*
($\forall e \in$ N) H$\land$B $\not\models$ e *(crisp-consistency of H)*

In the previous chapter we defined concepts necessary to formulate the FILP task (i.e. fuzzy Herbrand interpretation, fuzzy definite clause, fuzzy model ...). These allow us to define the FILP task taking into account that it has to be a generalization of the classical ILP task. We face a problem. A straightforward rewriting of classical ILP definition does not make sense because we have no clear positive and negative examples. From the semantics of truth values (see previous chapter) it is clear, that e:$\alpha \in$ E holds in all degrees $\alpha' \leq \alpha$ and need not hold in all degrees $\alpha'' > \alpha$. Thus the conditions of completeness and consistency will be different from the classical ones.

When learning from fuzzy entailment, given is a set of fuzzy examples E (fuzzy facts). Given is the fuzzy background knowledge B (fuzzy definite program). The task is to find a fuzzy hypothesis H (fuzzy definite clauses), such that the following conditions hold:

($\forall e.\alpha \in$ E) H$\land$B $\models_{FLP}$ e.α *(fuzzy-completeness of H)*
($\forall e.\alpha \in$ E) ($\forall \beta > \alpha$) H$\land$B $\not\models_{FLP}$ e.β *(fuzzy-consistency of H)*

Nevertheless, these definitions seem to be very similar but they are still very different. First, the fuzzy meaning of a model, entailment, fact, definite program and definite clause differ from the classical meaning of these concepts. Second, in the FILP task we do not have only positive and negative examples. Indeed we have examples with truth values belonging to the interval [0, 1]. However, the FILP task differs more from the classical ones it still remains its generalization (the proof is in [10]).

As we see, the deductive part of FLP is computationally not difficult, because we know all truth functions of connectives and aggregations. In the inductive part it is the opposite. In the beginning of induction we have just the known connectives or aggregations. But these need not to fit the data we are learning from. There can be (infinitely) many unknown types of connectives and aggregations (and thus hypotheses) our data correspond to.

There can be several approaches to solve the FILP task. For example, we can use just the known connectives, aggregations, and try to find some hypotheses. Another approach can be the genetic algorithms, where we can find some previously unknown connectives, aggregations in rules. We can construct several approaches by this way. All these approaches need to implement an own deductive part, because the inference is different from the classical Prolog inference (even though the fuzzy inference rules are the generalization of the Prolog inference rules).

Our approach to FILP task is to induce Generalized Annotated Programs (GAP) where we use the equivalence of FLP and GAP and the fact that GAP deals just with crisp connectives.

We construct an alternative approach to our FILP task as follows: we transform FILP task to Inductive Generalized Annotated Programming (IGAP) task [10]. We find an IGAP hypothesis (GAP program) which we transform back to FILP hypothesis (FLP program).

When learning from GAP entailment, given is a set of GAP examples E (GAP facts). Given is the GAP background knowledge B (GAP definite program). The task is to find a GAP hypothesis H (GAP definite clauses), such that the following conditions hold:

$$(\forall e.\alpha \in E) \; H \wedge B \models_{GAP} e.\alpha \; (\textit{gap-completeness of } H)$$
$$(\forall e.\alpha \in E) \; (\forall \beta > \alpha) \; H \wedge B \not\models_{GAP} e.\beta \; (\textit{gap-consistency of } H)$$

3   Methods

In previous chapter we have introduce semantic models. Nevertheless these are not very efficient when implemented. In this chapter we describe methods which were implemented and tested and still preserving the semantics of our FLP and GAP programs.

3.1   Learning Local Preferences

First step needed in our method is the monotonization of data. For each body attribute A_i we have to find an ordering $<_{A_i}^{u_j}$ (generating fuzzy function $<_{f_{A_i}^{u_j}}$ resp.) which enables to find monotone GAP rules explaining to global object evaluation. Main problem is whether the overall evaluation of a hotel depends on the price according to some ordering (e.g. expressed by fuzzy linguistic values small, large, medium,…).

There are several known methods for monotonization, for example we can use linear (e.g. giving fuzzy functions small or large) or quadratic regression (e.g. giving fuzzy functions medium (cup) or boundary (cap)). These methods return the fuzzy function, which is then used as the ordering of domain. However, when data are not distributed uniformly across the attribute domain, regression may make wrong results. Suppose that we have much more hotels with small price than hotels with medium price and hotels with large price are only few. With least square regression, each hotel is treated equivalently, so the regression will fit mostly to cheap hotels, while more costly hotels are neglected. The error of regression however will be acceptable, because there are only few costly hotels.

Discretization of attribute domain. Because of these reasons, we propose a new method to handle complicated distributions of objects across the attribute domain. We illustrate our method on determining the ordering of the attribute domain price for user 1 and user 2. First, we need to discretize the attribute domain. Neither equidistant nor equipotent method is good for our purpose. The best are intervals corresponding to overall notion of small, medium and large price (we do not consider fuzzy partitions in this paper). We obtain intervals $[35,70),[70,100)$ and $[100,150)$. We associate a number with each rating – poor = 1, good = 2 and excellent = 3. Then the process continues with computing the average of all ratings of hotels with the price in a certain interval.

$$\text{Pref}_{User1}([35,70)) = \frac{\sum\limits_{\substack{h \in Hotels \\ price(h) \in [35,70)}} \text{Pref}_{User1}(h)}{\sum\limits_{\substack{h \in Hotels \\ price(h) \in [35,70)}} 1} = (3*3+1*2)/4 = 10/4$$

Computation above is made for all intervals, thus we get a representative rating for every interval for every user.

Determining the ordering of discretized domain. Now, on a discretized attribute domain, a traditional method for regression is used, working with representants for each interval. The problem is what values to use as x-coordinate of representants of interval i. The middle of interval i may be used, but more suitable will be the average price of hotels in i (or some other clustering method). Then, the tuple {representant, the average price of hotels in i} forms the centroid of hotels in i.

As we can see in Figure 3, the trend is clearly decreasing for User 1, while for User 2, his/her ordering is more complicated, corresponding to fuzzy border values.

As we work only with four types of fuzzy functions (small, large, medium, border), the quadratic regression is most suitable for us.

Note that main purpose of our attribute ordering is to monotonize our data and make the inductive rule learning better corresponding to user preferences. So measures of learning quality are the parameter we optimize here.

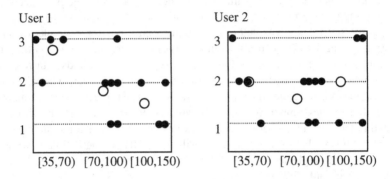

Fig. 3. Representants for different users

3.2 IGAP

Our approach to IGAP is based on multiple use of a classical ILP system with monotonicity axioms in the background knowledge (illustrated in algorithm 1 [10]).

Algorithm 1. Our fuzzy completion translation method for IGAP

Input: Annotated E, Annotated B, Ordering of Attributes.
Output: Annotated H.
  1. Initialize the two-valued hypothesis $H^* = \varnothing$.
  2. Find out every n classes of truth values which are present in E ($TV_1 < \ldots < TV_n$).
  3. Find out every $m_1, \ldots, m_k$ classes of truth values which are present in B for every predicate $p_1, \ldots, p_k$ ($TVp_{1,1} < \ldots < TVp_{1,m1}, \ldots, TVp_{k,1} < \ldots < TVp_{k,mk}$).
  4. Transform the annotated background knowledge B to a two-valued background knowledge B^* by an extra attribute TV ($p_i(x_1, \ldots, x_{is}):TVp_{i,j} \Rightarrow p_i(x_1, \ldots, x_{is}, TVp_{i,j})$).
  5. Add monotonicity axioms to B^* for every annotated predicate p_i, $i \in \{1, \ldots, k\}$
      ($p_i(x_1, \ldots, x_{is}, X) \leftarrow le(X, Y), p_i(x_1, \ldots, x_{is}, Y).,$
      $le(TVp_{i,1}, TVp_{i,2})., \ldots, le(TVp_{i,mi-1}, TVp_{i,mi}).$)
  6. For all TV_i, where $1 < i \leq n$ do the following:
      a. split the example set E to negative $E- = \{e:\alpha \in E|\alpha < TV_i\}$ and positive $E+ = \{e:\alpha \in E|\alpha \geq TV_i\}$ parts.
      b. With the ILP system compute the hypothesis H_i^* for the two-valued background knowledge B, positive E+, and negative E- examples.
      c. Add the hypothesis H_i^* to H^*.
  7. Transform two-valued hypothesis H^* to annotated hypothesis H by transforming the extra attributes TV in literals back ($p_i(x_1, \ldots, x_{is}, TVp_{i,j}) \Rightarrow p_i(x_1, \ldots, x_{is}):TVp_{i,j}$).

Informally, we search every present truth values of examples and background knowledge predicates. Then we transform predicates in B to crisp form, thus achieving crisp background knowledge B^*. Then we extend B^* with the "monotonicity axioms" which states that if the predicate holds with truth Y it also holds in truth X less or equal to Y. Predicates "le" states the relation less or equal. This corresponds to natural meaning of truth values to B^*. Then we split the example set to positive and negative parts according to truth values present in E as follows: learning rules that guarantee our annotation function has value at least α, every example higher or equal than α belongs to positive example set, the others create the negative example set (note that when learning witness for α in B* all truth values take part). Thus, the hypothesis for the grade α holds in grade "at least" α, what agree with the natural meaning of truth in GAP.

Notice, that it can happen that we do not cover all example e:α right in the grade α, but in grade $\delta<\alpha$. So, that means, that our algorithm can find hypotheses that are not complete. On the other hand, the consistency condition is always fulfilled (proved in [10]).

4 Implementation

In this Section we describe experimental implementation of main parts of our system.

4.1 Heuristics for Top-k Search

We base our work in deductive step on [5], which introduced a top-k search. There are other methods for flexible search, such that proposed in [20], [14], [11] or [8].

Top-k search is a method of finding k best objects according to user criteria (an aggregation function) without the need of ranking and ordering all objects in database. There are several algorithms proposed in [5], also proved to be instance optimal. However, in practice, instance optimality is often not sufficient – performance is not satisfying. In [7], we have proposed some heuristics for these algorithms, which improve the speed of algorithms.

The paradigm of top-k search is working with ordered lists. Each list corresponds to an attribute A_i and it contains objects ordered by user preference on D_i. The ordering of a domain according to an arbitrary fuzzy function was discussed in [4]. The overall score of an object is computed from its attributes values.

We obtain data from lists with sequential access. Reducing the number of sequential accesses is the first task. Some algorithms use also direct access similar to a new query to database, which returns the attribute value for an object. This direct access is mostly very costly, so reducing the number of direct accesses is another goal.

Because of space limitations, we can not explain heuristics in more detail; they are however presented in Section 5.

4.2 TOKAF

We proposed and implemented a system Tokaf [26] for performing top-k queries over RDF data. The system is aimed to be used as a middleware; its possible integrations are proposed in Figure 4. As a Java library, Tokaf can be used either on the server side, for example in a Web service, or on the client side. In both cases, it gathers information from local or Web data sources and combines them into one ordered list. Further manipulation and presentation of this list to the user is not the aim of Tokaf.

There are several implemented classes for standard user scoring functions, normalizers for Jena and Sesame, all five algorithms proposed in [5] and heuristics described in [7].

In the future we plan to incorporate our system into Semantic Web Infrastructure described in [24].

4.3 IGAP

Our algorithm is implemented in Java. It does not read any inputs from file or database. Objects are represented in form similar to RDF format *attribute(object, value)*. This representation enables us to easily handle missing attribute values. We use ILP system ALEPH [21] with standard settings. We use ALEPH because it is able to work with rules in the background knowledge what is important in case we want to introduce monotonicity axioms.

IGAP contains several packages for preprocessing: There are implemented several methods on discretisation of continuous attribute domains (equidistant, equipotent). For attribute ordering detection there are implemented methods of regression (linear, polynomial) and qualitative models (QUIN algorithm [1]).

Hypotheses are represented in following structures:

hypotheses(hypothesis, time_of_computing, accuracy), rules(hypothesis, rule, rule_coverage), attributes(hypothesis, rule, attribute, value), where value states for truth value (in case of fuzzy attribute) or real value (in case of crisp attribute). Notice, that the head attribute is included in this structure too.

5   Experiments

We present results of experiments of one of our new heuristics - MissingValues. This heuristic is compared to the direct implementation of algorithm from [5], which is denoted as Parallel access in Figure 5. Experiments was done in local environment with a testing set of 100 000 objects with five attributes, which were stored in RDF database Sesame [25].

We can see from Figure 5 that the number of accesses is much lower for MissingValues, especially for smaller values of k. This is reasonable, because users want a small set of recommendations; no one will go through the list of 1000 objects. The number of accesses can not exceed the number of objects, which is 100 000.

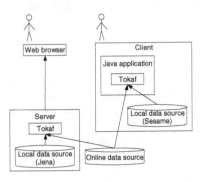

Fig. 4. Use cases of Tokaf

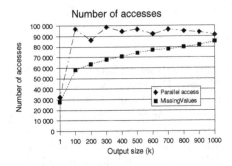

Fig. 5. Testing MissingValues heuristic

We further experimented with attribute domain ordering detection module in IGAP. First we tried linear regression. This method is the fastest but not suitable to detect ordering types, where middle or marginal values are preferable.

There is another method to attribute domain ordering detection using IGAP itself. This proceed as follows: we try to learn a hypothesis separately for every of the four *basic types of orderings* (lower-best, higher-best, middle-best and marginal-best) using just one attribute (for what we try to detect the domain ordering) in learning process for objects. ALEPH does not learn any rule for the wrong type of ordering. If ALEPH learns some rules for more than one type of ordering, we use that ordering type where the hypothesis has higher accuracy. Nevertheless this method turned out to be not satisfactory. We detect the ordering of the domain of attribute price for the user 2 as "lower-best" instead of "marginal-best" what should be the correct ordering (giving higher accuracy of learning). The reason is, we did not find right coordinates of minima of fuzzy function.

Finally, we used quadratic polynomial regression to ordering detection as follows. We compute the quadratic polynomial and its global maximum respectively minimum. This point we mark as the *"middle point"* from what the middle-best respectively marginal-best types of orderings can be detected. If the middle point is out of used domain or lies in its margins we can assume lower-best or higher-best ordering types. The results can be seen on Figure 6.

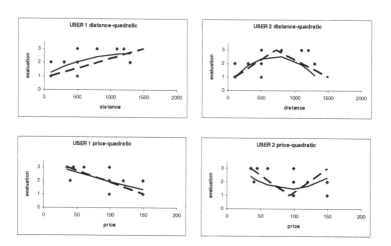

Fig. 6. Detected basic types of orderings by using polynomial regression

The computation with these basic types of orderings (local preferences) from figure 6 gives us following results for the user 2 (for user 1 the results are similar to those in table 2):

```
excellent(A) :- distance(A, 0.3), price(A, 1.0).    [Accuracy = 1]
good(A) :- distance(A, 0.3).                         [Accuracy = 1]
```

We interpret these rules as following:

```
user_2_evaluation = excellent  IF distance ∈ <300;1100> AND price ∈
<35;35> ∪ <149;149>

user_2_evaluation = good IF distance ∈ <300;1100>
```

As can be seen, the results are very similar to results for user 2 from the table 2. All the rules have high accuracy.

Global quality of learning was measured by accuracy weighted average (weighted by truth value annotating the head of the rule). The idea is, that learning bad rules for excellent hotel (in focus of user) is more punished than learned bad rules for hotels not that much interesting for user. This measure was the highest by above mentioned orderings for both users.

6 Related Work and Conclusion

To create a more suitable set of rules using ILP in [2] an algorithm called FS FOIL was developed, that extends the original FOIL algorithm, modified to be able to handle first order fuzzy predicates where cover compares confidence and support of fuzzy predicates. A version of FOIL that handles membership degree has already been developed in [19] but the rules induced still keep a classical meaning. In [16] a system enriching relational learning with several types of fuzzy rules - flexible, gradual and certainty - was introduced. In this approach a fuzzy rule is associated by crisp rules where the truth of a head is the same or complementary of the truth of a body (on an α-cut). These types of rules are considered in [17], too, where hypotheses are computed by a fixed T-norm and are more flexible as in [16]. All these approaches are using vague linguistic hedges and are implemented in FOIL. These approaches have some disadvantages: [19] uses only Lukasiewicz logic, [17] and [19] deals with fixed types of fuzzy rules, moreover in [17] the truth values of the head of a rule and the body have the same truth value (or they are complements α and $1-\alpha$) while in [19] a fixed t-norm (aggregation) is used in learning.

We do not know about any inductive GAP system.

Our FILP task does not consider probability distributions as in probabilistic models [18, 6]. Embedding of FILP to Bayesian Logic Programs (BLP) is studied in [22] . In [23] the transformations of GAP to several frameworks are introduced.

To conclude, we have presented models, methods and experimental implementation of a system supporting top-k answers to user fuzzy preference queries. Main contributions of this paper are a method for monotonization of data using user preferences. This enables to use our inductive method for generalized annotated programs working on a fuzzy completion of data. Efficient heuristics for finding top-k answers was implemented and tested too.

Acknowledgement. Supported by Czech projects 1ET100300517 and 1ET 100300419 and Slovak projects NAZOU and VEGA 1/3129/06.

References

[1] Bratko, I., Šuc, D.: Learning qualitative models. AI Magazine 24, 107–119 (2003)
[2] Bodenhofer, U., Drobics, M., Klement, E-P.: FS-FOIL: An Inductive learning method for extracting interpretable fuzzy descriptions. Int.J. Approximate Reasoning 32, 131–152 (2003)
[3] Džeroski, S., Lavrač, N.: An introduction to inductive logic programming. In: Džeroski, S., Lavrač, N. (eds.) Relational data mining, pp. 48–73. Springer, Heidelberg (2001)
[4] Eckhardt, A., Pokorný, J., Vojtáš, P.: A system recommending top-k objects for multiple users preferences. In: Proc. of Fuzz-IEEE, London (to appear, 2007)
[5] Fagin, R., Lotem, A., Naor, M.: Optimal Aggregation Algorithms for Middleware. In: Extended abstract appeared in Proc. PODS 2001, pp. 102–113 (2001)
[6] Getoor, L., et al.: Learning probabilistic relational models. In: Džeroski, S., Lavrač, N. (eds.) Relational data mining, pp. 307–335. Springer, Heidelberg (2001)
[7] Gurský, P., Lencses, R., Vojtáš, P.: Algorithms for user dependent integration of ranked distributed information. In: Böhlen, M.H., Gamper, J., Polasek, W., Wimmer, M.A. (eds.) TCGOV 2005. LNCS (LNAI), vol. 3416, pp. 123–130. Springer, Heidelberg (2005)
[8] Güntzer, U., Balke, W., Kiessling, W.: Optimizing Multi-Feature Queries for Image Databases. In: Proc. of the 26th VLDB Conference, Cairo, Egypt (2000)
[9] Hájek, P.: Metamathematics if fuzzy logic. Kluwer, Dordrecht (1999)
[10] Horváth, T., Vojtáš, P.: Induction of Fuzzy and Annotated Logic Programs. In: Muggleton, S., Otero, R., Tamaddoni-Nezhad, A. (eds.) ILP 2006. LNCS(LNAI), vol. 4455, pp. 260–274. Springer, Heidelberg (2007)
[11] Ilyas, I.F., Aref, W.G., Elmagarmid, A.K.: Supporting top-k join queries in relational database. In: Proc. of VLDB, pp. 754–765, Berlin (2003)
[12] Kifer, M., Subrahmanian, V.S.: Theory of generalized annotated logic programming and its applications. J. Logic Programing 12, 335–367 (1992)
[13] Krajči, S., Lencses, R., Vojtáš, P.: A comparison of fuzzy and annotated logic programming. Fuzzy Sets and Systems 144, 173–192 (2004)
[14] Papadias, D., Tao, Y., Fu, G., Seeger, B.: Progressive skyline computation in database systems. ACM Trans. Database Syst. 30(1), 41–82 (2005)
[15] Pokorný, J., Vojtáš, P.: A data model for flexible querying. In: Caplinskas, A., Eder, J. (eds.) ADBIS 2001. LNCS, vol. 2151, pp. 280–293. Springer, Heidelberg (2001)
[16] Prade, H., Richard, G., Serrurier, M.: Enriching relational Learning with fuzzy predicates. In: Lavrač, N., Gamberger, D., Todorovski, L., Blockeel, H. (eds.) PKDD 2003. LNCS (LNAI), vol. 2838, pp. 399–410. Springer, Heidelberg (2003)
[17] Prade, H., Richard, G., Dubois, D., Sudkamp, T., Serrurier, M.: Learning first order fuzzy rules with their implication operator. In. Proc. of IPMU (2004)
[18] De Raedt, L., Kersting, K.: Probabilistic Inductive Logic Programming. In: Ben-David, S., Case, J., Maruoka, A. (eds.) ALT 2004. LNCS (LNAI), vol. 3244, pp. 19–36. Springer, Heidelberg (2004)
[19] Shibata, D., et al.: An induction algorithm based on fuzzy logic programming. In: Zhong, N., Zhou, L. (eds.) Methodologies for Knowledge Discovery and Data Mining. LNCS (LNAI), vol. 1574, pp. 268–273. Springer, Heidelberg (1999)
[20] Tao, T., Zhai, C.: Best-k Queries on Database Systems. In: Proceedings of the 15th ACM international conference on Information and knowledge management (2006)
[21] Srinavasan, A.: The Aleph Manual. Technical Report, Comp.Lab. Oxford University

[22] Vojtáš, P., Vomlelová, M.: Transformation of deductive and inductive tasks between models of logic programming with imperfect information. In: Proceedings of IPMU, 2004: Editrice Universita La Sapienza, Roma, pp. 839–846 (2004)

[23] Vojtáš, P., Vomlelová, M.: On models of comparison of multiple monotone classifications. In: Proc. IPMU 2006, Paris, France, Éditions EDK, Paris, pp. 1236–1243 (2006)

[24] Yaghob, J., Zavoral, F.: Semantic Web Infrastructure using DataPile. In: IEEE/WIC/ACM WI 2006, Los Alamitos, California, pp. 630–633 (2006) ISBN 0-7695-2749-3

[25] http://www.openrdf.org

[26] Sources and libraries of Tokaf system, http://sourceforge.net/projects/tokaf//

Composable Markov Building Blocks

Sander Evers, Maarten M. Fokkinga, and Peter M.G. Apers

University of Twente, The Netherlands

Abstract. In situations where disjunct parts of the same process are described by their own first-order Markov models and only one model applies at a time (activity in one model coincides with non-activity in the other models), these models can be joined together into one. Under certain conditions, nearly all the information to do this is already present in the component models, and the transition probabilities for the joint model can be derived in a purely analytic fashion. This composability provides a theoretical basis for building scalable and flexible models for sensor data.

1 Introduction

In order to deal with time series of sensor data, it is useful to have a statistical model of the observed process. This helps to smooth noisy readings, detect faulty observations, or fill in incomplete data, by keeping track of in what states the process is most likely to be. For example, in object localization, if we have a sequence of position observations 3–2–4–18–5–4 and a model that assigns a low likelihood to objects moving back and forth fast, we know we can disregard the 18 reading. The parameters of such a statistical model can be obtained from domain expert knowledge or by (supervised or unsupervised) *learning* from data.

When the state space of a statistical model is large and heterogeneous, these parameters become hard to obtain. Therefore, like in all large and complex problems, it is fruitful to look for *composability* of statistical models; composability is often the key to flexibility and scalability. In this article, we consider a specific opportunity for composability, where several *disjunct parts* of the state space can be described by their own first-order Markov models (we have investigated first-order Markov models because these are the most simple). We present a mathematical result about the conditions under which these models are composable, and the method to perform this composition.

In order to illustrate this result, we use a running example about activity recognition, where the heterogeneity of the state space stems from the fact that different types of sensors are used for several subclasses of activities. This particular example actually has a very small state space, and we stress the fact that it is used only for illustration of the mathematical procedure; it is not meant as a realistic application.

Fig. 1a shows this example, which consists of three component models body, object and computer, which are associated with three different types of sensors:

H. Prade and V.S. Subrahmanian (Eds.): SUM 2007, LNAI 4772, pp. 131–142, 2007.

- Motion sensors on the body are used to classify the activities walking and climbing stairs.
- Sensors on a coffee cup and a book register interaction with these objects, and are used to classify coffee drinking and book reading.
- From desktop computer interactions, the activities logging in, reading mail, reading an article, and writing a document are classified.

Each is a first-order Markov model that, in addition to the states just mentioned, contains a state of *non-activity*. In this state the monitored person is considered to be doing 'something else', which cannot be observed more precisely in that model. Furthermore, *there can only be one activity at a time*, i.e. the activities of one model coincide with non-activity in the other models. Our goal is to compose these models together into one.

We have investigated the conditions under which this model composition can happen in a purely analytic fashion, without assuming or adding any other information apart from the *structure* of the transition graph between the component models (Fig. 1b). The main result is that when this structure is 'sparse enough', all inter-component transition probabilities can be deduced from the component models. The technique that we present checks this condition and deduces the probabilities, and is novel to the best of our knowledge.

The remainder of this article is structured as follows. In Sect. 2, we formalize the problem; Sect. 3 reduces it to a set of linear equations; in Sect. 4 we present a specialized method to solve this system; in Sect. 5 we apply this method to our problem; Sect. 6 discusses some related work and Sect. 7 concludes.

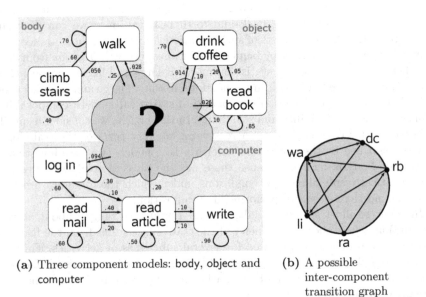

(a) Three component models: body, object and computer

(b) A possible inter-component transition graph

Fig. 1. Running example: activity recognition

2   Markov Models and Pseudo-aggregated Components

In this section, we give a quick introduction to Markov models, and we formalize the relation between a global Markov model G and its component models.

Consider a process that can be in one of the states of a finite set S_G at each subsequent point in (discrete) time. One of the simplest and most used models that probabilistically relates the states in such a series to each other is the *homogeneous first-order Markov model*. Informally, the *first-order Markov condition* means that the state at time $\tau + 1$ (represented by the stochastic variable $X_{\tau+1}$) is only dependent on X_τ, i.e. for guessing the next state, knowledge of the current state obsoletes all knowledge of previous states. Formally, this is expressed using *conditional independence*:

$$\mathsf{P}(X_{\tau+1} = t | X_\tau = s) = \mathsf{P}(X_{\tau+1} = t | X_{0..\tau} = (x_0, x_1, \ldots, x_{\tau-1}, s))$$

The parameters of a first-order Markov model consist of the conditional probabilities $\mathsf{P}(X_{\tau+1} = t | X_\tau = s)$ with $s, t \in S_G$. We consider *homogeneous* models, which means that these conditional probabilities are the same for all values of τ. This allows one to specify all these parameters using a transition function G, in which $G(s, t) = \mathsf{P}(X_{\tau+1} = t | X_\tau = s)$. Often, this function is represented by a matrix, for which we will also use the symbol G; furthermore, we will also use G to refer to the corresponding Markov model itself. In the remainder of this article, when we mention a Markov model, a first-order heterogeneous Markov model is implied.

The probabilities in a Markov model can be interpreted as observation frequencies. An observation of G consists of a consecutive sequence $[x_0, x_1, x_2, \ldots]$ of states ($x_i \in S_G$); each subsequence $[s, t]$ corresponds to an observed transition from s to t. We denote the number of distinct $[s, t]$ subsequences by $\#[s, t]$. The longer the sequence we observe, the more the frequency $\#[s, t]/\#[s, \_]$ converges to $G(s, t)$. (We use $[s, \_]$ to denote any observed transition from s; $\#[s, \_]$ is almost equal to the number of s occurrences in the sequence.)

Learning a model from the data works the other way around: the $G(s, t)$ parameters are estimated by using the observed frequencies $\#[s, t]/\#[s, \_]$. In principle, to check the Markov condition for the observed data, one should also calculate the frequencies with added prefixes to ensure e.g. that $\#[r, s, t]/\#[r, s, \_] \approx G(s, t)$; but in practice, Markov models are also successfully used when this condition does not hold.

Now, consider the situation in which we assume the data originates from a Markov model G with states $\{1, \ldots, n\}$, but we cannot distinguish between the states m through n (with $m < n$) in our observations. For example, our body sensor can only distinguish between three states: climbing stairs, walking, and a "rest state" of non-activity. When we use the observed transition frequencies to estimate a Markov model, we arrive at a different model C with $|S_C| = n$ states. This model is called the *pseudo-aggregation* of G with respect to the partition $S_C = \{\{1\}, \{2\}, \ldots, \{m-1\}, \{m, \ldots, n\}\}$. (In the formal definition of pseudo-aggregation[1], the parameters of the pseudo-aggregated model C are directly defined in terms of the G parameters, i.e. without referring to observations.)

The goal of this article is to reconstruct the unknown global Markov model G (in our running example, $S_G = \{cs, wa, dc, rb, li, rm, ra, wr\}$; each activity is abbreviated to two letters) from several known pseudo-aggregations, the *component models*, which have a special form:

- Each partition S_C consists of one or more singleton states and exactly one non-singleton "rest" state. In our running example:
  - $S_{body} = \{\{cs\}, \{wa\}, \{dc, rb, li, rm, ra, wr\}\}$,
  - $S_{object} = \{\{dc\}, \{rb\}, \{cs, wa, li, rm, ra, wr\}\}$, and
  - $S_{computer} = \{\{li\}, \{rm\}, \{ra\}, \{wr\}, \{cs, wa, dc, rb\}\}$.
- Each state s from S_G corresponds to a singleton state $\{s\}$ in exactly one of the S_C partitions. We say that the state *belongs to* a specific C model. The model to which state s belongs is written C_s. For example, $C_{cs} = $ body.

For clarity of exposition we will hereafter slightly transcend this formalization and identify the singleton states with their only member, so cs can actually mean $\{cs\}$. Also, we will abbreviate the non-singleton state of each pseudo-aggregation to *rest*.

To illustrate the situation, consider the example global observation sequence shown in Fig. 2, with its three corresponding component sequences. Because of the special partitioning form, at each point τ, the accurate current state is observed by one component; the other components observe their *rest* state. By calculating frequencies, each of the component sequences gives rise to a C model; the goal is to reconstruct the G model from only these C models. Of course, if we would be able to use the C sequences directly, we could paste them together into the G sequence and use that to construct the G model. However, this assumes an important condition, namely that the C sequences are recorded at the same time. If this is not the case, we can not reconstruct a global sequence; this article shows that under certain conditions one can do without it, and just use the probabilities (frequencies) from the C models.

Note that, even if the Markov condition holds for the global observation data, it generally does not hold for the local observation data. For example, if the $(dc, rest)$ transition in the object component always corresponds to (dc, li) in the global model, and there is no (li, dc) transition possible, then (in an object sequence) $\#[dc, rest, dc]/\#[dc, rest, \_] = 0$, although $\#[rest, dc]/\#[rest, \_] > 0$. *Pseudo*-aggregation means we treat it as a Markov chain regardless. This does not invalidate our approach, because pseudo-aggregation does not affect the stationary distribution (see next section).

τ	0	1	2	3	4	5	6	7	8	...
global	[cs,	wa,	wa,	dc,	li,	rm,	ra,	rb,	wa,	...]
body	[cs,	wa,	wa,	*rest*,	*rest*,	*rest*,	*rest*,	*rest*,	wa,	...]
object	[*rest*,	*rest*,	*rest*,	dc,	*rest*,	*rest*,	*rest*,	rb,	*rest*,	...]
computer	[*rest*,	*rest*,	*rest*,	*rest*,	li,	rm,	ra,	*rest*,	*rest*,	...]

Fig. 2. Global and component observation sequences

The 'certain conditions' that we mentioned pertain chiefly to the graph of possible transitions between the components. We introduce some terminology for this:

- If the states $s, t \in S_G$ belong to the same component model ($C_s = C_t$), we will call the transition from s to t an *intra-component* transition; otherwise ($C_s \neq C_t$), it is called an *inter-component* transition.
- A *possible* transition (s, t) is one with $G(s, t) > 0$.
- A state that is involved in at least one possible inter-component transition is called a *border state*.
- The directed graph consisting of all border states as vertices and all possible inter-component transitions (s, t) as edges is called the *inter-component transition graph*.

In the remainder of the article, we will show how to reconstruct G when:

- we know the inter-component transition graph (i.e. we know which inter-component transitions are have $G(s, t) > 0$), and
- this inter-component transition graph does not contain direction-alternating cycles (a concept that we will explain in section 4).

In our example, the border states are {wa,dc,rb,li,ra}. An example inter-component transition graph is shown in Fig. 1b. Note that it is not derived from the component models; it is extra information that we add.

3   Transforming to the Domain of Long-Run Frequencies

In the global model G, the transition probabilities $G(s, t)$ for *intra*-component transitions can be taken directly from the C model to which the states belong: $G(s, t) = C_s(s, t)$. The problem lies with the *inter*-component transitions: we know for which transitions $G(s, t) > 0$, but we don't know the exact values. However, the information about transitions from and to the rest states in the C models can make it possible to deduce them in a completely analytic fashion. To do this, we first transform the problem from the domain of conditional probabilities $G(s, t)$ into (unconditional) long-run frequencies $F(s, t)$. In Sect. 5, we will transform the solution back.

The unconditional long-run frequency $F(s, t)$ is the frequency with which a transition from s to t would occur compared to the *total* number of transitions (instead of to the transitions from s). To transform conditional frequencies into unconditional frequencies, we need to know the proportion of the total time spent in each state. These proportions are known[2] to be equal to the stationary distribution π_G, which is the normalized left eigenvector of the transition matrix G corresponding to eigenvalue 1, i.e. the solution to:

$$\pi_G G = \pi_G$$
$$\sum_s \pi_G(s) = 1$$

The existence and uniqueness of π_G are guaranteed when the Markov model is irreducible and ergodic. (We will come back to these notions in Sect. 7.) It is well known how to calculate a stationary distribution given a transition matrix, but we cannot calculate π_G directly because we do not know the complete G matrix. Instead, we use the stationary distributions of the C matrices; it is known ([1], Lemma 4.1) that even though C is a *pseudo*-aggregation (which 'illegitimately' assumes the Markov condition), π_C is equivalent to π_G up to aggregation. For each state s, we use the model C_s to which it belongs:

$$\pi_G(s) = \pi_{C_s}(s)$$

Using this, we can simply calculate $F(s,t)$ for all *intra*-component transitions from $C_s(s,t)$ by multiplying it by the proportion of time spent in s:

$$F(s,t) = \pi_G(s) \cdot C_s(s,t)$$

We need to solve $F(s,t)$ for *inter*-component transitions. From the inter-component transition graph, we know which of these frequencies are 0. We solve the rest of them by equating, for each border state s, the summed frequencies of incoming transitions (including self-transitions) to the proportion of time spent in s (because every time unit spent in s is preceded by a transition to s), and doing the same for the outgoing transitions (because every time unit spent in s is followed by a transition from s):

$$\sum_r F(r,s) = \pi_G(s)$$

$$\sum_t F(s,t) = \pi_G(s)$$

Moving all the known quantities to the right-hand side gives:

$$\sum_{r|C_r \neq C_s} F(r,s) = \pi_G(s) - \sum_{r|C_r = C_s} F(r,s)$$

$$\sum_{t|C_s \neq C_t} F(s,t) = \pi_G(s) - \sum_{t|C_s = C_t} F(s,t)$$

We are then left with a system of linear equations, with twice as much equations as there are border states, and as much unknowns as there are inter-component transitions. In principle, we could solve these equations using a standard method such as Gauss-Jordan elimination, but in the next section we present a technique that is tailored to the special structure of this system. It has the benefit that it directly relates the conditions under which the system has one unique solution to the inter-component transition graph, and that it checks these conditions (and solves the equations) in a time proportional to the number of inter-component transitions.

4   Distributing Vertex Sum Requirements

In this section, we abstract from the Markov model problem, and present a method for solving a system of linear equations associated with a directed graph: each edge corresponds to an unknown, and each vertex corresponds to two equations (one for the incoming and one for the outgoing edges).

Formally, we represent the system by a directed graph $G = (V, E)$, with vertex set V and edge set $E \subseteq V \times V$, and two vertex sum requirements $f^+, f^- : V \to \mathbb{R}$, which specify for each $v \in V$ the sum of the weights on its outgoing and incoming edges, respectively (loops count for both). A solution to the system is a weight distribution $f : E \to \mathbb{R}$ matching these requirements, i.e.

$$f^+(v) = \sum_{w | (v,w) \in E} f(v, w)$$

$$f^-(v) = \sum_{u | (u,v) \in E} f(u, v)$$

for all $v \in V$. In this section, we present a necessary and sufficient condition on the structure of G for the uniqueness of such a distribution, and an algorithm to determine it (if it exists at all). For the proof and algorithm, we use an undirected representation of G, which we call its uncoiled graph.

Definition 1. *Given directed graph $G = (V, E)$ with n vertices $\{v_1, v_2, \ldots, v_n\}$, we define its* uncoiled graph *$U = (S + T, E')$. U is an undirected bipartite graph with partitions $S = \{s_1, s_2, \ldots, s_n\}$ and $T = \{t_1, t_2, \ldots, t_n\}$ of equal size $|S| = |T| = n$, representing each vertex v_i twice: as a source s_i and as a target t_i. E' contains an undirected edge $\{s_i, t_j\}$ iff E contains a directed edge (v_i, v_j). Furthermore, we represent f^+ and f^- together by a function $f^\pm : S + T \to \mathbb{R}$:*

$$f^\pm(s_i) \stackrel{def}{=} f^+(v_i)$$

$$f^\pm(t_i) \stackrel{def}{=} f^-(v_i)$$

The transformation to an uncoiled graph is just a matter of representation; from U and $f^\pm$, the original G and f^-, f^+ can easily be recovered. An example directed graph G and its uncoiled graph U in two different layouts are shown in Fig. 3. Every vertex v_i in G corresponds to two vertices s_i and t_i in U (in Fig. 3b, these are kept close to the spot of v_i; Fig. 3c more clearly shows the partitioning in S and T). Every edge in G corresponds to an edge in U; if it leaves from v_i and enters v_j, its corresponding edge in U is incident to s_i and t_j.

Fig. 3a also shows partial vertex sum requirements for G: $f^+(v_1) = 5$ and $f^-(v_1) = 3$, and a partial weight distribution that matches these requirements: $f(v_1, v_1) = 3$ and $f(v_1, v_2) = 2$. In fact, this f has been deduced from f^- and f^+: because v_1 has only one incoming edge, we can solve $f(v_1, v_1) = f^-(v_1) = 3$. With this information, we can also solve $f(v_1, v_2) = f^+(v_1) - f(v_1, v_1) = 5 - 3 = 2$. This illustrates the basic principle of how Algorithm 1 works.

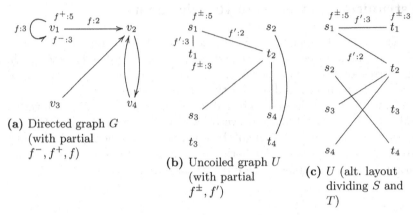

(a) Directed graph G (with partial f^-, f^+, f)

(b) Uncoiled graph U (with partial $f^\pm, f'$)

(c) U (alt. layout dividing S and T)

Fig. 3. Uncoiling

For graph U, these same requirements and distribution are represented by $f^\pm$ and f', respectively (see Fig. 3b, 3c). The assertion that f' matches $f^\pm$ is

$$\forall v \in S + T. \quad f^\pm(v) = \sum_{w | \{v,w\} \in E'} f'\{v, w\}$$

The algorithm works on this new representation: it solves f' from $f^\pm$. Afterwards, the solution f' is translated to the corresponding f. We now state the sufficient condition to find this solution: U should not contain a cycle.

Lemma 1. *A cycle in U represents a direction-alternating cycle in G and vice versa. A direction-alternating cycle is a sequence of an even number of distinct directed edges $(e_1, e_2, \ldots, e_{2m})$ in which:*

- *e_1 and e_{2m} have a common source*
- *e_i and e_{i+1} have a common target, for odd i*
- *e_i and e_{i+1} have a common source, for even i (smaller than $2m$)*

Theorem 2. *For each directed graph G without direction-alternating cycles and weight-sum functions f^+ and f^-, if there exists a matching weight distribution f, it is unique. Algorithm 1 decides whether it exists; if so, it produces the solution.*

Proof. The algorithm works on the uncoiled graph U, which contains no cycles because of Lemma 1; hence, it is a forest. For each component tree, we pick an arbitrary element as root and recurse over the subtrees. The proof is by induction over the tree structure; the induction hypothesis is that after a call SolveSubtree(*root, maybeparent*), the unique matching distribution on all the edges in the subtree rooted in *root* has been recorded in f'. To satisfy the hypothesis for the next level, we consider the $f^\pm$ requirements for the roots

---

Input: directed graph $G = (V, E)$ and weight sums f^+, f^-
Output: unique weight distribution f that matches the sums

$(V', E') \leftarrow$ uncoiled graph of G (as in Def. 1)
$f^\pm \leftarrow$ projection of f^+, f^- on V' (as in Def. 1)
$f' \leftarrow$ the empty (partial) function
$visited \leftarrow \emptyset$

while $visited \neq V'$ **do**
    $root \leftarrow$ an arbitrary element of $(V' - visited)$
    SolveSubtree($root, \emptyset$)
    if $f^\pm(root) \neq \sum_w f'\{root, w\}$ **then error** 'no distribution exists'
end
foreach $(v_i, v_j) \in E$ **do** $f(v_i, v_j) \leftarrow f'\{s_i, t_j\}$

procedure SolveSubtree($root, maybeparent$)
    // *maybeparent* records the node we came from, to prevent going back
    if $root \in visited$ **then error** 'cycle detected'
    $visited \leftarrow visited \cup \{root\}$
    foreach $v \in (V' - maybeparent)$ **such that** $\{root, v\} \in E'$ **do**
        SolveSubtree($v, \{root\}$)
        $f'\{root, v\} \leftarrow f^\pm(v) - \sum_w f'\{v, w\}$
    end
end

Algorithm 1. Finding the unique weight distribution

of the subtrees. By the induction hypothesis, these all have one unknown term, corresponding to the edge to their parent: thus, we find a unique solution for each edge at the current level. □

Remark. The algorithm contains two additional checks:

- When the root of a component is reached, the $f^\pm$ equation for this root is checked. If it holds, the *existence* of a matching distribution f is established (for this component).
- When visiting a node, it is checked whether it was visited before. If it was, U contains a cycle. As we will show next, this means that no *unique* matching distribution exists.

Theorem 3. *A directed graph G with a direction-alternating cycle has no unique weight distribution matching a given f^+, f^-.*

Proof. Given such a cycle $(e_1, e_2, \ldots, e_{2m})$ and a matching weight distribution f, we construct another matching weight distribution g:

$$g(e_i) = f(e_i) + c, \quad \text{for all odd } i$$
$$g(e_i) = f(e_i) - c, \quad \text{for all even } i$$
$$g(e) = f(e), \quad \text{for all other edges } e$$

□

5   Finishing the Transition Model Construction

In Sect. 3, we ended with a set of equations to solve, namely

$$\sum_{r|C_r \neq C_s} F(r,s) = \pi_G(s) - \sum_{r|C_r = C_s} F(r,s)$$

$$\sum_{t|C_s \neq C_t} F(s,t) = \pi_G(s) - \sum_{t|C_s = C_t} F(s,t)$$

for all border states s. To solve these, we use Algorithm 1, with (V, E) the inter-component transition graph: vertices V are the border states, and edges E are the inter-component transitions. The unknown inter-component transition probabilities that we want to solve correspond to the edge weights in f, and the vertex sum requirements correspond to the right-hand sides of the above equations:

$$f^-(s) = \pi_G(s) - \sum_{r|C_r = C_s} F(r,s)$$

$$f^+(s) = \pi_G(s) - \sum_{t|C_s = C_t} F(s,t)$$

The weight distribution f that the algorithm yields gives us the unknown F values. So, we now know $F(s,t)$ for all (s,t):

$F(s,t) = \pi_{C_s}(s) \cdot C_s(s,t)$ for all intra-component (s,t) transitions

$F(s,t) = \quad f(s,t) \quad$ for (s,t) in the inter-component transition graph

$F(s,t) = \quad\quad 0 \quad\quad$ for other (s,t) (for which $G(s,t) = 0$)

We arrive at the desired matrix G of conditional probabilities by normalizing the rows:

$$G(s,t) = \frac{F(s,t)}{\sum_x F(s,x)}$$

6   Related Work

A probabilistic model with a state space of n variables that can each take k values requires, in the general case, k^n parameters (one for each possible combination of values), so scales exponentially in n. A widely used method to avoid this problem is using a graphical model like a Bayesian network[3,4]; because it assumes many conditional independences between variables, the number of parameters can grow linearly with the number of variables (each variable is represented by a node in the graph; if a node has a maximum of p parents, the model has at most $(k-1)k^p n$ parameters). However, in this article we are not concerned with scalability in the number of variables; we assume one (process) variable, and are concerned with scalability in k, the number of values. Even if we would model the sets of values that can be distinguished by the component models as a separate variables, constructing a (dynamic) Bayesian network would be of no use: the fact that the process can be in one state at a time constitutes a very clear dependence between all the variables.

To summarize, instead of a condition on the dependence graph between variables, we investigated a condition on the transition graph between values of the same (process) variable. Presently, we are not familiar with any other work in this direction.

7   Conclusion and Future Work

We have presented a technique to compose Markov models of disjunct parts of a state space into a large Markov model of the entire state space. We review the conditions under which we can apply this technique:

- The inter-component transition graph should be known, and should not contain any direction-alternating cycles.
- The Markov chain G should be irreducible and ergodic, in order to calculate the stationary distribution π_G. We refer to [2] for the definition of these terms; for finite chains, it suffices that all states are accessible from each other (i.e. the transition graph is strongly connected) and that all states are *aperiodic*: the possible numbers of steps in which you can return to a given state should not be only multiples of $n > 1$.

An example class of inter-component transition graphs satisfying these conditions is formed by those with symmetric edges (only two-way transitions), that forms a *tree* when the two-way connections are represented by an undirected edge.

In this article, we have only considered the theoretical situation where the C models are perfect pseudo-aggregations of one model G. In practice, this will probably never be the case. Even when the observation sequences are generated by a perfect Markov model, they would have to be infinitely long to guarantee this. The consequence using imperfect pseudo-aggregations is that the stationary distributions π_C will not perfectly agree with another, and π_G is only *approximated*. We leave it to future research to determine when an acceptable approximation can be reached. A second open question is how to deal with inter-model transition graphs which *do* contain some direction-alternating cycles. Perhaps some additional information could be used to determine the best solution (in a maximum likelihood sense); without this information, the distribution of maximum entropy could be used.

Acknowledgements

This research is funded by NWO (Nederlandse Organisatie voor Wetenschappelijk Onderzoek; Netherlands Organisation for Scientific Research), under project 639.022.403. The authors would like to thank Richard Boucherie for his comments on the article.

References

1. Rubino, G., Sericola, B.: Sojourn times in finite Markov processes. Journal of Applied Probability 26(4), 744–756 (1989)
2. Ross, S.M.: Introduction to Probability Models, 8th edn. Academic Press, London (2003)
3. Charniak, E.: Bayesian networks without tears. AI Magazine 12(4), 50–63 (1991)
4. Russell, S., Norvig, P.: Artificial Intelligence: A Modern Approach, 2nd edn. Prentice-Hall, Englewood Cliffs (2004)

Tractable Probabilistic Description Logic Programs

Thomas Lukasiewicz*

Dipartimento di Informatica e Sistemistica, Sapienza Università di Roma
Via Ariosto 25, I-00185 Roma, Italy
lukasiewicz@dis.uniroma1.it

Abstract. We propose tractable probabilistic description logic programs (or *probabilistic dl-programs*) for the Semantic Web, which combine tractable description logics, normal programs under the answer set semantics, and probabilities. In particular, we introduce the *total well-founded semantics* for probabilistic dl-programs. Contrary to the previous answer set and well-founded semantics, it is defined for all probabilistic dl-programs and all probabilistic queries. Furthermore, tight (resp., tight literal) query processing under the total well-founded semantics coincides with tight (resp., tight literal) query processing under the previous well-founded (resp., answer set) semantics whenever the latter is defined. We then present an anytime algorithm for tight query processing in probabilistic dl-programs under the total well-founded semantics. We also show that tight literal query processing in probabilistic dl-programs under the total well-founded semantics can be done in polynomial time in the data complexity and is complete for EXP in the combined complexity. Finally, we describe an application of probabilistic dl-programs in probabilistic data integration for the Semantic Web.

1 Introduction

During the recent five years, formalisms for dealing with probabilistic uncertainty have started to play an important role in research related to the Web and the *Semantic Web* (which is an extension of the current Web by standards and technologies that help machines to understand the information on the Web so that they can support richer discovery, data integration, navigation, and automation of tasks; see [1]). For example, the order in which Google returns the answers to a web search query is computed by using probabilistic techniques. Besides web search and information retrieval, other important web and semantic web applications of formalisms for dealing with probabilistic uncertainty are especially data integration [18] and ontology mapping [15].

The Semantic Web consists of several hierarchical layers, where the *Ontology layer*, in form of the *OWL Web Ontology Language* [19], is currently the highest layer of sufficient maturity. OWL consists of three increasingly expressive sublanguages, namely, *OWL Lite*, *OWL DL*, and *OWL Full*, where OWL Lite and OWL DL are essentially very expressive description logics with an RDF syntax. As shown in [11], ontology entailment in OWL Lite (resp., OWL DL) reduces to knowledge base (un)satisfiability in the description logic $\mathcal{SHIF}(\mathbf{D})$ (resp., $\mathcal{SHOIN}(\mathbf{D})$). As a next step in the development of the Semantic Web, one aims especially at sophisticated reasoning capabilities for the *Rules*, *Logic*, and *Proof layers* of the Semantic Web.

---

* Alternative address: Institut für Informationssysteme, Technische Universität Wien, Favoritenstraße 9-11, A-1040 Wien, Austria; e-mail: lukasiewicz@kr.tuwien.ac.at.

H. Prade and V.S. Subrahmanian (Eds.): SUM 2007, LNAI 4772, pp. 143–156, 2007.

In particular, there is a large body of work on integrating rules and ontologies, which is a key requirement of the layered architecture of the Semantic Web. One type of integration is to build rules on top of ontologies, that is, for rule-based systems that use vocabulary from ontology knowledge bases. Another form of integration is to build ontologies on top of rules, where ontological definitions are supplemented by rules or imported from rules. Both types of integration have been realized in recent hybrid integrations of rules and ontologies, called *description logic programs* (or *dl-programs*), which are of the form $KB = (L, P)$, where L is a description logic knowledge base, and P is a finite set of rules involving queries to L in a loose coupling [7,8] (see also [7] for more background, detailed examples, and further references on dl-programs).

Other research efforts are directed towards formalisms for *uncertainty reasoning in the Semantic Web*: An important recent forum for uncertainty in the Semantic Web is the annual *Workshop on Uncertainty Reasoning for the Semantic Web (URSW)* at the *International Semantic Web Conference (ISWC)*; there also exists a W3C Incubator Group on *Uncertainty Reasoning for the World Wide Web*. There are especially extensions of description logics [10], ontology languages [6,17], and dl-programs [14] by probabilistic uncertainty (to encode ambiguous information, such as "John is a student with the probability 0.7 and a teacher with the probability 0.3", which is very different from vague/fuzzy information, such as "John is tall with the degree of truth 0.7").

In particular, the probabilistic dl-programs in [14] are one of the most promising approaches to probabilistic dl-programs for the Semantic Web, since they faithfully generalize two well-established logic programming and uncertainty formalisms, namely, answer set programming and Bayesian networks. They also generalize Poole's independent choice logic (ICL) [16], which is a powerful representation and reasoning formalism for single- and also multi-agent systems. The ICL combines logic and probability, and generalizes many important uncertainty formalisms, in particular, influence diagrams, Bayesian networks, Pearl's causal models, Markov decision processes, and normal form games. Moreover, it allows for natural notions of causes and explanations as in Pearl's causal models. It is also closely related to other seminal approaches to probabilistic logic programming, such as P-log [2] and Bayesian logic programs [12].

Since the Web contains a huge amount of data, an important feature of web and semantic web formalisms should be that they allow for efficient algorithms. However, no such algorithms are known so far for the probabilistic dl-programs in [14].

In this paper, we try to fill this gap. We propose an approach to probabilistic dl-programs that is defined on top of tractable description logics (rather than $\mathcal{SHIF}(\mathbf{D})$ and $\mathcal{SHOIN}(\mathbf{D})$ as in [14]), and show that this approach allows for tight query processing with polynomial data complexity. In the course of this, we also provide some other new results around probabilistic dl-programs, which are summarized as follows:

- We provide novel reductions of tight query processing and of deciding consistency in probabilistic dl-programs to computing the answer sets of the underlying normal dl-programs. These reductions significantly simplify previous reductions of [14], which additionally require to solve two (in general quite large) linear optimization problems resp. to decide the solvability of these linear optimization problems.
- We define a novel well-founded semantics of probabilistic dl-programs, called the *total well-founded semantics*, since it defines tight answers for *all* probabilistic

queries, contrary to the previous well-founded semantics of [14], which defines tight answers only for a quite restricted class of probabilistic queries. The total well-founded semantics is defined for all probabilistic dl-programs, contrary to the answer set semantics, which is only defined for consistent probabilistic dl-programs.

- As for other nice semantic features of the total well-founded semantics, we show that the tight answers under the total well-founded semantics coincide with the tight answers under the well-founded semantics of [14], if the latter are defined. For literal queries, the tight answers under the total well-founded semantics coincide with the tight answers under the answer set semantics, if the latter are defined.

- We provide an anytime algorithm for tight query processing in probabilistic dl-programs under the total well-founded semantics, along with a precise characterization of its anytime error. Furthermore, we show that tight query processing under the total well-founded semantics can be done in polynomial time in the data complexity and is complete for EXP in the combined complexity.

- We describe an application of probabilistic dl-programs in probabilistic data integration for the Semantic Web, where probabilistic dl-programs allow for dealing with probabilistic uncertainty and inconsistencies. We especially discuss different types of probabilistic data integration that can be realized with our approach.

2   Description Logics

The probabilistic dl-programs of this paper assume that the underlying description logic allows for decidable conjunctive query processing. The tractability and complexity results of this paper (see Section 8) additionally assume that the underlying description logic allows for conjunctive query processing in polynomial data complexity. We use *DL-Lite* here, but the tractability and complexity results also hold for the variants of *DL-Lite* in [5]. In this section, we recall the syntax and semantics of *DL-Lite*. Intuitively, description logics model a domain of interest in terms of concepts and roles, which represent classes of individuals resp. binary relations between classes of individuals.

Syntax. We first define concepts and axioms and then knowledge bases and conjunctive queries in *DL-Lite*. We assume pairwise disjoint sets $\mathbf{A}$, $\mathbf{R}$, and $\mathbf{I}$ of *atomic concepts*, *(atomic) roles*, and *individuals*, respectively. We use $\mathbf{R}^-$ to denote the set of all inverses R^- of roles $R \in \mathbf{R}$. A *basic concept* B is either an atomic concept $A \in \mathbf{A}$ or an exists restriction $\exists R$, where $R \in \mathbf{R} \cup \mathbf{R}^-$. An *axiom* is either (1) a concept inclusion axiom $B \sqsubseteq \phi$, where B is a basic concept, and ϕ is either a basic concept B or its negation $\neg B$, or (2) a *functionality axiom* (funct R), where $R \in \mathbf{R} \cup \mathbf{R}^-$, or (3) a concept membership axiom $B(a)$, where B is a basic concept and $a \in \mathbf{I}$, or (4) a role membership axiom $R(a, c)$, where $R \in \mathbf{R}$ and $a, c \in \mathbf{I}$. A *(description logic) knowledge base* L is a finite set of axioms. A *conjunctive query* over L is of the form $Q(\mathbf{x}) = \exists \mathbf{y} \, (conj(\mathbf{x}, \mathbf{y}))$, where $\mathbf{x}$ and $\mathbf{y}$ are tuples of distinct variables, and $conj(\mathbf{x}, \mathbf{y})$ is a conjunction of assertions $B(z)$ and $R(z_1, z_2)$, where B and R are basic concepts and roles from $\mathbf{R}$, respectively, and z, z_1, and z_2 are individuals from $\mathbf{I}$ or variables in $\mathbf{x}$ or $\mathbf{y}$.

Example 2.1. A university database may use a knowledge base L to characterize students and exams. E.g., suppose (1) every bachelor student is a student; (2) every master student is a student; (3) professors are not students; (4) only students give exams and only exams are given; (5) *john* is a student, *mary* is a master student, *java* is an exam, and *john* has given it. These relationships are encoded by the following axioms in L:

(1) *bachelor_student* $\sqsubseteq$ *student*; (2) *master_student* $\sqsubseteq$ *student*;

(3) *professor* $\sqsubseteq$ ¬*student*; (4) ∃*given* $\sqsubseteq$ *student*; ∃*given*$^{-1}$ $\sqsubseteq$ *exam*;

(5) *student*(*john*); *master_student*(*mary*); *exam*(*java*); *given*(*john*, *java*).

Semantics. The semantics of *DL-Lite* is defined as usual in first-order logics. An *interpretation* $\mathcal{I} = (\Delta^{\mathcal{I}}, \cdot^{\mathcal{I}})$ consists of a nonempty *domain* $\Delta^{\mathcal{I}}$ and a mapping $\cdot^{\mathcal{I}}$ that assigns to each $A \in \mathbf{A}$ a subset of $\Delta^{\mathcal{I}}$, to each $o \in \mathbf{I}$ an element of $\Delta^{\mathcal{I}}$ (such that $o_1 \neq o_2$ implies $o_1^{\mathcal{I}} \neq o_2^{\mathcal{I}}$), and to each $R \in \mathbf{R}$ a subset of $\Delta^{\mathcal{I}} \times \Delta^{\mathcal{I}}$. We extend $\cdot^{\mathcal{I}}$ to all concepts and roles, and we define the *satisfaction* of an axiom F in $\mathcal{I}$, denoted $\mathcal{I} \models F$, as usual. A tuple **c** of individuals from **I** is an *answer* for a conjunctive query $Q(\mathbf{x}) = \exists \mathbf{y} \, (conj(\mathbf{x}, \mathbf{y}))$ to a knowledge base L iff for every $\mathcal{I} = (\Delta^{\mathcal{I}}, \cdot^{\mathcal{I}})$ that satisfies all $F \in L$, there exists a tuple **o** of elements from $\Delta^{\mathcal{I}}$ such that all assertions in $conj(\mathbf{c}, \mathbf{o})$ are satisfied in $\mathcal{I}$. In *DL-Lite*, computing all such answers has a polynomial data complexity.

3 Description Logic Programs

We adopt the description logic programs (or dl-programs) of [7,8], which consist of a description logic knowledge base L and a generalized normal program P, which may contain queries to L (called dl-queries). Note that these dl-programs can be extended by queries to other formalisms, such as RDF theories. We first define the syntax of dl-programs and then their answer set and their well-founded semantics. Note that in contrast to [7,8], we assume here that dl-queries may be conjunctive queries to L.

Syntax. We assume a function-free first-order vocabulary Φ with finite nonempty sets of constant and predicate symbols Φ_c and Φ_p, respectively, and a set of variables $\mathcal{X}$. We assume that (i) Φ_c is a subset of **I** (since the constants in Φ_c may occur in concept and role assertions of dl-queries) and that (ii) Φ and **A** (resp., **R**) have no unary (resp., binary) predicate symbols in common (and thus dl-queries are the only interface between L and P). A *term* is a constant symbol from Φ or a variable from $\mathcal{X}$. If p is a predicate symbol of arity $k \geqslant 0$ from Φ, and $t_1, \ldots, t_k$ are terms, then $p(t_1, \ldots, t_k)$ is an *atom*. A *literal* is an atom a or a default-negated atom *not* a. A *(normal) rule* r is of the form

$$a \leftarrow b_1, \ldots, b_k, not \, b_{k+1}, \ldots, not \, b_m, \tag{1}$$

where $a, b_1, \ldots, b_m$ are atoms and $m \geqslant k \geqslant 0$. We call a the *head* of r, denoted $H(r)$, while the conjunction $b_1, \ldots, b_k, not \, b_{k+1}, \ldots, not \, b_m$ is the *body* of r; its *positive* (resp., *negative*) part is $b_1, \ldots, b_k$ (resp., *not* $b_{k+1}, \ldots, not \, b_m$). We define $B(r)$ as the union of $B^+(r) = \{b_1, \ldots, b_k\}$ and $B^-(r) = \{b_{k+1}, \ldots, b_m\}$. A *(normal) program* P is a finite set of normal rules. We say P is *positive* iff it is "*not*"-free.

A *dl-query* $Q(\mathbf{t})$ is a conjunctive query. A *dl-atom* has the form $DL[S_1 \uplus p_1, \ldots,$ $S_m \uplus p_m; Q(\mathbf{t})]$, where each S_i is a concept or role, p_i is a unary resp. binary predicate symbol, $Q(\mathbf{t})$ is a dl-query, and $m \geqslant 0$. We call $p_1, \ldots, p_m$ its *input predicate symbols*. Intuitively, $\uplus$ increases S_i by the extension of p_i. A *(normal) dl-rule* r is of the form (1), where any $b \in B(r)$ may be a dl-atom. A *(normal) dl-program* $KB = (L, P)$ consists of a description logic knowledge base L and a finite set of dl-rules P. We say $KB = (L, P)$ is *positive* iff P is positive. *Ground terms, atoms, literals*, etc., are defined as usual. We denote by $ground(P)$ the set of all ground instances of dl-rules in P relative to Φ_c.

Example 3.1. A dl-program $KB = (L, P)$ is given by L as in Example 2.1 and P consisting of the following dl-rules, which express that (1) the relation of propaedeutics enjoys the transitive property, (2) if a student has given an exam, then he/she has given all exams that are propaedeutic to it, (3) if two students have a given exam in common, then they have given the same exam, and (4) *unix* is propaedeutic for *java*, and *java* is propaedeutic for *programming_languages*:

(1) $propaedeutic(X, Z) \leftarrow propaedeutic(X, Y), propaedeutic(Y, Z)$;

(2) $given\_prop(X, Z) \leftarrow DL[given(X, Y)], propaedeutic(Z, Y)$;

(3) $given\_same\_exam(X, Y) \leftarrow DL[given \uplus given\_prop; \exists Z(given(X, Z) \land given(Y, Z))]$;

(4) $propaedeutic(unix, java); propaedeutic(java, programming\_languages)$.

Answer Set Semantics. The *Herbrand base* HB_Φ is the set of all ground atoms constructed from constant and predicate symbols in Φ. An *interpretation* I is any $I \subseteq HB_\Phi$. We say I is a *model* of $a \in HB_\Phi$ under a description logic knowledge base L, denoted $I \models_L a$, iff $a \in I$. We say I is a *model* of a ground dl-atom $a = DL[S_1 \uplus p_1, \ldots, S_m \uplus p_m; Q(\mathbf{c})]$ under L, denoted $I \models_L a$, iff $L \cup \bigcup_{i=1}^{m} A_i(I) \models Q(\mathbf{c})$, where $A_i(I) = \{S_i(\mathbf{e}) \mid p_i(\mathbf{e}) \in I\}$. We say I is a *model* of a ground dl-rule r iff $I \models_L H(r)$ whenever $I \models_L B(r)$, that is, $I \models_L a$ for all $a \in B^+(r)$ and $I \not\models_L a$ for all $a \in B^-(r)$. We say I is a *model* of a dl-program $KB = (L, P)$, denoted $I \models KB$, iff $I \models_L r$ for all $r \in ground(P)$.

Like ordinary positive programs, each positive dl-program KB has a unique least model, denoted M_{KB}, which naturally characterizes its semantics. The *answer set semantics* of general dl-programs is then defined by a reduction to the least model semantics of positive ones, using a reduct that generalizes the ordinary Gelfond-Lifschitz reduct [9] and removes all default-negated atoms in dl-rules: For dl-programs $KB = (L, P)$, the *dl-reduct* of P relative to L and an interpretation $I \subseteq HB_\Phi$, denoted P_L^I, is the set of all dl-rules obtained from $ground(P)$ by (i) deleting each dl-rule r such that $I \models_L a$ for some $a \in B^-(r)$, and (ii) deleting from each remaining dl-rule r the negative body. An *answer set* of KB is an interpretation $I \subseteq HB_\Phi$ such that I is the unique least model of (L, P_L^I). A dl-program is *consistent* iff it has an answer set.

The answer set semantics of dl-programs has several nice features. In particular, for dl-programs $KB = (L, P)$ without dl-atoms, it coincides with the ordinary answer set semantics of P. Answer sets of a general dl-program KB are also minimal models of KB. Furthermore, positive and locally stratified dl-programs have exactly one answer set, which coincides with their canonical minimal model.

Well-Founded Semantics. Rather than associating with every dl-program a (possibly empty) set of two-valued interpretations, the well-founded semantics associates with every dl-program a unique three-valued interpretation.

A *classical literal* is either an atom a or its negation $\neg a$. For sets $S \subseteq HB_\Phi$, we define $\neg S = \{\neg a \mid a \in S\}$. We define $Lit_\Phi = HB_\Phi \cup \neg HB_\Phi$. A set of ground classical literals $S \subseteq Lit_\Phi$ is *consistent* iff $S \cap \{a, \neg a\} = \emptyset$ for all $a \in HB_\Phi$. A *three-valued interpretation* is any consistent $I \subseteq Lit_\Phi$. We define the well-founded semantics of dl-programs $KB = (L, P)$ via a generalization of the operator γ^2 for ordinary normal programs. We define the operator γ_{KB} as follows. For every $I \subseteq HB_\Phi$, we define $\gamma_{KB}(I)$ as the least model of the positive dl-program $KB^I = (L, P_L^I)$. The operator γ_{KB} is anti-monotonic, and thus the operator γ_{KB}^2 (defined by $\gamma_{KB}^2(I) = \gamma_{KB}(\gamma_{KB}(I))$, for every $I \subseteq HB_\Phi$) is monotonic and has a least and a greatest fixpoint, denoted $lfp(\gamma_{KB}^2)$ and $gfp(\gamma_{KB}^2)$, respectively. Then, the *well-founded semantics* of the dl-program KB, denoted $WFS(KB)$, is defined as $lfp(\gamma_{KB}^2) \cup \neg(HB_\Phi - gfp(\gamma_{KB}^2))$.

As an important property, the well-founded semantics for dl-programs approximates their answer set semantics. That is, for all consistent dl-programs KB and $\ell \in Lit_\Phi$, it holds that $\ell \in WFS(KB)$ iff ℓ is true in every answer set of KB.

4   Probabilistic Description Logic Programs

In this section, we recall probabilistic dl-programs from [14]. We first define the syntax of probabilistic dl-programs and then their answer set semantics. Informally, they consist of a dl-program (L, P) and a probability distribution μ over a set of total choices B. Every total choice B along with the dl-program (L, P) then defines a set of Herbrand interpretations of which the probabilities sum up to $\mu(B)$.

Syntax. We now define the syntax of probabilistic dl-programs and queries addressed to them. We first define choice spaces and probabilities on choice spaces.

A *choice space* C is a set of pairwise disjoint and nonempty sets $A \subseteq HB_\Phi$. Any $A \in C$ is called an *alternative* of C, and any element $a \in A$ is called an *atomic choice* of C. Intuitively, every alternative $A \in C$ represents a random variable and every atomic choice $a \in A$ one of its possible values. A *total choice* of C is a set $B \subseteq HB_\Phi$ such that $|B \cap A| = 1$ for all $A \in C$ (and thus $|B| = |C|$). Intuitively, every total choice B of C represents an assignment of values to all the random variables. A *probability* μ on a choice space C is a probability function on the set of all total choices of C. Intuitively, every probability μ is a probability distribution over the set of all variable assignments. Since C and all its alternatives are finite, μ can be defined by (i) a mapping $\mu: \bigcup C \to [0, 1]$ such that $\sum_{a \in A} \mu(a) = 1$ for all $A \in C$, and (ii) $\mu(B) = \Pi_{b \in B} \mu(b)$ for all total choices B of C. Intuitively, (i) defines a probability over the values of each random variable of C, and (ii) assumes independence between the random variables.

A *probabilistic dl-program* $KB = (L, P, C, \mu)$ consists of a dl-program (L, P), a choice space C such that (i) $\bigcup C \subseteq HB_\Phi$ and (ii) no atomic choice in C coincides with the head of any $r \in ground(P)$, and a probability μ on C. Intuitively, since the total choices of C select subsets of P, and μ is a probability distribution on the total choices of C, every probabilistic dl-program is the compact encoding of a probability distribution on a finite set of normal dl-programs. Observe here that P is fully general and not necessarily stratified or acyclic. An *event* α is any Boolean combination of atoms (that is, constructed from atoms via the Boolean operators "$\wedge$" and "$\neg$"). A *conditional event* is of the form $\beta|\alpha$, where α and β are events. A *probabilistic query* has the form $\exists(\beta|\alpha)[r, s]$, where $\beta|\alpha$ is a conditional event, and r and s are variables.

Example 4.1. Consider $KB = (L, P, C, \mu)$, where L and P are as in Examples 2.1 and 3.1, respectively, except that the following two (probabilistic) rules are added to P:

$$friends(X, Y) \leftarrow given\_same\_exam(X, Y), DL[master\_student(X)],$$
$$DL[master\_student(Y)], choice_m ;$$
$$friends(X, Y) \leftarrow given\_same\_exam(X, Y), DL[bachelor\_student(X)],$$
$$DL[bachelor\_student(Y)], choice_b .$$

Let $C = \{\{choice_m, not\_choice_m\}, \{choice_b, not\_choice_b\}\}$, and let the probability μ on C be given by μ: $choice_m, not\_choice_m, choice_b, not\_choice_b \mapsto 0.9, 0.1, 0.7,$ 0.3. Here, the new rules express that if two master (resp., bachelor) students have given the same exam, then there is a probability of 0.9 (resp., 0.7) that they are friends. Note that probabilistic facts can be encoded by rules with only atomic choices in their body. Our wondering about the entailed tight interval for the probability that $john$ and $bill$ are friends can then be expressed by the probabilistic query $\exists(friends(john, bill))[R, S]$.

Answer Set Semantics. We now define a probabilistic answer set semantics of probabilistic dl-programs, and the notions of consistency and tight answers.

Given a probabilistic dl-program $KB = (L, P, C, \mu)$, a *probabilistic interpretation* Pr is a probability function on the set of all $I \subseteq HB_\Phi$. We say Pr is an *answer set* of KB iff (i) every interpretation $I \subseteq HB_\Phi$ with $Pr(I) > 0$ is an answer set of $(L, P \cup \{p \leftarrow \mid p \in B\})$ for some total choice B of C, and (ii) $Pr(\bigwedge_{p \in B} p) = \mu(B)$ for every total choice B of C. Informally, Pr is an answer set of $KB = (L, P, C, \mu)$ iff (i) every interpretation $I \subseteq HB_\Phi$ of positive probability under Pr is an answer set of the dl-program (L, P) under some total choice B of C, and (ii) Pr coincides with μ on the total choices B of C. We say KB is *consistent* iff it has an answer set Pr.

Given a ground event α, the *probability* of α in a probabilistic interpretation Pr, denoted $Pr(\alpha)$, is the sum of all $Pr(I)$ such that $I \subseteq HB_\Phi$ and $I \models \alpha$. We say $(\beta|\alpha)[l, u]$ $(l, u \in [0, 1])$ is a *tight consequence* of a consistent probabilistic dl-program KB under the answer set semantics iff l (resp., u) is the infimum (resp., supremum) of $Pr(\alpha \wedge \beta) / Pr(\alpha)$ subject to all answer sets Pr of KB with $Pr(\alpha) > 0$ (note that this infimum (resp., supremum) is naturally defined as 1 (resp., 0) iff no such Pr exists). The *tight answer* for a probabilistic query $Q = \exists(\beta|\alpha)[r, s]$ to KB under the answer set semantics is the set of all ground substitutions θ (for the variables in Q) such that $(\beta|\alpha)[r, s]\theta$ is a tight consequence of KB under the answer set semantics. For ease of presentation, since the tight answers for probabilistic queries $Q = \exists(\beta|\alpha)[r, s]$ with non-ground $\beta|\alpha$ can be reduced to the tight answers for probabilistic queries $Q = \exists(\beta|\alpha)[r, s]$ with ground $\beta|\alpha$, we consider only the latter type of probabilistic queries in the following.

5   Novel Answer Set Characterizations

In this section, we give novel characterizations of (i) the consistency of probabilistic dl-programs and (ii) tight query processing in consistent probabilistic dl-programs under the answer set semantics in terms of the answer sets of normal dl-programs.

As shown in [14], a probabilistic dl-program $KB = (L, P, C, \mu)$ is consistent iff the system of linear constraints $LC_\top$ (see Fig. 1) over y_r ($r \in R$) is solvable. Here, R is the union of all sets of answer sets of $(L, P \cup \{p \leftarrow \mid p \in B\})$ for all total choices B of C. But observe that $LC_\top$ is defined over a set of variables R that corresponds to the set of all answer sets of the underlying normal dl-programs, and thus R is in general quite

$$\sum_{r\in R,\, r\not\models\bigwedge B} -\mu(B)\, y_r \;+\; \sum_{r\in R,\, r\models\bigwedge B} (1-\mu(B))\, y_r \;=\; 0 \quad \text{(for all total choices } B \text{ of } C)$$

$$\sum_{r\in R,\, r\models\alpha} y_r \;=\; 1$$

$$y_r \;\geqslant\; 0 \quad \text{(for all } r\in R)$$

Fig. 1. System of linear constraints LC_α

large. The following theorem shows that the consistency of probabilistic dl-programs can be expressed in terms of answer sets of normal dl-programs only, without additionally deciding whether a system of linear constraints is solvable.

Theorem 5.1 (Consistency). *Let $KB = (L, P, C, \mu)$ be a probabilistic dl-program. Then, KB is consistent iff, for every total choice B of C such that $\mu(B) > 0$, the dl-program $(L, P \cup \{p \leftarrow | p \in B\})$ is consistent.*

Similarly, as shown in [14], computing tight answers for probabilistic queries can be reduced to computing all answer sets of normal dl-programs and solving two linear optimization problems. More specifically, let $KB = (L, P, C, \mu)$ be a consistent probabilistic dl-program, and let $Q = \exists(\beta|\alpha)[r, s]$ be a probabilistic query with ground $\beta|\alpha$. Then, the tight answer for Q to KB is given by $\theta = \{r/l,\ s/u\}$, where l (resp., u) is the optimal value of the subsequent linear program (2) over y_r $(r \in R)$, if (2) has a solution, and it is given by $\theta = \{r/1,\ s/0\}$, if (2) has no solution.

$$\min \text{ (resp., max) } \sum_{r\in R,\, r\models\alpha\wedge\beta} y_r \quad \text{subject to } LC_\alpha \text{ (see Fig. 1).} \tag{2}$$

But the linear program (2) is defined over the same (generally quite large) set of variables as the system of linear constraints LC_T above. The following theorem shows that the tight answers can also be expressed in terms of answer sets of normal dl-programs only, without additionally solving two linear optimization problems.

Theorem 5.2 (Tight Query Processing). *Let $KB = (L, P, C, \mu)$ be a consistent probabilistic dl-program, and let $Q = \exists(\beta|\alpha)[r, s]$ be a probabilistic query with ground $\beta|\alpha$. Let a (resp., b) be the sum of all $\mu(B)$ such that (i) B is a total choice of C and (ii) $\alpha \wedge \beta$ is true in every (resp., some) answer set of $(L, P \cup \{p \leftarrow | p \in B\})$. Let c (resp., d) be the sum of all $\mu(B)$ such that (i) B is a total choice of C and (ii) $\alpha \wedge \neg\beta$ is true in every (resp., some) answer set of $(L, P \cup \{p \leftarrow | p \in B\})$. Then, the tight answer θ for Q to KB under the answer set semantics is given as follows:*

$$\theta = \begin{cases} \{r/1,\ s/0\} & \text{if } b=0 \text{ and } d=0; \\ \{r/0,\ s/0\} & \text{if } b=0 \text{ and } d\neq 0; \\ \{r/1,\ s/1\} & \text{if } b\neq 0 \text{ and } d=0; \\ \{r/\frac{a}{a+d},\ s/\frac{b}{b+c}\} & \text{otherwise.} \end{cases} \tag{3}$$

6 Total Well-Founded Semantics

In this section, we define a novel well-founded semantics for probabilistic dl-programs, called the *total well-founded semantics*, since it is defined for all probabilistic queries to probabilistic dl-programs, as opposed to the well-founded semantics of [14], which is only defined for a very limited class of probabilistic queries. Furthermore, the total well-founded semantics is defined for all probabilistic dl-programs, as opposed to the answer set semantics, which is only defined for consistent probabilistic dl-programs.

More concretely, given a probabilistic dl-program $KB = (L, P, C, \mu)$ and a probabilistic query $Q = \exists(\beta|\alpha)[r, s]$ with ground $\beta|\alpha$, the tight answer θ for Q to KB under the well-founded semantics of [14] *exists* iff both ground events $\alpha \wedge \beta$ and α are defined in every $S = WFS(L, P \cup \{p \leftarrow | p \in B\})$ such that B is a total choice of C. Here, a ground event ϕ is *defined* in S iff either $I \models \phi$ for every interpretation $I \supseteq S \cap HB_\Phi$, or $I \not\models \phi$ for every interpretation $I \supseteq S \cap HB_\Phi$. If α is false in every $WFS(L, P \cup \{p \leftarrow | p \in B\})$ such that B is a total choice of C, then the tight answer is defined as $\theta = \{r/1, s/0\}$; otherwise, the tight answer (if it exists) is defined as $\theta = \{r/\frac{u}{v}, s/\frac{u}{v}\}$, where u (resp., v) is the sum of all $\mu(B)$ such that (i) B is a total choice of C and (ii) $\alpha \wedge \beta$ (resp., α) is true in $WFS(L, P \cup \{p \leftarrow | p \in B\})$.

We define the total well-founded semantics as follows, taking inspiration from the novel answer set characterization of tight answers in the previous section.

Definition 6.1 (Total Well-Founded Semantics). Let $KB = (L, P, C, \mu)$ be a probabilistic dl-program, and let $Q = \exists(\beta|\alpha)[r, s]$ be a probabilistic query with ground $\beta|\alpha$. Let a (resp., b^-) be the sum of all $\mu(B)$ such that (i) B is a total choice of C and (ii) $\alpha \wedge \beta$ is true (resp., false) in $WFS(L, P \cup \{p \leftarrow | p \in B\})$. Let c (resp., d^-) be the sum of all $\mu(B)$ such that (i) B is a total choice of C and (ii) $\alpha \wedge \neg\beta$ is true (resp., false) in $WFS(L, P \cup \{p \leftarrow | p \in B\})$. Let $b = 1 - b^-$ and $d = 1 - d^-$. Then, *the tight answer θ for Q to KB under the total well-founded semantics ($TWFS(KB)$)* is defined by Eq. (3).

The following theorem shows that for probabilistic queries $Q = \exists(\ell)[r, s]$, where ℓ is a ground literal, the tight answers under the total well-founded semantics coincide with the tight answers under the answer set semantics (if they exist). This result is a nice semantic feature of the total well-founded semantics. It also paves the way for an efficient computation of tight answers to such queries under the answer set semantics via the bottom-up fixpoint iteration of the well-founded semantics of normal dl-programs.

Theorem 6.1. *Let $KB = (L, P, C, \mu)$ be a consistent probabilistic dl-program, and let $Q = \exists(\ell)[r, s]$ be a probabilistic query with ground literal ℓ. Then, the tight answer for Q to KB under the total well-founded semantics coincides with the tight answer for Q to KB under the answer set semantics.*

The next theorem shows that the total well-founded semantics generalizes the well-founded semantics of [14], that is, the tight answers under the former coincide with the tight answers under the latter, as long as the tight answers under the latter exist.

Theorem 6.2. *Let $KB = (L, P, C, \mu)$ be a probabilistic dl-program, and let $Q = \exists(\beta | \alpha)[r, s]$ be a probabilistic query with ground $\beta|\alpha$. Then, the tight answer for Q to KB under the total well-founded semantics coincides with the tight answer for Q to KB under the well-founded semantics of [14] (if it exists).*

7   Algorithms

In this section, we provide an anytime algorithm for tight query processing in probabilistic dl-programs under the total answer set semantics.

Algorithm tight_answer

Input: probabilistic dl-program $KB = (L, P, C, \mu)$, probabilistic query $Q = \exists(\beta|\alpha)[r, s]$
with ground $\beta|\alpha$, and error threshold $\epsilon \in [0, 1]$.

Output: $\theta = \{r/l', s/u'\}$ such that $|l - l'| + |u - u'| \leqslant \epsilon$, where $\{r/l, s/u\}$ is the tight
answer for Q to KB under the total well-founded semantics.

Notation: $B_1, \ldots, B_k$ is a sequence of all total choices B of C with $\mu(B_1) \geqslant \cdots \geqslant \mu(B_k)$.

1. $a := 0;\ b := 1;\ c := 0;\ d := 1;\ v := 1;\ i := 1;$
2. **while** $i \leqslant k$ and $v > 0$ and $\frac{v \cdot \max(a,d)}{(a+d) \cdot (a+d+v)} + \frac{v \cdot \max(b,c)}{(b+c) \cdot (b+c+v)} > \epsilon$ **do begin**
3. $S := WFS(L, P \cup \{p \leftarrow\ |\ p \in B_i\});$
4.   **if** $\alpha \wedge \beta$ is true in S **then** $a := a + \mu(B_i)$
5.   **else if** $\alpha \wedge \beta$ is false in S **then** $b := b - \mu(B_i);$
6.   **if** $\alpha \wedge \neg\beta$ is true in S **then** $c := c + \mu(B_i)$
7.   **else if** $\alpha \wedge \neg\beta$ is false in S **then** $d := d - \mu(B_i);$
8. $v := v - \mu(B_i);$
9. $i := i + 1$
10. **end**;
11. **if** $b = 0$ and $d = 0$ **then return** $\theta = \{r/1, s/0\}$
12.   **else if** $b = 0$ and $d \neq 0$ **then return** $\theta = \{r/0, s/0\}$
13.   **else if** $b \neq 0$ and $d = 0$ **then return** $\theta = \{r/1, s/1\}$
14.   **else return** $\theta = \{r/\frac{a}{a+d}, s/\frac{b}{b+c}\}$.

Fig. 2. Algorithm tight_answer

By Definition 6.1, computing the tight answer for a probabilistic query to a probabilistic dl-program $KB = (L, P, C, \mu)$ under $TWFS(KB)$ can be reduced to computing
the well-founded models of all normal dl-programs $(L, P \cup \{p \leftarrow\ |\ p \in B\})$ such that B
is a total choice of C. Here, the number of all total choices B is generally a non-neglec-
table source of complexity. We thus propose (i) to compute the tight answer only up to
an error within a given threshold $\epsilon \in [0, 1]$, (ii) to process the B's along decreasing probabilities $\mu(B)$, and (iii) to eventually stop the computation after a given time interval.

Given a (not necessarily consistent) probabilistic dl-program $KB = (L, P, C, \mu)$, a
probabilistic query $Q = \exists(\beta|\alpha)[r, s]$ with ground $\beta|\alpha$, and an error threshold $\epsilon \in [0, 1]$,
algorithm tight_answer (see Fig. 2) computes some $\theta = \{r/l', s/u'\}$ such that $|l - l'| +
|u - u'| \leqslant \epsilon$, where $\{r/l, s/u\}$ is the tight answer for Q to KB under $TWFS(KB)$.
More concretely, it computes the bounds l' and u' by first initializing the variables a,
b, c, and d (which play the same role as in Definition 6.1). It then computes the well-
founded semantics S of the normal dl-program $(L, P \cup \{p \leftarrow\ |\ p \in B_i\})$ for every total
choice B_i of C, checks whether $\alpha \wedge \beta$ and $\alpha \wedge \neg\beta$ are true or false in S, and updates a,
b, c, and d accordingly. If the possible error in the bounds falls below ϵ, then it stops
and returns the bounds computed thus far. Hence, in the special case where $\epsilon = 0$, the
algorithm computes in particular the tight answer for Q to KB under $TWFS(KB)$. The
following theorem shows that algorithm tight_answer is sound.

Theorem 7.1. *Let KB be a probabilistic dl-program, let $Q = \exists(\beta|\alpha)[r, s]$ be a proba-
bilistic query with ground $\beta|\alpha$, and let $\theta = \{r/l, s/u\}$ be the tight answer for Q to KB*

under $TWFS(KB)$. Let $\theta' = \{r/l', s/u'\}$ be the output computed by tight_answer for the error threshold $\epsilon \in [0, 1]$. Then, $|l - l'| + |u - u'| \leqslant \epsilon$.

Algorithm tight_answer is actually an *anytime algorithm*, since we can always interrupt it, and return the bounds computed thus far. The following theorem shows that these bounds deviate from the tight bounds with an exactly measurable error (note that it can also be shown that the possible error is decreasing along the iterations of the while-loop). For this reason, algorithm tight_answer also iterates through the total choices B_i of C in a way such that the probabilities $\mu(B_i)$ are decreasing, so that the error in the computed bounds is very likely to be low already after few iteration steps.

Theorem 7.2. *Let KB be a probabilistic dl-program, let $Q = \exists(\beta|\alpha)[r, s]$ be a probabilistic query with ground $\beta|\alpha$, let $\epsilon \in [0, 1]$ be an error threshold, and let $\theta = \{r/l, s/u\}$ be the tight answer for Q to KB under $TWFS(KB)$. Suppose we run tight_answer on KB, Q, and ϵ, and we interrupt it after line (9). Let the returned $\theta' = \{r/l', s/u'\}$ be as specified in lines (11) to (14). Then, if $v = 0$, then $\theta = \theta'$. Otherwise,*

$$|l - l'| + |u - u'| \leqslant \frac{v \cdot \max(a,d)}{(a+d) \cdot (a+d+v)} + \frac{v \cdot \max(b,c)}{(b+c) \cdot (b+c+v)}.$$

The algorithm is based on two finite fixpoint iterations for computing the well-founded semantics of normal dl-programs, which are in turn based on a finite fixpoint iteration for computing the least model of positive dl-programs, as usual.

8   Complexity

In this section, we finally provide tractability and complexity results.

The following theorem shows that tight query processing in probabilistic dl-programs $KB = (L, P, C, \mu)$ in *DL-Lite* (where L is in *DL-Lite*) under $TWFS(KB)$ can be done in polynomial time in the data complexity. The result follows from the polynomial data complexity of (a) computing the well-founded semantics of a normal dl-program (see above) and (b) conjunctive query processing in *DL-Lite*. Here, $|C|$ is bounded by a constant, since C and μ define the probabilistic information of P, which is fixed as a part of the program in P, while the ordinary facts in P are the variable input.

Theorem 8.1. *Given a probabilistic dl-program KB in DL-Lite and a probabilistic query $Q = \exists(\ell)[r, s]$ with ground literal ℓ, the tight answer $\theta = \{r/l, s/u\}$ for Q to KB under $TWFS(KB)$ can be computed in polynomial time in the data complexity.*

The next theorem shows that computing tight answers is EXP-complete in the combined complexity. The lower bound follows from the EXP-hardness of datalog in the combined complexity, and the upper bound follows from Theorem 7.1.

Theorem 8.2. *Given a probabilistic dl-program KB in DL-Lite and a probabilistic query $Q = \exists(\beta|\alpha)[r, s]$ with ground $\beta|\alpha$, computing the tight answer $\theta = \{r/l, s/u\}$ for Q to KB under $TWFS(KB)$ is EXP-complete in the combined complexity.*

9   Probabilistic Data Integration

A central aspect of the Semantic Web is data integration. To some extent, dl-programs already perform some form of data integration, since they bring together rules and ontologies, and also allow for connecting to other formalisms, such as RDF theories. In this section, we illustrate that probabilistic dl-programs allow for data integration with probabilities. Thus, probabilistic dl-programs are a very promising formalism for probabilistic data integration in the Rules, Logic, and Proof layers of the Semantic Web.

In addition to expressing probabilistic knowledge about the global schema and about the source schema, the probabilities in probabilistic dl-programs can especially be used for specifying the probabilistic mapping in the data integration process. Below we illustrate two different types of probabilistic mappings, depending on whether the probabilities are used as *trust* or as *mapping probabilities*.

The simplest way of probabilistically integrating several data sources is to weight each data source with a *trust probability* (which all sum up to 1). This is especially useful when several redundant data sources are to be integrated. In such a case, pieces of data from different data sources may easily be inconsistent with each other.

Example 9.1. Suppose that we want to obtain a weather forecast for a certain place by integrating the potentially different weather forecasts of several weather forecast institutes. For ease of presentation, suppose that we only have three weather forecast institutes A, B, and C. In general, one trusts certain weather forecast institutes more than others. In our case, we suppose that our trust in the institutes A, B, and C is expressed by the trust probabilities 0.6, 0.3, and 0.1, respectively. That is, we trust most in A, medium in B, and less in C. In general, the different institutes do not use the same data structure to represent their weather forecast data. For example, institute A may use a single relation $forecast(place, date, weather, temperature, wind)$ to store all the data, while B may have one relation $forecastPlace(date, weather, temperature, wind)$ for every place, and C may use several different relations $forecast\_weather(place, date, weather)$, $forecast\_temperature(place, date, temperature)$, and $forecast\_wind(place, date, wind)$. Suppose that the global schema G has the relation $forecast\_rome(date, weather, temperature, wind)$, which may e.g. be posted on the web by the tourist information of Rome. The probabilistic mapping of the source schemas of A, B, and C to the global schema G can then be specified by the following $KB_M = (\emptyset, P_M, C_M, \mu_M)$:

$$P_M = \{forecast\_rome(D, W, T, M) \leftarrow forecast(rome, D, W, T, M), inst_A;$$
$$forecast\_rome(D, W, T, M) \leftarrow forecastRome(D, W, T, M), inst_B;$$
$$forecast\_rome(D, W, T, M) \leftarrow forecast\_weather(rome, D, W),$$
$$forecast\_temperature(rome, D, T), forecast\_wind(rome, D, M), inst_C\};$$
$$C_M = \{\{inst_A, inst_B, inst_C\}\};$$
$$\mu_M : inst_A, inst_B, inst_C \mapsto 0.6, 0.3, 0.1.$$

The mapping assertions state that the first, second, and third rule above hold with the probabilities 0.6, 0.3, and 0.1, respectively. This is motivated by the fact that three institutes may generally provide conflicting weather forecasts, and our trust in the institutes A, B, and C are given by the trust probabilities 0.6, 0.3, and 0.1, respectively.

When integrating several data sources, it may be the case that the relationships between the source schema and the global schema are *purely probabilistic*.

Example 9.2. Suppose that we want to integrate the schemas of two libraries, and that the global schema contains the predicate symbol *logic_programming*, while the source schemas contain only the concepts *rule-based_systems* resp. *deductive_databases*.

These predicate symbols and concepts are overlapping to some extent, but they do not exactly coincide. For example, a randomly chosen book from *rule-based_systems* (resp., *deductive_databases*) may belong to the area *logic_programming* with the probability 0.7 (resp., 0.8). The probabilistic mapping from the source schemas to the global schema can then be expressed by the following $KB_M = (\emptyset, P_M, C_M, \mu_M)$:

$$P_M = \{logic\_programming(X) \leftarrow DL[rule\text{-}based\_systems(X)],\ choice_1\,;$$
$$logic\_programming(X) \leftarrow DL[deductive\_databases(X)],\ choice_2\}\,;$$
$$C_M = \{\{choice_1, not\_choice_1\}, \{choice_2, not\_choice_2\}\}\,;$$
$$\mu_M:\ choice_1, not\_choice_1, choice_2, not\_choice_2 \mapsto 0.7,\ 0.3,\ 0.8,\ 0.2\,.$$

10   Conclusion

We have proposed tractable probabilistic dl-programs for the Semantic Web, which combine tractable description logics, normal programs under the answer set semantics, and probabilities. In particular, we have introduced the total well-founded semantics for probabilistic dl-programs. Contrary to the previous answer set and well-founded semantics, it is always defined. Furthermore, tight (resp., tight literal) query processing under the total well-founded semantics coincides with tight (resp., tight literal) query processing under the previous well-founded (resp., answer set) semantics in all cases where the latter is defined. We have then presented an anytime algorithm for tight query processing in probabilistic dl-programs under the total well-founded semantics. Note that the total well-founded semantics and the anytime algorithm are not limited to *DL-Lite* as underlying description logic; they hold for all probabilistic dl-programs on top of description logics with decidable conjunctive query processing. We have also shown that tight query processing in probabilistic dl-programs under the total well-founded semantics can be done in polynomial time in the data complexity and is complete for EXP in the combined complexity. Finally, we have described an application of probabilistic dl-programs in probabilistic data integration for the Semantic Web.

Instead of being based on the loosely integrated normal dl-programs $KB = (L, P)$ of [7,8], probabilistic dl-programs can also be developed as a generalization of the *tightly integrated* normal dl-programs $KB = (L, P)$ of [13] (see [4]). Essentially, rather than having dl-queries to L in rule bodies in P (which also allow for passing facts as dl-query arguments from P to L) and assuming that Φ and $\mathbf{A}$ (resp., $\mathbf{R}$) have no unary (resp., binary) predicate symbols in common (and so that dl-queries are the only interface between L and P), the tightly integrated normal dl-programs of [13] have no dl-queries, but Φ and $\mathbf{A}$ (resp., $\mathbf{R}$) may very well have unary (resp., binary) predicate symbols in common, and so the integration between L and P is of a much tighter nature. Nearly all the results of this paper carry over to such tightly integrated probabilistic dl-programs. As an important feature for the Semantic Web, they also allow for expressing in P probabilistic relations between the concepts and roles in L, since we can freely use concepts and roles from L as unary resp. binary predicate symbols in P.

An interesting topic for future research is to investigate whether one can also develop an efficient top-k query technique for the presented probabilistic dl-programs: Rather than computing the tight probability interval for a given ground literal, such a technique returns k most probable ground instances of a given non-ground expression.

Acknowledgments. This work has been supported by the German Research Foundation (DFG) under the Heisenberg Programme and by the Austrian Science Fund (FWF) under the project P18146-N04. I thank the reviewers for their constructive and useful comments, which helped to improve this work.

References

1. Berners-Lee, T.: Weaving the Web. Harper, San Francisco, CA (1999)
2. Baral, C., Gelfond, M., Rushton, J.N.: Probabilistic reasoning with answer sets. In: Proc. LPNMR-2004, pp. 21–33 (2004)
3. Calì, A., Lukasiewicz, T.: An approach to probabilistic data integration for the Semantic Web. In: Proc. URSW-2006 (2006)
4. Calì, A., Lukasiewicz, T.: Tightly integrated probabilistic description logic programs for the Semantic Web. In: Dahl, V., Niemelä, L. (eds.) ICLP 2007. LNCS, vol. 4670, pp. 428–429. Springer, Heidelberg (2007)
5. Calvanese, D., De Giacomo, G., Lembo, D., Lenzerini, M., Rosati, R.: Data complexity of query answering in description logics. In: Proc. KR-2006, pp. 260–270 (2006)
6. da Costa, P.C.G., Laskey, K.B.: PR-OWL: A framework for probabilistic ontologies. In: Proc. FOIS-2006, pp. 237–249 (2006)
7. Eiter, T., Lukasiewicz, T., Schindlauer, R., Tompits, H.: Combining answer set programming with description logics for the Semantic Web. In: Proc. KR-2004, pp. 141–151 (2004)
8. Eiter, T., Lukasiewicz, T., Schindlauer, R., Tompits, H.: Well-founded semantics for description logic programs in the Semantic Web. In: Antoniou, G., Boley, H. (eds.) RuleML 2004. LNCS, vol. 3323, pp. 81–97. Springer, Heidelberg (2004)
9. Gelfond, M., Lifschitz, V.: Classical negation in logic programs and deductive databases. New Generation Computing 17, 365–387 (1991)
10. Giugno, R., Lukasiewicz, T.: P-$\mathcal{SHOQ}$(**D**): A probabilistic extension of $\mathcal{SHOQ}$(**D**) for probabilistic ontologies in the Semantic Web. In: Flesca, S., Greco, S., Leone, N., Ianni, G. (eds.) JELIA 2002. LNCS (LNAI), vol. 2424, pp. 86–97. Springer, Heidelberg (2002)
11. Horrocks, I., Patel-Schneider, P.F.: Reducing OWL entailment to description logic satisfiability. J. Web Sem. 1(4), 345–357 (2004)
12. Kersting, K., De Raedt, L.: Bayesian logic programs. CoRR, cs.AI/0111058 (2001)
13. Lukasiewicz, T.: A novel combination of answer set programming with description logics for the Semantic Web. In: Franconi, E., Kifer, M., May, W. (eds.) ESWC 2007. LNCS, vol. 4519, pp. 384–398. Springer, Heidelberg (2007)
14. Lukasiewicz, T.: Probabilistic description logic programs. Int. J. Approx. Reason. 45(2), 288–307 (2007)
15. Pan, R., Ding, Z., Yu, Y., Peng, Y.: A Bayesian network approach to ontology mapping. In: Cruz, I., Decker, S., Allemang, D., Preist, C., Schwabe, D., Mika, P., Uschold, M., Aroyo, L. (eds.) ISWC 2006. LNCS, vol. 4273, pp. 563–577. Springer, Heidelberg (2006)
16. Poole, D.: The independent choice logic for modelling multiple agents under uncertainty. Artif. Intell. 94(1–2), 7–56 (1997)
17. Udrea, O., Deng, Y., Hung, E., Subrahmanian, V.S.: Probabilistic ontologies and relational databases. In: Meersman, R., Tari, Z. (eds.) OTM 2005. LNCS, vol. 3760, pp. 1–17. Springer, Heidelberg (2005)
18. van Keulen, M., de Keijzer, A., Alink, W.: A probabilistic XML approach to data integration. In: Proc. ICDE-2005, pp. 459–470 (2005)
19. W3C. OWL web ontology language overview, W3C Recommendation (February 10, 2004), Available at www.w3.org/TR/2004/REC-owl-features-20040210/

Valued Hesitation in Intervals Comparison

Meltem Öztürk[1] and Alexis Tsoukiàs[2]

[1] CRIL Université d'Artois
ozturk@cril.univ-artois.fr
[2] LAMSADE - CNRS, Université Paris Dauphine
tsoukias@lamsade.dauphine.fr

Abstract. The paper presents a valued extension of the recently introduced concept of PQI interval order. The main idea is that, while comparing objects represented by interval of values there is a zone of hesitation between strict difference and strict similarity which could be modelled through valued relations. The paper presents suitable definitions of such valued relations fulfilling a number of interesting properties. The use of such a tool in data analysis and rough sets theory is discussed in the paper.

Keywords: interval orders, PQI interval orders, valued relations, valued similarity, uncertainty modelling.

1 Introduction

Comparing objects described under form of intervals dates back to the work of Luce, [1], where difference of utilities are perceived only when beyond a threshold (for a comprehensive discussion on the concepts of semi-order and interval order see [2,3]). The basic idea introduced in such works is that when we compare objects under form of intervals they can be considered as different (preferred) iff their associated intervals have an empty intersection. Otherwise they are similar (indifferent). However, such an approach does not distinguish the specific case where one interval is "more to the right" (in the sense of the reals) of the other, but they have a non empty intersection. Such a situation can be viewed as an hesitation (denoted Q) between preference (dissimilarity, denoted P) and indifference (similarity, denoted I) and merits a specific attention.

Recently Tsoukiàs and Vincke [4] gave a complete characterisation of such a structure (denoted as PQI interval order), while in [5] and [6] a polynomial algorithms for the detection of such a structure in an oriented graph are provided. In this paper we extend such results considering the situation of hesitation under a continuous valuation of preference and indifference. The idea is that the intersection of the two intervals can be more or less large thus resulting in a more or less large hesitation represented by a value in the interval [0,1] for preference and indifference.

The paper is organised as follows. In the next section we introduce the basic notation and results on regular interval orders and semi-orders. In section 3 we introduce the concept of PQI interval order and semi-order. In section 4 we present a general frame work for the characterisation of preference structures with three binary relations (P, Q and I) and introduce a functional representation for preference (dissimilarity) and

H. Prade and V.S. Subrahmanian (Eds.): SUM 2007, LNAI 4772, pp. 157–170, 2007.

indifference (similarity) fulfilling a number of nice properties. Further research directions are included in the conclusions. The paper updates and extends results appeared originally in [7].

2   Interval Orders

In the following we will consider objects represented under form of intervals of values. Given a finite set A of objects we associate to each element of A two functions $l : A \mapsto \mathbb{R}$ and $u : A \mapsto \mathbb{R}$ (the left and right extreme of x respectively) such that $\forall x\ l(x) < u(x)$. Such a representation is equivalent to the one where to each element x of A is associated a function $g(x)$ and threshold function $t(x)$. We have $l(x) = g(x)$ and $u(x) = g(x) + t(x)$. In the rest of the paper we will only use the $(l(x), u(x))$ representation. Given the finite structure of set A, when we compare intervals we can restrict inequalities to their strict part without loss of any generality.

Further we consider a structure of two binary relations $P \subseteq A \times A$ and $I \subseteq A \times A$ (respectively named preference and indifference). From a data analysis point of view we can consider indifference as a similarity relation and the union of preference and its inverse as a dissimilarity relation. Hereafter, for sake of simplicity, we will only use the terms of preference and indifference such that: P is asymmetric and irreflexive, I is symmetric and reflexive, $P \cup I$ is complete and $P \cap I = \emptyset$.

Given any two binary relations V, W on the set A we denote $V.W(x, y)$ if and only if $\exists z :\ V(x, z) \wedge W(z, y)$. We denote $V \subseteq W$ for the formula $\forall x, y\ V(x, y) \Rightarrow W(x, y)$.

We are now able to give some basic definitions and theorems.

Definition 1. *[2]. A $\langle P, I \rangle$ preference structure on a set A is a PI interval order iff* $\exists\ l, u : A \mapsto \mathbb{R}$ *such that:*
$\forall\ x :\ u(x) > l(x)$;
$\forall\ x, y : P(x, y)\ \Leftrightarrow\ l(x) > u(y)$;
$\forall\ x, y : I(x, y)\ \Leftrightarrow\ l(x) < u(y)$ *and* $l(y) < u(x)$.

Definition 2. *[2]. A $\langle P, I \rangle$ preference structure on a set A is a PI semi order iff* $\exists\ l :$ $A \mapsto \mathbb{R}$ *and a positive constant k such that:*
$\forall\ x, y : P(x, y)\ \Leftrightarrow\ l(x) > l(y) + k$;
$\forall\ x, y : I(x, y)\ \Leftrightarrow\ |l(x) - l(y)| < k$.

Such structures have been extensively studied in the literature (see for example [2]). We recall here below the two fundamental results which characterise interval orders and semi orders.

Theorem 1. *[2]. A $\langle P, I \rangle$ preference structure on a set A is a PI interval order iff* $P.I.P \subset P$.

Theorem 2. *[2]. A $\langle P, I \rangle$ preference structure on a set A is a PI semi order iff $P.I.P$ $\subset P$ and $I.P.P \subset P$.*

3 *PQI* Interval Orders

Recently [4] suggested that, while the conditions under which the relation P holds could be considered fixed, the conditions under which the relation I holds contain two different situations: One called "indifference" (where one interval is included to the other) and the other called "weak preference" or "hesitation between indifference and preference" (where the intersection of the two intervals is non empty, but one interval is "more to the right of the other"). More formally we consider preference structures composed of three preference relations: P (which is asymmetric and irreflexive), Q (which is asymmetric and irreflexive) and I (which is symmetric and reflexive), $P \cup Q \cup I$ being complete and mutual intersections being empty and we have the following results.

Definition 3. *[4] A* $\langle P, Q, I \rangle$ *preference structure on a finite set A is a PQI interval order, iff* $\exists\, l, u : A \mapsto \mathbb{R}$ *such that,* $\forall x, y \in A, x \neq y$:
- $u(x) > l(x)$;
- $P(x, y) \Leftrightarrow u(x) > l(x) > u(y) > l(y)$;
- $Q(x, y) \Leftrightarrow u(x) > u(y) > l(x) > l(y)$;
- $I(x, y) \Leftrightarrow u(x) > u(y) > l(y) > l(x)$ *or* $u(y) > u(x) > l(x) > l(y)$.

Theorem 3. *[4] A* $\langle P, Q, I \rangle$ *preference structure on a finite set A is a PQI interval order, iff there exists a partial order I_l such that:*
i) $I = I_l \cup I_u \cup I_o$ *where* $I_o = \{(x, x),\ x \in A\}$ *and* $I_u = I_l^{-1}$;
ii) $(P \cup Q \cup I_l)P \subset P$;
iii) $P(P \cup Q \cup I_u) \subset P$;
iv) $(P \cup Q \cup I_l)Q \subset P \cup Q \cup I_l$;
v) $Q(P \cup Q \cup I_u) \subset P \cup Q \cup I_u$.

Definition 4. *[4] A PQI semi order is a PQI interval order such that* $\exists\, k > 0$ *constant for which* $\forall x:\ u(x) = l(x) + k$.

In other words, a PQI semi order is a $\langle P, Q, I \rangle$ preference structure for which there exists a real valued function $l : A \mapsto \mathbb{R}$ and a positive constant k such that $\forall\, x, y$:
- $P(x, y) \Leftrightarrow l(x) > l(y) + k$;
- $Q(x, y) \Leftrightarrow l(y) + k > l(x) > l(y)$;
- $I(x, y) \Leftrightarrow l(x) = l(y)$; (in fact I reduces to I_o).

Theorem 4. *[4] A* $\langle P, Q, I \rangle$ *preference structure is a PQI semi order iff:*
i) *I is transitive*
ii) $PP \cup PQ \cup QP \subset P$;
iii) $QQ \subset P \cup Q$;

4 Valued Hesitation

The existence of a zone of hesitation between strict preference and indifference and the introduction of valued relations in order to take in account such an hesitation has been first considered by Roy ([8,9]) in the case of the so-called pseudo-orders and extensively studied in [10]. However, in this case they consider preference structures with two thresholds which is equivalent to a representation with intervals whose length is within an interval of values. The hesitation occurs between the extremities of this second interval.

In our case we consider preference structures with only one threshold. The hesitation is due to the interval structure of the information associated to each object. The above results however, although introduce the idea that comparing objects represented by intervals implies the existence of a zone of hesitation between preference and indifference, are unable to give a "measure" of such an hesitation.

Consider three objects whose cost is for the first (x) in the interval $[10, 18]$, for the second (y) in the interval $[11, 20]$ and for the third (z) in the interval $[17, 20]$. Using the previous approach we get $Q(x, y)$, $Q(x, z)$ and $I(y, z)$. However, it is intuitively clear that the hesitation which occurs when objects x and y are compared is not the same with the hesitation which occurs when objects x and z are compared. Moreover, although objects y and z are considered indifferent it is again intuitively clear that they are indifferent to some extend and not identical.

The basic idea introduced is that the extend to which the two intervals have a non empty intersection could be a "measure" of the hesitation between preference and indifference. Such an idea dates back to Dubois and Prade ([11]), but applied to conventional preference structures where a distribution of possibility can be associated to alternatives under the form of a fuzzy number. In this approach we consider flat distributions of uncertainty in the sense that any value of the interval has the same possibility to represent the "real" value. From this point of view it is meaningful to compare lengths of intervals in order to have a "measure" of the uncertainty. The approach however, easy generalises in the case of specific uncertainty distributions.

First of all we will present a general framework for the fuzzification of preference structures having the three relations P, Q and I and then we will propose a model in order to calculate the evaluation of each relation.

We begin by introducing some basic notions and notations: We are going to use the symbols of T and S in order to represent T-norms and T-conorms respectively as continuous representations of conjunction and disjunction operators in the case of continuous valuations. n will represent the negation operator (for a discussion about such operators in the frame of fuzzy sets theory see [12]).

T-norms and T-conorms are related by duality. Pairs of t-norms and t-conorms satisfy the generalisation of the De Morgan law as in the following:

Definition 5 (De Morgan Triplets). *Let T be a t-norm, S a t-conorm and n a strict negation then $\langle T, S, n \rangle$ is a De Morgan triple iff $\forall x, y \in [0, 1]$:*

$$n(S(x, y)) = T(n(x), n(y)).$$

Several De Morgan Triplets have been suggested in the literature. Zadeh and Lukasiewicz triplets (see [12]) are the most used ones in preference modelling. We denote them respectively by (T_{min}, S_{min}, n) and (LT, LS, n) (see Table 4). The extension of the properties of binary relations in the valued case is straightforward and omitted for sake of space in this paper. The reader can see the relevant details in [13]

Table 1. De Morgan triplets

Names	t-norms	t-conorms
Zadeh	$min(x, y)$	$max(x, y)$
Lukasiewicz	$max(x + y - 1, 0)$	$min(x + y, 1)$

and [14]. We only introduce in the following two notions that we need for the rest of the paper:

Definition 6 (Zero divisor). *[15] An element $x \in]0, 1[$ is called a zero divisor of a t-norm T iff $\exists y \in]0, 1[$ $T(x, y) = 0$. A t-norm without zero divisors is called positive.*

Definition 7 (Archimedean). *[15] A continuous t-norm T is Archimedean iff $\forall x \in]0, 1[$ $T(x, x) < x$.*

It is easy to see that Lukasiewicz t-norms have a zero divisor and are Archimedean and that the minimum operator is positive.

We are ready now to give the characterisation of a fuzzy preference structure having P, Q and I that we call fuzzy $\langle P, Q, I \rangle$ preference structure. Our study is inspired from the work of De Baets et al. ([16]) concerning the case of partial preference structures fuzzification.

Definition 8 (Fuzzy $\langle P, Q, I \rangle$ preference structure). *Consider a de Morgan triplet $M = (T, S, n)$ and three valued binary relations P, Q and I. A $\langle P, Q, I \rangle$ structure on the set A is a fuzzy preference structure w.r.t. M iff:*

1. *P and Q are irreflexive and T-asymmetric,*
2. *I is reflexive and symmetric,*
3. *$T(P, I) = 0$, $T(P, Q) = 0$ and $T(Q, I) = 0$,*
4. *$S(P, S(Q, I))$ is S-complete.*

We show by the help of the two next propositions that in order to have a real fuzzy preference structure defined in the whole unit interval $[0, 1]$, continuous, Archimedean t-norms having zero divisors must be used.

Proposition 1. *Consider a de Morgan triplet $M = (T, S, n)$ with a t-norm without zero divisors. If all the conditions of definition 8 are satisfied for a fuzzy $\langle P, Q, I \rangle$ structure with M, then the fuzzy relations P, Q and I are crisp.*

Proof. see [17]. ■

Hence, it is better to have a zero divisor in order to have fuzzy relations. In this case we know another result concerning non-Archimedean t-norms.

Proposition 2. *Consider a de Morgan triplet $M = (T, S, n)$ with a continuous non-Archimedean t-norm with zero divisors. If all the conditions of definition 8 are satisfied for a fuzzy $\langle P, Q, I \rangle$ structure with M, then $\exists x_\varsigma \in [0, 1[$ such that $\forall x, y$,*

$$p(x, y) < 1 \implies p(x, y) < x_\varsigma,$$
$$q(x, y) < 1 \implies q(x, y) < x_\varsigma,$$
$$i(x, y) < 1 \implies i(x, y) < x_\varsigma.$$

Proof. see [17]. ■

Hence, in order to use the whole unit interval $[0, 1]$, continuous, Archimedean t-norms having zero divisors must be used. Such t-norms are called nilpotent and are ϕ-transform of the Lukasiewicz t-norm. For that reason an alternative definition of fuzzy $\langle P, Q, I \rangle$ preference structure can be given:

Definition 9 (L-Fuzzy $\langle P, Q, I \rangle$ preference structure). *Consider a Lukasiewicz triplet* $L = (LT, LS, n)$ *and three valued binary relations* P, Q *and* I. *A* $\langle P, Q, I \rangle$ *structure on the set A is a L-fuzzy preference structure w.r.t. L if:*

1. *P and Q are irreflexive and LT-asymmetric,*
2. *I is reflexive and symmetric,*
3. $LT(P, I) = 0$, $LT(P, Q) = 0$, $LT(Q, I) = 0$, $LT(P, Q^{-1}) = 0$, *(exclusivity),*
4. $LS(P, LS(Q, I))$ *is LS-complete.*

Although the definition 9 utilizes the whole unit interval, it presents some weaknesses. Three critics can be done:

1. The asymmetry condition with a t-norm having zero divisor allows the co-existence of strictly positive $p(x, y)$ and $p(y, x)$ for the same couple which can be contradictory to the semantics of preference relation or must be avoided in some situations.
2. The exclusivity condition with a t-norm having zero divisor do not permit us to forbid the co-existence of relations with contradictory semantics. For example, depending on the context of preference modelling, one may want to forbid the co-existence of P and Q^{-1}, since in the majority of cases if there some credibility for the sentence "x is strictly preferred to y", the sentence "y is weakly preferred to x" should not be credible at all.
3. Finally, within some context or for some decision maker it may be important to have a stronger completeness, in the sense that for every couple x, y, the characteristic relation or its converse should take the value 1. Again, positive t-conorms do not satisfy such conditions.

For all these reasons, we propose the use of different triangular norms for each condition.

Definition 10 (Flexible Fuzzy $\langle P, Q, I \rangle$ preference structure). *Consider De Morgan triplets* $M_i = (T_i, S_i, n_i)$ *with* $i \in \{1, \dots, 6\}$. *A* $\langle P, Q, I \rangle$ *structure on the set A is a flexible fuzzy preference structure w.r.t* M_i *if:*

1. *P and Q are irreflexive, P is T_1-asymmetric and Q is T_2-asymmetric,*
2. *I is reflexive and symmetric,*
3. $T_3(P, I) = 0$, $T_4(P, Q) = 0$, $T_5(Q, I) = 0$ *and* $T_6(P, Q^{-1}) = 0$, *(exclusivity),*
4. $S_1(P, S_1(Q, I))$ *is S_1-complete.*

We define the characteristic relation R as $R = S_1(P, S_1(Q, I))$.

Before analysing all the possibilities concerning the use of different t-norms, we make some assumptions:

i. The asymmetry conditions use the min operator: $T_1 = T_2 = \min$,
ii. The exclusivity between P and Q^{-1} makes use of the min operator: $T_6 = \min$,

iii. $\forall x, y$, if $r(x, y) = 1$ and $r(y, x) = 0$ then $p(x, y) = 1, q(x, y) = 0, i(x, y) = 0$,
iv. $\forall x, y$, if $r(x, y) = 1$ and $r(y, x) = 1$ then $i(x, y) = 1, p(x, y) = 0, q(x, y) = 0$.

Assumptions i and ii are related to the critics 1 and 2 and assumptions iii and iv are natural conditions very frequently used in preference modelling and decision analysis. Unfortunately they are not sufficient to conclude our analysis. The determinations of T_3, T_4, T_5 and S_1 are less natural and need more detailed study.

We begin by the completeness condition. Considering the characteristic relation R one can distinguish three different states: $r(x, y) = 1, r(x, y) = 0$ and $0 < r(x, y) < 1$. R is S_1-complete means that $\forall x, y$, $S_1(R(x, y), R(y, x)) = 1$. Therefore, we analyse different permutations of the states of R and R^{-1} and we obtain nine cases where some of them are already defined by the previous assumptions (see Table 2).

Table 2. Values of p, q and i whit our hypotheses

$R\backslash R^{-1}$	0	$]0, 1[$	1
0	?	?	P^{-1}
$]0, 1[$	?	?	?
1	P	?	I

Now we are interested in unknown cases. For the completeness condition there are two possibilities. S_1 may be positive (S_1^+) or negative[1] (S_1^-):

- If S_1 is positive, then
  - if $r(x, y) = 0$ then $r(y, x) = 1$ because R is S-complete: $S_1^+(r(x, y), r(y, x)) = S_1^+(0, r(y, x)) = r(y, x) = 1$,
  - if $r(x, y) = 1$ then $0 \leq r(y, x) \leq 1$ because in this case there is no condition on $r(y, x)$,
  - if $0 < r(x, y) < 1$ then $r(y, x) = 1$ because of the definition of positive t-norms.

  These results allow us to complete some cases of the Table 2, especially the ones which do not satisfy the completeness condition and we obtain the first collum of Table 3.
- If S_1 is negative, then
  - if $r(x, y) = 0$ then $r(y, x) = 1$ because R is S-complete: $S_1^-(r(x, y), r(y, x)) = S_1^-(0, r(y, x)) = r(y, x) = 1$,
  - if $r(x, y) = 1$ then $0 \leq r(y, x) \leq 1$ because in this case there is no condition on $r(y, x)$,
  - if $0 < r(x, y) < 1$ then $0 < r(y, x) \leq 1$ because S_1^- is negative and has a zero divisor.

  Like in the previous case, we complete the Table 2 thanks to these results and we obtain the second collum of Table 3.

In order to complete our analysis, exclusivity conditions must be studied for the five cases expressed in Table 3 by " ? ". Before beginning the analysis, let us mention that

---

[1] A De Morgan triplet with an involutive negation which is not positive.

Table 3. Values of p, q and i when r is S^+-complete and S^--complete

$R\backslash R^{-1}$	0	]0,1[	1
0	incomplete	incomplete	P^{-1}
]0,1[	incomplete	incomplete	?
1	P	?	I

$R\backslash R^{-1}$	0	]0,1[	1
0	incomplete	incomplete	P^{-1}
]0,1[	incomplete	?	?
1	P	?	I

some symmetries and similarities can help us to decrease the number of cases to analyse: cases $(r(x,y) = 1, 0 < r(y,x) < 1)$ and $(r(y,x) = 1, 0 < r(x,y) < 1)$ are symmetric and provide similar results. Thus, analysing the cases $(r(x,y) = 1, 0 < r(y,x) < 1)$ for positively and negatively completeness and $(0 < r(x,y) < 1, 0 < r(y,x) < 1)$ for positively completeness will be sufficient in order to finalise our analysis.

As in the completeness condition, for each t-norm of exclusivity conditions $(T_3, T_4$ and $T_5)$, there are two possibilities: T_i $(i = 3,4,5)$ can be positive (and will be denoted by T_i^+) or negative (and will be denoted by T_i^-). All the permutation of these two possibilities for three t-norms (there are $2^3 = 8$ of them) are analysed and the results are presented in Table 4 (the detailed analysis of these cases are not presented in this paper for the sake of space, an interested reader can see in [17]). Remark that in each case of Table 4 we present only relations which can be valued. For example having an empty case, like the first case of the first line, means that in this case we can only have crisp relations. When there are some relations in a case, like the second column of the first line, it means that these relations can be valued while the remaining ones are crisp. In the case of the second column of the first line, the indifference can be valued while P and Q are crisp.

Briefly, we remark in Table 4 that lines 1 and 3 correspond to crisp $\langle P, Q, I \rangle$ preference structures or $\langle P, Q, I \rangle$ preference structures having only the indifference relation as a valued one. Cases 6 and 8 do not have a natural interpretation. Lines 2, 7, 4 and 5 provide fuzzy $\langle P, Q, I \rangle$ preference structures with one crisp and two valued relations. In lines 2 and 7, there are some relative positions having $Q = 1$ and some others $0 < I \le 1$ and $0 < P \le 1$ while lines 4 and 5 provide some relative positions having $P = 1$ and some others $0 < I \le 1$ and $0 < Q \le 1$. The interpretations of the two first cases are not so natural (how to interpret the fact of having a valued "strict preference" while the weak preference is always crisp?). With lines 4 and 7, the strict preference appears as an upper bound of the weak preference relation where the preference becomes sure. For all these reasons lines 4 and 5 appear as the most favorable ones, between the eight ones, in order to fuzzify $\langle P, Q, I \rangle$ preference structures. Such structures are strongly related to fuzzy $\langle P, I \rangle$ preference structures but may have additional utility for the construction of models where the strict preference needs to be marked strongly.

As an example, we propose in the following a model used for the comparison of intervals where the situation of two disjoint intervals must be presented by a crisp strict preference relation, while other situations may have valued presentation.

Let x and y be two elements of a finite set A, having an interval representation such that $x : [l(x), u(x)]$ and $y : [l(y), u(y)]$ with $\forall x$, $l(x) < u(x)$. We define first of all the characteristic relation of our model:

Table 4. Relations which can be valued when different T_3, T_4, T_5 and S_1 are used

Exclusivity	Positively or negatively complete and $r(x,y) = 1, 0 < r(y,x) < 1$	Positively complete and $0 < r(x,y) < 1, 0 < r(y,x) < 1$
1) $T_3^+(P,I) = 0$ $T_4^+(P,Q) = 0$ $T_5^+(Q,I) = 0$		I
2) $T_3^-(P,I) = 0$ $T_4^+(P,Q) = 0$ $T_5^+(Q,I) = 0$	P,I	P,I,P^{-1}
3) $T_3^+(P,I) = 0$ $T_4^-(P,Q) = 0$ $T_5^+(Q,I) = 0$		I
4) $T_3^+(P,I) = 0$ $T_4^+(P,Q) = 0$ $T_5^-(Q,I) = 0$	Q,I	Q,I,Q^{-1}
5) $T_3^+(P,I) = 0$ $T_4^-(P,Q) = 0$ $T_5^-(Q,I) = 0$	Q,I	Q,I,Q^{-1}
6) $T_3^-(P,I) = 0$ $T_4^+(P,Q) = 0$ $T_5^-(Q,I) = 0$	P,I Q,I	P,I,P^{-1} Q,I,Q^{-1}
7) $T_3^-(P,I) = 0$ $T_4^-(P,Q) = 0$ $T_5^+(Q,I) = 0$	P,I	P,I,P^{-1}
8) $T_3^-(P,I) = 0$ $T_4^-(P,Q) = 0$ $T_5^-(Q,I) = 0$	P,Q,I	P,Q,I,Q^{-1},P^{-1}

Definition 11. *The credibility of the assertion "x is at least as good as y $(r(x,y))$" is such that*

$$\forall x, y \in A, \ r(x,y) = \max(0, \min(1, \max(\frac{u(x) - l(y)}{u(y) - l(y)}, \frac{u(x) - l(y)}{u(x) - l(x)}))).$$

Different values of the relation R for different interval comparison case are presented in Table 5.

The characteristic relation covers the strict preference, the indifference and the hesitation among the two previous relations. The second step is to define all these valued relations in terms of R. For this purpose we make use of the symmetric and the asymmetric part of R:

$$R^a(x,y) = \min \left[1, \max \left(0, \min \left(\frac{u(x) - u(y)}{u(x) - l(x)}, \frac{l(x) - l(y)}{u(y) - l(y)} \right) \right) \right],$$ (1)

$$R^s(x,y) = \frac{\max \left[0, (\min(u(x) - l(y), u(x) - l(x), u(y) - l(y), u(y) - l(x))) \right]}{\min(u(x) - l(x), u(y) - l(y))}$$ (2)

As in the crisp case, R is the union of P, Q and I where P, Q are asymmetric and I is symmetric. For that reason, we propose to define R^a and R^s such as:

$$R^a = S(P, Q) \text{ and } R^s = I.$$

The indifference can be directly obtained from equation 2. For P and Q we have to separate the relation R^a. For this purpose we add a new hypothesis which says that the strict preference P exists only in the case of two disjoint intervals:

$$\forall x, y \in A, \ p(x,y) \Longleftrightarrow l(x) \geq u(y).$$

As a result we define our three relations as in the following:

$$p(x,y) = \begin{cases} R_I^a(x,y) \text{ if } l(x) \geq u(y), \\ 0 \qquad \text{ifnot}; \end{cases}$$ (3)

$$q(x,y) = \begin{cases} R_I^a(x,y) \text{ if } l(x) < u(y), \\ 0 \qquad \text{ifnot}; \end{cases}$$ (4)

$$i(x,y) = R_I^s(x,y).$$ (5)

Table 5 illustrates all the values of the three relations for each interval comparison case.

Such a model has nice properties:

Proposition 3. *Suppose that a binary relation P and valued relations Q and I are defined as in equations 3-5, then*
i. P and Q are irreflexive and min-asymmetric,
ii. I is reflexive and symmetric,
iii. $T_{min}(P, I) = 0, \ T_{min}(P, Q) = 0, \ LT(Q, I) = 0, \ T_{min}(P, Q^{-1}) = 0$,
iv. $LS(P, LS(Q, I))$ is LS-complete.

Proof. see [17].   ■

The relations between the characteristic relation R and the three preference relations are presented in the following proposition.

Proposition 4. *Suppose that the three valued relations P, Q and I are defined as in equations 3-5, then:*
  i. $LS(P,Q) = R^d$
  ii. $I = min(R, R^{-1})$
or explicitly, $\forall (x,y) \in A \times A$
  i. $p(x,y) + q(x,y) = 1 - r(y,x)$
  ii. $i(x,y) = min\{r(x,y), r(y,x)\}$

Proof. see [17]. ∎

Table 5. Relations of the interval comparison with valued hesitation

	$r(x,y)$	$p(x,y)$	$q(x,y)$	$i(x,y)$
	1	1	0	0
	1	0	$min\left(\frac{a}{\|x\|}, \frac{b}{\|y\|}\right)$	$max\left(\frac{c}{\|x\|}, \frac{c}{\|y\|}\right)$
	1	0	0	1
	1	0	0	1
	1	0	0	1
	$max\left(\frac{c}{\|x\|}, \frac{c}{\|y\|}\right)$	0	0	$max\left(\frac{c}{\|x\|}, \frac{c}{\|y\|}\right)$
	0	0	0	0

5   Discussion

What do we get with such results? What can we do with such valued relation? We consider two cases.

The first, obvious, case concerns the domain of preference modelling. Having a functional representation of the type described in the above section enables to give an explicit representation of the uncertainty and hesitation which appears when we compare intervals and to overcome the difficulty associated to the use of crisp thresholds. In fact if a discrimination problem exists this will concern any type of comparison. Therefore even if we fix a discrimination threshold there always exists an interval around the threshold for which a discrimination problem has to be considered (and that recursively for any new threshold introduced). The valued representation solves this problem. In this particular case the solution does not require the introduction of two thresholds, but gives a valued version for preference and indifference in all cases intervals are compared.

The second case concerns more generally the problem of comparing objects not necessarily for preference modelling reasons. As already introduced we can always consider the concept of indifference equivalent to the one of similarity, the concept of preference becoming a directed dissimilarity. Establishing the similarity among objects is a crucial problem for several research fields such as statistics, data analysis (in archeology, geology, medical diagnosis etc.), information theory, classification, case based reasoning, machine learning etc. A specific area of interest in the use of similarity relations is in rough sets theory ([18]).

In rough sets we consider objects described under a set of attributes and we establish a relation of indiscernibility (which is a crisp equivalence relation) in order to take in account our limited descriptive capability. In other terms real objects might be different, but due to our limited descriptive capability (represented by the set of attributes) we might be obliged to consider them as identical (indiscernible). Indiscernibility classes are then used in order to induce classification rules. However, equivalence relations can be very restrictive for several real cases where the more general concept of similarity is more suitable (see [19,20]). The use of a valued similarity has been considered in [21,22,23,24] for several different cases. Thanks to such a relation it is possible to induce classification rules to which a credibility degree is associated. By this way it is possible to enhance the classification capability of a data set although a confidence degree inferior to 1 has to be accepted. The approach described in this paper enables to give a theoretical foundation for the case where objects have to compared on attributes with continuous scales and where either a discrimination threshold has to be considered or the objects are represented by intervals.

6   Conclusion

In this paper we present some results concerning the extension of PQI interval orders under continuous valuation. Particularly we propose a general frame work for the characterization of fuzzy preference structures with P, Q and I and give the functional representation for these three relations such that the portion of interval which is common is considered as a "measure" of the hesitation associated to the interval comparison. Such functions fulfill a number of nice properties in the sense that they correspond to a fuzzy preference structure as defined in [14].

The use of such valued preference relations not only enhance the toolkit of preference modelling, but enables a more flexible representation in all cases where a similarity among objects is under question. The particular case of rough sets theory is discussed in the paper. Several research directions remain open such as:

- the problem of aggregating such valued relations in order to obtain a comprehensive relation (crisp or valued) when several attributes or criteria are considered;
- a further analysis of the formal properties fulfilled by such valued relations;
- the analysis of such preference structures under the positive/negative reasons framework as introduced in [25] and discussed in [26].

References

1. Luce, R.D.: Semiorders and a theory of utility discrimination. Econometrica 24, 178–191 (1956)
2. Fishburn, P.C.: Interval Orders and Interval Graphs. J. Wiley, Chichester (1985)
3. Pirlot, M., Vincke, Ph.: Semi Orders. Kluwer Academic, Dordrecht (1997)
4. Tsoukiàs, A., Vincke, Ph.: A characterization of pqi interval orders. Discrete Applied Mathematics 127(2), 387–397 (2003)
5. Ngo The, A., Tsoukiàs, A., Vincke, Ph.: A polynomial time algorithm to detect PQI interval orders. International Transactions in Operational Research 7, 609–623 (2000)
6. Ngo The, A., Tsoukiàs, A.: Numerical representation of pqi interval orders. Discrete Applied Mathematics 147, 125–146 (2005)
7. Oztürk, M., Tsoukiàs, A.: Positive and negative reasons in interval comparisons: Valued pqi interval orders. In: Proceedings of IPMU 2004, pp. 983–989 (2004)
8. Roy, B., Vincke, P.: Relational systems of preference with one or more pseudo-criteria: Some new concepts and results. Management Science 30, 1323–1335 (1984)
9. Roy, B., Vincke, Ph.: Pseudo-orders: definition, properties and numerical representation. Mathematical Social Sciences 14, 263–274 (1987)
10. Perny, P., Roy, B.: The use of fuzzy outranking relations in preference modelling. Fuzzy Sets and Systems 49, 33–53 (1992)
11. Dubois, D., Prade, H.: Decision making under fuzziness. In: Advances in fuzzy set theory and applications, pp. 279–302. North Holland, Amsterdam (1979)
12. Dubois, D., Prade, H.: Fuzzy sets and systems - Theory and applications. Academic press, New York (1980)
13. Fodor, J., Roubens, M.: Fuzzy preference modelling and multicriteria decision support. Kluwer Academic Publishers, Dordrecht (1994)
14. Perny, P., Roubens, M.: Fuzzy preference modelling. In: Słowiński, R. (ed.) Fuzzy sets in decision analysis, operations research and statistics, pp. 3–30. Kluwer Academic, Dordrecht (1998)
15. Ovchinnikov, S.N.: Modelling valued preference relation. In: Kacprzyk, J., Fedrizzi, M. (eds.) Multiperson decion making usingfuzzy sets and possibility theory, pp. 64–70. Kluwer, Dordrecht (1990)
16. Van De Walle, B., De Baets, B., Kerre, E.: Charaterizable fuzzy preference structures. Annals of Operations Research 80, 105–136 (1998)

17. Ozturk, M.: Structures mathématiques et logiques pour la comparaison des intervalles. Thése de doctorat, Université Paris-Dauphine (2005)
18. Pawlak, Z.: Rough Sets. Theoretical Aspects of Reasoning about Data. Kluwer, Dordrecht (1991)
19. Slowinski, R., Vanderpooten, D.: Similarity relation as a basis for rough approximations. In: P., W., (eds) Advances in Machine Intelligence & Soft-computing, Bookwrights, Raleigh, pp. 17–33 (1997)
20. Slowinski, R., Vanderpooten, D.: A generalized definition of rough approximations based on similarity. IEEE Transactions on Data and Knowledge Engineering 12, 331–336 (2000)
21. Greco, S., Matarazzo, B., Slowinski, R.: Handling missing values in rough set analysis of multi-attribute and multi-criteria decision problems. In: Zhong, N., Skowron, A., Ohsuga, S. (eds.) New Directions in Rough Sets, Data Mining, and Granular-Soft Computing. LNCS (LNAI), vol. 1711, pp. 146–157. Springer, Heidelberg (1999)
22. Stefanowski, J., Tsoukiàs, A.: On the extension of rough sets under incomplete information. In: Zhong, N., Skowron, A., Ohsuga, S. (eds.) RSFDGrC 1999. LNCS (LNAI), vol. 1711, pp. 73–81. Springer, Heidelberg (1999)
23. Stefanowski, J., Tsoukiàs, A.: Valued tolerance and decision rules. In: Ziarko, W., Yao, Y. (eds.) RSCTC 2000. LNCS (LNAI), vol. 2005, pp. 212–219. Springer, Heidelberg (2001)
24. Stefanowski, J., Tsoukiàs, A.: Incomplete information tables and rough classification. Computational Intelligence 17, 454–466 (2001)
25. Perny, P., Tsoukiàs, A.: On the continuous extension of a four valued logic for preference modelling. In: Proceedings of the IPMU 1998 conference, Paris, pp. 302–309 (1998)
26. Tsoukiàs, A., Perny, P., Vincke, Ph.: From concordance/discordance to the modelling of positive and negative reasons in decision aiding. In: Bouyssou, D., Jacquet-Lagrèze, E., Perny, P., Słowiński, R., Vanderpooten, D., Vincke, P. (eds.) Aiding Decisions with Multiple Criteria: Essays in Honour of Bernard Roy, pp. 147–174. Kluwer Academic, Dordrecht (2002)

Aggregates in Generalized Temporally Indeterminate Databases

Octavian Udrea[1], Zoran Majkić[2], and V.S. Subrahmanian[1]

[1] University of Maryland College Park, Maryland 20742 USA
[2] Universitá di Roma La Sapienza, Via Salaria 113 I-00198, Rome, Italy
{udrea,vs}@umiacs.umd.edu, zmajkic@dis.uniroma.it

Abstract. Dyreson and Snodgrass as well as Dekhtyar et. al. have provided a probabilistic model (as well as compelling example applications) for why there may be temporal indeterminacy in databases. In this paper, we first propose a formal model for aggregate computation in such databases when there is uncertainty not just in the temporal attribute, but also in the ordinary (non-temporal) attributes. We identify two types of aggregates: event correlated aggregates, and non event correlated aggregations, and provide efficient algorithms for both of them. We prove that our algorithms are correct, and we present experimental results showing that the algorithms work well in practice.

1   Introduction

In many application domains, we cannot be sure of the exact time an event would occur. For example, even though Fedex may tell us that a package will be delivered sometime today, if our *chronon* is "minute", then there is uncertainty about exactly at what time the package will be delivered. Dyreson and Snodgrass [1] present a large set of convincing examples ranging from carbon-dating of archeological artifacts to scheduling applications where such uncertainty is the norm, not the exception, followed by an excellent framework for reasoning about such temporal indeterminacy. Later, Dekhtyar et. al. [2] built a rich temporal-probabilistic database algebra in which they could do away with many assumptions (e.g. independence) that extended the framework of Dyreson and Snodgrass.

Both the preceding works are *time centric* in the sense that uncertainty only exists in the temporal attributes of a relation. However, there are many applications where uncertainty can occur either in the temporal attributes or in the data (non-temporal) attributes, or in both. Our first major contribution is the concept of a "Generalized Probabilistic Temporal (GPT)" database that can handle both kinds of uncertainty. For example, almost every manufacturing company around today uses statistical models to estimate demand for a given product [3, chap.4] - independently of whether the product is high end (e.g. energy) or technology focused (e.g. digital cameras) or plain simple food (e.g. pasta). Such models estimate demand over time. They may estimate other parameters as well (e.g. price). Likewise, the entire agricultural sector is a poster child for temporal probabilistic data. Statistical models are used to predict how much of a particular crop (e.g. wheat) may be available, what the prices are likely to be, and so on. Such

H. Prade and V.S. Subrahmanian (Eds.): SUM 2007, LNAI 4772, pp. 171–186, 2007.

models are used by market analysts to make investments (e.g. into grain futures), by governments to decide what to import and when and in what quantity, and so forth [3]. In general, almost all applications involving economic principles are subject to uncertainty about supply, uncertainty about demand. Most of these uncertainties vary with time (e.g. demand for winter coats is usually small in the summer months).

Table 1 shows a sample data set about an energy market (virtually all US energy is sold by energy producers to energy distributors one day ahead using very complex statistical estimates of supply and demand). In this application, an energy producer is estimating demand (the **Quantity** field) for a given market as well as the **Price** (per unit of energy) to be charged for that quantity. For example, the quantity estimated for tomorrow in New York may be 5600 or 5700 units (with some probabilities) and the price per unit in the NY market may be be 115,600 or 115,700 per unit. Natural queries that corporate executives may be interested in include:

Q1: What is the expected demand in NY tomorrow?
Q2: What is my expected income tomorrow ?
Q3: On which day during the next 2 weeks period will I have the highest income?

Table 1. Day-ahead energy market example

Event Id	Market	Price	Quantity	TP-case statement
1	NY	5600 [.6, .7] 5700 [.3, .4]	115600 [.5, .7] 115700 [.4, .6]	$\{\langle(10 \sim 14),(10 \sim 14), 0.4, 0.8, u\rangle\}$
2	Bos	5500 [.1, .1] 5600 [.2, .2]	104300 [.6, .8] 105000 [.3, .4]	$\{\langle(11 \sim 13),(11 \sim 13), 0.5, 0.9, u\rangle\}$
3	Wash	5650 [.5, .7] 5700 [.3, .5]	90500 [.5, .7] 92000 [.4, .6]	$\{\langle(10 \sim 12),(10 \sim 12), 0.4, 0.8, u\rangle\}$

All of these queries are aggregate queries. Our second major contribution is the development of a declarative semantics for *aggregate queries* in GPT databases. Aggregates are of obvious interest in applications such as the above - a government might want to know the total expected wheat production in a given time period, while a manufacturer might want to know which market has the maximum profit margins.

Aggregate queries involving temporal probabilistic attributes fall into two general categories. Non-event correlated aggregates (NECA) are aggregates where all tuples in a GPT-relation are treated in "one pass." For example, queries (Q1) and (Q2) above fall into this category. In contrast, an event-correlated aggregate (ECA) is really an "aggregate over an aggregate." Query (Q3) falls into this category because we first need to find, for each day, the expected income for that day (this is an aggregate) and then we need to find the day that maximizes the expected income (which is an aggregate over the previously computed aggregates). Our third major contribution is the *development of algorithms* to efficiently compute NECA queries and ECA queries on GPT databases. In particular, we should mention that ECA queries can be speeded up by a "pre-aggregate" computation.

Our fourth major contribution is a *prototype implementation* of our algorithms together with an experimental evaluation showing that our algorithms are very efficient. For instance, a SUM event-correlated aggregate can be computed in about 1.7 seconds over a database of 15,000 events in a disk-resident DB; when the number is increased to 500,000 disk-resident events, this can be done in about 5.1 seconds.

In this paper, we first extend the TP database model of Dekhtyar et. al. [2] to incorporate uncertainty in both the temporal and the data attributes – this is done in Section 2. We then develop a declarative definition of NECA and ECA aggregate queries in Section 4. Section 5 provides algorithms to compute the answers to NECA and ECA queries. Section 6 describes our prototype implementation.

2   GPT Database Model

2.1   Technical Preliminaries

This section provides a brief overview of temporal probabilistic databases from [2]. We assume that $\tau = \{1, 2, \ldots, N\}$ for some integer N denotes the set of all legal time points — this time is discrete and modeled by the natural numbers. Throughout this paper, we will assume that τ is arbitrary but fixed. We assume the existence of a set of *time point variables* ranging over τ.

Definition 1 (Temporal constraint)

(i) *If t_i is a time point variable,* op $\in \{<, \leq, =, \neq, \geq, >\}$, $v \in \tau$, *then $(t_i$ op $v)$ is a temporal constraint.*

(ii) *If $t_1, t_2 \in \tau$ and $t_1 \leq t_2$, then $(t_1 \sim t_2)$ is a temporal constraint (shorthand for $(t_1 \leq t \leq t_2)$; we abuse notation and write (t_1) instead of $(t_1 \sim t_1)$).*

(iii) *If C_1 and C_2 are temporal constraints then so are $(C_1 \wedge C_2)$, $(C_1 \vee C_2)$ and $(\neg C_1)$.*

We use $\mathcal{S}_\tau$ to denote the set of all temporal constraints. The set $\text{sol}(C)$ of solutions of a temporal constraint C is defined in the usual way. For example, $\text{sol}((12 \sim 14) \vee (18 \sim 23)) = \{12, 13, 14, 18, 19, 20, 21, 22, 23\}$.

Definition 2 (Probability Distribution Function (PDF)). *A function $\wp : \mathcal{S}_\tau \times \tau \rightarrow [0, 1]$ is a PDF if $(\forall D \in \mathcal{S}_\tau) (\forall t \notin \text{sol}(D)) (\wp(D, t) = 0)$. Furthermore, $\wp$ is a restricted PDF if $(\forall D \in \mathcal{S}_\tau) (\sum_{t \in \text{sol}(D)} \wp(D, t) \leq 1)$.*

This definition of a PDF is rich enough to capture almost all probability mass functions (e.g. uniform, geometric, binomial, Poisson, etc.)[4]. Furthermore, probability density functions can be approximated by PDFs via a process of quantization.

Definition 3 (TP-case). *A TP-case is a 5-tuple $\langle C, D, L, U, \delta \rangle$ where (i) C and D are temporal constraints, (ii) $\emptyset \subset \text{sol}(C) \subseteq \text{sol}(D)$, (iii) $0 \leq L \leq U \leq 1$, and (iv) δ is a restricted PDF.*

The last column of Table 1 shows TP-cases for each of the three events. Consider the first event shown there - the associated TP-case $\{\langle (10 \sim 14), (10 \sim 14), 0.4, 0.8, u \rangle\}$ says that the event with Event Id 1 will be true at some time between 10 and 14 with 40 to 80% probability. In general, C specifies the time points when an event is valid while D specifies the time points over which the PDF δ is applicable. Since $\text{sol}(C) \subseteq \text{sol}(D)$, it follows that δ assigns a probability to each time point $t \in \text{sol}(C)$.

Table 2. Probabilistic flattening of a GPT-tuple

Event Id	Market	L_1, U_1	Price	L_2, U_2	Quantity	L_3, U_3	TP-case statement
1	NY	[1,1]	5600	[.6,.7]	115600	[.5,.7]	$\{\langle(10 \sim 14),(10 \sim 14),0.4,0.8,u\rangle\}$
1	NY	[1,1]	5600	[.6,.7]	115700	[.4,.6]	$\{\langle(10 \sim 14),(10 \sim 14),0.4,0.8,u\rangle\}$
1	NY	[1,1]	5700	[.3,.4]	115600	[.5,.7]	$\{\langle(10 \sim 14),(10 \sim 14),0.4,0.8,u\rangle\}$
1	NY	[1,1]	5700	[.3,.4]	115700	[.4,.6]	$\{\langle(10 \sim 14),(10 \sim 14),0.4,0.8,u\rangle\}$

Definition 4 (TP-case statement). *A TP-case statement Γ is a set of TP-cases, where* $(\forall \gamma_i, \gamma_j \in \Gamma)((i \neq j) \rightarrow \text{sol}(\gamma_i.C \land \gamma_j.C) = \emptyset)$. *We define* $\text{sol}(\Gamma) = \bigcup\{\text{sol}(\gamma_i.C) \mid \gamma_i \in \Gamma\}$.

The last column of Table 1 shows TP-cases for each of the three events in that relation.

Definition 5 (P-tuple). *Suppose $[R] = (A_1, ..., A_k)$ is a relation scheme in 1NF. A P-tuple over $[R]$ is a k-tuple $pt = (\langle V_1, f_1 \rangle, ..., \langle V_k, f_k \rangle)$ where for all $i \in [1, k]$, $V_i \subseteq \text{dom}(A_i)$ and f_i is a function that maps each value in V_i to a probability interval (i.e., a closed subinterval of $[0, 1]$). For each attribute A_i we will call V_i the value set for that attribute.*

If we eliminate the last column of Table 1, we would have a P-relation.

2.2 GPT Relations

In the following, we define a GPT tuple (or event) as a complex structure composed of an unique identifier, its temporal information Γ, and the set of probabilistic data (a P-tuple). For a relation R, we denote by $[R]$ the relation scheme of R.

Definition 6 (GPT tuples and relations). *A general probabilistic temporal tuple over the relation scheme $[R] = (A_1, ..., A_k)$ is a tuple $gpt = (Id, pt, \Gamma)$, where Id is the event's identifier, $pt = (\langle V_1, f_1 \rangle, ..., \langle V_k, f_k \rangle)$ is a P-tuple and Γ is a TP-case statement. A GPT-relation over R is a finite set of GPT-tuples over R.*

Example 1. The example given in Table 1 is a GPT-relation.

Definition 7 (FP-scheme). *Suppose $[R] = (A_1, ..., A_k)$ is a relation scheme in 1NF and L and U are probabilistic attributes where $\text{dom}(L) = \text{dom}(U) = [0, 1]$. We say that $[fpR] = (A_1 : [L_1, U_1], ..., A_k : [L_k, U_k])$ is an FP-scheme over $[R]$ with data attributes $A_1, ..., A_k$ and their probability intervals $[L_i, U_i]$, $i \in [1, k]$.*

An FP-scheme resembles a simple relational scheme, but each attribute is "tied" to a probability interval. We now show how a given GPT relation can be "flattened" to an FP-scheme.

Definition 8 (Probabilistic flattening of GPT tuples). *For a given GPT-tuple $gpt = (Id, pt, \Gamma)$, where $pt = (\langle V_1, f_1 \rangle, ..., \langle V_k, f_k \rangle)$, the probabilistic flattened relation, TP (gpt) of gpt, is given by: $TP(gpt) = \{(Id, \langle v_1, L_1, U_1 \rangle, ..., \langle v_k, L_k, U_k \rangle, \Gamma) \mid (v_1, ..., v_k) \in V_1 \times ... \times V_k \land [L_i, U_i] = f_i(v_i)\}$. The probabilistic flattening of a GPT-relation is the union of the probabilistic flattening of its GPT-tuples.*

Intuitively, we can flatten the P-tuple part of a GPT-tuple by taking the cartesian product of all the V_i's. We then append the TP-case part of the P-tuple to each of the resulting tuples to get a flattened GPT-tuple.

Example 2. The probabilistic flattened relation (*TP relation*) of the event with $Id = 1$ in Table 1 is shown in Table 2.

Remark. Each tuple in the probabilistic flattening of an event can be regarded as a TP-tuple. We will call such a tuple an *FPT-tuple* to emphasize that it was obtained through flattening and therefore its tuple data is an FP-scheme - meaning each data attribute is tied to a probability interval.

We now introduce the notion of a semi-annotated version of an FPT-tuple. This is done by taking each solution of a TP-case associated with that tuple and replacing the TP-case part of the FPT-tuple by that solution. In addition, the probabilities associated with that time point (solution of TP-case constraints) are added to the tuple.

Definition 9 (Semi annotation). *Let* $fpt = (Id, d, \Gamma)$ *be a TP-tuple over the relational scheme* $[R] = (A_1, ..., A_k)$ *with* $d = (\langle v_1, L_1, U_1 \rangle, ..., \langle v_k, L_k, U_k \rangle)$ *as its data tuple. Then the* semi-annotated relation *for* fpt, *denoted* $SANN(fpt)$, *is defined as follows:* $SANN(fpt) = \{(Id, d, eTime, L_t, U_t) \mid \exists \gamma_i = \langle C_i, D_i, L_i, U_i, \delta_i \rangle \in \Gamma$, *s.t.* $(eTime \in sol(C_i)) \wedge ([L_t, U_t] = [L_i \cdot x, U_i \cdot x], x = \delta_i(D_i, eTime))\}$. *The semi annotated relation of an event* $gpt = (Id, pt, \Gamma)$, *denoted* $SANN(gpt)$, *is the union of all semi-annotated relations of its* FPT-tuples.

Table 3 shows part of the semi-annotated version of the GPT-relation shown in Figure 1.

Table 3. Semi-annotated relation (partial)

Event Id	Market	L_1, U_1	Price	L_2, U_2	Quantity	L_3, U_3	eTime	L_t, U_t
1	NY	[1,1]	5600	[.6,.7]	115600	[.5,.7]	10	[.08,.016]
1	NY	[1,1]	5600	[.6,.7]	115600	[.5,.7]	11	[.08,.016]
1	NY	[1,1]	5600	[.6,.7]	115700	[.4,.6]	10	[.08,.016]
1	NY	[1,1]	5600	[.6,.7]	115700	[.4,.6]	11	[.08,.016]
1	NY	[1,1]	5700	[.3,.4]	115600	[.5,.7]	10	[.08,.016]
1	NY	[1,1]	5700	[.3,.4]	115600	[.5,.7]	11	[.08,.016]
1	NY	[1,1]	5700	[.3,.4]	115700	[.4,.6]	10	[.08,.016]
1	NY	[1,1]	5700	[.3,.4]	115700	[.4,.6]	11	[.08,.016]

All operations of the temporal probabilistic algebra proposed in [2] can be extended to GPT-relations. We do not do this here as the focus of this paper is on aggregates which, to our knowledge, have never been defined for temporally indeterminate databases.

3   Probabilistic Context

As we have seen in the previous section, the GPT model represents uncertainty both at the event and tuple data levels. As such, the computation of aggregates requires that we "combine" probability intervals. In other words, if $price_{NY} = 5600$ with probability in $[.6, .7]$ and $price_{Bos} = 5500$ with probability $[.1, .1]$, what is the probability that

$price_{NY} + price_{Bos} = 11,100$? Clearly, this depends upon the relationship between prices in Boston and NY. If, for example, there are some power plants that can provide power to both Boston and NY, then there should be a correlation in price. On the other hand, if Boston and NY share no common power plants, then the prices are probably independent of each other.

Lakshmanan et. al. [5,6] have proposed a very general notion of *conjunction and disjunction strategies*. Given two events e_1, e_2, each with probability intervals I_1, I_2 respectively, they define a conjunction strategy $\otimes$ to be an associative, commutative function that returns a probability interval $I_1 \otimes I_2$ for the conjunction $e_1 \wedge e_2$. Conjunction strategies are required to satisfy several other axio that we do not mention here. Disjunction strategies $\oplus$ do the same for disjunction. They show that these strategies are rich enough to express a wide variety of relationships between events such as independence, ignorance, positive and negative correlations, etc.

We will now define the concept of a *probabilistic context* that describes in precise terms how probability intervals for data (and temporal) attributes can be combined. For the rest of the paper, let S_C be the set of probabilistic conjunctive strategies and S_D the set of disjunctive strategies.

A probabilistic context (defined below) associates a conjunction and disjunction strategy with any set of attributes.

Definition 10. *(Probabilistic context) Let* $[R]$ *be a GPT relation scheme and* $2^{[R]}$ *be the power set of the set of attributes in* $[R]$*. A probabilistic context over* $[R]$ *denoted by* $ctx(R)$ *is a pair* $\langle \otimes_{ctx}, \oplus_{ctx} \rangle$*, where:*

(1) $\otimes_{ctx} : 2^{[R]} \rightarrow S_C$ *is a function that maps a set of attributes to a probabilistic conjunction strategy. Intuitively, for* $W \in 2^{[R]}$ *probability intervals would be combined using* $\otimes_{ctx}(W)$ *for any* $|W|$*-ary operator applied to values of the attributes in* W*. For singleton subsets* $\{A\} \subseteq [R]$*,* $\otimes_{ctx}(\{A\})$ *would be used in aggregate computations on* A*.*

(2) $\oplus_{ctx} : 2^{[R]} \rightarrow S_D$ *is a function that maps a set of attributes to a probabilistic disjunctive strategy.*

For the example described at the beginning of this section, using the independence conjunction strategy the result of $price_{NY} + price_{Bos}$ would be $\langle 11100, [.06, .07] \rangle$.

4   Temporal Probabilistic Aggregates Declarative Semantics

In this section, we define the formal semantics for the event and non-event correlated aggregation operators and show how these relate to aggregates on semi-annotated GPT relations. *We should note that even though the semantics for event correlated aggregation are based on their semi-annotated counterpart, our implementation computes such aggregates directly on GPT relations.* We start off with some simple examples that illustrate the differences between the two types of aggregation.

Example 3. Consider the relation shown in Table 1. We would like to answer the query *What is the total expected demand?* Let us assume that events are mutually independent (i.e. the independence conjunctive strategy is used for aggregation over the *Quantity* attribute). Then the result of this query is the value $\langle V, f \rangle$, where $V = \{310400, 311900, 311100, \ldots\}$ and $f(310400) = [.15, .392]$, $f(311900) = [.12, .336]$, $f(311100) = [.06, .168]$, and so on. The TP-cases do not play a role in answering this query. When computing such aggregates, we only need ensure that different values from any single value set of the *Quantity* attribute are not aggregated. We will denote this type of aggregation **non-event correlated aggregation**.

Example 4. Let us consider the same relation, but with the query *When does the maximum demand occur?* One way to answer this query is via the following steps: (i) we find the set of time points T such that each time point in T is a solution to at least one TP-case in the relation; (ii) for each such time point $t \in T$, we add up the value of the *Quantity* attributes for all events e that have $t \in sol(e.\Gamma)$; (iii) choose the time point with the largest value for the aggregated attribute. Step (i) would give us $T = \{10, 11, 12, 13, 14\}$. For step (ii), part of the result is shown in Table 4(a) - again, assuming events are mutually independent. We call this type of aggregation **event correlated aggregation**.

Note: The reader may also notice that the query for this example actually includes two different aggregates - a *SUM* and a *MAX* operator; we use a combination of the two to illustrate why grouping by time points is relevant to the problem. In later sections, we will provide a much more efficient algorithm called **ECA-interval** that does not require examining each time point that is a solution of a TP-case.

Table 4. (a) Event correlated aggregation; (b) Non event correlated aggregation

eTime	SumOfQuantity
10	206100 [.25, .49]
	207600 [.2, .42]
	206200 [.2, .42]
	207700 [.16, .36]
. . .	. . .
14	115600 [.5, .7]
	115700 [.4, .6]

eTime	Sum(Price)
$\{\langle(10 \sim 14), (10 \sim 14), 0.4, 0.8, u\rangle,$	16750 [.03,.049]
$\langle(10 \sim 11), (10 \sim 11), 0.4, 0.8, u\rangle,$	16800 [.018,.035]
$\langle(10 \sim 12), (10 \sim 12), 0.4, 0.8, u\rangle\}$	16850 [.06,.126]
	16900 [.036,.09]
	16950 [.03,.056]
	17000 [.018,.04]

4.1 Aggregation Operators

Definition 11 (Aggregation operator). *An aggregation operator agg is a function that takes a GPT-relation gpR and an attribute $A \in [gpR]$ as input and returns a GPT-relation gpR' containing **at most one** data attribute $A_{agg} = \langle V_{agg}, f_{agg} \rangle$. The values of A_{agg} are only over the values of attribute A.*

An aggregation operator produces a GPT-relation. For non-event correlated aggregation, the temporal attribute can be a simple union of all TP-case statements in gpR and the resulting relation would contain at most one tuple. For event correlated aggregation, gpR' may contain multiple tuples, each with its own event ID and set of TP-case statements. If the aggregation is performed over a data attribute in gpR, then gpR' would contain one data attribute with the aggregation result. However, if the aggregation is performed over the temporal attribute[1], gpR' will not contain any data attributes. Since aggregation on data attributes is a much more challenging problem, we will focus on such aggregates for the rest of the paper.

Due to the generality of aggregate operators as defined above, we believe an informal classification is in order. Useful temporal aggregate operators are most likely to include *min, max* and *count*; sums or average computations over time points do not make sense. Data aggregate operators can be classified into **base** operators such as *sum, min, max, count* and **derived** aggregate operators such as *avg* or *stdev*. Derived operators are usually expressions involving base aggregates, data values and constants; for example, $avg = \frac{sum}{count}$. Computing such expressions is straightforward given the probabilistic context and the methods for combining probabilistic value sets that we have already informally described.

In this paper we focus on base aggregate operators such as *SUM, MIN*, etc. For notation purposes, for an aggregation operator agg we denote by agg_r the corresponding relational aggregation operator. We denote by op_{agg} the corresponding arithmetic operator used to compute agg_r. For instance, if $agg = SUM$, $op_{agg} = +$. We expect that the binary op_{agg} operator is commutative and associative. Finally, we denote by op^*_{agg} the extension of op_{agg} to multisets of real numbers.

4.2   Non Event Correlated Aggregation

This section will explore how non-event correlated aggregation can be performed on GPT tuples. As mentioned before, we will consider data tuple aggregates, as temporal data aggregates are straightforward problem.

Definition 12 (Non-event correlated GPT-aggregation). *Suppose R is a GPT-relation with probability context $ctx(R)$, $A \in [R]$ be an attribute and agg is an aggregation operator. For each tuple $t \in R$, we denote by $\langle V_t, f_t \rangle$, the value set and probability function for attribute A. Then, $agg(R, A) =_{def} \{(Id_*, \langle V, f \rangle, \Gamma)\}$, where:*

(i) Id_* is a new, dynamically created event ID.
(ii) $V = \{op^*_{agg}(V') \mid V' \in \mathbf{X}_{t \in R} V_t\}$, where $\mathbf{X}$ is the cartesian product operator.
(iii) Let $\otimes = \otimes_{ctx}(\{A\})$ and $\oplus = \oplus_{ctx}(\{A\})$. Then $\forall\, v \in V$, the function f is defined by $f(v) = \bigoplus \{ f(v_1) \otimes \ldots \otimes f(v_N) \mid (v_1, \ldots, v_N) \in \mathbf{X}_{t \in R} V_t$ and $op^*_{agg}(\{v_1, \ldots, v_N\}) = v \}$, where $\bigoplus$ is the extension of $\oplus$ to sets of probability intervals.
(iv) $\forall \Gamma' \in [R].\Gamma, \forall t_i \in sol(\Gamma'), t_i \in sol(\Gamma)$.

This definition gives a method of computing non-event correlated probabilistic aggregates directly on GPT-relations. The reader may note that the intuition given in Example 3 is formalized here. The corresponding definition for non-event correlated aggregation for semi annotated relations is straightforward.

Example 5. For the GPT relation in Table 1, we choose $\otimes_{ctx}(\{Price\})$ to be the independence conjunction strategy and $\oplus_{ctx}(\{Price\})$ to be the ignorance disjunctive strategy defined in [5] as $[l_1, u_1] \oplus_{ig} [l_2, u_2] = [max(l_1, l_2), min(1, u_1 + u_2)]$. The result of the SUM non-event correlated aggregate over the $Price$ attribute can be found in Table 4(b).

---

[1] Example: What is the number of time points when the expected demand will exceed a certain threshold?

4.3   Event Correlated Aggregation

We now define event correlated aggregation based on its semi-annotated counterpart. There are several advantages of defining aggregation for GPT relations in terms of its semi-annotated version: (i) correctness (i.e. commutativity with the semi-annotation function) is implied and (ii) the definition is less restrictive as to the form of the resulting GPT relation, which allows for more freedom in choosing an appropriate algorithm.

Definition 13 (World). *Let R be a GPT relation and let $R' = SANN(R)$ be its semi-annotated form. Let $ctx(R)$ be the probability context over R, let $A_k \in [R]$ be a data attribute in $[R]$ and let $[L_k, U_k]$ be the probability interval for A_k in R'. Suppose $x \in \tau$ is a time point. A* world *for x, R and A_k is any subset w of the set $\pi_{(Id, eTime, A_k, L_k, U_k)}(\sigma_{(eTime=x)}(R'))$ such that $\forall\, t_1, t_2 \in w, t_1.Id \neq t_2.Id\,^2$. A* maximal world *for a time point x is a world w' such that $\not\exists w''$ another world for x such that $w' \subset w''$.*

Intuitively, a maximal world for a time point represents a possible combination of values from the value sets for A_k. This is conceptually similar to an element in the cartesian product present in Definition 12. Furthermore, a maximal world contains tuples for all possible events that contain such values. For a time point x, a relation R and an attribute $A \in [R]$, we denote by $\mathcal{W}_x(R, A)$ the set of maximal worlds over R and A w.r.t. x. Furthermore, given an aggregate operator agg and its relational counterpart agg_r, we denote by $agg_r(\mathcal{W}_x(R, A)) = \{y | \exists\, w \in \mathcal{W}_x(R, A) \text{ s.t. } agg^r(w, A) = y\}$. In short, $agg_r(\mathcal{W}_x(R, A))$ is the set of all possible values obtainable through relational aggregation through agg_r over any maximal world w and the attribute A. Similarly, we define $agg_r^{-1}(y, \mathcal{W}_x(R, A)) = \{w \in \mathcal{W}_x(R, A) | agg_r(w, A) = y\}$.

Definition 14 (Semi annotated aggregation). *Let R be a GPT relation and let $R' = SANN(R)$ be its semi-annotated form. Let $ctx(R)$ be the probability context over R, let $A_k \in [R]$ be a data attribute in $[R]$ and let $[L_k, U_k] \in [R']$ be its corresponding probabilistic attribute in the semi-annotated form. Let agg be an aggregation operator and agg_r the corresponding relational aggregate. We define the semi-annotated version of agg as $agg_{FL}(R', A_k) = \{t | t = (Id_*, eTime, A_k^{agg}, [L_k, U_k]^{agg})\}$, where $\forall\, x \in R'.eTime, \forall\, y \in agg_r(\mathcal{W}_x(R, A)), \exists!\, t \in agg_{FL}(R', A_k), t = (Id_*, eTime, A_k^{agg}, [L_k, U_k]^{agg})$ such that:*

(1) $t.Id_*$ is a new, dynamically generated event identifier.
(2) $t.eTime = x$ and $t.A_k^{agg} = y$.
(3) Let $\otimes = \otimes_{ctx}(\{A_k\})$ and $\oplus = \oplus_{ctx}(\{A_k\})$. Let $\bigoplus$ be the extension of $\oplus$ to a multiset of probability intervals and $\bigotimes$ the similar extension of $\otimes$. For a world $w \in \mathcal{W}_x(R, A_k)$, let $w.[L_k, U_k]$ be the multiset of probability intervals that appear in that world. Let $\mathcal{I}$ be the multiset $\{[L, U] | \exists\, w \in agg_r^{-1}(y, \mathcal{W}_x(R, A)) \text{ s.t. } [L, U] \in w.[L_k, U_k]\}$. Then $t.[L_k, U_k]^{agg} = \bigoplus(\mathcal{I})$.

This definition formalizes the intuition given in Example 4 for the semi-annotated version of the GPT relation. In short, we perform all possible combinations of values in

---

^{2} Note that w is a set, therefore duplicate tuples for the values in A_k are ignored.

the value set of A_k, while grouping them by time point and insuring that two different values from the same value set do not participate in the same aggregate value. We can now define event correlated aggregation for GPT relations. We denote by π_{-Id} the projection operation that selects all attributes of a GPT relation except the event Id.

Definition 15 (Event correlated aggregation). *Let R be a GPT relation, let $A \in [R]$ be a data attribute in $[R]$. Let $ctx(R)$ be the probabilistic context over R, let agg be an aggregate operator and let agg_{FL} be its semi-annotated counterpart. The result of the application of agg to attribute A in $[R]$ is a GPT relation that satisfies the following:*
$$\pi_{-Id}(SANN(agg(R, A))) = \pi_{-Id}(agg_{FL}(SANN(R, A))).$$

5   Algorithms for Computing Aggregates

Aggregate computation in the GPT model poses a series of new challenges due to the presence of uncertainty both in temporal and regular attributes.

Problem 1. NECA aggregation is directly defined on GPT relations. ECA aggregation on the other hand is defined w.r.t. the semi-annotated version of a GPT-relation. However, semi-annotation involves an significant space blowup which we would like to avoid. As such, our algorithms (both for NECA and ECA aggregation) work directly with GPT relations.

Problem 2. Let us consider a GPT relation R and an attribute $A \in [R]$ such that $\forall t \in R$, $t.A = \langle V_t, f_t \rangle$, $|V| \leq c$, where c is an arbitrary constant. Let agg be an aggregation operator. According to Definition 12 (for NECA) and Definitions 14 and 15, in the worst case scenario the space complexity of the result would be $\mathcal{O}(c^N)$, where $N = |R|$.

It is obvious that in the case of Problem 2, an exponential complexity (both in space and time) is unacceptable. Furthermore, it is unlikely that a result with a data size exponential in the size of the initial relation would be of any use to an end user. As such, we see two possible scenarios: either the size of the input relation is limited by a selection query (as is usually the case with aggregates on relational data) or aggregate computations are run in sequence, as is the case in Example 4. For the sake of generality, we will assume the existence of a *restrict* method [3] that restricts the set of values V_t that are to be considered for further computation for any tuple t at any intermediate step. We assume the existence of such a method for both event and non-event correlated aggregations.

5.1   NECA Algorithm

We now present the *NECA* algorithm for computing non-event correlated aggregates on GPT-relations. The algorithm takes advantage of our earlier assumption that op_{agg} is associative and commutative. Likewise, Lakshmanan et. al. [5] assume that all conjunctive and disjunctive strategies are associative and commutative - something we assume as well.

---

[3] If aggregates are run in sequence, then the *restrict* method can be easily provided by the query planner. For Example 4, we would only look at the maximum value from any value set V_t for a tuple t, knowing that a *MAX* query is to be applied next. If the selection query case holds, then the *restrict* method can simply let all values in V_t go through.

Algorithm: NECA(R,A,agg,$ctx(R)$)
Input: GPT relation R, attribute $A \in [R]$,aggregation operator agg, probabilistic context $ctx(R)$.
Output: GPT relation R_{agg} representing the result of non-event correlated aggregation.
Notation: $\otimes = \otimes_{ctx}(\{A\})$, $\oplus = \oplus_{ctx}(\{A\})$;
1. $\Gamma \leftarrow \emptyset$;
2. $V \leftarrow \emptyset$;
3. $f \leftarrow null$;
4. **for all** $t \in R$ **do**
5. $\Gamma \leftarrow \Gamma \cup t.\Gamma$;
6.   **if** $V = \emptyset$ **then**
7. $\langle V, f \rangle \leftarrow t.A$;
8.   **else**
9. $V' \leftarrow V \mathbf{X} t.A.V$;
10. $V \leftarrow \emptyset$;
12.   **for all** $(v_1, v_2) \in V'$ **do**
13. $V \leftarrow V \cup \{v_1 \ op_{agg} \ v_2\}$;
14. $V \leftarrow restrict(V)$;
15.   **for all** $v \in V$ **do**
16. $f(v) \leftarrow 0$;
17.   **for all** $(v_1, v_2) \in V'$ s.t. $v_1 \ op_{agg} \ v_2 = v$ **do**
18. $f(v) \leftarrow f(v) \oplus (f(v_1) \otimes t.A.f(v_2))$;
19.   **endfor**
20.   **endif**
21. **endfor**
22. $R_{agg} \leftarrow \{(Id_*, \Gamma, \langle V, f \rangle)\}$;
23. **return** R_{agg};

Algorithm: ECA-timepoint(R,A,agg,$ctx(R)$)
Input: GPT relation R, attribute $A \in [R]$,aggregation operator agg, probabilistic context $ctx(R)$.
Output: GPT relation R_{agg} representing the result of event correlated aggregation.
Notation: (t, L, U) is the TP-case statement that only contains t as a solution.
1. $R_{agg} \leftarrow \emptyset$;
2. **for all** $t \in \tau$ **do**
3. $R' \leftarrow \sigma_{t \in sol(\Gamma)}(R)$;
4. $R'' \leftarrow NECA(R', A, agg, ctx(R))$;
5. $[L, U] \leftarrow [1, 1]$;
6.   **for all** $u \in R'$ and $\gamma \in u.\Gamma$ **do**
7.   **if** $t \in sol(\gamma)$ **then**
8. $[L, U] \leftarrow [L, U] \oplus_{ctx} (\{\Gamma\}) [\gamma.L \cdot \delta(\gamma.D, t), \gamma.U \cdot \delta(\gamma.D, t)]$;
9.   **endfor**
10. $Ragg \leftarrow Ragg \cup \{(Id_*, (t, L, U), R''.A_{agg}\}$;
11. **endfor**
12. **return** R_{agg};

Fig. 1. (a) The NECA algorithm; (b) The ECA-timepoint algorithm

The algorithm performs an incremental computation by analyzing one tuple in the input relation at a time and maintaining an intermediate result. The *restrict* method is used at each step to restrict the number of values from the intermediate value set that are to be considered further during the computation. As an example if the query planner can determine that a *MIN* aggregate is to be executed on this result, the *restrict* method would only select the smallest value computed at each step.

Theorem 1 (NECA correctness). *The NECA algorithm terminates and the resulting GPT relation is correct w.r.t. Definition 12 when $restrict$ is the identity function.*

Let us assume that the set returned by the *restrict* method is bounded by $\mathcal{O}(r)$ and the size of the value sets for attribute A are bounded by an arbitrary constant c. For each tuple, at most $\mathcal{O}(r)$ values held in the intermediate result are combined with at most $\mathcal{O}(c)$ values from the new tuple. This operation is performed for each tuple in the input relation, therefore the complexity of the *NECA* algorithm is $\mathcal{O}(n) \cdot \mathcal{O}(c \cdot r)$

5.2 ECA Algorithms

In this section, we present two algorithms to compute ECA aggregates. We remind the reader that even thought the declarative semantic in Definition 15 is based on the semi-annotated corresponding aggregate, our methods avoid the space blowup required by semi-annotation and compute aggregates directly on GPT relations. The first algorithm, *ECA-timepoint*, is a simple method for computing event correlated aggregation. The second algorithm *ECA-Interval*, is far more efficient.

ECA-timepoint is based on the *NECA* algorithm. A simple probabilistic flattening of the result of the *ECA-timepoint* yields the corresponding semi-annotated aggregate. However, as our experiments will show, the *ECA-timepoint* algorithm is resource consuming both in terms of execution time and space, as the result is dependent on the granularity of temporal information.

The correctness of the *ECA-timepoint* algorithm follows directly from Definition 15 as the probabilistic flattening of the resulting relation yields the same result as semi-annotated aggregation. The complexity of the algorithm is clearly $\mathcal{O}(|\tau|) \cdot \mathcal{O}(NECA)$, since the for loop on line 6 is run only for events that have t as a solution, while the complexity of the *NECA* algorithm is higher.

We try to address the disadvantages of *ECA-timepoint* with the more advanced *ECA-interval* algorithm which makes use of interval constraints to perform the computation of each aggregate value only once. The *ECA-interval* algorithm uses a *pre-aggregation* relation that contains partial information to be included in the result. Simply put, a pre-aggregate is a GPT relation that contains temporal data (Γ) and an IDS attribute. Each tuple in the pre-aggregate corresponds to a tuple in the result **independent** of the aggregate operator used. The result will replicate the temporal attribute and aggregate all events whose IDs are in the IDS set[4].

Table 5. Pre-aggregate relation

Γ	IDS
$\{\langle(10),.2,.38\rangle\}$	$\{1,3\}$
$\{\langle(11),.34,.57\rangle,$ $\langle(12),.34,.57\rangle\}$	$\{1,2,3\}$
$\{\langle(13),.23,.41\rangle\}$	$\{1,2\}$
$\{\langle(14),.08,.16\rangle\}$	$\{1\}$

Example 6. For the GPT relation in Table 1, we choose $\oplus_{ctx}(\Gamma)$ to be the independence disjunction strategy. The pre-aggregate relation for this case is shown in Table 5.

Theorem 2. *The* ECA-interval *algorithm terminates and produces a correct result w.r.t. Definition 15 when* restrict *is the identity function.*

6   Experimental Results

We have developed a 6570 line Java implementation of the algorithms described in this paper. Our experiments were run on a Pentium 4 3.2Ghz machine with 1GB of RAM. The GPT database was built on top of PostgreSQL 8.0. The series of experiments described in this section were run on synthetically generated data with between 14,500 events and 500,000 events, all data being stored on disk. During the experiments we have identified several factors that impact the performance and storage space requirements for our algorithms. Among these were: (i) the data size; (ii) the type of aggregate query - SUM queries are much more expensive than MIN, MAX, $COUNT$; this

---
[4] In a non-event correlated manner.

method pre_aggregate($R,ctx(R)$)
Input: GPT relation R, probabilistic context $ctx(R)$.
Output: GPT relation Pre with attributes Γ and IDS. The IDS attribute contains a set of event IDs that correspond to the TP-case statements in the tuple.
Notation: $\otimes = \otimes_{ctx}(\{Gamma\})$; $\oplus = \oplus_{ctx}(\{Gamma\})$; (t, L, U) is the TP-case statement that only contains t as a solution.
Comments: The *computeLU* method for a time point used here follows the computation of L,U for a time point in line 8 of the *ECA-timepoint* algorithm [5].

1. $Pre \leftarrow \emptyset$;
2. **for** all $t \in R$ **do**
3. $\Gamma \leftarrow t.\Gamma$;
4.   **for** all $u \in Pre$ **do**
5.   **if** $sol(\Gamma) \cap sol(u.\Gamma) \neq \emptyset$ **then**
6.   **for** all $\gamma_1 \in \Gamma, \gamma_2 \in u.\Gamma$ s.t. $sol(\gamma_1) \cap sol(\gamma_2) \neq \emptyset$ **do**
7. $u.\Gamma \leftarrow u.\Gamma - \{\gamma_2\}$;
8. $u.\Gamma \leftarrow u.\Gamma \cup \{\langle x, computeLU(x)\rangle | x \in$
                $sol(\gamma_2) - sol(\gamma_1)\}$;
9. $\Gamma \leftarrow \Gamma - \{\gamma_1\}$;
10. $\Gamma \leftarrow \Gamma \cup \{\langle x, computeLU(x)\rangle | x \in sol(\gamma_1) - sol(\gamma_2)\}$;
11. $\Gamma' \leftarrow \{\langle x, computeLU(x)\rangle | x \in sol(\gamma_1) \cap sol(\gamma_2)\}$;
12. $Pre \leftarrow Pre \cup \{\Gamma', u.IDS \cup \{t.Id\}\}$;
13.   **goto** 4;
14.   **endfor**
15.   **endif**
16.   **endfor**
17. $Pre \leftarrow Pre \cup \{(\Gamma, \{t.Id\})\}$;
18. **endfor**
19. **return** Pre;

Algorithm: ECA-interval($R,A,agg,ctx(R)$)
Input: GPT relation R, attribute $A \in [R]$,aggregation operator agg, probabilistic context $ctx(R)$.
Output: GPT relation R_{agg} representing the result of event correlated aggregation.

1. $Pre \leftarrow pre\_aggregate(R, ctx(R))$;
2. **for** all $t \in Pre$ **do**
3. $R' \leftarrow NECA(\sigma_{Id \in t.IDS}(R), A, agg, ctx(R))$;
4. $R_{agg} \leftarrow R_{agg} \cup \{Id_*, t.\Gamma, R'.A_{agg}\}$;
5. **endfor**
6. **return** R_{agg}.

Fig. 2. The ECA-interval algorithm

also involves the $restrict$ method bounds; (iii) the "overlapping" factor l - which measures the degree of temporal overlap between events. Strictly speaking, l was computed as an average on the multiset $\{x | \exists\, t \in \tau$ s.t. $\exists\, x\ different\ events\ with\ t\ as\ a\ solution\}$.

Impact of Size. We measured the impact of the input relation size on the running time of queries. We fixed the $restrict$ method to select only the maximum value from each value set, similarly to Example 4. The overlapping factor was $l \approx 8.5$. We applied a SUM aggregate both in non-event and event correlated manner, plotting the running time for each of the three algorithms. The time taken to construct the pre-aggregate relation was measured independently. Figure 3(a) shows the experimental results. We can easily see that the non-event correlated aggregation is only slightly faster than the *ECA-interval* algorithm. The reason for this is that in the *ECA-interval* case, once the pre-aggregated relation is computed, the *NECA* algorithm is applied to small subsets of the tuples in the input relation, whereas in the *NECA* case, the algorithm is applied to the whole relation. We can also see that the *ECA-interval* outperforms the *ECA-timepoint*

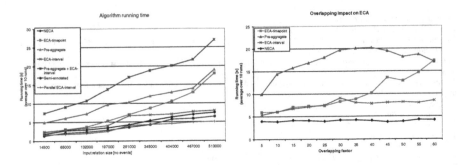

Fig. 3. (a) Running time analysis; (b) Overlap impact on performance

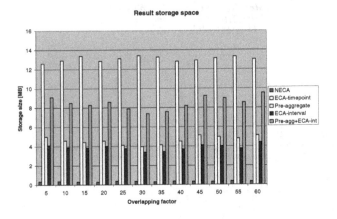

Fig. 4. Overlap impact on storage space

algorithm. Moreover, the parallelized version of the *ECA-interval* algorithm using 40 worker threads is as efficient as the semi-annotated version of the aggregation.

Impact of Overlapping Factor. We fixed the input relation size to 255000 events and we measured the impact of the overlapping factor on the relative performance of the *ECA-interval* and *ECA-timepoint* algorithms. The *NECA* algorithm is not affected by these experiments, as it does not consider temporal information in the process of computing an aggregate value. The $restrict$ method was the same as mentioned above. The results in Figure 3(b) show that once the overlapping factor starts to increase, the *ECA-interval* algorithm slowly tends toward the same running time as *ECA-timepoint* due to the increased number of single time point constraints in the pre-aggregation relation. However, as the overlapping factor increases over a certain threshold, more events will correspond to the same tuple in the result - since τ is finite, it can only mean the size of the overlapping intervals increases, meaning *ECA-interval* is much more efficient than *ECA-timepoint.*

Size of output. We measured the storage space needed for the results of the aggregation. The critical factor here is again the overlapping factor. The *NECA* algorithm only produces one tuple, and thus is storage space is minimal with a reasonable $restrict$ method

- the only variations are due to the representation of a compact union of all temporal information. The overlapping factor was fixed to the same value as in the first set of experiments. The *ECA-timepoint* is the most inefficient from this point of view, since it stores one tuple for each time point, whereas the *ECA-interval* algorithm minimizes the storage space for event correlated aggregation. The results can be seen in Figure 4.

7   Related Work and Conclusions

The business world is full of economic models that are full of uncertainty about supply (of a resource) and demand (for the resource). Supply and demand usually have a temporal aspect to them - supply and demand for sweaters is far greater in the winter months than in the summer. In this paper, we have used a real-world energy model [7] that we have worked on to motivate the need for reasoning about uncertainty in domains where time plays a role.

Though there has been a long history of work on uncertainty in databases [8,5], the first to recognize the subtle interplay between time and uncertainty were Dyreson and Snodgrass [1] who, in a pioneering paper, laid out a large set of motivating examples and proposed a probabilistic model for temporal data. They extended temporal relational DBMSs to include probabilities about when an event might occur. They proposed an extension of SQL to query such databases and came up with elegant structures to store PDFs. Their work assumed that events were independent. To address this, Dekhtyar et. al. [2] proposed a temporal-probabilistic DB algebra in which they showed how such independence assumptions could be eliminated. The formalisms of both [1,2] assume that uncertainty occurs only in the temporal attributes. In this paper, our GPT model allows uncertainty to occur both in the temporal attributes, as well as in the data attributes of relations. Our notion of a probabilistic context allows the user to make assumptions about the relationships between events when he asks a query - the GPT data model supports answering queries based on any such probabilistic context.

Our second (and really the primary) contribution focuses on aggregate computations in GPT-databases. Past work on aggregates focused either solely on temporal data [9,10,11] or on probabilistic data [12].

We should add that there has been a long history of work on reasoning about both time and uncertainty in the AI community [13,14,15,16] but none of this work addresses aggregate computation.

In short, in this paper, we have proposed a model for aggregate computation in GPT databases that allows us to represent, for example, the output of statistical models of supply and demand in a database and then to process all kinds of interesting aggregate queries. Our algorithms have all been implemented and work very efficiently.

References

1. Dyreson, C.E., Snodgrass, R.T.: Supporting valid-time indeterminacy. ACM Trans. Database Syst. 23, 1–57 (1998)
2. Dekhtyar, A., Ross, R., Subrahmanian, V.S.: Probabilistic temporal databases, I: algebra. ACM Trans. Database Syst. 26, 41–95 (2001)

3. Wilkinson, N.: Managerial Economics: A Problem-Solving Approach. Cambridge University Press, Cambridge (2005)
4. Ross, S.M.: A first course on probability. Prentice Hall College Div. Englewood Cliffs (1997)
5. Lakshmanan, L.V.S., Leone, N., Ross, R., Subrahmanian, V.S.: Probview: a flexible probabilistic database system. ACM Trans. Database Syst. 22, 419–469 (1997)
6. Lakshmanan, L.V.S., Shiri, N.: A parametric approach to deductive databases with uncertainty. IEEE Transactions on Knowledge and Data Engineering 13, 554–570 (2001)
7. Wolfram, C.D.: Strategic bidding in a multi-unit auction: An empirical analysis of bids to supply electricity. RAND Journal of Economics 29(4), 703–772 (1998)
8. Lakshmanan, L.V.S., Shiri, N.: A parametric approach to deductive databases with uncertainty. Knowledge and Data Engineering 13, 554–570 (2001)
9. Yang, J., Widom, J.: Incremental computation and maintenance of temporal aggregates. The VLDB Journal 12, 262–283 (2003)
10. Gendrano, J.A.G., Huang, B.C., Rodrigue, J.M., Moon, B., Snodgrass, R.T.: Parallel algorithms for computing temporal aggregates. In: ICDE 1999, pp. 418–427 (1999)
11. Zhang, D., Markowetz, A., Tsotras, V.J., Gunopulos, D., Seeger, B.: Efficient computation of temporal aggregates with range predicates. In: Symposium on Principles of Database Systems (2001)
12. Ross, R., Subrahmanian, V.S., Grant, J.: Aggregate operators in probabilistic databases. J. ACM 52, 54–101 (2005)
13. Baral, C., Tran, N., Tuan, L.: Reasoning about actions in a probabilistic setting. In: Proc. of AAAI'02, Edmonton, Alberta, Canada, pp. 507–512. AAAI Press (2002)
14. Dean, T., Kanazawa, K.: Probabilistic Temporal Reasoning. In: Proceedings AAAI, St. Paul, MN, USA, pp. 524–529. AAAI Press / The MIT Press (1988)
15. Dubois, D., Prade, H.: Processing Fuzzy Temporal Knowledge. IEEE Transactions on Systems, Man and Cybernetics 19, 729–744 (1989)
16. Lehmann, D., Shelah, S.: Reasoning with time and chance. Information and Control 53, 165–198 (1982)

An Indexing Technique for Fuzzy Numerical Data

Carlos D. Barranco[1], Jesús R. Campaña[2], and Juan M. Medina[2]

[1] Division of Computer Science, School of Engineering, Pablo de Olavide University,
Ctra. de Utrera Km. 1, 41013 Sevilla, Spain
`cbarranco@upo.es`
[2] Dept. of Computer Science and Artificial Intelligence, University of Granada,
Daniel Saucedo Aranda s/n, 18071 Granada, Spain
`{jesuscg,medina}@decsai.ugr.es`

Abstract. This paper introduces an indexing technique for fuzzy numerical data which relies on the classical, well-known and well-spread B+tree index data structure. The proposed indexing technique is specifically devised to increase the performance of query processing when a possibility measured flexible condition is involved. The proposal relies on the use of an indexing data structure implemented in virtually every database management system. This feature makes the proposal a good candidate to be used, with very low implementation effort, in a fuzzy database management system created as an extension of a classical one. The paper includes a performance analysis of the proposed indexing technique in contrast with other purpose equivalent techniques in order to evaluate the suitability of the proposal.

1 Introduction

The fuzzy set theory provides computer science scholars and practitioners with a good tool for managing imprecise and vague data. This tool is used to develop novel applications that are able to manage *fuzzy* data, and which usually perform better in classical and non-classical problems than crisp solutions. Many of these *fuzzy* applications are prototypes that have not usually been conceived to process a large amount of data, and for this reason, the fuzzy data management subsystem has largely been overlooked in application design and implementation. These applications usually manage and store the fuzzy data directly using files with some proprietary or text format. When a database management system (DBMS) is used for this task, the DBMS is generally unable to manage fuzzy data so the applications must include a bridge to store fuzzy data as crisp data components. This bridge encloses fuzzy data management and query methods at the application layer and is generally poorly optimized.

As these novel applications prove their potential, they are likely to be incorporated into real-world environments. This kind of environment requires high performance, scalability and availability for applications.

If we focus on data access, the poor fuzzy data management subsystems of these applications do not contribute to providing the required performance, scalability and availability levels. The former case, when fuzzy data is directly stored

H. Prade and V.S. Subrahmanian (Eds.): SUM 2007, LNAI 4772, pp. 187–200, 2007.
© Springer-Verlag Berlin Heidelberg 2007

and managed in files, is clearly inappropriate and does not deserve further discussion as the first step to improving these systems is moving towards a DBMS. In the second case, when fuzzy data is stored in a crisp DBMS, applications should take advantage of the high performance, scalability and availability provided by the DBMS. However, this increase in performance, scalability and availability provided by the DBMS is reduced since all fuzzy data processing is carried out at the application level. This increases data traffic between the DBMS and the bridge and its computational power requirements as flexible query results are determined in this component so all the potential results of the fuzzy query must be retrieved from the DBMS. Moreover, the bridge is usually a specific development which is generally poorly optimized and unable to work in scalable configurations, and so the fuzzy data bridge becomes a new bottle-neck.

A DBMS with fuzzy data (imprecise and uncertain) processing capabilities, i.e. a fuzzy DBMS (FDBMS), is a very convenient solution. Since building a complete and efficient DBMS requires a lot of effort, authors believe that it should not be developed from scratch. The performance of current DBMS could be harnessed if a FDBMS is built on top of them. The article [1] proposes the idea of taking advantage of the extension mechanism of current object-relational DBMS in order to create user-defined data types to seamlessly store, query and manage fuzzy data as native database objects.

Although this kind of FDBMS inherits the desirable features of the host DBMS, specific indexing mechanisms for fuzzy data would be required to achieve a significant increase in performance. While there has been much research into fuzzy database models, there has been less work on indexing mechanisms for efficiently accessing fuzzy data. Moreover, existing fuzzy data indexing proposals are hard to implement using the extension mechanisms of current DBMSs as the proposals generally require specific data structures and algorithms.

This paper proposes an indexing technique for fuzzy numerical data which is devised to improve the processing performance of a query including a possibility measured atomic flexible condition. The proposal relies on a B+tree data structure. As this data structure has not been specifically designed (nor is it optimal) for fuzzy numerical data indexing, a lower performance than other proposals which rely on specific data structures should be expected. Nevertheless, it is also simple and well optimized and virtually available in every current DBMS, which would reduce implementation, integration and optimization efforts if the proposed technique is incorporated into a FDBMS from the extension of a crisp DBMS. In our opinion, the difference in performance is not likely to be significant, and would be offset by the reduction in the implementation effort required. The paper measures and analyzes the performance of the proposal.

This paper introduces the concepts of *fuzzy numerical data* and *possibility measured atomic flexible conditions* which are used throughout this paper in Sect. 2. In Sect. 3, related work on fuzzy data indexing and the indexing principle, on which this paper and other considered proposals are based, are described. Section 4 presents the considered and proposed indexing techniques. Section 5 studies the procedure for evaluating the performance of these indexing techniques. Section 6 analyzes the performance results. Finally, Section 7 includes our concluding remarks and suggests our future lines of research.

2   Basic Concepts

The proposed indexing technique was described in the previous section as a technique for *fuzzy numerical data* to improve the performance of query processing when a *possibility measured atomic flexible condition* is involved. This section defines these concepts in the context of this paper.

A *fuzzy numerical value*, for the purposes of this paper, is a convex possibility distribution on an underlying domain in which a linear order relation is defined.

Also for the purposes of this paper, a *fuzzy condition* is a restriction imposed on the values of an attribute which contains a fuzzy numerical value for each row. This restriction is specified as a fuzzy numerical value to which the restricted attribute value must be equal. A fuzzy condition can be partially fulfilled. When a fuzzy condition is applied on an attribute of a table containing fuzzy numerical values, it results in two fuzzy sets of rows: those *possibly* satisfying the condition and those *necessarily* satisfying it.

This paper only focuses on possibility measured conditions since necessity measured conditions, which can take advantage of a more efficient indexing schema, warrant specific work. Nevertheless, as the possibility degree is always greater than or equal to the necessity degree, the proposed indexing schema can be used as a preselection filter for the resulting rows of a necessity measured atomic flexible condition.

The possibility degree is therefore called the fulfillment degree of the condition in the rest of the paper. This degree is computed as shown in (1), where $D(A)$ is the underlying domain associated to the fuzzy attribute A, $\Pi_{A(r)}$ is the possibility distribution which describes the fuzzy value of the attribute A for the row r, and μ_C the membership function defining the fuzzy condition C.

$$\Pi(C/r) = \sup_{d \in D(A)} \left(\Pi_{A(r)}(d) \wedge \mu_C(d) \right). \tag{1}$$

A fuzzy condition is combined with a crisp relational comparator to set a threshold for its fulfillment degree. This minimum specifies the degree of flexibility in which the fuzzy condition is applied, from 1 (no flexibility) to 0 (maximum flexibility). The typical expression for applying a threshold T is $\Pi(C/r) \geq T$, except when the threshold is 0. In the latter case, the expression $\Pi(C/r) > T$ is applied. The combination of a fuzzy condition with a threshold is called an *atomic flexible condition* for the purposes of this paper and is notated $\langle C, T \rangle$.

An example of a query including a possibility measured atomic flexible condition is the following:

```
SELECT * FROM tbl WHERE FEQ(f,[a,b,c,d])>=T
```

The previous query is expressed using the SDS [1] query language. It returns a table containing the rows from tbl table whose value for the attribute f is possibly equal to the fuzzy numerical constant value represented as a trapezoidal possibility distribution $[a, b, c, d]$, with a fulfillment degree which is greater than or equal to the threshold value T.

3   Related Work

The seminal paper [2] claims the need for specific indexing techniques for fuzzy databases, and proposes two indexing principles for flexible querying using possibility and necessity measures on fuzzy attributes described as possibility distributions. This section introduces briefly the currently proposed indexing techniques and describes the aforementioned indexing principle for possibility measured flexible conditions and includes some discussion about it.

3.1   Fuzzy Data Indexing Techniques

Two fuzzy data indexing techniques are proposed in [3,4] and [5,6,7]. The first technique creates one index structure for each fuzzy predicate associated to a fuzzy attribute, whereas the second is based on a crisp multidimensional indexing technique. Unfortunately, these indexing techniques are only applicable when the number of potential flexible conditions which can be used to build queries is finite and low, and this is not the case with fuzzy numerical values.

The paper [8] proposes an indexing technique for convex possibility distributions defined on an ordered domain that relies on a crisp multidimensional indexing method. This technique is suitable for numerical fuzzy data indexing, on which this paper focuses, and is described in Sect. 4.

3.2   Indexing Principle for Possibility Measured Flexible Conditions

The latter indexing technique and this paper's proposal are based on the indexing principles proposed in [2]. The following is a brief introduction to it.

Preselection Criteria. The indexing principle allows the rows which do not satisfy an atomic flexible condition to be filtered out of a table.

Recalling (1), in the basic case when the threshold of an atomic flexible condition is zero, a row r possibly satisfies a fuzzy condition C if, and only if, the expression in (2) is satisfied, where $supp(A(r))$ and $supp(C)$ are the support of the fuzzy sets $A(r)$ and C. The support of a fuzzy set S on D characterized by the membership function μ_S is defined as $supp(S) = \{d \in D, \mu_S(d) > 0\}$.

$$\Pi(C/r) > 0 \iff \exists d \in D, d \in A(r), d \in C \iff A(r) \cap C \neq \emptyset \iff \\ supp(A(r)) \cap supp(C) \neq \emptyset . \tag{2}$$

If the threshold of the atomic flexible condition is greater than zero, (2) can be reformulated as shown by (3). In this equation $A(r)_T$ and C_T are T-cuts of

$A(r)$ and C, respectively. A T-cut of a fuzzy set S is defined as $S_T = \{d \in D, \mu_S(d) \geq T\}$.

$$\Pi(C/r) \geq T \iff \exists d \in D, \mu_{A(r)}(d) \geq T, \mu_C(d) \geq T \iff A(r)_T \cap C_T \neq \emptyset. \tag{3}$$

Equation 2 is an effective indexing principle, as every row which satisfies it must be included in the set of rows satisfying the flexible condition. In order to apply this principle it is only necessary to index the support of the data on the restricted attribute in a fast access data structure. Equation 3, on the other hand, is not an effective indexing principle for flexible conditions with a threshold greater than zero. The application of the indexing principle requires every possible T-cut (i.e. for every possible value for T inside $[0,1]$) to be indexed. To overcome this drawback the weakened indexing principle in (4), which only requires the support of the fuzzy numerical data to be indexed, is defined. As it is a weakened principle, it is otherwise only useful to preselect the resulting rows of a query as false positives must be filtered out.

$$A(r)_T \cap C_T \neq \emptyset \Rightarrow supp(A(r)) \cap C_T \neq \emptyset. \tag{4}$$

A Unified Preselection Criterion. In our opinion, the previous preselection criteria defined in (2) and (4) can be generalized and reformulated as the unified preselection criterion shown in (5), where the preselection function ps is defined in (6). In the latter, *base* is defined as (7) shows. Henceforth, the interval resulting from (7) when applied to a flexible condition $\langle C, T \rangle$ will be called the *base* of the flexible condition.

$$\langle C, T \rangle \Rightarrow ps(C/r, T), 0 \leq T \leq 1. \tag{5}$$

$$ps(C/r, T) \iff supp(A(r)) \cap base(\langle C, T \rangle) \neq \emptyset, 0 \leq T \leq 1. \tag{6}$$

$$base(\langle C, T \rangle) = \begin{cases} supp(C), & T = 0 \\ C_T, & 0 < T \leq 1 \end{cases}. \tag{7}$$

When the fuzzy data and the fuzzy conditions are modeled using convex possibility distributions defined over a linearly ordered underlying domain, their support and every T-cut is an interval. In this case, the preselection criteria can be reformulated as a conjunction of range conditions as shown in (8). For this equation, $\inf(S)$ and $\sup(S)$ correspond, respectively, to the infimum and the supremum of a crisp set S.

$$ps(C/r, T) \iff \sup(supp(A(r))) \geq \inf(base(\langle C, T \rangle)) \wedge \\ \inf(supp(A(r))) \leq \sup(base(\langle C, T \rangle)). \tag{8}$$

The previous indexing principle relies on the assumption that each attribute value and fuzzy condition is represented by a possibility distribution whose support is a closed interval.

4   Considered and Proposed Indexing Techniques

This paper contrasts the performance of two fuzzy data indexing techniques based on the previously described indexing principle. The following subsections will describe these techniques.

4.1   Fuzzy Data Indexing with a G-Tree

The article [8] proposes the use of a G-tree [9] for indexing the lower and upper bounds of the interval representing the support of the possibility distributions modelling the indexed fuzzy data. A G-tree is a combination of a B-tree and a grid file for indexing multidimensional data points. This index structure supports single point queries as well as range queries.

In this approach, an interval corresponds to a two-dimensional data point. For each interval $[l, u]$, a point (l, u) is inserted in the indexing structure. The preselection row set of a flexible condition $\langle C, T \rangle$ is obtained by retrieving all entries in the index satisfying the range query $m \leq x \leq u_{base(\langle C,T \rangle)}, l_{base(\langle C,T \rangle)} \leq y \leq M$, where m and M are the minimum and maximum values of the attribute domain. This range condition is a translation of the preselection criteria of (8) to the described two-dimensional mapping scheme. For the rest of the paper, this technique is called GT for the sake of conciseness.

4.2   Fuzzy Data Indexing with B+Trees

The seminal idea of this alternative proposal was depicted in [10]. This paper reformulates it so that its performance may easily be compared with GT. This technique takes advantage of classical B+tree indexing structures [11,12] for indexing the intervals representing the support of the indexed fuzzy numerical data. Throughout the remainder of this paper this technique is called 2BPT.

2BPT indexes an interval by means of two B+tree structures: one indexes the values of the lower bound of the indexed intervals, whereas the other indexes upper bound values.

The preselection row set for a flexible condition $\langle C, T \rangle$ is calculated by following these steps:

1. The range condition $\sup(supp(A(r))) \geq \inf(base(\langle C, T \rangle))$ from the preselection criterion of (8) is applied by using the B+tree that indexes the upper bound values of data support. The resulting set is named $U_{\langle C,T \rangle}$.
2. Likewise, the range condition $\inf(supp(A(r))) \leq \sup(base(\langle C, T \rangle))$ from (8) is applied. This range condition will be processed by using the B+tree that indexes the lower bound values of data support. The resulting set is named $L_{\langle C,T \rangle}$.
3. The preselection row set $PS_{\langle C,T \rangle}$ is populated by the rows satisfying the two previous range conditions. Thus, this set is $PS_{\langle C,T \rangle} = U_{\langle C,T \rangle} \cap L_{\langle C,T \rangle}$.

It can easily be seen that 2BPT doubles the overhead due to tree traverse because it uses two trees, and this should lead to lower performance in comparison with GT, which only uses one. Otherwise, 2BPT does not suffer from

GT's performance degradation caused by low bucket usage due to its partitioning method, which is extremely sensitive to data distribution because of its fixed nature. The counteraction of these factors enables the proposed fuzzy indexing technique to perform in a similar way to the G-tree based technique.

5   Performance Evaluation of Fuzzy Indexing Techniques

A quantitative performance evaluation must be carried out in order to assess to what extent 2BPT performs like GT. This section describes the index performance measures used, the influential factors on index performance which have been taken into account, and the experiments carried out to assess these measures.

5.1   Performance Measures

Index performance is measured as the saving in time when a query is processed by taking advantage of it, in contrast to the case when the query is processed using sequential access. Obviously, this time saving is inversely related to the time required to apply the indexing mechanism, which can be divided into the time necessary to access index data and the time to process this data.

As the data of a large index is usually stored in the secondary memory, the time required to access this data is much greater than the time to process it, and so the data processing time is generally neglected.

The data access time is clearly dependent on the amount of data. Since secondary storage devices are block-based, the data block is their information transfer unit instead of bytes or bits. In order to achieve an independent performance measure of the indexing techniques, a performance measure based on the number of data blocks accessed by the index technique would be appropriate. Any hardware or OS-dependent techniques for reducing the access time are ignored because the amount of data, not the time to access it, is taken into account. Such a performance measure should also consider the cardinality of the query results, as the amount of data accessed by the index causes a smaller impact when processing high cardinality queries.

A candidate performance measure that meets the previous consideration is the *index efficiency*. This measure is defined as (9) shows, where d is the minimum number of data blocks in which the result set can be fitted, and i is the number of blocks of index data accessed by the technique. Since this measure considers the minimum number of data blocks which fits the query result (rather than the real number which is dependent on the physical layout of the data due to DBMS and operating system policies), it therefore corresponds to the worst performance case.

$$eff = \frac{d}{d+i} \,. \tag{9}$$

5.2   Index Performance Influential Factors

A large number of factors affect the performance of the indexing techniques for fuzzy data. On the one hand, there is the set of physical and logical factors related to the classical indexing techniques on which these indexes for fuzzy data are based. Although these factors could increase index efficiency when tuned, they are basically hardware or particular case dependent and so studying them does not provide a good insight into the general performance of the considered indexing techniques under general conditions. On the other hand, there is a set of factors related to the indexed data and the processed queries which would affect index performance. The indexing principle, on which both studied techniques are based, computes the preselection set as the intersection of two intervals: the fuzzy data support and the flexible condition base. For this reason, as the extent of these intervals together with the amount of indexed data grows, the number of resulting rows is greater and so the impact of the index overhead is smaller.

The extent of the support of a fuzzy set is measured as proposed in (10), where $u_{supp(S)}$ and $l_{supp(S)}$ are the upper and lower bounds of the interval representing the support of the fuzzy set S and, D_M and D_m are the maximum and minimum values of the domain D on which the fuzzy set S is defined. For the purpose of this paper, the result of this formula is called the *imprecision degree* of the fuzzy set S.

$$impr(S) = \frac{u_{supp(S)} - l_{supp(S)}}{D_M - D_m} . \tag{10}$$

The imprecision factor of the fuzzy set modeling a flexible condition is not the only one related to the extent of the base of a flexible query. This extent is reduced as the threshold of the flexible query increases. The speed of this reduction is determined by the sharpness of the transition of the possibility distribution from values of low possibility to values of high possibility.

The proposed way to measure the sharpness of fuzzy sets defined by a possibility distribution on an ordered underlying domain is the one defined in (11), where $u_{supp(S)}$ and $l_{supp(S)}$ are the upper and lower bounds of the interval representing the support of the fuzzy set S, $core(S) = \{d \in D, \mu_S(d) = 1\}$ is the core of a fuzzy set, and $u_{core(S)}$ and $l_{core(S)}$ are the upper and lower bounds of the interval representing the core of the fuzzy set S. For the purposes of this paper, this value is called the *fuzziness degree* of the fuzzy set S.

$$fuzz(S) = \frac{u_{core(S)} - l_{core(S)}}{u_{supp(S)} - l_{supp(S)}} . \tag{11}$$

To sum up, five influential factors on the fuzzy index performance have been identified. These are the amount of indexed data, the imprecision of the fuzzy data and the imprecision, the fuzziness and the threshold of flexible queries.

5.3   Experiments

The performance of the two compared fuzzy data indexing techniques has been assessed taking into account different data and query scenarios.

Different data sets have been employed to create different data scenarios. In order to evaluate the influence of the amount of indexed data, the cardinality of data sets has been fixed to 6,250, 12,500, 25,000, 50,000 and 100,000 data elements. The data of each one is randomly generated using a uniform distributed random generator in the interval $[-1000000, 1000000]$ and ensuring that each data element has the same fixed imprecision and fuzziness degree for the entire set. 110 data sets for each cardinality have been evaluated, each with a fixed imprecision degree ranging from 0 to 0.9 and a fixed fuzziness degree ranging from 0 to 1, at 0.1 increments. The imprecision degree 1 is ignored because in this case all data elements in the data set are the same. A total 550 data sets comprising a total 21,312,500 random fuzzy data elements are considered in this experiment.

In the same way, different flexible query scenarios have been considered. Each data set has been queried using randomly generated atomic flexible conditions. In order to ensure that the influential parameter spectrum has been equally considered, the possibility distributions modeling the applied flexible condition are generated thereby ensuring fixed imprecision and fuzziness degrees. Similarly, the spectrum of threshold values is explored by fixing threshold values ranging from 0 to 1 at 0.1 steps. For each fixed combination of imprecision, fuzziness degree and threshold, 20 atomic fuzzy conditions are randomly generated. A total of 26,620 random queries are applied to each data set, which results in an evaluation of 14,641,000 queries.

The experiment is isolated from physical and logical factors relating to the underlying indexing techniques by fixing the same factor values for both indexing techniques. The values for these factors are chosen to minimize the row size, which generates worse case performance measures.

6   Results

Our results yield a global approximation of the efficiency of the indexing techniques of 0.42 with a 0.9 standard deviation for 2BPT, and 0.43 with a 0.6 standard deviation for GT. This means that there is a difference of approximately 2%.

In order to assess the importance of the considered influential factors, a deeper analysis of the results has been conducted. The first considered factor is the database size which results in larger index structures and may result in an increase in the cardinality of the results. Figure 1 shows the mean efficiency of the compared techniques for different database sizes. The figure shows that even though GT is slightly more efficient than 2BPT, the performance of the 2BPT technique is quite similar. The fluctuation of the efficiency for GT is related with the fluctuation of block usage in its indexing data structure as will be shown below.

Another important factor for index efficiency is the imprecision degree of the indexed data. Figure 2 shows the mean efficiency measured for different imprecision degrees of the considered data sets. It can be seen that the efficiency of 2BPT is similar, and in some cases greater, than of GT for data sets comprising highly imprecise data. The efficiency is much different for data sets composed of slightly imprecise data, especially when the data sets consist exclusively of crisp data, which is a very extreme case of a fuzzy database. Once again, fluctuation of efficiency for GT can be observed.

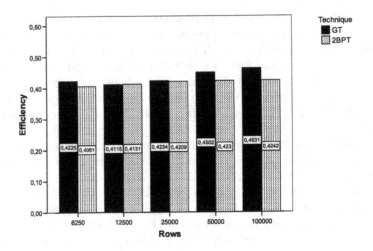

Fig. 1. Comparison of efficiency under different database sizes

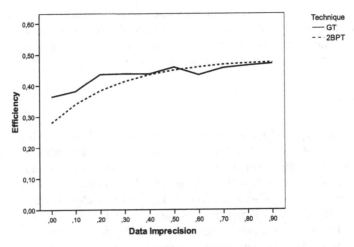

Fig. 2. Comparison of efficiency under different data imprecision degrees

Figure 3 shows the aforementioned imprecision fluctuation of GT in contrast with the stability of 2BPT. The block usage of GT is strongly data dependent, as this indexing technique does not ensure minimum block usage. In contrast, 2BPT ensures a minimum block usage of 0.5, which results in an average block usage of 0.73, whereas an average block usage of 0.52 is measured for GT. Figure 4 shows a fluctuation in block usage in the case of GT (with its subsequent fluctuation in efficiency) in contrast to the stability of 2BPT in block usage and therefore in its efficiency.

With regards to the set of influential query factors, Figure 5 shows the relation between query imprecision and index efficiency. It can be seen that 2BPT is more

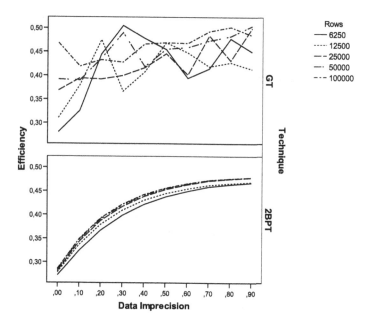

Fig. 3. Comparison of efficiency stability under different database sizes and data imprecision degrees

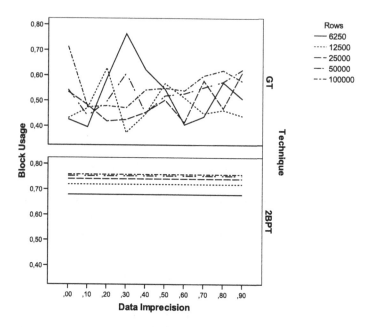

Fig. 4. Comparison of block usage stability under different database sizes and data imprecision degrees

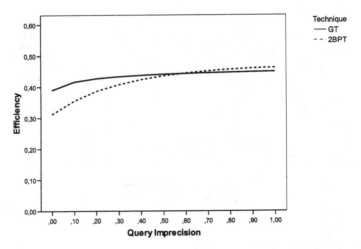

Fig. 5. Comparison of efficiency under different query imprecision degrees

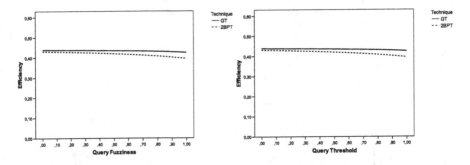

Fig. 6. Comparison of efficiency and different query fuzzyness and threshold degrees

affected by this factor than GT. Nevertheless, 2BPT is equally efficient with the exception of very low imprecision queries and crisp ones in particular.

Query fuzziness is another considered factor in index efficiency. A small influence of this factor for 2BPT and a negligible influence for GT have been observed. Similarly, the results show that the query threshold has a slight effect on the efficiency of 2BPT, and practically none on the efficiency of GT. Figure 6 shows a graphical representation of the influence of these factors.

7   Concluding Remarks and Future Work

This paper proposes an indexing technique which improves the performance of query processing when it involves a possibility measured atomic flexible condition which is used to query fuzzy numerical data. Experimental results show that the mean performance of 2BPT is similar to GT. In addition, results reveal that

2BPT is a more stable indexing method than GT since it is extremely sensitive to data distribution issues that lead to a low block usage.

The insignificant difference of efficiency observed and the enormous difference of implementation effort of GT in contrast with 2BPT makes the latter a good candidate to be implemented in an FDBMS, particularly when it is built as an extension of a classical DBMS where the B+tree indexing technique is available. 2BPT offers a practically immediate indexing mechanism (with a low implementation cost) for fuzzy numerical data with an almost similar index efficiency, whereas GT requires a specific data structure and algorithm implementation.

This paper focuses on possibility measured atomic flexible conditions. Future work would focus on providing and studying indexing mechanisms for queries involving necessity measured conditions, which should be aimed at reducing implementation costs as this proposal does. Additionally, further research effort should be spent on indexing mechanisms for other imprecis and uncertain data types, such as scalar fuzzy data, fuzzy objects and fuzzy collections.

Acknowledgment

This work has been partially supported by the Ministry of Education and Culture of Spain ("Ministerio de Educación y Cultura") and the European Social Fund under the grant TIC2003–08687–C02-2, and by the Council for Innovation, Science and Corporations of Andalusia (Spain) ("Consejería de Innovación Ciencia y Empresa") under the grant TIC–1570.

References

1. Cubero, J.C., Marín, N., Medina, J.M., Pons, O., Vila, M.A.: Fuzzy object management in an object-relational framework. In: Proceedings of X Intl. Conf. on Information Processing and Management of Uncertainty in Knowledge-Based Systems (IPMU), pp. 1767–1774 (2004)
2. Bosc, P., Galibourg, M.: Indexing principles for a fuzzy data base. Information Systems 14(6), 493–499 (1989)
3. Bosc, P., Pivert, O.: Fuzzy querying in conventional databases. In: Fuzzy logic for the management of uncertainty, pp. 645–671. John Wiley & Sons, Inc. Chichester (1992)
4. Petry, F.E., Bosc, P.: Fuzzy databases: principles and applications. International Series in Intelligent Technologies. Kluwer Academic Publishers, Dordrecht (1996)
5. Yazici, A., Cibiceli, D.: An index structure for fuzzy databases. In: Proceedings of the Fifth IEEE International Conference on Fuzzy Systems, vol. 2, pp. 1375–1381 (1996)
6. Yazici, A., Cibiceli, D.: An access structure for similarity-based fuzzy databases. Information Sciences 115(1-4), 137–163 (1999)
7. Yazici, A., Ince, C., Koyuncu, M.: An indexing technique for similarity-based fuzzy object-oriented data model. In: Christiansen, H., Hacid, M.-S., Andreasen, T., Larsen, H.L. (eds.) FQAS 2004. LNCS (LNAI), vol. 3055, pp. 334–347. Springer, Heidelberg (2004)

8. Liu, C., Ouksel, A., Sistla, P., Wu, J., Yu, C., Rishe, N.: Performance evaluation of g-tree and its application in fuzzy databases. In: CIKM '96: Proceedings of the fifth international conference on Information and knowledge management, pp. 235–242. ACM Press, New York (1996)

9. Kumar, A.: G-tree: a new data structure for organizing multidimensional data. IEEE Transactions on Knowledge and Data Engineering 6(2), 341–347 (1994)

10. Barranco, C.D., Campaña, J.R., Medina, J.M.: On an indexing mechanism for imprecise numerical data for fuzzy object relational database management systems. In: Proceedings of 11th Int.l Conf. on Information Processing and Management of Uncertainty in Knowledge-Based Systems (IPMU), vol. 2, pp. 2205–2212 (2006)

11. Bayer, R., McCreight, E.M.: Organization and maintenance of large ordered indexes. Acta Informatica 1(3), 173–189 (1972)

12. Comer, D.: Ubiquitous b-tree. ACM Comput. Surv. 11(2), 121–137 (1979)

Combining Uncertain Outputs from Multiple Ontology Matchers

Ying Wang, Weiru Liu, and David Bell

School of Electronics, Electrical Engineering and Computer Science,
Queen's University Belfast, Belfast, BT7 1NN, UK
{ywang14,w.liu,da.bell}@qub.ac.uk

Abstract. An ontology matching method (or a matcher) aims at matching every entity (or concept) in one ontology to the most suitable entity (or entities) in another ontology. Usually it is almost impossible to find a perfect match in the second ontology for every entity in the first ontology, so a matcher generally returns a set of possible matches with some weights (uncertainty) attached to each pair of match. In order to improve a matching result, several matchers can be used and the matched results from these matchers are combined with suitable approaches. In this paper, we first propose two new matchers among three matchers we use. We then address the need of dealing with uncertainties in mapping by investigating how some uncertainty reasoning frameworks can be used to combine matching results. We apply both the Dempster Shafer theory of evidence (DS theory) and Possibility Theory to merge the results computed by different matchers. Our experimental results and comparisons with related work indicate that integrating these theories to deal with uncertain ontology matching is a promising way to improve the overall matching results.

1 Introduction

Ontology mapping (or matching) is a very important task in the Semantic Web and it has attracted a large amount of effort (e.g., [1,2,3,4,5,6]). Good surveys on recent developments of ontology mapping can be found in [7,8]. Most of the earlier work in this area did not consider uncertainty or imprecision in a mapping, however, in most cases, the mappings produced are imprecise and uncertain. For instance, most automatic ontology mapping tools use heuristics or machine-learning techniques, which are imprecise by their very nature. Even experts are sometimes unsure about the exact matches between concepts and typically assign some certainty rating to a match [9], so a matching result is often associated with a weight which can express how close the two entities are as a match. The need to consider the uncertainty in a mapping began to emerge in a number of papers (e.g., [10,11,12,13,14]) in which Dempster Shafer theory, Bayesian Networks, and rough sets theory are used to deal with different aspects of mapping or ontology descriptions (e.g., concept subsumptions).

In this paper, we further investigate how to combine the weights associated with matchers. We first propose two new matchers, a *linguistic-based matcher*

H. Prade and V.S. Subrahmanian (Eds.): SUM 2007, LNAI 4772, pp. 201–214, 2007.

which extends Lin's approach [15] by considering the path length of two words in the WordNet as a punishment coefficient to adjust a similarity measure from Lin's approach, and a *structure-based matcher* which utilizes the similarity measures between two words (w_1 and w_2), a father node of w_1 with w_2 and all the child nodes of w_1 with w_2. This matcher takes both the semantics and the structure of an ontology into account. We then discuss how the mapping results from different matchers can be combined. We consider both the Dempster Shafer theory of evidence (DS theory) and Possibility Theory and apply them to combine the outcomes obtained by three different and independent matchers (the above two plus the standard *edit distance-based matcher*).

Each matcher returns a match with a weight. We interpret these weights in terms of both DS theory and Possibility Theory and then use their corresponding merging operators to merge the matched results. Our study shows that these two theories are suitable for different situations and using both theories significantly improves the matching results in terms of precision and recall, as illustrated in our experiments. Therefore, integrating uncertainty merging methods into ontology mapping is promising to improve the quality of mapping.

The rest of the paper is organized as follows. Section 2 introduces the basic concepts. Section 3 describes the main ideas in our approach and the mapping matchers used. Section 4 gives the background information about the experiments and the results. Section 5 discusses related work. Section 6 concludes the paper with discussions on future research.

2   Background

2.1   Ontologies and Ontology Mapping

There are many definitions about ontologies and a commonly used one is "An ontology is a formal, explicit specification of a shared conceptualization." [16]. We use the following notation to formally define an ontology. An ontology O is defined as a tuple: $O = (C, R, F, A, I)$ where C is a set of concepts, such as cars or persons; R is a set of relations, such as $mother - of(x, y)$ denotes that y is x's mother; F is a set of functions; A is a set of axioms and I is a set of instances, namely objects appearing in concepts in C, such as *Alan*. In this paper an entity of an ontology is defined as follows: e_{ij} are entities of O_i with $e_{ij} \in \{C_i, R_i, I_i\}$, and entity index $j \in N$ [1].

The overall objective of ontology mapping can be described as in [6]: given two ontologyies O_1 and O_2, for each entity e (or element, concept) in ontology O_1 finding the corresponding element(s) in ontology O_2, which has/have the same or similar semantics with e, and vice versa. Ontology mapping functions and some relative functions that will be used are:

- $map\ O_{i_1} \to O_{i_2}$: representing the mapping function between the two ontologies
- $map(e_{i_1 j_1}) = e_{i_2 j_2}$: representing the mapping of two entities

- $sim(e_{i_1j_1}, e_{i_2j_2})$: representing the degree of similarity between two entities computed by a matcher
- $sim(e_{i_1j_1}^f, e_{i_2j_2})$: representing the degree of similarity between father node $(e_{i_1j_1}^f)$ of $e_{i_1j_1}$ and $e_{i_2j_2}$ computed by a matcher
- $sim(e_{i_1j_1}^c, e_{i_2j_2})$: representing the degree of similarity between a child node $(e_{i_1j_1}^c)$ of $e_{i_1j_1}$ and $e_{i_2j_2}$ computed by a matcher

2.2 Uncertainty Theories

Uncertainty is pervasive in information. Uncertain information is usually modeled numerically using Probability Theory, Possibility Theory, or DS theory.

The Dempster-Shafer theory of evidence: DS theory defines mass functions on frame of discernment denoted $\Theta = \{\theta_1, \theta_2, \ldots, \theta_n\}$ which contains mutually exclusive and exhaustive possible answers to a question. A mass function assigns some positive values in $[0, 1]$ to some subsets of Θ. If a mass function gives a positive value to a subset A, then this value represents the probability mass of an agent's belief that the true value of the answer is exactly in A excluding any of its subsets. Since A can be a subset with more than one element, DS theory can be regarded as a generalization of probability theory in which a probability value has to be assigned to individual elements. When multiple mass functions are provided from independent sources on the same frame of discernment, the combined impact of these mass functions is obtained using a mathematical formula called *Dempster's combination rule*. DS theory provides a flexible way to model uncertain information and a convenient mechanism to combine two or more distinct pieces of evidence [17,18].

Possibility Theory: Possibility Theory was developed out of Zadeh's fuzzy set theory [19], it is a simple yet powerful theory for modeling and reasoning with uncertain and imprecise knowledge or information. At the semantic level, a basic function in Possibility Theory [20] is a possibility distribution denoted as π which assigns each possible word in the frame of discernment Ω - a value in $[0, 1]$ (or a set of graded values). From a possibility distribution, two measures are derived, a possibility measure (demoted as Π) and a necessity measure (denoted as N). The former estimates to what extent the true event is believed to be in the subset and the latter evaluates the degree of necessity that the subset is true. In terms of merging, there are two main families of merging operators for merging possibility distributions, namely, conjunctive and disjunctive. A typical conjunctive merging operation is the minimum (min) and a typical disjunctive one is the maximum (max).

3 Ontology Matching

Many mapping approaches make use of different aspects of information to discover mappings between ontologies. In this paper, we design our mapping method by utilizing three different matchers, two of which are name-based matchers and one is a structure-based matcher.

3.1   Name-Based Matchers

They are often used to match names and name descriptions of ontology entities. The names of ontology entities are composed of several words, so first we
adopt two different matchers based on name-based method: *Edit distance-based
matcher* and *Linguistic-based matcher* to compute similarity of two words, then
we exploit a method to compute a similarity of the names of ontology entities
based on this.

Edit distance-based matcher: *Edit distance* is a simply implemented method
to compare the degree of similarity of two words. It takes two strings and computes the edit distance between these two strings. That is, the number of in-
sertions, deletions, and substitutions of characters required to transform one
string into another. For example, the edit distance between **test** and **tent** is
1. In this paper, we develop an edit distance-based matcher which uses edit
distance method to compute the similarity between two words. The similarity
measurement between words w_1 and w_2 is defined as:

$$sim_{ed}(w_1, w_2) = \frac{1}{1 + ed(w_1, w_2)} \qquad (1)$$

where $ed(w_1, w_2)$ denotes the edit distance of two words. We choose the form
stated above because it returns a similarity value in [0,1].

Linguistic-based matcher: *Linguistic-based matcher* uses common knowledge
or domain specific thesauri to match words and this kind of matchers has been
used in many papers [21,22]. In this paper, we use an electronic lexicon Word-
Net for calculating the similarity values between words. WordNet is a lexical
database developed by Princeton University which is now commonly viewed as
an ontology for natural language concepts. It is organized into taxonomic hierarchies. Nouns, verbs, adjectives and adverbs are grouped into synonym sets
(synsets), and the synsets are organized into senses (i.e., corresponding to different meanings of the same concept). The synsets are related to other synsets
at the higher or lower levels in the hierarchy by different types of relationships.
The most common relationships are the Hyponym/Hypernym (i.e., Is-A relationships) and the Meronym/Holonym (i.e., Part-Of relationships) [23]. In this
paper, we only use the Hyponym/Hypernym relationships from WordNet.

Lin in [15] proposed a probabilistic model which depends on corpus statistics to calculate the similarity values between words using the WordNet. This
method is based on statistical analysis of corpora, so it considers the probability
of $word_1$ ($sense_1$) and $word_2$ ($sense_2$) and their most specific common subsumer
$lso(w_1, w_2)$ appearing in the general corpus. However, since the words in given
ontologies are usually application specific, this general corpus statistics obtained
using the WordNet can not reflect the real possibility of domain-specific words.
To improve Lin's method, we propose to calculate a punishment coefficient according to the ideas in the path length method [24]. The path length method
regards WordNet as a graph and measures the similarity between two concepts

(words) by identifying the minimum number of edges linking the concepts. It provides a simple approach to calculating similarity values and does not suffer from the disadvantage that Lin's method does, so we integrate Lin's method and a punishment coefficient to calculate the similarity values between words. First, we outline Lin's approach. The main formulas in this method are as follows:

$$sim_{Lin}(s_1, s_2) = \frac{2 \cdot \log(p(s_1, s_2))}{\log(p(s_1)) + \log(p(s_2))} \tag{2}$$

$$p(s) = \frac{freq(s)}{N} \tag{3}$$

$$freq(s) = \sum_{n \in words(s)} count(n) \tag{4}$$

where: $p(s_1, s_2)$ is the probability that the same hypernym of sense s_1 and sense s_2 occurs, $freq(s)$ denotes the word counts in sense s, $p(s)$ expresses the probability that sense s occurs in some synset and N is the total number of words in WordNet.

The punishment coefficient which is based on the theory of path length of WordNet is denoted as: $\frac{1}{2}\alpha^l$. Its meaning is explained as follows: α is a constant between 0 and 1 and is used to adjust the decrease of the degree of similarity between two senses when the path length between them is deepened and l expresses the longest distance either sense s_1 or sense s_2 passes by in a hierarchical hypernym structure. Because sense s_1 and sense s_2 occupy one of the common branches, this value has to be halved.

Therefore in our method, the similarity value calculated by Lin's method is adjusted with this coefficient to reflect more accurate degree between two senses s_1 and s_2. The revised calculation is:

$$sim_{new}(s_1, s_2) = \frac{2 \cdot \log(p(s_1, s_2))}{\log(p(s_1)) + \log(p(s_2))} \bullet \frac{1}{2}\alpha^l \tag{5}$$

Word w_1 and word w_2 may have many senses, we use $s(w_1)$ and $s(w_2)$ to denote the sets of senses for word w_1 and word w_2 respectively as $s(w_1) = \{s_{1i} \mid i = 1, 2, ..., m\}, s(w_2) = \{s_{1j} \mid j = 1, 2, ..., n\}$. where the numbers of senses that word w_1 and word w_2 contain are m and n. We decide to choose the maximum similarity value between two words w_1 and w_2, so the similarity between words is:

$$sim(w_1, w_2) = \max(sim_{new}(s_{1i}, s_{2j})), \ 1 \leq i \leq m, 1 \leq j \leq n \tag{6}$$

Calculating similarities of names of ontology entities: We can compute similarities between pairs of words according to two matchers stated above, next we calculate similarities of names of ontology entities based on the results obtained from the two matchers separately. The names of ontology entities are composed of several words, for instance, **PersonList**, actually is **Person** and **List**. We preprocess these kinds of names before we start to calculate the similarities of these names. We split a phrase (name of entity) and put the individual words into a set like $set = \{Person, List\}$ and then we deal with these words as follows:

1. Calculate similarities of every pair of words within both sets by using one of the matchers (Edit distance-based matcher or Linguistic-based matcher).
2. For each word in one set, compute similarity values between this word and every word from the other set and then pick out the largest similarity value. Finally attach this value to the word. Repeat this step until all of the words in the two sets have their own values.
3. Compute the final degree of similarity of names using the sum of similarity values of all words from two sets divided by the total counts of all words.

For example, we calculate similarity of two phrases: **PersonName** and **Person-Sex**. First, we split these two phrases into two sets: $set_1 = \{Person, Name\}$, $set_2 = \{Person, Sex\}$. Second, we calculate similarity values of each pair from two sets, such as the similarity value between **Person** in set_1 and **Person** in set_2, the similarity value between **Person** in set_1 and **Sex** in set_2, then choose the largest value from these two values and attach this value to **Person** in set_1. Repeat this step until *Name, Person* (in set_2) and *Sex* have their own largest value. Finally, the sum of these four similarity values is divided by the total cardinality (i.e. four) of these words.

3.2   Structure-Based Matcher

We regard each ontology as a model of tree, and in terms of tree structure we propose a *Structure-based Matcher* which determines the similarity between two nodes (entities) based on the similarities of their father nodes and children nodes. Such similarity values are obtained using a path length method based on WordNet, so we first introduce the method. We take WordNet as a hierarchical structure and the idea of the path length method is to find the sum of the shortest path passing from two concepts (words) to their common hypernym. We measure the similarity between two words by using the inverse of the sum length of the shortest paths:

$$sim_{path}(w_1, w_2) = \frac{1}{llength + rlength} \qquad (7)$$

where: *llength* is the shortest path from word node w_1 to its common hypernym with word node w_2 and *rlength* denotes the shortest path from w_2 to its common hypernym with w_1. After calculating similarities between words, we can obtain similarities between names of entities.

Given two names of entities which belong to different ontologies, we can calculate the values of $sim_{path}(e_{i_1 j_1}, e_{i_2 j_2})$, $sim_{path}(e^f_{i_1 j_1}, e_{i_2 j_2})$ and $sim_{path}(e^c_{i_1 j_1}, e_{i_2 j_2})$. Then our *Structure-based matcher* is defined to calculate similarities between two entities utilizing these values with suitable weights: α_1, α_2 and α_3

$$sim_{str}(e_{i_1j_1}, e_{i_2j_2}) = \begin{cases} \alpha_1 * sim_{path}(e_{i_1j_1}, e_{i_2j_2}) + \alpha_2 * sim_{path}(e^f_{i_1j_1}, e_{i_2j_2}) + \\ \alpha_3 * \sum sim_{path}(e^c_{i_1j_1}, e_{i_2j_2}) \\ \exists father\ node\ and\ children\ nodes; \\ \alpha_1 * sim_{path}(e_{i_1j_1}, e_{i_2j_2}) + \alpha_2 * sim_{path}(e^f_{i_1j_1}, e_{i_2j_2}) \\ \exists father\ node\ and\ \not\exists children\ nodes; \\ \alpha_1 * sim_{path}(e_{i_1j_1}, e_{i_2j_2}) + \alpha_3 * \sum sim_{path}(e^c_{i_1j_1}, e_{i_2j_2}) \\ \exists children\ nodes\ and\ \not\exists father\ nodes; \\ \alpha_1 * sim_{path}(e_{i_1j_1}, e_{i_2j_2}) \\ \not\exists father\ node\ and\ children\ nodes. \end{cases}$$

$$(8)$$

where $\alpha_1, \alpha_2, \alpha_3$ separately denotes different weights distributed to similarities between $e_{i_1j_1}$ and $e_{i_2j_2}$, the father node of $e_{i_1j_1}$ and $e_{i_2j_2}$, a child node of $e_{i_1j_1}$ and $e_{i_2j_2}$. In formula (8), $\sum \alpha_i = 1$. We assign different values to these three weights as follows

$$\begin{cases} \alpha_1 = 0.5, \alpha_2 = 0.3, \alpha_3 = 0.2 \ \exists father\ node\ and\ children\ nodes; \\ \alpha_1 = 0.5, \alpha_2 = 0.5 \qquad\qquad \exists father\ node\ and\ \not\exists children\ nodes; \\ \alpha_1 = 0.5, \alpha_3 = 0.5 \qquad\qquad \exists children\ nodes\ and\ \not\exists father\ node; \\ \alpha_1 = 1, \qquad\qquad\qquad\qquad \not\exists father\ node\ and\ children\ nodes. \end{cases}$$

3.3 Combining Mapping Results from Three Matchers

Using Dempster Shafer Theory of Evidence to combine the three matchers: We deploy DS theory to model and combine the outputs from the three ontology matchers described above in Sections 3.1 and 3.2.

Definition 1 (Frame of Discernment). *A set is called a frame of discernment (or simply a frame) if it contains mutually exclusive and exhaustive possible answers to a question. The set is usually denoted as* Θ.

Definition 2 (Mass Function). *A function m: is called a mass function on frame* Θ *if it satisfies the following two conditions:*

1. $m(\emptyset) = 0$
2. $\sum_A m(A) = 1$

where $\emptyset$ *is the empty set and* A *is a subset of* Θ.

Definition 3 (Dempster's Combination Rule). *If* m_1 *and* m_2 *are two mass functions on frame* Θ *from distinct sources, then* $m = m_1 \oplus m_2$ *is the resulting mass function after combing* m_1 *and* m_2.

In terms of ontology mapping, let O_1 and O_2 be two ontologies. For an entity $e_{i_1j_1}$ in O_1, we get its mappings with all the names in O_2, and the frame of discernment is $\Theta = e_{i_1j_1} \times O_2$.

Based on this frame, we have three mass functions m_1, m_2 and m_3 representing the normalized similarity values which are in [0,1] of all the possible mappings between $e_{i_1 j_1}$ and all the entities in O_2 form the three matchers respectively. In this situation, we interpret the similarity value between a pair of names as the mass value assigned to this pair, an element of the frame. After combining these three mass functions using Dempster's combination rule, a unified mapping result is obtained taking into account the result from each matcher.

Using Possibility Theory to combine the three matchers: Possibility theory and the body of aggregation operations from fuzzy set theory provide some tools to address the problem of merging information coming from several sources. In possibility theory, a possibility distribution $\pi_1(u) : \Theta \to [0, 1]$ assigns each element in Θ a value in $[0, 1]$ representing the possibility that this element is the true world, where Θ is a frame of discernment. There are two families of merging operators to combine two possibility distributions: the conjunctive operators (e.g., minimum operator) and the disjunctive operators (e.g., the maximum operator) [25]. We use the normalized minimum operator to combine two sets of matching data.

Definition 4. *Let π_1 and π_2 be two possibility distributions and π be the combined distribution with minimum operator, then*

$$\forall \omega, \pi(\omega) = min(\pi_1(\omega), \pi_2(\omega)) \tag{9}$$

Definition 5. *Let the degree of consistency of π_1 and π_2 be defined as*

$$h(\pi_1, \pi_2) = sup_{\omega \in \Omega} \pi_1(\omega) * \pi_2(\omega) = \max(\min(\pi_1(\omega), \pi_2(\omega))) \tag{10}$$

When using this theory, we interpret the similarity values as degrees of possibility of element in a frame - a frame of the form $e_{i_1 j_1} \times O_2$, where $e_{i_1 j_1}$ is an entity in O_1. From the three matchers, we get three possibility distributions π_1, π_2 and π_3 and we combine them using the minimum operator as showed above. An advantage of using this theory is that we do not have the restriction that the two pieces of information must come from distinct sources as required by Dempster's combination rule.

4   Experiments

4.1   Dataset

We have proposed two different ways to combine mapping results from three matchers. We now present the experimental results that demonstrate the performance of our matchers and combination methods on the OAEI 2006 Benchmark Tests. In our experiments, we only focus on classes and properties in ontologies.

Generally, almost all the benchmark tests in OAEI 2006 describe Bibliographic references except Test 102 which is about wine and they can be divided into five groups [26] in terms of their characteristics: Test 101-104, Test 201-210, Test 221-247, Test 248-266 and Test 301-304. A brief description is given below.

- **Test 101-104:** These tests contain classes and properties with either exactly the same or totally different names.
- **Test 201-210:** The tests in this group change some linguistic features compared to Test 101-104. For example, some of the ontologies in this group have no comments or names, names of some ontology have been replaced with synonyms.
- **Test 221-247:** The structures of the ontologies have been changed but the linguistic features have been maintained.
- **Test 248-266:** Both the structures and names of ontologies have been changed and the tests in this group are the most difficult cases in all the benchmark tests.
- **Test 301-304:** Four real-life ontologies about BibTeX.

In our evaluation, we choose **Test 101**, **Test 103**, **Test 104**, **Test 205**, **Test 223** and **Test 302** of OAEI 2006 Benchmark Tests and take **Test 101** as the reference ontology. All the other ontologies are compared with **Test 101**. The reason for selecting them as test cases are:

1. They are well known in the field of ontology mapping.
2. They have normal classes, object properties and datatype properties hierarchy, so we can obtain regular results by using these three matchers.
3. Test 101-104 have similar structures and names of entities, while the structures and names of Test 205, 223, 302 are different from the reference ontology, i.e. Test 101, so we can use these datasets to test performance of matchers and combination methods.

For Test 101, Test 103, Test 104 and Test 205 each test contains 33 classes and 64 properties; Test 223 has 66 classes and 65 properties; Test 302 has 13 classes and 30 properties.

4.2 Experimental Evaluation Metrics

To evaluate the performance of mapping, like many other papers that use retrieval metrics, *Precision*, *Recall* and *f-measure* to measure a mapping method, we use these measures to evaluate our methods as well. *Precision* describes the number of correctly identified mappings versus the number of all mappings discovered by the three approaches. *Recall* measures the number of correctly identified mappings versus the number of possible existing mappings discovered by hand. *f-measure* is defined as a combination of the *Precision* and *Recall*. Its score is in the range $[0, 1]$.

$$precision = \frac{|m_m \cap m_a|}{|m_a|} \tag{11}$$

$$recall = \frac{|m_m \cap m_a|}{|m_m|} \tag{12}$$

$$f - measure = \frac{2 * precision * recall}{precision + recall} \tag{13}$$

where m_m and m_a represent the mappings discovered by hand and by a method proposed in our paper respectively.

4.3 Single Matchers vs. Combination of Matchers

Figure 1 shows the *f-measure* of the three single matchers and combination methods on the five datasets, which includes Test 101 vs Test 103, Test 101 vs Test 104, Test 101 vs Test 205, Test 101 vs Test 223, Test 101 vs Test 302. Each single matcher is marked as follows: *Ed* for Edit distance-based matcher; *L* for Linguistic-base matcher; *S* for *Structure-based matcher*; *DS* for Dempster's combination rule; *PT* for the minimum merging operator in Possibility Theory.

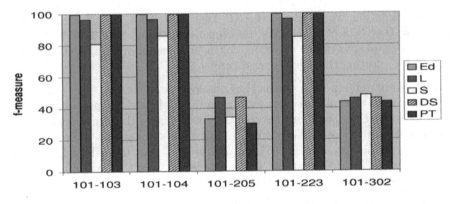

Fig. 1. Single matchers vs. combination methods

From Figure 1, we can see that almost for every group of tests, the f-measures of results using Dempster's combination rule is better than or equivalent to that of a single matcher, the minimum operator of Possibility Theory performs well except for Test101 vs Test 205, which has the results lower than other single matchers results. For Test 101 vs Test 103, Test 101 vs Test 104 and Test 101 vs Test 223, *Edit distance-based matcher* obtains better results than the other two single matchers because these three groups of tests have almost the same names of entities. For Test 101 vs Test 205 and Test 101 vs Test 302, *Linguistic-based matcher* gets better results than the other two single matchers because *Linguistic-based matcher* can obtain good results for those different names which have the same meaning.

4.4 Comparison of Systems Utilizing Different Matchers

We use the combination mechanisms in both DS theory and Possibility Theory to combine the matching results from our three matchers. We now compare the outputs from the two combination rules to the results obtained from *falcon, ola* and *ctxMatch2-1* algorithms which were used in the EON 2005 Ontology

Table 1. Comparison of Experiment Results

Datasets	DS			PT			falcon			ola			ctxMatch2-1		
	p	r	f	p	r	f	p	r	f	p	r	f	p	r	f
101-103	100	98.97	99.48	100	98.97	99.48	100	100	100	100	100	100	87	34	48
101-104	100	98.97	99.48	100	98.97	99.48	100	100	100	100	100	100	87	34	48.89
101-205	46.88	46.39	46.63	30.29	29.90	30.09	88	87	87.5	43	42	42.5	36	4	7.2
101-223	100	98.97	99.48	100	98.97	99.48	100	100	100	100	100	100	83	31	45.14
101-302	45.83	45.83	45.83	43.75	43.75	43.75	97	67	79.26	37	33	34.89	0	0	0

Alignment Contest [1], and the details are given in Table 1. In Table 1, p for precision, r for recall, f for f-measure, DS for Dempster's combination rule, and PT for the minimum merging operator in Possibility Theory. Overall, we believe that the two combination rules we use are very satisfactory, with Dempster's combination rule outperforming the minimum rule in Possibility Theory slightly for pair 101 vs 205. Although on every pair of ontologies, our results of two combination rules are less ideal than the *falcon* system, however, our results are better than *ola* system on two out of five pairs of matching, and the results are much better than the *ctxMatch2-1* system. The performances of these five different approaches are all very good for Test 101 vs 103 and vs 104 and Test 101 vs Test 223, but none of the systems performed exceptionally well for Test 205 and Test 302. Below we analyze the reasons for this.

For Test 101 vs 103 and vs 104, the two ontologies to be matched contain classes and properties with exactly the same names and structures, so every system that deploys the computation of similarities of names of entities can get good results. Test 223 has more classes than Test 101 to 104 and the structure of its ontology is changed although the linguistic features remains the same and its class names are generally the same as the reference ontology. These similarities in the linguistic features and class names enable these matching systems to perform well.

Test 205 describes the same kind of information as other ontologies, i.e. publications, however, the class names in it are very different from those in the reference ontology Test 101. Even though we employed three matchers to calculate similarities between names, the results are still not very satisfactory. Test 302 is a real-life BibTeX ontology which also includes different words compared to Test 101 describing publications so the results are similar to Test 205, so we do not get good results from these two datasets.

Our linguistic-based matcher does not consider the structures between words and assumes that all the words are equally important. However, different words in a name have different degrees of importance, therefore, this is one aspect that we will need to improve further. In our structure-based matcher, we adopt the idea of assigning different weights to different aspects when matching two words. The weights are predefined but we think these could be learned in our next step of research.

---

[1] http://oaei.ontologymatching.org/2005/results/

5   Related Work

In a mapping process, if only syntactic or element-level matching is performed, as in the case for name matching without the use of a thesaurus, inaccuracies can occur [27]. This affects the results of mapping, but so far only a few ontology mapping methods have considered dealing with the uncertainty issue.

Nagy et al [10] and Besana [11] both recognized the importance of uncertainty in ontology mapping, and both of them used DS theory to assist mapping. They believed that different matchers have uncertainties associated with them, so they combine the results obtained from different matchers using DS theory and it is possible to give a uniform interpretation, consistent with the uncertainty inherited in the problem. Although Nagy et al utilized Dempster's combination rule into ontology mapping, it is not clear how they applied the theory. For example, they did not explicitly define a *Frame of Discernment*. Besana [11] exploited DS theory into a more complicated process. He considers not only combining ontology matching results using DS theory, but also uncertain mappings using DS theory.

In [12] a Bayesian Networks based approach was designed and a system called BayesOWL was proposed. In this approach, the source and target ontologies are first translated into Bayesian networks (BN); the concept mapping between the two ontologies are treated as evidential reasoning between the two translated BNs. Probabilities, which are required for constructing conditional probability tables (CPT) during translation and for measuring semantic similarity during mapping, are learned using text classification techniques, where each concept in an ontology is associated with a set of semantically relevant text documents, which are obtained by ontology guided web mining. This approach used Bayesian Networks, but the networks are sophisticated and it is not easy to construct them from an ontology expressed by OWL.

Holi and Hyvönen [13] observed that in the real world, concepts are not always subsumed by each other, and cannot always be organized in a crisp subsumption hierarchies. Many concepts only partly overlap each other, so they present a new probabilistic method to model conceptual overlap in taxonomies, and an algorithm to compute the overlap between a selected concept and other concepts of a taxonomy by using Bayesian networks. This method focused on the uncertainty of description languages of ontologies. Although it is not related to the mapping, it can be used as a measure of semantic distance between concepts.

Zhao et al [14] proposed a novel similarity measure method based on rough set theory and formal concept analysis (RFCA) to realize ontology mapping tasks. The authors combined rough set theory into the similarity computation formula of formal concept analysis (FCA). Although the authors did not consider uncertainty in the process of mapping explicitly, they applied the rough set theory to measure the similarities of concepts of ontologies. So, in some case, they did consider the uncertainty problem.

6   Conclusion

In this paper, we utilize three independent matchers to deal with ontology mapping and they are: *Edit distance-based matcher*, *Linguistic-based matcher* and *Structure-based matcher*. In the *Linguistic-based matcher*, we improved Lin's method which computes similarity value between words. In the *Structure-based matcher*, we adopt the structure of ontology to calculate similarity values between two entities and it considers the impact of the direct relative nodes (father and/or children) to one entity.

Following this, we investigated how the problem of uncertainty in ontology mapping can be dealt with. We considered both the Dempster-Shafer theory and Possibility Theory to combine the uncertain mapping results from different matchers stated above. We applied our ontology mapping systems (two combination rules with three matchers) to a set of ontologies used for ontology mapping competitions. The experimental results show that it is efficient and feasible to exploit these uncertainty theories to deal with uncertainty factors in the process of ontology mapping.

As future work, on the one hand, we will design new matchers to handle some situations that are not considered here, for example, how to get accurate *n:1*, *1:n* or *n:n* mapping results. On the other hand, we will continue investigating the uncertainty issues in ontology mapping and consider how to use different uncertainty theories to deal with different situations in ontology mapping.

References

1. Ehrig, M., Sure, Y.: Ontology mapping - an integrated approach. In: Bussler, C.J., Davies, J., Fensel, D., Studer, R. (eds.) ESWS 2004. LNCS, vol. 3053, pp. 76–91. Springer, Heidelberg (2004)
2. Ehrig, M., Staab, S.: Qom - quick ontology mapping. In: McIlraith, S.A., Plexousakis, D., van Harmelen, F. (eds.) ISWC 2004. LNCS, vol. 3298, pp. 683–697. Springer, Heidelberg (2004)
3. Noy, N.F., Musen, M.A.: Prompt: Algorithm and tool for automated ontology merging and alignment. In: Proceedings of the 17th National Conference on Artificial Intelligence and 12th Conference on Innovative Applications of Artificial Intelligence (AAAI/IAAI 2000), pp. 450–455 (2000)
4. Noy, N.F., Musen, M.A.: Anchor-prompt: Using non- local context for semantic matching. In: Workshop on Ontologies and Information Sharing at the 17th International Joint Conference on Articial Intelligence (IJCAI 2001) (2001)
5. Kalfoglou, Y., Schorlemmer, W.M.: Information-flow-based ontology mapping. In: Proceedings of the International Federated Conferences (CoopIS/DOA/ODBASE 2002), pp. 1132–1151 (2002)
6. Su, X., Gulla, J.A.: Semantic enrichment for ontology mapping. In: Meziane, F., Métais, E. (eds.) NLDB 2004. LNCS, vol. 3136, pp. 217–228. Springer, Heidelberg (2004)
7. Rahm, E., Bernstein, P.A.: A survey of approaches to automatic schema matching. Journal of VLDB 10(4), 334–350 (2001)
8. Shvaiko, P., Euzenat, J.: A survey of schema-based matching approaches. Journal of Data Semantics 4, 146–171 (2005)

9. Choi, N., Song, I.Y., Han, H.: A survey on ontology mapping. SIGMOD Record. 35(3), 34–41 (2006)
10. Nagy, M., Maria Vargas-Vera, E.M.: Dssim-ontology mapping with uncertainty. In: Cruz, I., Decker, S., Allemang, D., Preist, C., Schwabe, D., Mika, P., Uschold, M., Aroyo, L. (eds.) ISWC 2006. LNCS, vol. 4273, Springer, Heidelberg (2006)
11. Besana, P.: A framework for combining ontology and schema matchers with demp- ster shafer. In: Cruz, I., Decker, S., Allemang, D., Preist, C., Schwabe, D., Mika, P., Uschold, M., Aroyo, L. (eds.) ISWC 2006. LNCS, vol. 4273, pp. 196–200. Springer, Heidelberg (2006)
12. Pan, R., Ding, Z., Yu, Y., Peng, Y.: A bayesian network approach to ontology mapping. In: Gil, Y., Motta, E., Benjamins, V.R., Musen, M.A. (eds.) ISWC 2005. LNCS, vol. 3729, pp. 563–577. Springer, Heidelberg (2005)
13. Markus Holi, E.H.: Modeling degrees of conceptual overlap in semantic web on- tologies. In: Gil, Y., Motta, E., Benjamins, V.R., Musen, M.A. (eds.) ISWC 2005. LNCS, vol. 3729, pp. 98–99. Springer, Heidelberg (2005)
14. Zhao, Y., Wang, X., Halang, W.A.: Ontology mapping based on rough formal concept analysis. In: Proceedings of the Advanced International Conference on Telecommunications and International Conference on Internet and Web Applica- tions and Services (AICT/ICIW'06), p. 180 (2006)
15. Lin, D.: An information-theoretic definition of similarity. In: Proceedings of the 15th International Conference on Machine Learning (ICML'98), pp. 296–304 (1998)
16. Gruber, T.R.: A translation approach to portable ontology specifications. Knowl- edge Acquisition Journal 5(2), 199–220 (1993)
17. Liu, W.: Propositional, Probabilistic and Evidential Reasoning: Integrating Nu- merical and Symbolic Approaches (2001)
18. Liu, W.: Analyzing the degree of conflict among belief functions. Journal of Arti- ficial Intelligence. 170(11), 909–924 (2006)
19. Zadeh, L.A.: Fuzzy sets as a basis for a theory of possibility. Journal of Fuzzy Sets and Systems 100, 9–34 (1999)
20. Dubois, D., Prade, H.: Possibility Theory (1988)
21. Tang, J., 0003, Y.L., Li, Z.: Multiple strategies detection in ontology mapping. In: Proceedings of the 14th international conference on World Wide Web (WWW'05) (Special interest tracks and posters) pp. 1040–1041 (2005)
22. Madhavan, J., Bernstein, P.A., Rahm, E.: Generic schema matching with cu- pid. In: Proceedings of 27th International Conference on Very Large Data Bases (VLDB'01), pp. 49–58 (2001)
23. Varelas, G., Voutsakis, E., Raftopoulou, P., Petrakis, E.G.M., Milios, E.E.: Seman- tic similarity methods in wordnet and their application to information retrieval on the web. In: Proceedings of 7th ACM International Workshop on Web Information and Data Management (WIDM 2005), pp. 10–16 (2005)
24. Resnik, P.: Using information content to evaluate semantic similarity in a taxon- omy. In: Proceedings of 14th International Joint Conference for Artificial Intelli- gence (IJCAI'95), pp. 448–453 (1995)
25. Dubois, D., Prade, H.: Possibility theory in information fusion. In: the 11th Inter- national Workshop on Non-Monotonic Reasoning (NMR'02), pp. 103–116 (2002)
26. Qu, Y., Hu, W., Cheng, G.: Constructing virtual documents for ontology matching. In: Proceedings of 15th World Wide Web Conference (WWW'06), pp. 23–31 (2006)
27. Cross, V.: Uncertainty in the automation of ontology matching. In: Proceed- ings of the 4th International Symposium on Uncertainty Modeling and Analysis (ISUMA'03), pp. 135–140 (2003)

Preferred Database Repairs Under Aggregate Constraints

Sergio Flesca, Filippo Furfaro, and Francesco Parisi

DEIS - Università della Calabria
Via Bucci - 87036 Rende (CS) Italy
{flesca,furfaro,fparisi}@deis.unical.it

Abstract. A framework for computing preferred repairs in numerical databases violating a given set of strong and weak aggregate constraints is introduced, which is based on a transformation into an Integer Linear Programming (ILP) instance. Aggregate constraints are linear inequalities on aggregates retrieved from the input data. While strong constraints express mandatory conditions, weak constraints define conditions which are expected to be satisfied, even if this is not mandatory. Thus, preferred repairs are repairs which make the data satisfy all the given strong constraints and as many weak constraints as possible. An experimental validation of the proposed approach is provided, proving its effectiveness.

1 Introduction

A great deal of attention has been devoted to the problem of extracting reliable information from databases containing pieces of information inconsistent w.r.t. integrity constraints. Several works in this area deal with "classical" forms of constraint (such as keys, foreign keys, functional dependencies), and propose different strategies for updating inconsistent data reasonably, in order to make it consistent by means of minimal changes. Indeed, these kinds of constraint often do not suffice to manage data consistency, as they cannot be used to define algebraic relations between stored values. In fact, this issue frequently occurs in several scenarios, such as scientific databases, statistical databases, and data warehouses, where numerical values of tuples are derivable by aggregating values stored in other tuples. In our previous work [12], we introduced a new form of integrity constraint, namely *aggregate constraint*, which enables conditions to be expressed on aggregate values extracted from the database. In that work, we addressed the problem of repairing and extracting reliable information from data violating a given set of aggregate constraints. The following example, which will be used throughout the rest of the paper, describes a scenario where aggregate constraints can be effectively used to check data consistency.

Example 1. Table 1 represents the *cash budget* of a company for year 2006, that is a summary of cash flows (receipts, disbursements, and cash balances). Values '*det*', '*aggr*' and '*drv*' in column *Type* stand for *detail*, *aggregate* and *derived*, respectively. Specifically, an item of the table is *aggregate* if it is obtained by aggregating items of type *detail* of the same section, whereas a *derived* item is an item whose value can be computed using the values of other items of any type and belonging to any section.

H. Prade and V.S. Subrahmanian (Eds.): SUM 2007, LNAI 4772, pp. 215–229, 2007.

Table 1. A cash budget for year 2006

	Section	Subsection	Type	Value
t_1	Receipts	beginning cash	drv	3000
t_2	Receipts	cash sales	det	2200
t_3	Receipts	receivables	det	650
t_4	Receipts	total cash receipts	aggr	2450
	...	...	...	...

		...		...	...	...	
	Disbursements	payment of accounts	det	1300	t_5
	Disbursements	capital expenditure	det	100	t_6
	Disbursements	long-term financing	det	600	t_7
	Disbursements	total disbursements	aggr	1000	t_8
	Balance	net cash inflow	drv	450	t_9
	Balance	ending cash balance	drv	3450	t_{10}

A cash budget must satisfy the following integrity constraints (which can be expressed by means of *aggregate constraints*):

κ_1 : for each section, the sum of the values of all *detail* items must be equal to the value of the *aggregate* item of the same section;

κ_2 : the net cash inflow must be equal to the difference between total cash receipts and total disbursements;

κ_3 : the ending cash balance must be equal to the sum of the beginning cash and the net cash inflow.

Table 1 was acquired by means of an OCR tool from a paper document. The original cash budget was consistent, but some symbol recognition errors occurred during the digitizing phase, as constraints 1) and 2) are not satisfied on the acquired data, that is:

a) in section *Receipts*, the aggregate value of *total cash receipts* is not equal to the sum of detail values of the same section: $2200 + 650 \neq 2450$;

b) in section *Disbursements*, the aggregate value of *total disbursements* is not equal to the sum of detail values of the same section: $1300 + 100 + 600 \neq 1000$;

c) the value of *net cash inflow* is not to equal the difference between *total cash receipts* and *total disbursements*: $2450 - 1000 \neq 450$. □

The strategy proposed in [12] for repairing data inconsistent w.r.t. a given set of aggregate constraints is based on the notions of value-update and *card*-minimal repair. According to this approach, a *card*-minimal repair is a set of value updates making data consistent and having minimum cardinality. Repairing data by means of *card*-minimal repairs is well-suited for several contexts dealing with numerical data acquired automatically, such as balance-sheet analysis and sensor networks, where assuming that the minimum number of errors occurred in the acquisition phase is often reasonable.

In general, there may be several *card*-minimal repairs for a database violating a given set of aggregate constraints. For instance, it is possible to repair the data reported in Table 1 by decreasing attribute *Value* in tuple t_2 down to 1800 and increasing attribute *Value* in tuple t_8 up to 2000. An alternative repair consists of decreasing attribute *Value* in tuple t_3 down to 250 and increasing attribute *Value* in tuple t_8 up to 2000. This work stems from the idea that exploiting well-established information on the context where the data acquisition takes place can allow us to choose the most reasonable repairs among those having minimum cardinality. As a matter of fact, consider our running example in the case that, for all the years preceding 2006, the value of *cash sales* was never less than 2000 and the value of *receivables* was never greater than 400. Then, the value of *cash sales* for the current year is not likely to be less than 2000, and the value of *receivables* is not likely to be greater than 400. These likely conditions can be interpreted as *weak constraints*, in the sense that their satisfaction is not mandatory. Weak constraints can be exploited for defining a repairing technique where inconsistent data are fixed in the "most likely" way. Specifically, the most likely ways of repairing inconsistent data are those corresponding to *card*-minimal repairs satisfying as many weak constraints as possible. For instance, if we consider the above-mentioned weak constraints in our running example, the repair decreasing attribute *Value* in tuple t_3 down to 250 can be reasonably preferred to that decreasing attribute *Value* in tuple t_2 down to 1800, since the former yields a database which satisfies both the weak constraints.

Related Work. Several works have investigated a number of issues related to repairing inconsistent data. Some of them [2,3,7,8,9,10,13,16,18] have addressed the consistent query answer (CQA) problem [1]. Informally, a tuple t is a consistent answer of a query q posed on D if t is in all the answers of q evaluated on every repaired database obtained from D. The above-cited works mainly differ on: (i) the type of integrity constraints considered (functional dependencies, inclusion dependencies, universal constraints, etc.), (ii) the type of update operations allowed in the repair (insertion/deletion of tuples, value updates). See [4,11] for a more detailed survey on these works.

In several contexts, such as the scenario presented in our running example, the problem of computing a repair (rather than computing the consistent answer of a single query) is relevant. This problem has been addressed in [5,6,14], where repairs consisting of value updates have been considered. Specifically, in [14], the computation of repairs has been studied for categorical data in the presence of constraints expressed as first order formulas. In [5], numerical data inconsistent w.r.t. denial constraints have been considered. In [6], repairs on categorical data in the presence of functional and inclusion dependencies have been studied. However, none of these work has investigated the repairing problem for data inconsistent w.r.t. strong and weak aggregate constraints. In our previous work [12], we only characterized the complexity of the CQA problem and the repair existence problem in the presence of strong aggregate constraints.

Main contributions. In this work we introduce the notion of *weak aggregate constraints*, expressing conditions which are likely to hold on aggregate information summarizing the actual data. We exploit weak aggregate constraints to define *preferred (card-minimal) repairs*, i.e., *card*-minimal repairs which are the most "reasonable" ones, in the sense that they satisfy as many weak aggregate constraints as possible. We first investigate some issues related to the existence of preferred repairs from a theoretical standpoint. Then, we tackle the problem of computing preferred *card*-minimal repairs. Specifically, we introduce a restricted but expressive class of aggregate constraints (namely, *steady* aggregate constraints), and define a transformation of the problem of computing preferred repairs in the presence of steady aggregate constraints to *Integer Linear Programming* (ILP). This transformation allows us to compute a preferred *card*-minimal repair by using any ILP solver. We also prove the effectiveness of the proposed approach through several experiments in a real-life scenario. These experiments show that, in practical cases, the computation of a preferred repair is fast enough to be used in (semi-)automatic data acquisition systems.

2   Preliminaries

We assume classical notions of database scheme, relation scheme, and relations. In the following we will also use a logical formalism to represent relational databases, and relation schemes will be represented by means of sorted predicates of the form $R(A_1 : \Delta_1, \ldots, A_n : \Delta_n)$, where $A_1, \ldots, A_n$ are attribute names and $\Delta_1, \ldots, \Delta_n$ are the corresponding domains. Each Δ_i can be either $\mathbb{Z}$ (infinite domain of integers) or $\mathbb{S}$ (strings). Attributes [resp. constants] defined over $\mathbb{Z}$ will be said to be *numerical attributes* [resp. *numerical constants*]. The set of attribute names $\{A_1, \ldots, A_n\}$ of relation scheme R will be denoted as $\mathcal{A}_R$, whereas the subset of $\mathcal{A}_R$ consisting of the names of the attributes which are a key for R will be denoted as $\mathcal{K}_R$. Given a ground atom t denoting a tuple, the value of attribute A of t will be denoted as $t[A]$.

Given a database scheme $\mathcal{D}$, we will denote as $\mathcal{M}_\mathcal{D}$ (namely, *Measure attributes*) the set of numerical attributes representing measure data. That is, $\mathcal{M}_\mathcal{D}$ specifies the set of attributes representing measure values, such as weights, lengths, prices, etc. For instance, in our running example, being $\mathcal{D}$ the database scheme consisting of the only relation scheme *CashBudget*, we have $\mathcal{M}_\mathcal{D} = \{\ Value\ \}$.

2.1   Aggregate Constraints

Given a relation scheme $R(A_1, \ldots, A_n)$, an *attribute expression* on R is defined recursively as follows:

- a numerical constant is an attribute expression;
- each numerical attribute A_i (with $i \in [1..n]$) is an attribute expression;
- $e_1 \psi e_2$ is an attribute expression on R, if e_1, e_2 are attribute expressions on R and ψ is an arithmetic operator in $\{+, -\}$;
- $c \times (e)$ is an attribute expression on R, if e is an attribute expression on R and c a numerical constant.

Let R be a relation scheme and e an attribute expression on R. An *aggregation function* on R is a function $\chi : (\Lambda_1 \times \cdots \times \Lambda_k) \to \mathbb{Z}$, where each Λ_i is either $\mathbb{Z}$ or $\mathbb{S}$, and is defined as follows:

$$\chi(x_1, \ldots, x_k) = \texttt{SELECT sum (e)}$$
$$\texttt{FROM}\quad \texttt{R}$$
$$\texttt{WHERE}\quad \alpha(x_1, \ldots, x_k)$$

where $\alpha(x_1, \ldots, x_k)$ is a boolean formula on $x_1, \ldots, x_k$, constants and attributes of R.

Example 2. The following aggregation functions are defined on the relational scheme *CashBudget(Section, Subsection, Type, Value)* of Example 1:

$$\chi_1(x, y) = \texttt{SELECT sum (Value)}$$
$$\texttt{FROM}\quad \texttt{CashBudget}$$
$$\texttt{WHERE}\quad \texttt{Section}=\texttt{x AND Type}=\texttt{y}$$

$$\chi_2(x) = \texttt{SELECT sum (Value)}$$
$$\texttt{FROM}\quad \texttt{CashBudget}$$
$$\texttt{WHERE}\quad \texttt{Subsection}=\texttt{x}$$

Function χ_1 returns the sum of *Value* of all the tuples having *Section* x, and *Type* z. For instance, χ_1('Disbursements', 'det') returns $1300 + 100 + 600 = 2000$, whereas χ_1('Receipts', 'aggr') returns 2450. Function χ_2 returns the sum of *Value* of all the tuples where *Subsection*$=y$. In our running example, as *Subsection* is a key for the tuples of *CashBudget*, the sum returned by χ_2 is an attribute value of a single tuple. For instance, χ_2('cash sales') returns 2200, whereas χ_2('receivables') returns 650.   □

Definition 1 (Aggregate constraint). *Given a database scheme $\mathcal{D}$, an aggregate constraint κ on $\mathcal{D}$ is an expression of the form:*

$$\kappa: \quad \forall x_1,\ldots,x_k \left(\phi(x_1,\ldots,x_k) \implies \sum_{i=1}^{n} c_i \cdot \chi_i(X_i) \leq K \right) \tag{1}$$

where:

1. $c_1,\ldots,c_n, K$ *are numerical constants;*
2. $\phi(x_1,\ldots,x_k)$ *is a (possible empty) conjunction of atoms containing the variables $x_1,\ldots,x_k$;*
3. *each $\chi_i(X_i)$ is an aggregation function, where X_i is a list of variables and constants, and variables appearing in X_i are a subset of $\{x_1,\ldots,x_k\}$.*

Given a database D and a set of aggregate constraints $\mathcal{AC}$, we will use the notation $D \models \mathcal{AC}$ [resp. $D \not\models \mathcal{AC}$] to say that D is consistent [resp. inconsistent] w.r.t. $\mathcal{AC}$.

Observe that aggregate constraints enable equalities to be expressed as well, since an equality can be viewed as a pair of inequalities. In the following, for the sake of brevity, equalities will be written explicitly.

Example 3. Constraint κ_1 defined in Example 1 can be expressed as follows:
$\kappa_1: \forall x,y,z,v \quad CashBudget(x,y,z,v) \implies \chi_1(x, \text{'det'}) - \chi_1(x, \text{'aggr'})=0$ □

For the sake of brevity, in the following any aggregate constraint whose body consists of an empty conjunction of atoms is denoted by writing only its head. For instance, the constraints κ_2 and κ_3 of Example 1 can be expressed as follows:

$\kappa_2: \chi_2(\text{'net cash inflow'}) - (\chi_2(\text{'total cash receipts'}) - \chi_2(\text{'total disbursements'})) = 0$

$\kappa_3: \chi_2(\text{'ending cash balance'}) - (\chi_2(\text{'beginning cash'}) + \chi_2(\text{'net cash balance'})) = 0$

We now introduce a restricted but expressive form of aggregate constraints, namely *steady aggregate constraints*. Before providing the definition of steady aggregate constraints, we introduce some preliminary notations. Given a relation scheme $R(A_1,\ldots,A_n)$ and a conjunction of atoms ϕ containing the atom $R(x_1,\ldots,x_n)$, where each x_j is either a variable or a constant, we say that the attribute A_j corresponds to x_j, for each $j \in [1..n]$. Given an aggregation function χ_i, we will denote as $\Omega(\chi_i)$ the union of the set of the attributes appearing in the WHERE clause of χ_i and the set of attributes corresponding to variables appearing in the WHERE clause of χ_i. Given an aggregate constraint κ where the aggregation functions $\chi_1,\ldots,\chi_n$ occur, we will denote as $\mathcal{A}(\kappa)$ the set of attributes $\bigcup_{i=1}^{n} \Omega(\chi_i)$. Given an aggregate constraint κ having the form (1), we will denote as $\mathcal{J}(\kappa)$ the set of attributes A corresponding to either variables shared by at least two atoms in ϕ, or constants appearing in atoms of ϕ.

Definition 2 (Steady aggregate constraint). *Given a database scheme* $\mathcal{D}$, *an aggregate constraint* κ *on* $\mathcal{D}$ *is said to be* steady *if* $\left(\mathcal{A}(\kappa) \cup \mathcal{J}(\kappa)\right) \cap \mathcal{M}_{\mathcal{D}} = \emptyset$.

Example 4. Consider the constraint κ_1 of our running example. Since $\mathcal{A}(\kappa_1) = \{Section, Type\}$, $\mathcal{J}(\kappa_1) = \emptyset$, and $\mathcal{M}_{\mathcal{D}} = \{Value\}$, κ_1 is a steady aggregate constraint. Reasoning analogously, it is easy to see that constraints κ_2 and κ_3 are steady too.   □

2.2 Repairing Inconsistent Databases

Updates at attribute-level will be used in the following as the basic primitives for repairing data violating aggregate constraints. Given a relation scheme R in the database scheme $\mathcal{D}$, let $\mathcal{M}_R = \{A_1, \ldots, A_k\}$ be the subset of $\mathcal{M}_{\mathcal{D}}$ containing all the attributes in R belonging to $\mathcal{M}_{\mathcal{D}}$.

Definition 3 (Atomic update). *Let* $t = R(v_1, \ldots, v_n)$ *be a tuple on the relation scheme* $R(A_1 : \Delta_1, \ldots, A_n : \Delta_n)$. *An* atomic update *on* t *is a triplet* $< t, A_i, v_i' >$, *where* $A_i \in \mathcal{M}_R$ *and* v_i' *is a value in* Δ_i *and* $v_i' \neq v_i$.

Update $u = < t, A_i, v_i' >$ replaces $t[A_i]$ with v_i', thus yielding the tuple $u(t) = R(v_1, \ldots, v_{i-1}, v_i', v_{i+1}, \ldots, v_n)$. We denote the pair $<tuple, attribute>$ updated by an atomic update u as $\lambda(u)$. For instance, performing $u = < t_5, Value, 300 >$ in the case of our running example, results in the tuple: $u(t_5) = CashBudget($'Disbursements', 'payment of accounts', 'det', 300$)$, and $\lambda(u) = < t_5, Value >$.

Definition 4 (Consistent database update). *Let* D *be a database and* $U = \{u_1, \ldots, u_n\}$ *be a set of atomic updates on tuples of* D. *The set* U *is said to be a* consistent database update *iff* $\forall j, k \in [1..n]$ *if* $j \neq k$ *then* $\lambda(u_j) \neq \lambda(u_k)$.

Informally, a set of atomic updates U is a consistent database update iff for each pair of updates $u_1, u_2 \in U$, either u_1 and u_2 do not work on the same tuples, or they change different attributes of the same tuple. The set of pairs $< tuple, attribute >$ updated by a consistent database update U will be denoted as $\lambda(U) = \cup_{u_i \in U} \{\lambda(u_i)\}$. Given a database D and a consistent database update U, performing U on D results in the database $U(D)$ obtained by applying all atomic updates in U.

Definition 5 (Repair). *Let* $\mathcal{D}$ *be a database scheme,* $\mathcal{AC}$ *a set of aggregate constraints on* $\mathcal{D}$, *and* D *an instance of* $\mathcal{D}$ *such that* $D \not\models \mathcal{AC}$. *A repair* ρ *for* D *is a consistent database update such that* $\rho(D) \models \mathcal{AC}$.

Example 5. A repair ρ_1 for *CashBudget* w.r.t. $\mathcal{AC} = \{\kappa_1, \kappa_2, \kappa_3\}$ consists of decreasing attribute *Value* in the tuple t_2 down to 1800 and increasing attribute *Value* in the tuple t_8 up to 2000, that is, $\rho_1 = \{ < t_2, Value, 1800 >, < t_8, Value, 2000 > \}$.   □

In general, given a database D inconsistent w.r.t. a set of aggregate constraints $\mathcal{AC}$, different repairs can be performed on D yielding a new consistent database. Indeed, they may not be considered "reasonable" the same. For instance, if a repair exists for D changing only one value in one tuple of D, any repair updating all values in all the tuples of D can be reasonably disregarded. To evaluate whether a repair should be considered "relevant" or not, we use the ordering criterion stating that a repair ρ_1 precedes a repair ρ_2 if the number of changes issued by ρ_1 is less than ρ_2.

Example 6. A repair for *CashBudget* is: $\rho' = \{< t_2, Value, 1800 >, < t_5, Value, 300 >, < t_9, Value, 1450 >, < t_{10}, Value, 4450 >\}$. Observe that ρ' consists of more atomic updates than ρ_1, where ρ_1 is the repair defined in Example 5. □

Definition 6 (*Card*-minimal repair). *Let $\mathcal{D}$ be a database scheme, $\mathcal{AC}$ a set of aggregate constraints on $\mathcal{D}$, and D an instance of $\mathcal{D}$. A repair ρ for D w.r.t. $\mathcal{AC}$ is a card-minimal repair iff there is no repair ρ' for D w.r.t. $\mathcal{AC}$ such that $|\lambda(\rho')| < |\lambda(\rho)|$.*

Example 7. In our running example, the set of *card*-minimal repairs is $\{\rho_1, \rho_2\}$, where ρ_1 is the repair defined in Example 5, and $\rho_2 = \{ < t_3, Value, 250 >, < t_8, Value, 2000 > \}$. The repair ρ' defined in Example 6 is not *card*-minimal as $|\lambda(\rho')| = 4 > |\lambda(\rho_1)|$. □

3 Preferred Repairs

Generally, several *card*-minimal repairs may exist for a database which is not consistent w.r.t. a given set of aggregate constraints. All the possible *card*-minimal repairs preserve as much information as possible, and in this sense they can be considered equally reasonable. Further information on the data to be repaired could be exploited to rank *card*-minimal repairs. For instance, in our running example, historical data retrieved from balance-sheets of past years could be exploited to find conditions which are likely to hold for the current-year balance-sheet, so that *card*-minimal repairs could be ordered according to the number of these conditions which are satisfied in the repaired database. These conditions can be expressed as *weak aggregate constraints*, that is aggregate constraints with a "weak" semantics: in contrast with the traditional "strong" semantics of aggregate constraints (according to which the repaired data *must* satisfy all the conditions expressed), weak aggregate constraints express conditions which reasonably hold in the actual data, although satisfying them is not mandatory.

Example 8. The two conditions defined in our running example (that is, "*it is likely that cash sales are greater than or equal to 2000*", and "*it is likely that receivables are less than or equal to 400*") can be expressed by the following weak aggregate constraints:

$\omega_1 : \chi_2(\text{'cash sales'}) \geq 2000$
$\omega_2 : \chi_2(\text{'receivables'}) \leq 400$

where χ_2 is the aggregation function defined in Example 2. □

Intuitively, a *card*-minimal repair satisfying n_1 weak constraints is preferred to any other *card*-minimal repair satisfying $n_2 < n_1$ weak constraints. We exploit this ordering criterion implied by weak constraints on the set of *card*-minimal repairs to define the notion of *preferred (card-minimal) repairs*.

Let $\mathcal{D}$ be a database scheme, D an instance of $\mathcal{D}$, and ω a weak aggregate constraint on $\mathcal{D}$ having the form (1) (see Definition 1). We denote the set of *ground weak constraints* obtained from the instantiation of ω on D as $gr(\omega, D)$, i.e., $gr(\omega, D) = \{\theta(\omega) \mid \theta$ is a substitution of variables $x_1, \ldots, x_k$ with constants such that $\phi(\theta x_1, \ldots, \theta x_k)$ is true in $D\}$. Given a set of weak constraints $\mathcal{W}$ on $\mathcal{D}$, we denote as $gr(\mathcal{W}, D)$ the set of ground weak constraints obtained from the instantiation of every

$\omega \in W$ on D, i.e., $gr(W, D) = \bigcup_{\omega \in W} \{gr(\omega, D)\}$. Let ρ be a *card*-minimal repair for D w.r.t. a set of aggregate constraints $\mathcal{AC}$ on $\mathcal{D}$, and W be a set of weak constraints on $\mathcal{D}$. We will denote as $\gamma(\rho, W, D)$ the number of ground weak constraints in $gr(W, \rho(D))$ which are not satisfied.

Definition 7 (Preferred repair). *Let $\mathcal{D}$ be a database scheme, $\mathcal{AC}$ a set of aggregate constraints on $\mathcal{D}$, W a set of weak aggregate constraints on $\mathcal{D}$, and D an instance of $\mathcal{D}$. A card-minimal repair ρ for D w.r.t. $\mathcal{AC}$ is said to be a* preferred *repair for D w.r.t. $\mathcal{AC}$ and W iff there is no card-minimal repair ρ' for D w.r.t. $\mathcal{AC}$ such that $\gamma(\rho', W, D) < \gamma(\rho, W, D)$.*

Example 9. As explained in Example 7, in our running example the set of *card*-minimal repairs is $\{\rho_1, \rho_2\}$. Let $W = \{\omega_1, \omega_2\}$ be the set of weak constraints defined in Example 8. Both ω_1 and ω_2 are ground weak constraints and $gr(W, D) = gr(W, \rho_1(D)) = gr(W, \rho_2(D)) = \{\omega_1, \omega_2\}$. Since both ω_1 and ω_2 are violated by $\rho_1(D)$, it holds that $\gamma(\rho_1, W, D) = 2$, whereas $\gamma(\rho_2, W, D) = 0$ since $\rho_2(D)$ satisfies both ω_1 and ω_2. Thus, ρ_2 is a preferred repair w.r.t. $\mathcal{AC}$ and W.   □

In our previous work [12], several issues related to the problem of repairing and extracting reliable information from data violating a given set of aggregate constraints has been investigated. Specifically, the complexity of the following two problems have been characterized: (i) the problem of deciding whether a repair exists (NP-complete), and (ii) the problem of checking whether a repair is *card*-minimal (coNP-complete). The following theorem extends these results to the case of preferred repairs.

Theorem 1. *Let $\mathcal{D}$ be a database scheme, $\mathcal{AC}$ a set of aggregate constraints on $\mathcal{D}$, W a set of weak constraints on $\mathcal{D}$, and D an instance of $\mathcal{D}$. The following hold:*

- *given an integer k, deciding whether there is a preferred repair ρ for D w.r.t. $\mathcal{AC}$ and W such that $\gamma(\rho, W, D) \geq k$ is in NP, and is NP-hard even in the case that $\mathcal{AC}$ and W consist of steady constraints only;*
- *given a repair ρ for D w.r.t. $\mathcal{AC}$, deciding whether ρ is a preferred repair for D w.r.t. $\mathcal{AC}$ and W is in coNP, and is coNP-hard even in the case that $\mathcal{AC}$ and W consist of steady constraints only.*

4   Computing a Preferred Repair

Although steady aggregate constraints are less expressive than (general) aggregate constraints, Theorem 1 states that both the preferred-repair existence problem and the preferred-repair checking problem are hard also in the presence of steady constraints only. From a practical standpoint, this loss in expressiveness is not dramatic, as steady aggregate constraints are expressive enough to model conditions ensuring data consistency in several real-life contexts. In fact, all the aggregate constraints used in our running example are steady.

In this section, we define a technique for computing preferred repairs for a database w.r.t a set of *steady aggregate constraints* and a set of *steady weak constraints*. This technique is based on the translation of the preferred-repair evaluation problem into an instance of Integer Linear Programming (ILP) problem [15]. Our technique exploits the restrictions imposed on steady aggregate constraints w.r.t. general aggregate constraints to accomplish the computation of a repair. As will be explained later, this approach does not work for (general) aggregate constraints.

We first show how a set of steady aggregate constraints can be expressed by means of a system of linear inequalities. Then, in order to model the problem of finding a preferred repair, we increment this system of inequalities with an appropriate set of linear inequalities and define an appropriate objective function, thus obtaining an optimization problem.

4.1   Expressing Steady Aggregate Constraints as a Set of Inequalities

Let $\mathcal{D}$ be a database scheme, $\mathcal{AC}$ a set of steady aggregate constraints on $\mathcal{D}$ and D an instance of $\mathcal{D}$. Let κ be a steady aggregate constraint in $\mathcal{AC}$. We recall that κ is of the form (1) (see Definition 1). Let $\Theta(\kappa)$ be a set containing every ground substitution θ of variables $x_1, \ldots, x_k$ with constants such that $\phi(\theta x_1, \ldots, \theta x_k)$ is true on D.

For the sake of simplicity, we assume that each attribute expression e_i occurring in an aggregation function χ_i appearing in κ is either an attribute in $\mathcal{M}_\mathcal{D}$ or a constant. We associate a variable z_{t,A_j} with each pair $\langle t, A_j \rangle$, where t is a tuple in D and A_j is an attribute in $\mathcal{M}_\mathcal{D}$. The variable z_{t,A_j} is defined on the same domain as A_j. For every ground substitution $\theta \in \Theta(\kappa)$, we will denote as $\mathcal{T}(\theta, \chi_i)$ the set of the tuples involved in the aggregation function χ_i. More formally, assume that the aggregation function χ_i is defined on the variables $x_{i_1}, \ldots, x_{i_m}$, where $x_{i_1}, \ldots, x_{i_m}$ is a subset of $\{x_1, \ldots, x_k\}$, and let r_i be an instance of relation R_i appearing in the aggregation function χ_i and α_i be the formula appearing in the WHERE clause of χ_i. The set $\mathcal{T}(\theta, \chi_i)$ is defined as follows: $\mathcal{T}(\theta, \chi_i) = \{t : t \in r_i \wedge t \models \alpha_i(\theta x_{i_1}, \ldots, \theta x_{i_m})\}$. For every ground substitution $\theta \in \Theta(\kappa)$, the translation of χ_i w.r.t. θ, denoted as $\mathcal{P}(\theta, \chi_i)$, is defined as follows:

$$\mathcal{P}(\theta, \chi_i) = \begin{cases} \sum_{t \in \mathcal{T}(\theta, \chi_i)} z_{t,A_j} & \text{if } e_i = A_j; \\ e_i \cdot |\mathcal{T}(\theta, \chi_i)| & \text{if } e_i \text{ is a constant.} \end{cases}$$

For every ground substitution θ in $\Theta(\kappa)$, we define $Q(\kappa, \theta)$ as $\sum_{i=1}^{n} c_i \cdot \mathcal{P}(\theta, \chi_i)$. The whole constraint κ is associated to the set $\mathcal{S}(\kappa)$ consisting of the inequalities $Q(\kappa, \theta) \leq K$ for each $\theta \in \Theta(\kappa)$. The translation of all aggregate constraints in $\mathcal{AC}$ produces a system of linear inequalities, denoted as $\mathcal{S}(\mathcal{AC}, D)$, consisting of the set of inequalities in $\{\cup_{\kappa \in \mathcal{AC}} \mathcal{S}(\kappa)\}$.

It is easy to see that this construction is not possible for a non-steady aggregate constraint. In fact, consider a repair ρ for D w.r.t. $\mathcal{AC}$, for each substitution $\theta \in \Theta(\kappa)$ it is possible that the set of tuples $\mathcal{T}(\theta, \chi_i)$ evaluated on D is different from the set of tuples $\mathcal{T}(\theta, \chi_i)$ evaluated on $\rho(D)$.

For the sake of simplicity, in the following we associate each pair $\langle t, A_j \rangle$ such that $t \in D$ and $A_j \in \mathcal{M}_\mathcal{D}$ with an integer index i. Therefore we will write z_i instead of z_{t,A_j}. The set of all indexes corresponding to pairs $\langle t, A_j \rangle$ such that z_{t,A_j} appears in $\mathcal{S}(\mathcal{AC}, D)$ will be denoted as $\mathcal{I}_{\mathcal{AC}}$. Thus, $\mathcal{S}(\mathcal{AC}, D)$ can be written as $\mathbf{A} \times \mathbf{Z} \leq \mathbf{B}$, where $\mathbf{Z}$ is the vector of variables z_i such that $i \in \mathcal{I}_{\mathcal{AC}}$.

Example 10. Consider the database *CashBudget* whose instance is shown in Table 1 and the set of aggregate constraints $\mathcal{AC} = \{\kappa_1, \kappa_2, \kappa_3\}$ of our running example. We associate the pair $\langle t_i, Value \rangle$, where t_i is the i-th tuple of relation *CashBudget* with the integer i. As every pair $\langle t_i, Value \}$ is involved in at least a constraint in $\mathcal{AC}$, it holds that $\mathcal{I}_{\mathcal{AC}} = \{1, \ldots, 10\}$. Thus, z_i (with $i \in \{1, \ldots, 10\}$) is the variable associated with $\langle t_i, Value \rangle$. The translation of constraints in $\mathcal{AC}$ is the following, where we explicitly write equalities instead of inequalities:

$$\mathcal{S}(\kappa_1) := \begin{cases} z_2 + z_3 = z_4 \\ z_5 + z_6 + z_7 = z_8 \end{cases} \qquad \mathcal{S}(\kappa_2) := \{ z_4 - z_8 = z_9 \qquad \mathcal{S}(\kappa_3) := \{ z_1 + z_9 = z_{10}$$

$\mathcal{S}(\mathcal{AC}, D)$ consists of the system obtained by assembling all the equalities reported above (basically, it is the intersection of systems $\mathcal{S}(\kappa_1)$, $\mathcal{S}(\kappa_2)$ and $\mathcal{S}(\kappa_3)$). $\qquad\square$

4.2 Evaluating Preferred Repairs

Let $\mathcal{D}$ be a database scheme, D be an instance of $\mathcal{D}$, $\mathcal{AC}$ be a set of steady aggregate constraints on $\mathcal{D}$, and $\mathcal{W}$ be a set of steady weak constraints on $\mathcal{D}$. In the following we will use the above-defined notations $\Theta(\kappa)$ and $Q(\kappa, \theta)$, for $\kappa \in \mathcal{AC} \cup \mathcal{W}$ and $\theta \in \Theta(\kappa)$. We will denote the current database value corresponding to the variable z_i as v_i (with $i \in \mathcal{I}_{\mathcal{AC}}$). That is, if z_i is associated with the pair $\langle t, A_j \rangle$, then $v_i = t[A_j]$. Every solution s of $\mathcal{S}(\mathcal{AC}, D)$ corresponds to a repair $\rho(s)$ for D w.r.t. $\mathcal{AC}$. In particular, for each variable z_i which is assigned a value $\widehat{z}_i$ different from v_i, repair $\rho(s)$ contains an atomic update assigning the value $\widehat{z}_i$ to the pair $\langle t, A_j \rangle$ which z_i corresponds to, that is $\rho(s)$ contains the atomic update $\langle t, A_j, \widehat{z}_i \rangle$. It is easy to see that, in general $\rho(s)$ is a non-minimal and non-preferred repair.

In order to decide whether a solution s of $\mathcal{S}(\mathcal{AC}, D)$ corresponds to a preferred repair, we must decide whether $\rho(s)$ is a *card*-minimal repair and whether $\gamma(\rho(s), \mathcal{W}, D)$ is minimum w.r.t. all others *card*-minimal repairs, i.e., $\rho(s)$ violates the minimum number of weak constraints in $gr(\mathcal{W}, D)$. To accomplish this, we must count the number of variables of s which are assigned a value different from the corresponding source value in D, and we must count the number of ground weak constraints which are not satisfied by $\rho(s)$. This is achieved as follows. For each $i \in \mathcal{I}_{\mathcal{AC}}$, we define a variable $y_i = z_i - v_i$ on the same domain as z_i. Variables y_i will be exploited for detecting whether z_i is assigned in a solution s of $\mathcal{S}(\mathcal{AC}, D)$ a value different from v_i. For each weak constraint $\omega \in \mathcal{W}$ having the form (1) (see Definition 1) and for each ground substitution $\theta \in \Theta(\omega)$, we define the variable $\sigma_{\omega,\theta} = K - Q(\omega, \theta)$. Variables $\sigma_{\omega,\theta}$ will be exploited for detecting whether for the substitution $\theta \in \Theta(\omega)$, the weak constraint ω is not satisfied: if in a solution s of $\mathcal{S}(\mathcal{AC}, D)$ the variables in $Q(\omega, \theta)$ are assigned values entailing that $\sigma_{\omega,\theta} < 0$ then the ground weak constraint $\theta(\omega)$ is not satisfied by repair $\rho(s)$. Consider the following system of linear (in)equalities:

$$\mathcal{S}(\mathcal{AC}, \mathcal{W}, D) := \begin{cases} \mathbf{A} \times \mathbf{Z} \leq \mathbf{B} \\ y_i = z_i - v_i & \forall i \in \mathcal{I}_{\mathcal{AC}} \\ \sigma_{\omega,\theta} = K - Q(\omega, \theta) & \forall \omega \in \mathcal{W} \text{ and } \theta \in \Theta(\omega) \end{cases}$$

As shown in [17], if a system of equalities has a solution, it has also a solution where each variable takes a value in $[-M, M]$, where M is a constant equal to $n \cdot (ma)^{2m+1}$, where m is the number of equalities, n is the number of variables and a is the maximum value among the modules of the system coefficients. It is straightforward to see that $\mathcal{S}(\mathcal{AC}, \mathcal{W}, D)$ can be translated into a system of linear equalities in augmented form with $m = |\mathcal{I}_{\mathcal{AC}}| + |gr(\mathcal{W}, D)| + r$ and $n = 2 \cdot |\mathcal{I}_{\mathcal{AC}}| + |var_{\mathcal{W}}| + r$, where r is the number of rows of $\mathbf{A}$ and $var_{\mathcal{W}}$ is the union of the sets of new variables appearing in equations $\sigma_{\omega, \theta} = K - Q(\omega, \theta)$, for $\omega \in \mathcal{W}$ and $\theta \in \Theta(\omega)$ [1].

In order to detect if a variable z_i is assigned (for each solution of $\mathcal{S}(\mathcal{AC}, \mathcal{W}, D)$ bounded by M) a value different from the original value v_i (that is, if $|y_i| > 0$), a new binary variable δ_i will be defined. Every δ_i will have value 1 if the value of z_i differs from v_i, 0 otherwise. Analogously, in order to detect if for a substitution θ the ground weak constraint $\theta(\omega)$ is not satisfied (that is, if $\sigma_{\omega, \theta} < 0$) a new binary variable $\mu_{\omega, \theta}$ will be defined. Every $\mu_{\omega, \theta}$ will have value 1 if $\theta(\omega)$ is not satisfied, 0 otherwise. To express these conditions, we add the following constraints to $\mathcal{S}(\mathcal{AC}, \mathcal{W}, D)$:

$$\begin{cases} y_i \leq M \cdot \delta_i & \forall i \in \mathcal{I}_{\mathcal{AC}} \\ -M \cdot \delta_i \leq y_i & \forall i \in \mathcal{I}_{\mathcal{AC}} \\ -M \cdot \mu_{\omega, \theta} \leq \sigma_{\omega, \theta} & \forall \omega \in \mathcal{W} \text{ and } \theta \in \Theta(\omega) \\ \delta_i \in \{0, 1\} & \forall i \in \mathcal{I}_{\mathcal{AC}} \\ \mu_{\omega, \theta} \in \{0, 1\} & \forall \omega \in \mathcal{W} \text{ and } \theta \in \Theta(\omega) \end{cases} \quad (2)$$

The system obtained by assembling $\mathcal{S}(\mathcal{AC}, \mathcal{W}, D)$ with inequalities (2) will be denoted as $\mathcal{S}'(\mathcal{AC}, \mathcal{W}, D)$. For each solution s' of $\mathcal{S}'(\mathcal{AC}, \mathcal{W}, D)$, the following hold: (i) for each z_i which is assigned in s' a value greater than v_i, the variable δ_i is assigned 1 (this is entailed by constraint $y_i \leq M \cdot \delta_i$); (ii) for each z_i which is assigned in s' a value less than v_i, the variable δ_i is assigned 1 (this is entailed by constraint $-M \cdot \delta_i \leq y_i$); (iii) for each $Q(\omega, \theta)$ whose variables are assigned in s' values such that $Q(\omega, \theta) > K$, the variable $\mu_{\omega, \theta}$ is assigned 1 (this is entailed by constraint $-M \cdot \mu_{\omega, \theta} \leq \sigma_{\omega, \theta}$). Moreover, for each z_i which is assigned in s' the same value as v_i (that is, $y_i = 0$), variable δ_i is assigned either 0 or 1, and for each $\sigma_{\omega, \theta}$ which is assigned in s a value greater than or equal to 0, variable $\mu_{\omega, \theta}$ is assigned either 0 or 1.

Obviously each solution of $\mathcal{S}'(\mathcal{AC}, \mathcal{W}, D)$ corresponds to exactly one solution for $\mathcal{S}(\mathcal{AC}, \mathcal{W}, D)$ (or, analogously, for $\mathcal{S}(\mathcal{AC}, D)$) with the same values for variables z_i. Vice versa, for each solution of $\mathcal{S}(\mathcal{AC}, D)$ whose variables are bounded by M there is at least one solution of $\mathcal{S}'(\mathcal{AC}, \mathcal{W}, D)$ with the same values for variables z_i. As solutions of $\mathcal{S}(\mathcal{AC}, D)$ correspond to repairs for D, each solution of $\mathcal{S}'(\mathcal{AC}, \mathcal{W}, D)$ corresponds to a repair ρ for D such that, for each update $u = \langle t, A, v \rangle$ in ρ it holds that $|v| \leq M$. Repairs satisfying this property will be said to be M-bounded repairs.

In order to consider only the solutions of $\mathcal{S}'(\mathcal{AC}, \mathcal{W}, D)$ where each δ_i is 0 if $y_i = 0$ and where each $\mu_{\omega, \theta}$ is 0 if $\sigma_{\omega, \theta} \geq 0$, we consider the following optimization problem $\mathcal{S}^*(\mathcal{AC}, \mathcal{W}, D)$, whose goal is minimizing the weighted sum of the values assigned to variables δ_i and $\mu_{\omega, \theta}$ (with $i \in \mathcal{I}_{\mathcal{AC}}$, $\omega \in \mathcal{W}$ and $\theta \in \Theta(\omega)$):

$$\mathcal{S}^*(\mathcal{AC}, \mathcal{W}, D) := \begin{cases} \min \left(\sum_{i \in \mathcal{I}_{\mathcal{AC}}} W \cdot \delta_i + \sum_{\omega \in \mathcal{W} \wedge \theta \in \Theta(\omega)} \mu_{\omega, \theta} \right) \\ \mathcal{S}'(\mathcal{AC}, \mathcal{W}, D) \end{cases}$$

---

[1] Observe that the size of M is polynomial in the size of the database, as it is bounded by $\log n + (2 \cdot m + 1) \cdot \log(ma)$.

where $S'(\mathcal{AC}, \mathcal{W}, D)$ is the system of inequalities defined above and $W = N_{\mathcal{W}} + 1$, where and $N_{\mathcal{W}}$ is the number of variables $\mu_{\omega,\theta}$, that is the cardinality of the set $\{\mu_{\omega,\theta} \mid \omega \in \mathcal{W} \wedge \theta \in \Theta(\omega)\}$. Basically, the objective function of $S^*(\mathcal{AC}, \mathcal{W}, D)$ entails that it is preferable that some δ_i is assigned 0 (i.e., a database value is not updated) with respect to assign 0 to all $\mu_{\omega,\theta}$ (i.e., all weak constraints are satisfied).

Theorem 2. *Let $\mathcal{D}$ be a database scheme $\mathcal{D}$, $\mathcal{AC}$ be a set of steady aggregate constraints on $\mathcal{D}$, $\mathcal{W}$ be a set of steady weak constraints on $\mathcal{D}$ and D be an instance of $\mathcal{D}$. Every (optimal) solution s^* of $S^*(\mathcal{AC}, \mathcal{W}, D)$ corresponds to a preferred repair $\rho(s^*)$ for D w.r.t. $\mathcal{AC}$ and $\mathcal{W}$.*

Basically, given an (optimal) solution s^* of $S^*(\mathcal{AC}, \mathcal{W}, D)$, the values $\hat{z}_i$, $\hat{y}_i$, $\hat{\delta}_i$, $\hat{\sigma}_{\omega,\theta}$, $\hat{u}_{\omega,\theta}$ of variables z_i, y_i, δ_i, $\sigma_{\omega,\theta}$, $u_{\omega,\theta}$ defines the set of atomic updates performed by the repair $\rho(s^*)$. The value $(\sum_{i \in \mathcal{I}_{AC}} \hat{\delta}_i)/W$ represents the number of atomic updates performed by any *card*-minimal repair for D w.r.t. $\mathcal{AC}$, whereas the value $\sum_{\omega \in \mathcal{W} \wedge \theta \in \Theta(\omega)} \hat{\mu}_{\omega,\theta}$ represents minimum number of the ground weak constraints which are not satisfied by any preferred repair.

Example 11. The optimization problem obtained for our running example where $\mathcal{AC} = \{\kappa_1, \kappa_2, \kappa_3\}$ and $\mathcal{W} = \{\omega_1, \omega_2\}$ is shown in Fig. 1, where θ is the empty substitution.

$$\min(\sum_{i=1}^{10} 3 \cdot \delta_i + \mu_{\omega_1,\theta} + \mu_{\omega_2,\theta})$$

$$\begin{cases}
z_2 + z_3 = z_4 & y_5 = z_5 - 1300 & y_i - M\delta_i \leq 0 & \forall i \in [1..10] \\
z_5 + z_6 + z_7 = z_8 & y_6 = z_6 - 100 & -y_i - M\delta_i \leq 0 & \forall i \in [1..10] \\
z_4 - z_8 = z_9 & y_7 = z_7 - 600 & -M \cdot \mu_{\omega_1,\theta} \leq \sigma_{\omega_1,\theta} & \\
z_1 - z_9 = z_{10} & y_8 = z_8 - 1000 & -M \cdot \mu_{\omega_2,\theta} \leq \sigma_{\omega_2,\theta} & \\
y_1 = z_1 - 3000 & y_9 = z_9 - 450 & z_i, y_i \in \mathbb{Z} & \forall i \in [1..10] \\
y_2 = z_2 - 2200 & y_{10} = z_{10} - 3450 & \delta_i \in \{0, 1\} & \forall i \in [1..10] \\
y_3 = z_3 - 650 & \sigma_{\omega_1,\theta} = z_2 - 2000 & \mu_{\omega_1,\theta} \in \{0, 1\} & \\
y_4 = z_4 - 2450 & \sigma_{\omega_2,\theta} = 400 - z_3 & \mu_{\omega_2,\theta} \in \{0, 1\} &
\end{cases}$$

Fig. 1. Instance of $S^*(\mathcal{AC}, \mathcal{W}, D)$ obtained for the running example

The problem above admits only one optimum solution wherein the value of the objective function is 6, as $\delta_i = 0$ for $i \in [1..10]$ except for $\delta_3 = \delta_8 = 1$, and $\mu_{\omega_1,\theta} = \mu_{\omega_2,\theta} = 0$. It is easy to see that this solution correspond to the preferred repair ρ_2. □

5   Experimental Results

We experimentally validated the proposed technique on database instances containing real-life balance-sheet data, and we used LINDO API 4.0 (available at www.lindo.com) as ILP solver. We considered three balance-sheets, which will be denoted as B_1, B_2, B_3, published by three different companies and sharing the same scheme. We defined (strong) aggregate constraints expressing the actual algebraic relations among the balance items defined in the standard. Moreover, for each balance sheet,

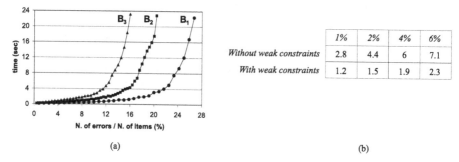

	1%	2%	4%	6%
Without weak constraints	2.8	4.4	6	7.1
With weak constraints	1.2	1.5	1.9	2.3

(a)   (b)

Fig. 2. Time needed (a) and average number of iterations (b) for computing a preferred repair

we defined weak constraints associating numerical intervals to each balance item (these intervals were retrieved from the balance-sheets published by the same companies in the previous 5 years).

Starting from the values reported in B_1, B_2, B_3, we generated the corresponding database instances D_1, D_2, D_3, containing 112, 256, and 378 tuples, respectively (each tuple contains exactly one measure attribute). Then, we simulated acquisition errors by randomly changing the measure values represented in the database instances. Specifically, for each D_i, we generated 100 database instances $D_i^1, \ldots, D_i^{100}$, containing a number of erroneous values between 0% and 30% of the number of items occurring in the source balance sheet B_i.

The diagram in Fig. 2(a) depicts the amount of time needed for computing a preferred repair vs. the percentage of erroneous values. From this experiment we can draw the conclusion that our technique can be effectively employed in real-life scenarios. In fact, the number of items occurring in a balance sheet is unlikely to be greater than 400, and the typical percentage of errors occurring in acquisition phase performed by means of OCR tools is less than 5% of acquired data. In this range, our prototype takes at most 1.5 seconds to compute a preferred repair.

Further experiments were conducted to test the practicality of using our technique as the core of a semi-automatic system for fixing data acquisition errors. We simulated the following iterative process. At each step, a preferred repair is computed, and it is validated by an user w.r.t. the original data. If the user finds that the repair does not reconstruct the original values, a new iteration is run, on the database instance where one of the wrongly re-constructed values is fixed. The process continues until an *accepted repair* is generated, i.e., the original data is re-constructed correctly. Therefore, we analyzed the impact of using weak constraints on the number of iterations needed for completing this process.

The table in Fig. 2(b) reports the average number of iterations which were necessary for returning an accepted repair, for different percentages of erroneous values (these results were obtained for B_2). The first row refers to the case that only strong aggregate constraints were considered, whereas the second row refers to the case that also weak aggregate constraints were considered. It is worth noting that the use of weak constraints considerably reduces the (average) number of iteration performed in the repairing process.

6 Conclusions and Future Works

We have introduced a framework for computing preferred repairs in numerical databases violating a given set of strong and weak aggregate constraints, which exploits a transformation into integer linear programming. Experimental results prove the effectiveness of the proposed approach. Further work will be devoted to investigating theoretical issues related to the CQA problem in the presence of weak aggregate constraints.

References

1. Arenas, M., Bertossi, L.E., Chomicki, J.: Consistent Query Answers in Inconsistent Databases. In: Proc. Symposium on Principles of Database Systems (PODS), pp. 68–79 (1999)
2. Arenas, M., Bertossi, L.E., Chomicki, J.: Answer Sets for Consistent Query Answering in Inconsistent Databases. Theory and practice of logic program 3(4-5), 393–424 (2003)
3. Arenas, M., Bertossi, L.E., Chomicki, J., He, X., Raghavan, V., Spinrad, J.: Scalar aggregation in inconsistent databases. Theoretical Computer Science 3(296), 405–434 (2003)
4. Bertossi, L.E., Chomicki, J.: Query Answering in Inconsistent Databases. In: Logics for Emerging Applications of Databases, pp. 43–83 (2003)
5. Bertossi, L., Bravo, L., Franconi, E., Lopatenko, A.: Complexity and Approximation of Fixing Numerical Attributes in Databases Under Integrity Constraints. In: Bierman, G., Koch, C. (eds.) DBPL 2005. LNCS, vol. 3774, pp. 262–278. Springer, Heidelberg (2005)
6. Bohannon, P., Flaster, M., Fan, W., Rastogi, R.: A Cost-Based Model and Effective Heuristic for Repairing Constraints by Value Modification. In: Proc. ACM SIGMOD, pp. 143–154 (2005)
7. Calì, A., Lembo, D., Rosati, R.: On the Decidability and Complexity of Query Answering over Inconsistent and Incomplete Databases. In: Proc. ACM Symposium on Principles of Database Systems (PODS), pp. 260–271 (2003)
8. Chomicki, J., Marcinkowski, J., Staworko, S.: Computing consistent query answers using conflict hypergraphs. In: Proc. International Conference on Information and Knowledge Management (CIKM), pp. 417–426 (2004)
9. Chomicki, J., Marcinkowski, J., Staworko, S., Hippo, A.: A System for Computing Consistent Answers to a Class of SQL Queries. In: Bertino, E., Christodoulakis, S., Plexousakis, D., Christophides, V., Koubarakis, M., Böhm, K., Ferrari, E. (eds.) EDBT 2004. LNCS, vol. 2992, pp. 841–844. Springer, Heidelberg (2004)
10. Chomicki, J., Marcinkowski, J.: Minimal-Change Integrity Maintenance Using Tuple Deletions. Information and Computation (IC) 197(1-2), 90–121 (2005)
11. Chomicki, J., Marcinkowski, J.: On the Computational Complexity of Minimal-Change Integrity Maintenance in Relational Databases. In: Inconsistency Tolerance, pp. 119–150 (2005)
12. Flesca, S., Furfaro, F., Parisi, F.: Consistent Query Answer on Numerical Databases under Aggregate Constraint. In: Bierman, G., Koch, C. (eds.) DBPL 2005. LNCS, vol. 3774, pp. 279–294. Springer, Heidelberg (2005)
13. Fuxman, A., Miller, R.J.: ConQuer: Efficient Management of Inconsistent Databases. In: Proc. ACM SIGMOD International Conference on Management of Data pp. 155–166 (2005)
14. Franconi, E., Laureti Palma, A., Leone, N., Perri, S., Scarcello, F.: Census Data Repair: a Challenging Application of Disjunctive Logic Programming. In: Nieuwenhuis, R., Voronkov, A. (eds.) LPAR 2001. LNCS (LNAI), vol. 2250, pp. 561–578. Springer, Heidelberg (2001)

15. Gass, S.I.: Linear Programming Methods and Applications. McGrawHill, New York (1985)
16. Greco, G., Greco, S., Zumpano, E.: A Logical Framework for Querying and Repairing Inconsistent Databases. IEEE TKDE 15(6), 1389–1408 (2003)
17. Papadimitriou, C.H.: On the complexity of integer programming. Journal of the Association for Computing Machinery (JACM) 28(4), 765–768 (1981)
18. Wijsen, J.: Database Repairing Using Updates. ACM Transactions on Database Systems (TODS) 30(3), 722–768 (2005)

Consistent Data Integration in P2P Deductive Databases

L. Caroprese and E. Zumpano

DEIS, Univ. della Calabria, 87030 Rende, Italy

{lcaroprese,zumpano}@deis.unical.it

Abstract. Data Integration in *Peer-to-Peer* (P2P) systems is concerned with the ability of physically connect autonomous sources (peer) for sharing and reuse information and for the creation of new information from existing one. In a P2P system a query can be posed to any peer and the answer is provided by integrating locally stored data with data provided from its neighbors. Anyhow, while collecting data for answering queries, imported data may corrupt the local database due to the violation of some integrity constraint, therefore inconsistencies have to be managed. This paper contributes to the proposal of a logic based framework for data integration and query answering in a *Peer-to-Peer* environment. It is based on [11,12] in which the *Preferred Weak Model Semantics*, capturing a different perspective for P2P data integration, has been proposed: just data not violating integrity constraints are exchanged among peers by using mapping rules. The motivation of this work stems from the observation that the complexity of computing preferred weak models in [11,12] does not let the approach to be implemented in practical applications. Therefore, a more pragmatic solution seems to be desirable for assigning semantics to a P2P system. First, the paper proposes a rewriting technique that allows modeling a P2P system, $\mathcal{PS}$, as a unique logic program, $Rew_t(\mathcal{PS})$, whose stable models correspond to the preferred weak models of $\mathcal{PS}$. Then, it presents the *Well Founded Model Semantics*, that allows obtaining a deterministic model whose computation is polynomial time. This is a (partial) stable model obtained by evaluating with a three-value semantics a logic program obtained from $Rew_t(\mathcal{PS})$. Finally, the paper provides results on the complexity of answering queries in a P2P system.

1 Introduction

Data Integration in *Peer-to-Peer* (P2P) systems is currently widely regarded as a significant area both in industry and academia. It is concerned with the ability of physically connect autonomous sources (peer) for sharing and reuse information and for the creation to new information from existing ones. This paper contributes to the proposal of a logic based framework for modeling P2P systems. Each peer, joining a P2P system, can both provide or consume data and has information about its neighbors, i.e. about the peers that are reachable and can provide data of interest. In a P2P system each peer exhibits a set of *mapping*

H. Prade and V.S. Subrahmanian (Eds.): SUM 2007, LNAI 4772, pp. 230–243, 2007.

rules, i.e. a set of semantic correspondences to its neighbor peers. Therefore, the entry of a new peer in the system is extremely simple as it just requires the definition of the mechanism for exchanging data within its neighborhood.

By using mapping rules as soon as it enters the system, a peer can participate and access all data available in its neighborhood, and through its neighborhood it becomes accessible to all the other peers in the system.

This paper extends previous works in [11,12] in which a different interpretation of mapping rules, that allows importing from other peers only tuples not violating integrity constraints, has been proposed. This new interpretation of mapping rules has led to the proposal of a semantics for a P2P system defined in terms of *Preferred Weak Models*. Under this semantics only facts not making the local databases inconsistent can be imported, and the preferred weak models are the consistent scenarios in which peers import maximal sets of facts not violating integrity constraints.

The following example will intuitively introduce the proposed semantics.

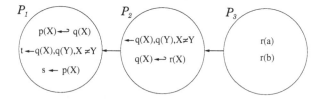

Fig. 1. A P2P system

Example 1. Consider the P2P system depicted in Fig. 1 consisting of three peers $\mathcal{P}_1$, $\mathcal{P}_2$ and $\mathcal{P}_3$ where:

- $\mathcal{P}_3$ contains two atoms: $r(a)$ and $r(b)$,
- $\mathcal{P}_2$ imports data from $\mathcal{P}_3$ using the mapping rule $q(X) \hookleftarrow r(X)$[1]. Moreover imported atoms must satisfy the constraint $\leftarrow q(X), q(Y), X \neq Y$ stating that the relation q may contain at most one tuple, and
- $\mathcal{P}_1$ imports data from $\mathcal{P}_2$, using the mapping rule $p(X) \hookleftarrow q(X)$. $\mathcal{P}_1$ also contains the rules $s \leftarrow p(X)$ stating that s is *true* if the relation p contains at least one tuple, and $t \leftarrow p(X), p(Y), X \neq Y$, stating that t is *true* if the relation p contains at least two distinct tuples.

The intuition is that, with $r(a)$ and $r(b)$ being *true* in $\mathcal{P}_3$, either $q(a)$ or $q(b)$ could be imported in $\mathcal{P}_2$ (but not both, otherwise the integrity constraint is violated) and, consequently, only one tuple is imported in the relation p of the peer $\mathcal{P}_1$. Note that, whatever is the derivation in $\mathcal{P}_2$, s is derived in $\mathcal{P}_1$ while t is not derived; thus the atoms s and t are, respectively, *true* and *false* in $\mathcal{P}_1$. □

Therefore, due to the specified mechanism for collecting data, a query, that can be posed to any peer in the system, is answered by using locally stored data and

---

[1] Please, note the special syntax we use for mapping rules.

all the information that can be imported, without corrupting the local database, from its neighbors.

The main motivation for this work relies in the observation that a P2P system may admit many preferred weak models and the computational complexity is prohibitive: in [11,12] it has been shown that i) deciding whether an atom is *true* in some preferred model is Σ_2^p-complete and ii) deciding whether an atom is *true* in every preferred model is Π_2^p-complete. Therefore, a more pragmatic solution for assigning semantics to a P2P system, that can be effectively implemented in current P2P systems, is needed. Based on this observation, the paper proposes an equivalent characterization of the Preferred Weak Model semantics, called *Total Stable Model Semantics*, that models a P2P system, $\mathcal{PS}$, with a unique disjunctive logic program, $Rew_t(\mathcal{PS})$, such that the preferred weak models of $\mathcal{PS}$ can be extracted from the stable models of $Rew_t(\mathcal{PS})$. Moreover, it presents the *Well Founded Model Semantics*, that allows obtaining a deterministic model, whose computation is polynomial time. This model is obtained by evaluating, with a three-value semantics, the logic program obtained from $Rew_t(\mathcal{PS})$. The paper also provides some results on the computational complexity of answering queries in a P2P system.

2   Background

It is assumed there are finite sets of *predicate symbols, constants* and *variables*. A *term* is either a constant or a variable. An *atom* is of the form $p(t_1, \ldots, t_n)$ where p is a predicate symbol and $t_1, \ldots, t_n$ are terms. A *literal* is either an atom A or its negation *not* A. A (*disjunctive*) *rule* is of the form $\mathcal{H} \leftarrow \mathcal{B}$, where $\mathcal{H}$ is a disjunction of atoms (*head* of the rule) and $\mathcal{B}$ is a conjunction of literals (*body* of the rule). A rule is *normal* if just an atom appears in its head. It is assumed that each rule is *safe*, i.e. variables appearing in the head or in negated body literals also appear in some positive body literal. A (*disjunctive*) *program* is a finite set of rules. A program $\mathcal{P}$ is *normal* if each rule in $\mathcal{P}$ is normal; it is *positive* if the body of each rule in $\mathcal{P}$ is negation-free. A term (resp. literal, rule, program) is *ground* is no variable appears in it. The set of all ground atoms obtained from predicate symbols and constants occurring in a program $\mathcal{P}$, is called *Herbrand base* of $\mathcal{P}$ and is denoted as $\mathcal{HB}(\mathcal{P})$. Given a rule r, $ground(r)$ denotes the set of all ground rules obtained from r by replacing variables with constants in all possible ways. Given a program $\mathcal{P}$, $ground(\mathcal{P}) = \bigcup_{r \in \mathcal{P}} ground(r)$. A rule with empty head is a *constraint*. A normal ground rule with empty body is a *fact*. In this case the implication symbol ($\leftarrow$) can be omitted. A ground program is *Head Cycle Free* (HCF) [3] if there are not two distinct atoms, occurring in the head of one of its rule, mutually dependent by positive recursion. A disjunctive program $\mathcal{P}$ is HCF if $ground(\mathcal{P})$ is HCF. An *interpretation* is a set of ground atoms. The *truth value* of a ground atom, a literal and a rule with respect to an interpretation M is as follows[2]: $val_M(A) = A \in M$, $val_M(not\ A) = not\ val_M(A)$, $val_M(L_1, \ldots, L_n) = min\{val_M\ (L_1), \ldots, val_M(L_n)\}$, $val_M(L_1 \vee \ldots \vee L_n) =$

---

[2] Assuming that $max(\emptyset) = false$ and $min(\emptyset) = true$.

$max\{val_M(L_1), \ldots, val_M(L_n)\}$ and $val_M(\mathcal{H} \leftarrow \mathcal{B}) = val_M(\mathcal{H}) \geq val_M(\mathcal{B})$, where A is an atom, $L_1, \ldots, L_n$ are literals, $H \leftarrow \mathcal{B}$ is a rule and $false < true$. An interpretation M is a *model* for a program $\mathcal{P}$ (or $M \models \mathcal{P}$), if all rules in $ground(\mathcal{P})$ are *true* w.r.t. M (i.e. $val_M(r) = true$ for each $r \in ground(\mathcal{P})$). A model M is said to be *minimal* if there is no model N such that $N \subset M$. The set of minimal models of a program $\mathcal{P}$ is denoted as $\mathcal{MM}(\mathcal{P})$. An interpretation M is a *stable model* of $\mathcal{P}$ if M is a minimal model of the positive program $\mathcal{P}^M$ (*reduct* of $\mathcal{P}$ w.r.t. M), where $\mathcal{P}^M$ is obtained from $ground(\mathcal{P})$ by (i) removing all rules r such that there exists a negative literal $not\ A$ in the body of r and $A \in M$ and (ii) removing all negative literals from the remaining rules [16]. It is well known that stable models are minimal models (i.e. $\mathcal{SM}(\mathcal{P}) \subseteq \mathcal{MM}(\mathcal{P})$) and that for positive programs, minimal and stable models coincide (i.e. $\mathcal{SM}(\mathcal{P}) = \mathcal{MM}(\mathcal{P})$). Given a program $\mathcal{P}$, its *normalized version*, denoted as $Normalized(\mathcal{P})$, is the normal program obtained from $\mathcal{P}$ by replacing each rule $A_1 \vee \ldots \vee A_h \leftarrow \mathcal{B}$, with $h > 1$, with the rules $A_i \leftarrow \mathcal{B}, not\ A_1, \ldots, not\ A_{i-1}, not\ A_{i+1}, \ldots, not\ A_h$, $\forall\ i \in [1, h]$. If $\mathcal{P}$ is HCF, its stable models coincide with the stable models of its normalized version, i.e. $\mathcal{SM}(\mathcal{P}) = \mathcal{SM}(Normalized(\mathcal{P}))$.

Partial stable models. Given a program $\mathcal{P}$, a *partial interpretation* assigns a definite truth value either *true* or *false* only to some atoms of $\mathcal{HB}(\mathcal{P})$ and assigns the *undefined* truth value to the rest of atoms in $\mathcal{HB}(\mathcal{P})$. Formally, a partial interpretation of a program $\mathcal{P}$ is a pair $\langle T, F \rangle$, where T and F are subsets of $\mathcal{HB}(\mathcal{P})$ such that $T \cap F = \emptyset$. The truth value of atoms in T (resp. F) is *true* (resp. *false*), whereas the truth value of atoms in $\mathcal{HB}(\mathcal{P}) - (T \cup F)$ is *undefined*. The truth values are ordered so that $false < undefined < true$; moreover $not\ undefined = undefined$. Given two partial interpretations $M_1 = \langle T_1, F_1 \rangle$ and $M_2 = \langle T_2, F_2 \rangle$, $M_1 \preceq M_2$ if $T_1 \subseteq T_2$ and $F_1 \supseteq F_2$. The truth value of rules with respect to a partial interpretation M is defined as previously specified. A *partial model* of $\mathcal{P}$ is a partial interpretation that satisfies all rules in $ground(\mathcal{P})$. A partial model $\langle T, F \rangle$ of $\mathcal{P}$ is *total* if it assigns to all atoms of $\mathcal{HB}(\mathcal{P})$ a definite truth value (i.e. $T \cup F = \mathcal{HB}(\mathcal{P})$). A partial model M is said to be *minimal* if there is no model N such that $N \neq M$ and $N \preceq M$. A partial (total) model $M = \langle T, F \rangle$ of $\mathcal{P}$ is *a stable partial (total) model* if it is a minimal model of $\mathcal{P}^M$, where $\mathcal{P}^M$ is obtained from $ground(\mathcal{P})$ by replacing all negative literals $not\ A$ with: (i) *true* if $not\ A$ is true in M, i.e. $A \in F$, (ii) *false* if $not\ A$ is false in M, i.e. $A \in T$, (iii) *undefined* if $not\ A$ is undefined in M, i.e. $A \notin (T \cup F)$. Note that, in the construction of $\mathcal{P}^M$ rules having a *false* atom in the body can be deleted, moreover *true* atom in the body can be deleted. Therefore, the above definition of $\mathcal{P}^M$ generalizes the one previously reported. It is well known that $\langle T, \mathcal{HB}(\mathcal{P}) - T \rangle$ is a total stable model of $\mathcal{P}$ under the three-value semantics if and only if T is a stable model of $\mathcal{P}$ under the two-value semantics. A partial stable model M of a program $\mathcal{P}$ *contradicts* another partial stable model N if there exists an atom that is *true* (resp. *false*) in M and *false* (resp. *true*) in N. A partial stable model M of a program $\mathcal{P}$ is a *deterministic partial stable model* if it does not contradict any other stable partial model. Given a program $\mathcal{P}$ and the set of its deterministic stable models, $\mathcal{DM}$, the algebraic structure $(\mathcal{DM}, \preceq)$

is a *lattice*. The set $\mathcal{DM}$ has a maximum, the *max-deterministic model*, and a minimum, the *well founded model*. If $\mathcal{P}$ is *normal*, its well founded model can be computed in polynomial time by using the *alternating fixpoint approach* [17,20].

3   P2P Systems: Syntax and Semantics

3.1   Syntax

A *(peer) predicate symbol* is a pair $i : p$, where i is a *peer identifier* and p is a predicate symbol. A *(peer) atom* is of the form $i : A$, where i is a *peer identifier* and A is a standard atom. A *(peer) literal* is a peer atom $i : A$ or its negation *not* $i : A$. A conjunction $i : A_1, \ldots, i : A_m, not\ i : A_{m+1}, \ldots, not\ i : A_n, \phi$, where ϕ is a conjunction of built-in atoms[3], will be also denoted as $i : \mathcal{B}$, with $\mathcal{B}$ equals to $A_1, \ldots, A_m, not\ A_{m+1}, \ldots, not\ A_n, \phi$.

A *(peer) rule* can be of one of the following three types:

1. STANDARD RULE. It is of the form $i : H \leftarrow i : \mathcal{B}$, where $i : H$ is an atom and $i : \mathcal{B}$ is a conjunction of atoms and built-in atoms.
2. INTEGRITY CONSTRAINT. It is of the form $\leftarrow i : \mathcal{B}$, where $i : \mathcal{B}$ is a conjunction of literals and built-in atoms.
3. MAPPING RULE. It is of the form $i : H \hookleftarrow j : \mathcal{B}$, where $i : H$ is an atom, $j : \mathcal{B}$ is a conjunction of atoms and built-in atoms and $i \neq j$.

In the previous rules $i : H$ is called *head*, while $i : \mathcal{B}$ (resp. $j : \mathcal{B}$) is called *body*. Negation is allowed just in the body of integrity constraints. The concepts of *ground rule* and *fact* are similar to those reported in Section 2. The definition of a predicate $i : p$ consists of the set of rules in whose head the predicate symbol $i : p$ occurs. A predicate can be of three different kinds: *base predicate*, *derived predicate* and *mapping predicate*. A base predicate is defined by a set of ground facts; a derived predicate is defined by a set of standard rules and a mapping predicate is defined by a set of mapping rules.

An atom $i : p(X)$ is a *base atom* (resp. *derived atom*, *mapping atom*) if $i : p$ is a base predicate (resp. standard predicate, mapping predicate). Given an interpretation M, $M[\mathcal{D}]$ (resp. $M[\mathcal{LP}]$, $M[\mathcal{MP}]$) denotes the subset of base atoms (resp. derived atoms, mapping atoms) in M.

Definition 1. P2P SYSTEM. A *peer* $\mathcal{P}_i$ is a tuple $\langle \mathcal{D}_i, \mathcal{LP}_i, \mathcal{MP}_i, \mathcal{IC}_i \rangle$, where (i) $\mathcal{D}_i$ is a set of facts (*local database*); (ii) $\mathcal{LP}_i$ is a set of standard rules; (iii) $\mathcal{MP}_i$ is a set of mapping rules and (iv) $\mathcal{IC}_i$ is a set of constraints over predicates defined by $\mathcal{D}_i$, $\mathcal{LP}_i$ and $\mathcal{MP}_i$. A *P2P system* $\mathcal{PS}$ is a set of peers $\{\mathcal{P}_1, \ldots, \mathcal{P}_n\}$.   □

Without loss of generality, we assume that every mapping predicate is defined by only one mapping rule of the form $i : p(X) \hookleftarrow j : q(X)$. The definition of a mapping predicate $i : p$ consisting of n rules of the form $i : p(X) \hookleftarrow \mathcal{B}_k$, with $k \in$

---

[3] A *built-in atom* is of the form $X\theta Y$, where X and Y are terms and θ is a comparison predicate.

$[1..n]$, can be rewritten into $2*n$ rules of the form $i:p_k(X) \hookleftarrow \mathcal{B}_k$ and $i:p(X) \leftarrow i:p_k(X)$, with $k \in [1..n]$. Given a P2P system $\mathcal{PS} = \{\mathcal{P}_1,\ldots,\mathcal{P}_n\}$, where $\mathcal{P}_i = \langle \mathcal{D}_i, \mathcal{LP}_i, \mathcal{MP}_i, \mathcal{IC}_i \rangle$, $\mathcal{D}, \mathcal{LP}, \mathcal{MP}$ and $\mathcal{IC}$ denote, respectively, the global sets of ground facts, standard rules, mapping rules and integrity constraints, i.e. $\mathcal{D} = \bigcup_{i \in [1..n]} \mathcal{D}_i$, $\mathcal{LP} = \bigcup_{i \in [1..n]} \mathcal{LP}_i$, $\mathcal{MP} = \bigcup_{i \in [1..n]} \mathcal{MP}_i$ and $\mathcal{IC} = \bigcup_{i \in [1..n]} \mathcal{IC}_i$. In the rest of this paper, with a little abuse of notation, $\mathcal{PS}$ will be also denoted both with the tuple $\langle \mathcal{D}, \mathcal{LP}, \mathcal{MP}, \mathcal{IC} \rangle$ and the set $\mathcal{D} \cup \mathcal{LP} \cup \mathcal{MP} \cup \mathcal{IC}$; moreover whenever the peer is understood, the peer identifier will be omitted.

3.2 Semantics

This section reviews the *Preferred Weak Model* semantics for P2P systems [11,12] which is based on a special interpretation of mapping rules. Observe that for each peer $\mathcal{P}_i = \langle \mathcal{D}_i, \mathcal{LP}_i, \mathcal{MP}_i, \mathcal{IC}_i \rangle$, the set $\mathcal{D}_i \cup \mathcal{LP}_i$ is a *positive normal program*, thus it admits just *one minimal model* that represents the *local knowledge* of $\mathcal{P}_i$. In this paper it is assumed that each peer is *locally consistent*, i.e. its local knowledge, say $\mathcal{K}_i$, satisfies $\mathcal{IC}_i$ ($\mathcal{K}_i \models \mathcal{IC}_i$). Therefore, inconsistencies may be introduced just when the peer imports data from other peers. The intuitive meaning of a mapping rule $i : H \hookleftarrow j : \mathcal{B} \in \mathcal{MP}_i$ is that if the body conjunction $j : \mathcal{B}$ is *true* in the source peer $\mathcal{P}_j$ the atom $i : H$ can be imported in $\mathcal{P}_i$ only if it does not imply (directly or indirectly) the violation of some integrity constraint in $\mathcal{IC}_i$. The following example will clarify the meaning of mapping rules.

Example 2. Consider the P2P system in Fig. 2. $\mathcal{P}_2$ contains the fact $q(b)$, whereas $\mathcal{P}_1$ contains the fact $s(a)$, the mapping rule $p(X) \hookleftarrow q(X)$, the standard rules $r(X) \leftarrow p(X)$ and $r(X) \leftarrow s(X)$ and the constraint $\leftarrow r(X), r(Y), X \neq Y$. If the fact $p(b)$ is imported in $\mathcal{P}_1$, the fact $r(b)$ will be derived. As $r(a)$ is already true in $\mathcal{P}_1$, because it is derived from $s(a)$, the integrity constraint is violated. Therefore, $p(b)$ cannot be imported in $\mathcal{P}_1$ as it indirectly violates an integrity constraint. □

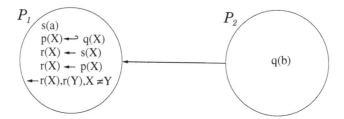

Fig. 2. A P2P system

Before formally presenting the preferred weak model semantics some notation is introduced. Given a mapping rule $r = H \hookleftarrow \mathcal{B}$, the corresponding standard logic rule $H \leftarrow \mathcal{B}$ will be denoted as $St(r)$. Analogously, given a set of mapping rules $\mathcal{MP}$, $St(\mathcal{MP}) = \{St(r) \mid r \in \mathcal{MP}\}$ and given a P2P system $\mathcal{PS} = \mathcal{D} \cup \mathcal{LP} \cup \mathcal{MP} \cup \mathcal{IC}$, $St(\mathcal{PS}) = \mathcal{D} \cup \mathcal{LP} \cup St(\mathcal{MP}) \cup \mathcal{IC}$.

Given an interpretation M, an atom H and a conjunction of atoms $\mathcal{B}$:

- $val_M(H \leftarrow \mathcal{B}) = val_M(H) \geq val_M(\mathcal{B})$,
- $val_M(H \hookleftarrow \mathcal{B}) = val_M(H) \leq val_M(\mathcal{B})$.

Therefore, if the body is *true*, the head of a standard rule *must* be *true*, whereas the head of a mapping rule *could* be *true*.

Intuitively, a *weak model* M of a P2P system $\mathcal{PS}$ is an interpretation that satisfies all standard rules, mapping rules and constraints of $\mathcal{PS}$ and such that each atom $H \in M[\mathcal{MP}]$ (i.e. each mapping atom) is *supported* from a mapping rule $H \hookleftarrow \mathcal{B}$ whose body $\mathcal{B}$ is satisfied by M. A *preferred weak model* is a weak model that contains a maximal subset of mapping atoms. This concept is justified by the assumption that it is *preferable* to import in each peer *as much knowledge as possible*.

Definition 2. (PREFERRED) WEAK MODEL. Given a P2P system $\mathcal{PS} = \mathcal{D} \cup \mathcal{LP} \cup \mathcal{MP} \cup \mathcal{IC}$, an interpretation M is a *weak model* for $\mathcal{PS}$ if $\{M\} = MM(St(\mathcal{PS}^M))$, where $\mathcal{PS}^M$ is the program obtained from $ground(\mathcal{PS})$ by removing all mapping rules whose head is *false* w.r.t. M.

Given two weak models M and N, M is said to *preferable* to N, and is denoted as $M \sqsupseteq N$, if $M[\mathcal{MP}] \supseteq N[\mathcal{MP}]$. Moreover, if $M \sqsupseteq N$ and $N \not\sqsupseteq M$, then $M \sqsupset N$. A weak model M is said to be *preferred* if there is no weak model N such that $N \sqsupset M$.

The set of weak models for a P2P system $\mathcal{PS}$ will be denoted by $\mathcal{WM}(\mathcal{PS})$, whereas the set of preferred weak models will be denoted by $\mathcal{PWM}(\mathcal{PS})$.   □

Observe that in the previous definition $St(\mathcal{PS}^M)$ is a positive normal program, thus it admits just one minimal model. Moreover, note that the definition of weak model presents interesting analogies with the definition of stable model.

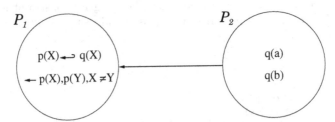

Fig. 3. The system $\mathcal{PS}$

Example 3. Consider the P2P system $\mathcal{PS}$ in Fig. 3. $\mathcal{P}_2$ contains the facts $q(a)$ and $q(b)$, whereas $\mathcal{P}_1$ contains the mapping rule $p(X) \hookleftarrow q(X)$ and the constraint $\leftarrow p(X), p(Y), X \neq Y$. The weak models of the system are $M_0 = \{q(a), q(b)\}$, $M_1 = \{q(a), q(b), p(a)\}$ and $M_2 = \{q(a), q(b), p(b)\}$, whereas the preferred weak models are M_1 and M_2.   □

An alternative characterization of the preferred weak model semantics, called *Preferred Stable Model* semantics, based on the rewriting of mapping rules into prioritized rules [7,25] has been proposed in [11,12].

4   Computing the Preferred Weak Model Semantics

The previous section has reviewed the semantics of a P2P system in terms of preferred weak models. This section presents an alternative characterization of the preferred weak model semantics that allows modeling a P2P system $\mathcal{PS}$ with a single logic program $Rew_t(\mathcal{PS})$. The logic program $Rew_t(\mathcal{PS})$ is then used as a computational vehicle to calculate the semantics of the P2P system as its (total) stable models correspond to the preferred weak models of $\mathcal{PS}$. With this technique the computation of the preferred weak models is performed in a *centralized way*, however the program $Rew_t(\mathcal{PS})$ will be used as a starting point for a *distributed technique*. Let's firstly introduce some preliminary concepts and definitions. Given an atom $A = i : p(x)$, A^t denotes the atom $i : p^t(x)$ and A^v denotes the atom $i : p^v(x)$. A^t will be called the *testing atom*, whereas A^v will be called the *violating atom*.

Definition 3. Given a conjunction

$$\mathcal{B} = A_1, \ldots, A_h, not\ A_{h+1}, \ldots, not\ A_n, B_1, \ldots, B_k, not\ B_{k+1}, \ldots, not\ B_m, \phi \quad (1)$$

where A_i $(i \in [1.. n])$ is a mapping atom or a derived atom, B_i $(i \in [1.. m])$ is a base atom and ϕ is a conjunction of built in atoms, we define

$$\mathcal{B}^t = A_1^t, \ldots, A_h^t, not\ A_{h+1}^t, \ldots, not\ A_n^t, B_1, \ldots, B_k, not\ B_{k+1}, \ldots, not\ B_m, \phi \quad (2)$$

□

From the previous definition it follows that given a negation free conjunction of the form

$$\mathcal{B} = A_1, \ldots, A_h, B_1, \ldots, B_k, \ldots, \phi \quad (3)$$

then

$$\mathcal{B}^t = A_1^t, \ldots, A_h^t, B_1, \ldots, B_k, \phi. \quad (4)$$

In the following, the rewriting of standard rules in $\mathcal{LP}$, mapping rules in $\mathcal{MP}$ and integrity constraints in $\mathcal{IC}$, is reported.

Definition 4. REWRITING OF A MAPPING RULE. Given a mapping rule[4] $m = H \leftarrowtail \mathcal{B}$, its rewriting is defined as $Rew_t(m) = \{H^t \leftarrow \mathcal{B};\ H \leftarrow H^t, not\ H^v\ \}.$ □

Intuitively, to check whether a mapping atom H generates some inconsistencies, if imported in its target peer, a testing atom H^t is imported in the same peer. Rather than violating some integrity constraint, it (eventually) generates the atom H^v. In this case H, cannot be inferred and inconsistencies are prevented.

Definition 5. REWRITING OF A STANDARD RULE.   Given a standard rule[4] $s = H \leftarrow \mathcal{B}$, its rewriting is defined as $Rew_t(s) = \{H \leftarrow \mathcal{B};\ H^t \leftarrow \mathcal{B}^t;\ A_1^v \vee \ldots \vee A_h^v \leftarrow \mathcal{B}^t, H^v\ \}.$ □

---

[4] Recall that $\mathcal{B}$ is of the form (3).

In order to find the mapping atoms that, if imported, generate some inconsistencies (i.e. in order to find their corresponding violating atoms), all possible mapping testing atoms are imported and the derived testing atoms are inferred. In the previous definition, if $\mathcal{B}^t$ (that is of the form (4)), is *true* and the violating atom H^v is *true*, then the body of the disjunctive rule is *true* and therefore it can be deduced that at least one of the violating atoms $A_1^v, \ldots, A_h^v$ is *true* (i.e. to avoid such inconsistencies at least one of atoms $A_1, \ldots, A_h$ cannot be inferred).

Definition 6. REWRITING OF AN INTEGRITY CONSTRAINT. Given an integrity constraint[5] $i = \ \leftarrow \mathcal{B}$, its rewriting is defined as $Rew_t(i) = \{A_1^v \vee \ldots \vee A_h^v \leftarrow \mathcal{B}^t\}$.   □

If the body $\mathcal{B}^t$ (that is of the form (2)), in the previous definition is *true*, then it can be deduced that at least one of the violating atoms $A_1^v, \ldots, A_h^v$ is *true*. This states that in order to avoid inconsistencies at least one of atoms $A_1, \ldots, A_h$ cannot be inferred.

Definition 7. REWRITING OF A P2P SYSTEM. Given a P2P system $\mathcal{PS} = \mathcal{D} \cup \mathcal{LP} \cup \mathcal{MP} \cup \mathcal{IC}$, then

- $Rew_t(\mathcal{MP}) = \bigcup_{m \in \mathcal{MP}} Rew_t(m)$
- $Rew_t(\mathcal{LP}) = \bigcup_{s \in \mathcal{LP}} Rew_t(s)$
- $Rew_t(\mathcal{IC}) = \bigcup_{i \in \mathcal{IC}} Rew_t(i)$
- $Rew_t(\mathcal{PS}) = \mathcal{D} \cup Rew_t(\mathcal{LP}) \cup Rew_t(\mathcal{MP}) \cup Rew_t(\mathcal{IC})$ □

Example 4. Consider again the P2P system $\mathcal{PS}$ presented in Example 3. From Definition (7) we obtain:

$Rew_t(\mathcal{PS}) = \{q(a); \ q(b);$
$\qquad\qquad p^t(X) \leftarrow q(X);$
$\qquad\qquad p(X) \leftarrow p^t(X), not \ p^v(X);$
$\qquad\qquad p^v(X) \vee p^v(Y) \leftarrow p^t(X), p^t(Y), X \neq Y\}$

The stable models of $Rew_t(\mathcal{PS})$ are:

$M_1 = \{q(a), q(b), p^t(a), p^t(b), p^v(a), p(b)\},$
$M_2 = \{q(a), q(b), p^t(a), p^t(b), p(a), p^v(b)\}.$ □

Definition 8. TOTAL STABLE MODEL. Given a P2P system, $\mathcal{PS}$, and a stable model M for $Rew_t(\mathcal{PS})$, the interpretation obtained by deleting from M its violating and testing atoms, denoted as $T(M)$, is a *total stable model* of $\mathcal{PS}$. The set of total stable models of $\mathcal{PS}$ is denoted as $TSM(\mathcal{PS})$.   □

Example 5. For the P2P system $\mathcal{PS}$ reported in Example 4, $TSM(\mathcal{PS}) = \{\{q(a), q(b), p(b)\}, \{q(a), q(b), p(a)\}\}.$ □

---

[5] Recall that $\mathcal{B}$ is of the form (1).

The following theorem shows the equivalence of preferred stable models and preferred weak models.

Theorem 1. *For every P2P system* $\mathcal{PS}$, $\mathcal{TSM}(\mathcal{PS}) = \mathcal{PWM}(\mathcal{PS})$.   □

Observe that this rewriting technique allows computing the preferred weak models of a P2P system with an arbitrary topology. The topology of the system will be encoded in its rewriting. As an example, if a system $\mathcal{PS}$ is *cyclic*, its rewriting $Rew_t(\mathcal{PS})$ could be *recursive*.

5   Well Founded Model Semantics

As stated before, a P2P system may admit many preferred weak models (total stable models) whose computational complexity has been shown to be prohibitive. Therefore, a more pragmatic solution for assigning semantics to a P2P system that can be effectively implemented, is needed. Based on this observation, this section proposes the use of the *Well Founded Model Semantics* as a mean to obtain a deterministic model whose computation is guaranteed to be polynomial time.

In more details, the rewriting presented in Section 4 allows modeling a P2P system by a single disjunctive logic program. By assuming that this program is HCF, it can be rewritten into an equivalent normal program for which a well founded model semantics can be adopted. Such a semantics allows computing a deterministic model describing the P2P system, in a polynomial time by capturing the intuition that if an atom is *true* in a total stable (or preferred weak) *model* of the P2P system $\mathcal{PS}$ and is *false* in another one, then it is *undefined* in the well founded model.

Theorem 2. *Let* $\mathcal{PS} = \mathcal{D} \cup \mathcal{LP} \cup \mathcal{MP} \cup \mathcal{IC}$ *be a P2P system, then* $Rew_t(\mathcal{PS})$ *is HCF iff there are not two distinct atoms occurring in the body of a rule in* $ground(\mathcal{LP} \cup \mathcal{IC})$ *mutually dependent by positive recursion.*   □

In the rest of this section, it is assumed that each P2P system $\mathcal{PS}$ is such that $Rew_t(\mathcal{PS})$ is HCF. Such a system $\mathcal{PS}$ will be called an *HCF P2P system*. From the previous hypothesis, it follows that $Rew_t(\mathcal{PS})$ can be normalized as $\mathcal{SM}(Rew_t(\mathcal{PS})) = \mathcal{SM}(Normalized(Rew_t(\mathcal{PS})))$.

Definition 9. REWRITING OF AN HCF P2P SYSTEM.   Given an HCF P2P system $\mathcal{PS}$, $Rew_w(\mathcal{PS}) = Normalized(Rew_t(\mathcal{PS}))$.   □

Therefore, the preferred weak models of an HCF P2P system, $\mathcal{PS}$, correspond to the stable models of the normal program $Rew_w(\mathcal{PS})$. The next step is to adopt for $Rew_w(\mathcal{PS})$ a three-valued semantics that allows computing *deterministic models* and in particular the *well founded model*.

Definition 10. WELL FOUNDED SEMANTICS.   Given an HCF P2P system, $\mathcal{PS}$, and the well founded model of $Rew_w(\mathcal{PS})$, say $\langle T, F \rangle$, the *well founded model semantics* of $\mathcal{PS}$ is given by $\langle \mathcal{T}(T), \mathcal{T}(F) \rangle$.   □

Example 6. Consider again the HCF P2P system, $\mathcal{PS}$, reported in Example 4. The rewriting of $\mathcal{PS}$ is:

$$Rew_w(\mathcal{PS}) = \{q(a);\ q(b);$$
$$p^t(X) \leftarrow q(X);$$
$$p(X) \leftarrow p^t(X), not\ p^v(X);$$
$$p^v(X) \leftarrow p^t(X), p^t(Y), X \neq Y, not\ p^v(Y);$$
$$p^v(Y) \leftarrow p^t(X), p^t(Y), X \neq Y, not\ p^v(X)\}$$

The well founded model of $Rew_w(\mathcal{PS})$ is $\langle \{q(a), q(b), p^t(a), p^t(b)\}, \emptyset \rangle$ and the well founded semantics of $\mathcal{PS}$ is given by $\langle \{q(a), q(b)\}, \emptyset \rangle$. The atoms $q(a)$ and $q(b)$ are *true*, while the atoms $p(a)$ and $p(b)$ are *undefined*.   □

The evaluation of the program $Rew_w(\mathcal{PS})$ allows computing the well founded semantics of $\mathcal{PS}$ in a *centralized way* and in a *polynomial time*. A future work will present a technique allowing to compute the well founded model in a distributed way.

6   Query Answers and Complexity

As regards the complexity of computing preferred weak models, the results have been presented in [11,12] by considering analogous results on stable model semantics for prioritized logic programs [25]. Specifically, it has been shown that deciding whether an atom is *true* in some preferred weak model is Σ_2^p-complete, whereas deciding whether an atom is *true* in every preferred weak model is Π_2^p-complete.

The rest of this section presents the corresponding results for HCF P2P systems.

Theorem 3. *Let* $\mathcal{PS}$ *be an HCF P2P system, then*

1. *Deciding whether an interpretation is a preferred weak model of* $\mathcal{PS}$ *is P-time.*
2. *Deciding whether an atom is* true *in some preferred weak model of* $\mathcal{PS}$ *is $\mathcal{NP}$-complete.*
3. *Deciding whether an atom is* true *in every preferred weak model of* $\mathcal{PS}$ *is co$\mathcal{NP}$-complete.*
4. *Deciding whether an atom is* true *in the well founded model of* $\mathcal{PS}$ *is P-time.*   □

Observe that the complexity of query answering reduces w.r.t. the general case presented in [11,12] of one level in the polynomial hierarchy. Moreover, if the well founded model semantics is adopted it becomes polynomial time. As for a further research it is planned to investigate, the structure of the P2P systems whose rewriting let to an HCF program.

7   Related Work

Recently, there have been several proposals considering the issue of managing the coordination, the integration of information as well as the computation of queries in an open ended network of distributed peers [4,5,8,10,14,15,21,23,27].

The problem of integrating and querying databases in a P2P environment has been investigated in [10,15]. In both works peers are modeled as autonomous agents which can export only data belonging to their knowledge, i.e. data which are *true* in all possible scenarios (models).

In [10] a new semantics for a P2P system, based on epistemic logic, is proposed. The paper also shows that the semantics is more suitable than traditional semantics based on FOL (First Order Logic) and proposes a sound, complete and terminating procedure that returns the certain answers to a query submitted to a peer.

In [15] a characterization of P2P database systems and a model-theoretic semantics dealing with inconsistent peers is proposed. The basic idea is that if a peer does not have models all (ground) queries submitted to the peer are *true* (i.e. are *true* with respect to all models). Thus, if some databases are inconsistent it does not mean that the entire system is inconsistent.

In [21] the problem of schema mediation in a Peer Data Management System (PDMS) is investigated. The semantics of query answering in a PDMS is defined by extending the notion of certain answer.

In [27] several techniques for optimizing the reformulation of queries in a PDMS are presented. In particular the paper presents techniques for pruning semantic paths of mappings in the reformulation process and for minimizing the reformulated queries. The design of optimization methods for query processing over a network of semantically related data is also investigated in [23].

As for a comparison with previous approaches in the literature, let's consider again the P2P system reported in Example 1. The approach, here proposed, states that either $q(a)$ or $q(b)$ could be imported in $\mathcal{P}_2$, otherwise a violation occurs. Anyhow, whatever is the derivation in $\mathcal{P}_2$, s is derived in $\mathcal{P}_1$ while t is not derived; thus the atoms s and t are, respectively, *true* and *false* in $\mathcal{P}_1$.

The epistemic semantics proposed in [10] states that both the atoms $q(a)$ and $q(b)$ are imported in the peer $\mathcal{P}_2$ which becomes inconsistent. In this case the semantics assumes that the whole P2P system is inconsistent and every atom is *true* as it belongs to all minimal models. Consequently, t and s are *true*.

The semantics proposed in [15] assumes that only $\mathcal{P}_2$ is inconsistent as it has no model. Thus, as the atoms $q(a)$ and $q(b)$ are *true* in $\mathcal{P}_2$ (they belong to all models of $\mathcal{P}_2$), then the atoms $p(a)$ and $p(b)$ can be derived in $\mathcal{P}_1$ and finally t and s are *true*.

8   Conclusion

This paper contributes to the proposal of a logic based framework for data integration and query answering in P2P systems. Each peer, participating in a

P2P system, can both provide or consume data and has information about its neighbors, i.e. about the peers that are reachable and can provide data of interest. Queries can be posed to any peer in the system and the answer is provided by using locally stored data and all the information that can be consistently imported from its neighbors. This paper, continues the work in [11,12] in which a new semantics, called the preferred weak model semantics, has been proposed. In more details, it stems from the observation that in practical applications a pragmatic solution, whose computational complexity does not result to be prohibitive, is needed for assigning semantics to a P2P system. To this aim, the paper has proposed a rewriting technique that allows modeling a P2P system $\mathcal{PS}$ into a unique logic program $Rew_t(\mathcal{PS})$, whose (total) stable models correspond to the preferred weak models of $\mathcal{PS}$. Moreover, the paper has presented the well founded model semantics, that allows obtaining a deterministic model whose computation is polynomial time. This model is obtained by evaluating the normal version of $Rew_t(\mathcal{PS})$, called $Rew_w(\mathcal{PS})$, with a three-valued semantics. The evaluation of the program $Rew_w(\mathcal{PS})$ allows computing the well founded semantics of $\mathcal{PS}$ in a *centralized way*. A future work will present a technique allowing to compute the well founded model in a distributed way. Finally, the paper has presented some results on the complexity of query answering under the proposed semantics.

References

1. Arenas, M., Bertossi, L., Chomicki, J.: Consistent Query Answers in Inconsistent Databases. In: Symposium on Principles of Database Systems, pp. 68–79 (1999)
2. Baral, C., Lobo, J., Minker, J.: Generalized Disjunctive Well-Founded Semantics for Logic Programs. Annals of Mathematics and Artificial Intelligence 5(2-4), 89–131 (1992)
3. Ben-Eliyahu, R., Dechter, R.: Propositional Sematics for Disjunctive Logic Programs. In: Joint International Conference and Symposium on Logic Programming, pp. 813–827 (1992)
4. Bernstein, P.A., Giunchiglia, F., Kementsietsidis, A., Mylopulos, J., Serafini, L., Zaihrayen, I.: Data Management for Peer-to-Peer Computing: A Vision. In: WebDB, pp. 89–94 (2002)
5. Bertossi, L., Bravo, L.: Query Answering in Peer-to-Peer Data Exchange Systems. In: Extending Database Technology Workshops (2004)
6. Brewka, G., Eiter, T.: Preferred Answer Sets for Extended Logic Programs. Artificial Intelligence 109(1-2), 297–356 (1999)
7. Brewka, G., Niemela, I., Truszczynski, M.: Answer Set Optimization. In: International Joint Conference on Artificial Intelligence, pp. 867–872 (2003)
8. Calì, A., Calvanese, D., De Giacomo, G., Lenzerini, M.: On the decidability and complexity of query answering over inconsistent and incomplete databases. In: Symposium on Principles of Database Systems, pp. 260–271 (2003)
9. Calvanese, D., De Giacomo, G., Lembo, D., Lenzerini, M., Rosati, R.: Inconsistency Tolerance in P2P Data Integration: an Epistemic Logic Approach. In: International Symposium on Database Programming Languages, pp. 692–697 (2004)

10. Calvanese, D., De Giacomo, G., Lenzerini, M., Rosati, R.: Logical foundations of peer-to-peer data integration. In: Symposium on Principles of Database Systems, pp. 241–251 (2004)
11. Caroprese, L., Greco, S., Zumpano, E.: A Logic Programming Approach to Querying and Integrating P2P Deductive Databases. In: The International Florida AI Research Society Conference, pp. 31–36 (2006)
12. Caroprese, L., Molinaro, C., Zumpano, E.: Integrating and Querying P2P Deductive Databases. In: International Database Engineering & Applications Symposium, pp. 285–290 (2006)
13. Fernàndez, J.A., Lobo, J., Minker, J., Subrahmanian, V.S.: Disjunctive LP + Integrity Constraints = Stable Model Semantics. Annals of Mathematics and Artificial Intelligence 8(3-4), 449–474 (1993)
14. Franconi, E., Kuper, G.M., Lopatenko, A., Zaihrayeu, I.: Queries and Updates in the coDB Peer to Peer Database System. In: International Conference on Very large Data Bases, pp. 1277–1280 (2004)
15. Franconi, E., Kuper, G.M., Lopatenko, A., Zaihrayeu, I.: A Robust Logical and Computational Characterisation of Perto-Peer Database Systems. In: International Workshop on Databases, Information Systems and Peer-to-Peer Computing, pp. 64–76 (2003)
16. Gelfond, M., Lifschitz, V.: The Stable Model Semantics for Logic Programming. In: Joint International Conference and Symposium on Logic Programming, pp. 1070–1080 (1988)
17. Van Gelder, A.: The Alternating Fixpoint of Logic Programs with Negation. In: Symposium on Principles of Database Systems, pp. 1–10 (1989)
18. Greco, G., Greco, S., Zumpano, E.: Repairing and Querying Inconsistent Databases. Transactions on Knowledge and Data Engineering, 1389–1408 (2003)
19. Gribble, S., Halevy, A., Ives, Z., Rodrig, M., Suciu, D.: What can databases do for peer-to-peer? In: WebDB, pp. 31–36 (2001)
20. Lonc, Z., Truszczynski, M.: On the Problem of Computing the Well-Founded Semantics. Computational Logic, 673–687 (2000)
21. Halevy, A., Ives, Z., Suciu, D., Tatarinov, I.: Schema mediation in peer data management systems. In: International Conference on Database Theory, pp. 505–516 (2003)
22. Lenzerini, M.: Data integration: A theoretical perspective. In: Symposium on Principles of Database Systems, pp. 233–246 (2002)
23. Madhavan, J., Halevy, A.Y.: Composing mappings among data sources. In: International Conference on Very Large Data Bases, pp. 572–583 (2003)
24. Pradhan, S., Minker, J.: Using Priorities to Combine Knowledge Bases. International Journal of Cooperative Information Systems 5(2-3), 333 (1996)
25. Sakama, C., Inoue, K.: Prioritized logic programming and its application to commonsense reasoning. Artificial Intelligence 123(1-2), 185–222 (2000)
26. Seipel, D., Minker, J., Ruiz, C.: Model Generation and State Generation for Disjunctive Logic Programs. Journal of Logic Programming 32(1), 49–69 (1997)
27. Tatarinov, I., Halevy, A.: Efficient Query reformulation in Peer Data Management Systems. In: SIGMOD, pp. 539–550 (2004)

Learning from Imprecise Granular Data Using Trapezoidal Fuzzy Set Representations

Ronald R. Yager

Machine Intelligence Institute
Iona College
New Rochelle, NY 10801
yager@panix.com

Abstract. We discuss the role and benefits of using trapezoidal fuzzy representations of granular information. We focus on the use of level sets as a tool for implementing many operations involving trapezoidal fuzzy sets. Attention is particularly brought to the simplification that the linearity of the trapezoid brings in that it often allows us to perform operations on only two level sets. We investigate the classic learning algorithm in the case when our observations are granule objects represented as trapezoidal fuzzy sets. An important issue that arises is the adverse effect that very uncertain observations have on the quality of our estimates. We suggest an approach to addressing this problem using the specificity of the observations to control its effect. Throughout this work particular emphasis is placed on the simplicity of working with trapezoids while still retaining a rich representational capability.

1 Introduction

The coming of age of the semantic web and other related technologies is making available huge amounts of granular, linguistic and imprecise, information. Our interest here is on the task of providing for the efficient representation and manipulation of granular information for learning and information fusion. We focus here on trapezoidal fuzzy subset as they can provide a very convenient object for the representation of granule information [1, 2] in many applications. This convenience is based on a number of features associated with trapezoidal fuzzy subsets.

One significant benefit of using trapezoidal representations occurs in the information input process where a user provides a formalization of some data or observation. Here starting with an imprecise perception or description of the value of some attribute the user must represent it in terms of some formal granular object. As noted by Zadeh [3, 4] this representation step affords the user considerable freedom in their selection of the representing granule. Various considerations can effect a user's choice of representation. Foremost among these is what Zadeh calls cointention [3], the ability of the representing object to convey the meaning of the concept it is being used to represent. We see that the form of the trapezoidal fuzzy subset allows the modeling of a wide class of granular type objects. Triangular, interval and point valued subsets are all special cases of trapezoids. Using trapezoids we also have the freedom of being or not having to be symmetric. Another positive feature of the trapezoid representation is

H. Prade and V.S. Subrahmanian (Eds.): SUM 2007, LNAI 4772, pp. 244–254, 2007.

the ease of acquiring the necessary parameters. Here we need only four parameters all of which are related to real features of the attribute being modeled. They are not cognitively complex features.

An additional consideration in selecting a representation of our datum is the facility with which the representing object can be manipulated in the context of the application. Many mathematical operations can easily be preformed using trapezoidal representations. Specifically many operations can be defined using level sets, which are intervals in the case of trapezoids. Furthermore these definitions often just make use of the end points of the intervals. Thus many operations on trapezoids can be performed just using the end points of intervals. A further significant advantage of the use of trapezoids is that working with level sets is greatly facilitated by the linearity of the trapezoid. There is a linear relationships between the bounding points of the level sets. This linearity often results in a situation in which we only need perform operations on two level sets to obtain a total implementation.

Our interest will be particularly on the role of trapezoids in the type of operations that occur in learning.

2 Basic Features of Trapezoidal Fuzzy Subsets

In figure 1 we show a standard normal trapezoidal fuzzy subset on the real line. As we see this fuzzy subset is specified by four parameters, a, b, c and d. An important feature of a trapezoid is its linear nature. Because of this many linear operations can be easily implemented with trapezoids.

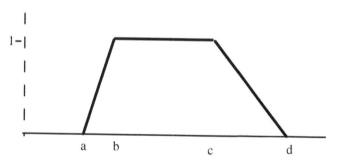

Fig. 1. Standard Normal Trapezoidal Fuzzy Subset

The membership grade F(x) of a normal trapezoidal fuzzy subset can be easily obtained from the four parameters, a, b, c, d

$$F(x) = 0 \quad x \leq a$$
$$F(x) = \frac{x - a}{b - a} \quad a < x \leq b$$
$$F(x) = 1 \quad b \leq x \leq c$$
$$F(x) = \frac{d - x}{d - c} \quad c < x \leq d$$
$$F(x) = 0 \quad x > d$$

The area under a standard trapezoidal fuzzy subset can be obtained using well know principles about the area of primary geometric figures. It is easy to shown that

$$\text{Area} = = 0.5 \, (c + d) - 0.5 \, (a + b)$$

In figure 2 we show some special cases of normal trapezoid fuzzy subsets. In figure 2.1 we see an interval fuzzy subset is a trapezoid where a = b and d = c. We see a triangular fuzzy subset is a trapezoid where b = c. We see a singleton is a trapezoid where a = b = c = d. In last figure is another special case trapezoidal fuzzy subset where where a = b. This is is clearly non–symmetric.

For the special cases of trapezoids the calculation of the area reduces to the following

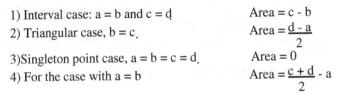

1) Interval case: a = b and c = d $\text{Area} = c - b$

2) Triangular case, b = c. $\text{Area} = \dfrac{d - a}{2}$

3)Singleton point case, a = b = c = d. $\text{Area} = 0$

4) For the case with a = b $\text{Area} = \dfrac{c + d}{2} - a$

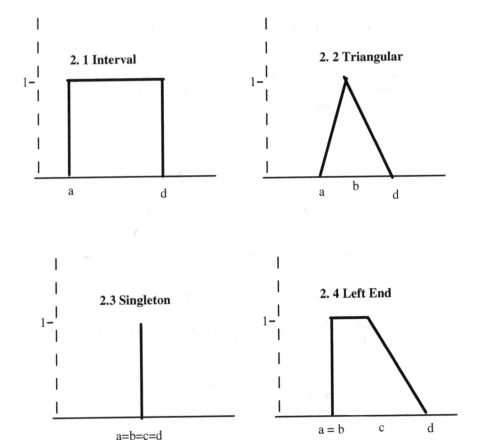

Fig. 2. Special Cases of Trapezoidal Fuzzy Sets

In point of fact the specification of a trapezoidal fuzzy subset requires five parameters rather than only four. In addition to a, b, c, and d we must also specify the largest membership grade α_{max}. In the preceding when we referred to normal fuzzy subsets we implicitly assumed $\alpha_{max} = 1$. In the sub-normal case, where $\alpha_{max} < 1$, while the general shape of the fuzzy subsets doesn't change the calculation of the membership grades and area must modified.

As can be easily shown in the case where $\alpha_{max} < 1$ then we get for the membership grade

$$E(x) = 0 \qquad\qquad\qquad\qquad x \leq a$$
$$E(x) = \alpha_{max}\left[\frac{x - a}{b - a}\right] \qquad\qquad a < x \leq b$$
$$E(x) = \alpha_{max} \qquad\qquad\qquad b < x \leq c$$
$$E(x) = \alpha_{max}\left[\frac{d - x}{d - c}\right] \qquad\qquad c < x \leq d$$
$$E(x) = 0 \qquad\qquad\qquad\qquad x > d$$

We see a very easy linear relationship between the membership grades of the normal fuzzy subset F and the subnormal fuzzy subset E, $E(x) = \alpha_{max}F(x)$. Here we see an example of the fundamental linearity of trapezoids.

An even more dramatic manifestation of the linear nature of trapezoids appears when we calculate the area under subnormal trapezoids. If E is a fuzzy subset the type shown in figure 1 except that its maximal membership grade is α_{max} then

$$\text{Area} = \alpha_{max}\left(\frac{c + d}{2} - \frac{a + b}{2}\right)$$

Here we clearly see the simplicity that the linearity associated with trapezoids brings.

3   Level Sets and Trapezoidal Fuzzy Subsets

It is the convenience and simplicity that the linearity associated with trapezoids brings to working with level sets that makes the trapezoidal fuzzy subset so useful for many applications. We recall that if F is a fuzzy subset the α-level set F_α is a crisp set such that $F_\alpha = \{x/F(x) \geq \alpha\}$.

We note that for any unimodal fuzzy subset of the real line, such as a trapezoid the level sets are interval subsets of the real line, $F_\alpha = [L_\alpha, U_\alpha]$. We note that for $\alpha_1 > \alpha_2$ then $F_{\alpha_1} \subseteq F_{\alpha_2}$. Here then $L_{\alpha_1} \geq L_{\alpha_2}$ and $U_{\alpha_1} \leq U_{\alpha_2}$.

Two special subsets associated with F are worth noting - the core and support of F, $\text{Core}(F) = \{x/F(x) = 1\}$ and $\text{Sup}(F) = \{x /F(x) \neq 0\}$. We see that since $F(x) \leq 1$ that the $\text{Core}(F) = \{x/F(x) \geq 1\} = F_1$. On the other hand $\text{Sup}(F) = F_\alpha$ as $\alpha \to 0$. By default we shall denote F_0 as $\text{Sup}(F)$.

In the following we shall assume normal fuzzy subsets, in this case $F_1 = [L_1, U_1] = [b, c]$ and $F_0 = [L_0, U_0] = [a, d]$.

As a result of the linearity of the trapezoid F any other level set can be obtained directly and easily from these two level sets. Consider $F_\alpha = [L_\alpha, U_\alpha]$ here with $1 - \alpha$ denoted as $\overline{\alpha}$ we have $L_\alpha = \alpha L_1 + \overline{\alpha} L_0 = \alpha b + \overline{\alpha} a$ and $U_\alpha = \alpha U_1 + \overline{\alpha} U_0 = \alpha c + \overline{\alpha} d$. Thus every α-level set can be obtained directly from the core and support of the trapezoid. Actually we can get the bounds of every level set from any two other level sets, F_{α_1} and F_{α_2}. Assume $F_{\alpha_1} = [L_{\alpha_1}, U_{\alpha_1}]$ and $F_{\alpha_2} = [L_{\alpha_2}, U_{\alpha_2}]$. We can show that for any $0 \le \alpha \le 1$

$$L_\alpha = \frac{1}{(\alpha_1 - \alpha_2)} [L_{\alpha_1} (\alpha - \alpha_2) + L_{\alpha_2} (\alpha_1 - \alpha)]$$

$$U_\alpha = \frac{1}{(\alpha_1 - \alpha_2)} [U_{\alpha_1} (\alpha - \alpha_2) + U_{\alpha_2} (\alpha_1 - \alpha)]$$

Thus we can uniquely specify the any trapezoidal fuzzy subset by providing any two level sets. From a pragmatic point of view it seems that requesting from a user the core set of F, F_1, and $F_{0.5} = \{x/F(x) \ge 0.5\}$ might be the most appropriate as users can more easily supply $F_{0.5}$ rather than F_0. We shall refer to the $F_{0.5}$ as the middle level set and denote it as F_m.

The specification of all level sets of a normal trapezoidal fuzzy subset can easily be to obtained using the middle and core sets. We see that if we have these two level sets $F_1 = [L_1, U_1] = [a, b]$ and $F_{0.5} = [L_{0.5}, U_{0.5}] = [g, h]$ then for any other α, $F_\alpha = [L_\alpha, U_\alpha]$ where $L_\alpha = 2 (a (\alpha - 0.5) + g (1 - \alpha))$ and $U_\alpha = 2 (b (\alpha - 0.5) + h (1 - \alpha))$.

Another important feature of the level sets is their role in the representation theorem. Let A be a fuzzy subset of X and let b [0, 1]. We define b ⊗ A to be a fuzzy subset E of X such that $E(x) = b A(x)$. Here we are multiplying the membership grades of A by b. Using this we can obtain the decomposition property of fuzzy sets [5]. Any fuzzy subset A can be expressed

$$A = \bigcup_{\alpha \in [0, 1]} \alpha \otimes A_\alpha$$

We see for any $x \in X$ that $A(x) = \underset{x \in A_\alpha}{\text{Max}} [\alpha]$.

4 Trapezoidal Preserving Operations

A useful feature for operations involving trapezoids is closure where an operation involving trapezoids results in another trapezoid. While the union and intersection of normal trapezoids are not trapezoids other operations satisfy this closure property. A particular interest here is on arithmetic operations.

The extension principle introduced by Zadeh [6] provides a method for extending arithmetic operators to fuzzy subsets [7]. Assume G: R × R → R is an arithmetic operation that is defined. Using the extension principle if A and B are two fuzzy subset of R then $G(A, B) = D$ where $D = \bigcup\limits_{x, y \in R} \{\frac{A(x) \wedge B(y)}{G(x, y)}\}$ and hence for any $z \in R$ we get

$$D(z) = \underset{\substack{\text{All } x, y \in R}}{\text{Max}} [A(x) \wedge B(y)].$$

$$\text{s}\cdot\text{t}\cdot$$

$$G(x, y) = z$$

It can be shown that this extended operator can be expressed in terms of level sets [6] if $D = G(A, B)$ then $D_\alpha = G(A_\alpha, B_\alpha)$. Since A_α and B_α are crisp subsets of R then $D_\alpha = \bigcup\limits_{\substack{x \in A_x \\ y \in B_x}} \{G(x, y)\}$. Thus the operation can be performed at each level. We further note that in the case of trapezoids since each level set is an interval the operation $D_\alpha = G(A_\alpha, B_\alpha)$ can be performed using interval operations. Here then if A and B are trapezoids then $A_\alpha = [L_{A_\alpha}, U_{A_\alpha}]$ and $B_\alpha = [L_{B_\alpha}, U_{B_\alpha}]$.

A question that naturally arises is what operations G always results in normal trapezoids when A and B are normal trapezoids. One necessary condition is that $D_\alpha = G(A_\alpha, B_\alpha)$ is always an interval. Another necessary condition is that with the core and support of D denoted respectively as $D_1 = [L_{D_1}, U_{D_1}]$ and $D_0 = [L_D, U_D]$ then for any other for any level set of D, $D_\alpha = [L_{D_\alpha}, U_{D_\alpha}]$ we have $L_{D_\alpha} = \alpha L_{D_1} + \overline{\alpha} L_D$ and $U_{D_\alpha} = \alpha U_{D_1} + \overline{\alpha} U_D$.

In order to see which operations are trapezoid preserving we must first provide some results from interval arithmetic. Consider two intervals $I_1 = [L_1, U_1]$ and $I_2 = [L_2, U_2]$. The basic operations of interval arithmetic are:

$$I_1 + I_2 = [L_1 + L_2, U_1 + U_2]$$
$$I_1 - I_2 = [L_1 - U_2, U_1 - L_2]$$
$$I_1 I_2 = [\text{Min}(L_1 L_2, L_1 U_2, U_1 L_2, U_1 U_2), \text{Max}((L_1 L_2, L_1 U_2, U_1 L_2, U_1 U_2)]$$
$$I_1 / I_2 = [\text{Min}(L_1/L_2, L_1/U_2, U_1/L_2, U_1/U_2), \text{Max}(L_1/L_2, L_1/U_2, U_1/L_2, U_1/U_2)]$$

If all the values are positive then we can simplify the calculations of $I_1 I_2$ and I_1/I_2. In particular $I_1 I_2 = [L_1 L_2, U_1 U_2]$ and $I_1/I_2 = [L_1/U_2, U_1/L_2]$.

Another property is that if $a \geq 0$ then $a I_1 = [aL_1, aU_1]$ and if $a < 0$ then $a I_1 = [aU_1, aL_1]$.

Furthermore $\text{Min}(I_1, I_2) = [\text{Min}(L_1, L_2), \text{Min}(L_1, L_2)]$ and $\text{Max}(I_1, I_2) = [\text{Max}(L_1, L_2), \text{Max}(L_1, L_2)]$.

We observe all the above arithmetic operations result in intervals.

We can consider some more complex operation. If w_1 and w_2 are non-negative values then

$$w_1I_1 + w_2I_2 = [w_1L_1 + w_2L_2, w_1U_1 + w_2U_2]$$
$$w_1I_1 - w_2I_2 = [w_1L_1 - w_2U_2, w_2U_1 - w_2U_2]$$

Let us now consider the trapezoidal preserving nature of these preceding operations. While the multiplication and division of trapezoids is not trapezoidal preserving.we now indicate an important operation which is trapezoidal preserving [8].

Theorem: If A and B are two trapezoids then $D = w_1A + w_2B$ is a trapezoid.

Essentially we have shown that for linear operators G, G(A, B) are trapezoids. More generally it can be shown that if A_1, A_1, ...A_n are normal trapezoids then

$$D = w_1A_1 + w_2A_2 + \ w_nA_n$$

is a normal trapezoid.

In the preceding we have indicated that linear arithmetic operations are trapezoidal preserving. That is operation such as weighted averages of trapezoids lead to trapezoids. Not only are they trapezoidal preserving but are easily implemented by simply performing the arithmetic operation on the end points of two level sets. With this facility it appears that trapezoidal fuzzy subsets can often provide a very useful representation of granular information. Furthermore we feel that the using the $\alpha = 1$ and $\alpha = 0.5$ level sets are perhaps the easiest level sets for a use to describe. Here they just must the end points of these represented interval.

5 Learning from Granular Observations

An important problem in many modern domains is learning from observations. This fundamental to data mining. We now show the facility for performing this task with granular observations using trapezoidal representations.

Assume V is variable whose domain X is a subset [a, b] of the real line. Let E be the current estimate of the value of V and let D be new observation of the value of V. In this case a common approach for obtaining a new estimate F of the value of V is [9, 10]

$$F = E + \lambda(D - E) = \lambda D + \bar{\lambda}E$$

where $\lambda \in [0, 1]$ is our learning rate. The larger λ the faster the learning but the more the system is prone to sporadic observations. We shall consider the situation in which our observations are granular. Here we shall use normal trapezoids as our representation of both the granular observations and the learned values. In the following we denote the level sets associated with E, F and D as $E_\alpha = [L\_E_\alpha, U\_E_\alpha]$, $F_\alpha = [L\_F_\alpha, U\_F_\alpha]$ and $D_\alpha = [L\_D_\alpha, U\_D_\alpha]$ respectively.

Since the calculation of $F = \lambda D + \bar{\lambda} E$ is a linear operation we can completely determine F by calculating F_α for any two level sets In this case any level set F_α can simply be obtained as

$$F_\alpha = [\lambda L\_D_\alpha + \bar{\lambda} L\_E_\alpha, \lambda U\_D_\alpha + \bar{\lambda} U\_E_\alpha]$$

Thus to completely determine F all we need calculate is

$$F_1 = [\lambda L\_D_1 + \bar{\lambda}\, L\_E_1,\ \lambda U\_D_1 + \bar{\lambda}\, U\_E_1]$$
$$F_{0.5} = [\lambda L\_D_{0.5} + \bar{\lambda}\, L\_E_{0.5},\ \lambda U\_D_{0.5} + \bar{\lambda}\, U\_E_{0.5}]$$

We illustrate the preceding with the following example

Example: In the following we let the domain of V, $X = [0, 10]$. Assume the current estimate E is expressed by the following two level set $E_1 = [4, 6]$ and $E_{0.5} = [3, 7]$. We further assume our granular observation D is described using the level sets $D_1 = [5, 8]$ and $D_{0.5} = [4, 10]$. Using a learning rate $\lambda = 0.2$ we obtain that our new estimate F has level sets

$$F_1 = [(.2)(5) + (.8)(4),\ ((2)8 + (.8)6] = [4.2, 6.4]$$
$$F_{0.5} = [(.2)(4) + (8)7,\ (.2)(10) + (.8)7] = [3.2, 7.6]$$

We further recall that if $F_1 = [L_1, U_1]$ and $F_{0.5} = [L_M, U_M]$ then for any level set $F_\alpha = [L_\alpha\ U_\alpha]$ we have

$$L_\alpha = (2L_1(\alpha - 1/2) + 2L_M(1 - \alpha)$$
$$U_\alpha = (2U_1(\alpha - 1/2) + 2U_M(1 - \alpha)$$

Thus in this case

$$L_\alpha = (2)(4.2)(\alpha - 1/2) + 2(3.2)(1 - \alpha) = 2.2 + 2\alpha$$
$$U_\alpha = (2)(6.4)(\alpha - 1/2) + 2(7.6)(1 - \alpha) = 8.8 - 2.4\alpha$$

Here then for example $F0 = [2.2, 8.8]$.

The simplicity of these calculations can not be over emphasized. Furthermore while we have worked with F_1 and $F_{0.5}$ the calculations could have just as easily been performed with with any level sets such as F_1 and F_0.

6 Managing the Imprecision in Granular Observations

When working with granular information as opposed to precise values there is one additional aspect that must be considered in the process of estimating the value of a variable. This aspect revolves around the uncertainty or quality associated with our estimate. Consider three examples of estimates of V, A, B, C. Assume there associated level sets are

$$A_1 = [5, 5] \text{ and } A_{0.5} = [5, 5]$$
$$B_1 = [4, 8] \text{ and } B_{0.5} = [3, 10]$$
$$C_1 = [0, 10] \text{ and } C_{0.5} = [0, 10]$$

It is clear that A provides more information about the value of V, it says it is precisely 5. While the case of B provides less information than A it is a better then that provided by C.

A well established measure of the amount of information contained in a fuzzy subset is the measure of specificity [11]. We shall use this to characterized the quality of information contained in our estimate. Let $A = [c, d]$ be an interval subset of the domain $X = [a, b]$. The specificity [11] of this interval valued fuzzy subset of is

$$Sp(A) = 1 - \frac{Length(A)}{b - a} = 1 - \frac{d - c}{b - a}$$

In this case of an interval it is simply inversely related to the size of the interval.

Using the extension principle we can extend this measure to a trapezoidal fuzzy subset F [8] .In particular it can be shown that

$$Sp(F) = 1 - \frac{Length(F_{0.5})}{b - a} = Sp(F_M)$$

It is simply the specificity of the 0.5 level set. This is very nice and simple.

As we noted the specificity is related to the uncertainty as well as the usefulness of the information. We see the bigger $Length(F_{0.5})$ the less specific.

Consider now the effect of learning on the specificity of the estimate. Using our learning algorithm with E our previous estimate, D our current observation and F our new estimate, all trapezoids, we have

$$F_\alpha = [\lambda L\_D_\alpha + \overline{\lambda} L\_E_\alpha, \lambda U\_D_\alpha + \overline{\lambda} U\_E_\alpha]$$

and hence

$$Length(F_\alpha) = \lambda(U\_D_\alpha L\_D_\alpha \overline{\lambda}(U\_E_\alpha - L\_E_\alpha)$$
$$Length(F_\alpha) = \lambda Length(D_\alpha) + \overline{\lambda} \, Length(E_\alpha)$$

Since $Sp(F) = 1 - \frac{Length(F_M)}{b - a}$ then

$$Sp(F) = 1 - \frac{\lambda \, Length(D_M) + \overline{\lambda} \, Length(E_M)}{b - c} = \lambda \, Sp(D) + \overline{\lambda} \, Sp(E)$$

Thus the specificity of the new estimate F is a weighted average of the specificity of the observation and the specificity of the current estimate.

What we can see is that very uncertain observations, those with small specificity (relatively large values for $Length(D_M)$) will tend to decrease the specificity of our estimate. As an extreme example consider the case when D is the completely uncertainty value, $D = [a, b]$. In this case $D_{0.5} = [a, b]$ and hence $Sp(D) = 0$. Thus here

$$Sp(F) = \lambda \, 0 + \overline{\lambda} \, Sp(E) = \overline{\lambda} \, Sp(E).$$

In this case we have just decreased our specificity without gaining any real information about the value of the variable.

It appears reasonable that we should try to reduce the effect of observations that are too imprecise on the learning process. In the following we shall suggest one method for accomplishing.

Consider the learning algorithm $F = E + \lambda(D - E)$ where λ is our learning rate, our openness to learn from the current observation D. We now suggest modifying the learning rate by a term $\sigma \in [0, 1]$ related to the specificities of D and E. We shall use as our modified learning algorithm

$$F = E + \lambda\sigma(D - E)$$

Here the σ is a term relating the specificities $Sp(E)$ and $Sp(D)$. Considerable possibilities exist for formulating σ here we shall just suggest some.

One possible form for σ is as shown in figure 3. In this we have

$$\sigma = 1 \qquad\qquad \text{if } Sp(D) \geq Sp(E)$$
$$\sigma = \frac{Sp(D)}{Sp(E)} \qquad \text{if } Sp(D) < Sp(E)$$

We can of course make the decay much slower when $Sp(D) \leq Sp(E)$. Instead of using $\frac{Sp(D)}{Sp(E)}$ we can use $(\frac{Sp(D)}{Sp(E)})^r$ where $r \in [0, 1]$.

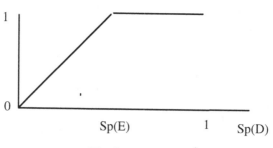

Fig. 3. Calculation of $\tilde{\sigma}$

More generally we can obtain σ using a fuzzy model [12] based on the relationship between $Sp(D)$ and $Sp(E)$. For example if

$$Sp(D) \text{ is } A_1 \text{ and } Sp(E) \text{ is } B_1 \text{ then } \sigma = g_1$$
$$Sp(D) \text{ is } A_2 \text{ and } Sp(E) \text{ is } B_2 \text{ then } \sigma = g_2$$
$$\dots\dots\dots\dots\dots$$
$$Sp(D) \text{ is } A_q \text{ and } Sp(E) \text{ is } B_q \text{ then } \sigma = g_q$$

We shall not discuss this further as we realize the method of determining σ may be context dependent. The important point we want to emphasize here is the need for controlling the effect of new observations based upon their uncertainty or quality.

7 Conclusion

We discussed the role and benefits of using trapezoidal representations of granular information. Throughout this work we emphasized the simplicity of working with trapezoids while still retaining a rich representational capability. Attention was particularly brought to the simplification that the linearity of the trapezoid brings by often allowing us to perform operations on only two level sets. We investigated the classic learning algorithm in the case when our observations are granule objects represented as trapezoidal fuzzy sets. An important issue that arose was the adverse effect that very uncertain observations have on the quality of our estimates. We suggested an approach to addressing this problem using the specificity of the observations to control its effect.

References

[1] Lin, T.S., Yao, Y.Y., Zadeh, L.A.: Data Mining, Rough Sets and Granular Computing. Physica-Verlag, Heidelberg (2002)

[2] Zadeh, L.A.: From imprecise to granular probabilities. Fuzzy Sets and Systems, 370–374 (2005)

[3] Zadeh, L.A.: Generalized theory of uncertainty (GTU)-principal concepts and ideas. Computational Statistics and Data Analysis (to appear)

[4] Zadeh, L.A.: Toward a generalized theory of uncertainty (GTU)-An outline. Information Sciences 172, 1–40 (2005)

[5] Zadeh, L.A.: Similarity relations and fuzzy orderings. Information Sciences 3, 177–200 (1971)

[6] Zadeh, L.: The concept of a linguistic variable and its application to approximate reasoning: Part 1. Information Sciences 8, 199–249 (1975)

[7] Dubois, D., Prade, H.: Operations on fuzzy numbers. International Journal of Systems Science 9, 613–626 (1978)

[8] Yager, R.R.: Using trapezoids for representing granular objects: applications to learning and OWA aggregation, Technical Report MII-2712 Machine Intelligence Institute, Iona College, New Rochelle, NY 10801 (2007)

[9] Zaruda, J.M.: Introduction to Artificial Neural Systems. West Publishing Co. St. Paul, MN (1992)

[10] Larose, D.T.: Discovering Knowledge in Data: An introduction to Data Mining. John Wiley and Sons, New York (2005)

[11] Yager, R.R.: On measures of specificity. In: Kaynak, O., Zadeh, L.A., Turksen, B., Rudas, I.J. (eds.) Computational Intelligence: Soft Computing and Fuzzy-Neuro Integration with Applications, pp. 94–113. Springer-Verlag, Berlin (1998)

[12] Yager, R.R., Filev, D.P.: Essentials of Fuzzy Modeling and Control. John Wiley, New York (1994)

Refining Aggregation Functions for Improving Document Ranking in Information Retrieval

Mohand Boughanem[1], Yannick Loiseau[2], and Henri Prade[1]

[1] IRIT-CNRS, Université de Toulouse, 118 route de Narbonne,
31062 Toulouse cedex9, France
{bougha,prade}@irit.fr
[2] LIMOS, Complexe scientifique des Cézeaux, 63177 Aubière cedex, France
loiseau@isima.fr

Abstract. Classical information retrieval (IR) methods use the sum for aggregating term weights. In some cases, this may diminish the discriminating power between documents because some information is lost in this aggregation. To cope with this problem, the paper presents an approach for ranking documents in IR, based on a refined vector-based ordering technique taken from multiple criteria analysis methods. Different vector representations of the retrieval status values are considered and compared. Moreover, another refinement of the sum-based evaluation that controls if a term is worth adding or not (in order to avoid noise effect) is considered. The proposal is evaluated on a benchmark collection that allows us to compare the effectiveness of the approach with respect to a classical one. The proposed method provides some improvement of the precision w.r.t Mercure IR system.

1 Introduction

The purpose of information retrieval (IR) is to find out documents that are relevant with respect to the user's information needs. The most commonly used method is to rank documents according to their relevance to a query stated by the user to represent these needs. The results of the performance evaluation of such a system depends on the rank of relevant documents among those retrieved by the IR system. The method used for rank-ordering the documents is therefore crucial for the result of the evaluation of a query.

In classical information retrieval systems, documents and queries are usually represented by sets of weighted terms. Term weights are computed from statistical analysis. More precisely, the weight of a term in a document is usually estimated by combining the term frequency tf in the document and the inverse document frequency of the term idf [1,2]. Weights in the query terms, on the other hand, express user preferences.

To evaluate to what extent a document is relevant to a query, a *retrieval status value* (rsv) is computed by aggregating the above weights for the terms present in the query, in a way that reflects the query structure (expressing disjunction or conjunction). Then documents are ranked on the basis of the *rsv*'s. Different

H. Prade and V.S. Subrahmanian (Eds.): SUM 2007, LNAI 4772, pp. 255–267, 2007.

kinds of aggregation functions have been discussed for combining the weights of the terms (pertaining to the same document) that are present in the considered query (assumed here to be without any user's preference weighting). Candidate operators for aggregation that are found in the literature are sum or average, similarity-based evaluation, p-norms [3,4], fuzzy logic conjunctive or disjunctive operations [5,6,7]. However, this type of approach leads to a loss of information (e.g. [8]), since individual keyword values are combined together.

A consequence is that it is impossible to discriminate documents having the same global relevance value. As an example, let us consider a three-terms query, aggregated by the average. This is only an example, and remarks similar to the ones below apply to other aggregation operators, including min and other fuzzy logic connectives. Let us suppose that the evaluation of the query $q = t_1 \wedge t_2 \wedge t_3$ on two documents d_1 and d_2 gives the following results (using normalized weights):

$$rsv(q, d_1) = \frac{w(t_1, d_1) + w(t_2, d_1) + w(t_3, d_1)}{3}$$
$$= \frac{0.1 + 0.7 + 0.7}{3} = 0.5;$$
$$rsv(q, d_2) = \frac{w(t_1, d_2) + w(t_2, d_2) + w(t_3, d_2)}{3}$$
$$= \frac{0.5 + 0.5 + 0.5}{3} = 0.5.$$

The issue is to know whether the user prefers a document with a medium relevance for all its criteria, or having a high relevance for most of them. This example not only raises an ambiguity problem between documents having apparently the same relevance, but more generally points out the problem of the impact of terms having weights much higher than others. If we want to privilege d_1 over d_2, this problem can be dealt with by using operators such as Ordered Weighted Average [5], which focus on the weights with high values and model quantifiers such as $most of$ [9,10,11], provided that such a quantifier is specified in the query. But this does not give a way of preferring d_2 to d_1 if we consider that one low weight can be a serious reason for discounting a document.

In this paper, we try another road. We no longer plan to aggregate the weights, but rather to rank-order the documents directly on the basis of the vectors of the weights of the terms present in the query, using decision making ideas that handle multiple criteria values (here replaced by the relevance value of each query term). The idea has been recently suggested by the authors in a conference paper [12], but new criteria for comparing vectors are considered, and a new experimentation is reported.

This alternative method is described in section 2. The section 3 presents the results of experiments carried out on CLEF collection [13].

2   Multicriteria Ranking

At least two approaches can be used to compare objects according to multiple criteria. The first one is to aggregate these criteria, then to compare the obtained values. This corresponds to the classical information retrieval approach, considering the relevance with respect to each query term relevance as a criterion to fulfil. The second method amounts to compare the criteria evaluation vectors directly by using a refinement of Pareto ordering ($(t_1, \ldots, t_n) >_{Pareto} (t'_1, \ldots, t'_n)$ iff $\forall i, t_i \geq t'_i$, and $\exists j, t_j > t'_j$). This later method is discussed in this paper. We briefly discuss the aggregation approach first.

2.1 Aggregation Schema

Query terms are usually weighted in order to allow the user to express his preferences and assess the importance of each term. Therefore, the result of the evaluation of a query on a document is a vector of the weights of the terms of the document present in the query, usually modified for taking into account preferences about the importance of the terms in the query. This is why classical IR aggregation methods use weighted conjunction (or disjunction) operators. In conjunctive queries, these operators can be weighted average or weighted minimum. Similar ideas apply to disjunctions as well.

However, this kind of aggregation is too restrictive. To relax the conjunction, ordered weighted operators, such as average (OWA[1] [5]) or minimum (OWmin [14]) have been introduced. The idea underlying this type of aggregation is to give low importance to the smallest weights in the evaluation vector, thus minimizing the impact of small terms, which amounts to model a *most of* quantifier (e.g. [11]).

The *OWmin* operator uses an auxiliary vector of levels of importance in order to minimize the impact of low weighted terms on the final relevance value. Thus, as for OWA, the term weights vectors are ordered and discounted by importance levels, using the minimum instead of the average for computing the global evaluation.

Two weighting methods are considered, based on Dienes implication and on Gödel implication respectively (e.g. [14]). For a vector $T = t_1, \ldots, t_n$ representing the indexing weights for a document, t_i is the relevance degree between the ith query term and the document. The vector is assumed to be decreasingly ordered (i.e. $t_i \geq t_{i+1}$). Let $W = (w_1, \ldots, w_n)$ be the level of importance vector, also assumed to be decreasingly ordered, i.e. $w_i \geq w_{i+1}$, with $w_1 = 1$. The idea is to give more importance (w_i high) to the terms with a high relevance degree. The *OWmin* aggregation using Dienes implication will be:

$$OWmin_D(T, W) = \min_i(\max(t_i, 1 - w_i))$$

while the Gödel implication is defined by

$$w_i \rightarrow t_i = \begin{cases} 1 \text{ if } w_i \leq t_i \\ t_i \text{ otherwise} \end{cases}$$

which gives:

$$OWmin_G(T, W) = \min_i(w_i \rightarrow t_i)$$

---

[1] Ordered weighted averaging operators.

In both cases, if the smallest w_i's are zero, these weighted aggregations amount in practice to restrict the minimum to the t_i's with high values (since small t_i's will be replaced by 1 in the aggregation, and the high values of t_i's, corresponding to values of w_i's equal or close to 1, will remain unchanged).

However, as already said, we want to rank-order documents by taking advantage of the full weights vector associated with each document, rather than using an aggregated value. This means that we keep the idea of using weights for modifying the indexing weights and restricting the focus of the evaluation, but we no longer compute an aggregated value (taken above as the minimum).

In order to compare vectors, the classical Pareto partial ordering has to be refined, since no pairs of documents should remain incomparable. In the following, we use refinements of the *min* or the *sum* operations, which do refine the Pareto ordering, to be compared with the sum operation, which is the classical operator used in IR.

2.2 Refining the Minimum Aggregation

There exist two noticeable refinements of the *min* operation, called *discrimin* and *leximin*, see e.g. [15,16]. They allow to distinguish between vectors having the same minimal value.

Discrimin: Two evaluation vectors are compared using only their distinct components. Thus, identical values having the same place in both vectors are dropped before aggregating the remaining values with a conjunction operator. Thus, only discriminating term weights are considered. In the context of information retrieval, given two vectors representing the weights of terms in query q for documents d_1 and d_2, expressing term-document relevance. For instance:

$$rsv(q, d_1) = (1, 0.5, 0.1, 0.3),$$
$$rsv(q, d_2) = (0.2, 0.7, 0.1, 1).$$

Using *min* as an aggregation, these two vectors would get the same score. The *discrimin* procedure "drops" the third term, giving $rsv(q, d_1) = 0.3$ and $rsv(q, d_2) = 0.2$ and allowing to rank these documents.

Leximin: It is a *discrimin* applied on vectors with increasingly re-ordered components. Considering two vectors:

$$rsv(q, d_1) = (1, 0.5, 0.1, 0.2),$$
$$rsv(q, d_2) = (0.2, 0.7, 0.1, 1).$$

Using the discrimin, both values are 0.2. Since the leximin sorts the values before comparing them, the 0.2 values are also dropped, giving $rsv(q, d_2) = 0.7$ and $rsv(q, d_1) = 0.5$, thus ranking d_2 before d_1.

Formally speaking, the *leximin* order between two vectors $W = (w_1, \ldots, w_n)$ and $w' = (w'_1, \ldots, w'_n)$ where the w'_is and the w''_is are increasingly ordered is defined by $W >_{lex} W'$ iff $w_1 > w'_1$ or $\exists k$ such that $\forall i = 1, k \ w_i = w'_i$ and $w_{k+1} > w'_{k+1}$.

Note that such a refinement will be sensitive to the way the computed weights w_i and w_i' are rounded, since this clearly influences the fact that two weights may be regarded as equal.

2.3   Refining the Sum Aggregation

Despite the sum is an efficient way to aggregate the terms weights better than min aggregation, its use may lead to some problems as described in the introduction.

In this paper, we test a way to refine the sum by keeping track of individual weights information to some extent. The operator used is a truncated sum that progressively misses weights according to their values. Given the ordered vector of term weights $W = (w_1, \ldots, w_n)$, it amounts to the lexicographic ordering of vectors of the form $(w_1 + \cdots + w_n, w_1 + \cdots + w_{n-1}, \ldots, w_1 + w_2, w_1)$, for $w_1 \leq w_2 \leq \ldots \leq w_n$. Such an ordering is closely related to the notion of Lorenz dominance (see, e.g. [17]). Therefore, the sum of all weights is first considered, as in classical systems, the sum of $n-1$ weights if the two sums are equal, and so on.

Several variants could be thought of. The first one, called $LexiSum$, is the above one; the second one, called $LexiSum_R$ uses the vector $(w_1 + \cdots + w_n, w_2 + \cdots + w_n, \ldots, w_{n-1} + w_n, w_n)$ that deletes small weights first. Lastly, two other variants might be considered based on the comparison of vectors of the form $(w_1, w_1 + w_2, \ldots, w_1 + \cdots + w_{n-1}, w_1 + \cdots + w_n)$ and of the form $(w_n, w_n + w_{n-1}, \ldots, w_n + \cdots + w_2, w_n + \cdots + w_1)$ that progressively cumulate weights.

However, we shall not report tests about these two last proposals since the first one is formally equivalent to $leximin$ (up to some possible rounding effects), while the other privileges the $maximum$ of the $w_i's$.

3   Experimental Results

In this section, we present the results of experiments on the English subset of the CLEF2001[2] collection, in order to evaluate the merit of the vector-based ranking of documents.

3.1   Description of the Experiments

The goal of the experiment is to evaluate the potential enhancement of the global performance of the information retrieval system, and to compare the results that are obtained using several ranking methods with the one provided by a classical approach. It compares results obtained with several aggregation strategies, namely the weighted sum aggregation underlying the classical approach (used in Mercure [18]) and the different vector refinements of the sum, and the leximin-based ranking method that refines the minimum(possibly applied with an $OWmin$).

---

[2] Cross Language Evaluation Forum: http://www.clef-campaign.org

The Mercure information retrieval system. The proposed refined methods are compared to the results of the Mercure system [18]. In this system, the weight w_t of a term t for a document is computed using a formula derived from the *Okapi* system [19]:

$$w_t = \frac{tf}{0.2 + 0.7 \times \frac{dl}{\Delta_l} + tf} \times (\log(\frac{n_{tot}}{n})) \qquad (1)$$

where tf is the term frequency in the document, dl is the document length, Δ_l is the average document length in the collection, n_{tot} is the size of the collection and n is the number of documents containing the term.

The final similarity degree S_{qd} between a query q and a document d, giving the relevance of the document for the query, is computed as:

$$S_{qd} = \sum_{t \in q} \lambda_t \times w_{td}$$

where λ_t is an importance weight for the term in the query (here always 1) and w_{td} is the index term weight for document d, given by equation 1.

3.2   CLEF Collection

The collection used in this experimentation is the English part of the CLEF2001 collection, containing more than 110,000 articles from the 1994 *Los Angeles Times*.

During the indexing stage, terms frequencies are computed for each document. These terms are stemmed using the Porter algorithm [20], and stop-words (i.e. words that bring no information) are removed.

Together with the collection of documents, a set of topics, which are evaluated on the given documents by human experts, are available. These topics, identified by a number, are described by a title, a short description of the topic, and a narrative part pointing out relevance criteria. They are used as a basis for generating the queries to be evaluated by the IR system. Moreover, the documents estimated to be relevant by experts are provided for each topic.

As an example, the topic 41 is defined as:

title: Pesticides in Baby Food
description: Find reports on pesticides in baby food.
narrative part: Relevant documents give information on the discovery of pesticides in baby food. They report on different brands, supermarkets, and companies selling baby food which contains pesticides. They also discuss measures against the contamination of baby food by pesticides.

It may also happen that the description is much richer than the title, as in the example:

title: Israel/Jordan Peace Treaty
description: Find reports citing the names of the main negotiators of the Middle East peace treaty between Israel and Jordan and also documents giving detailed information on the treaty.

narrative part: A peace treaty was signed between Israel and Jordan on 26 October 1994 opening up new possibilities for diplomatic relations between the two countries. Relevant documents will give details of the treaty and/or will name the principal people involved in the negotiations.

where the description specifies that the names of the negotiators must be in relevant document. Note that this information is not present in the title, and that using only titles to generate queries can lead to retrieved documents that were not judged relevant by experts. On the other hand, adding all description terms may be too restrictive, as seen in section 4.

3.3   Evaluations and Results

To evaluate the approach, we used a set of 50 queries automatically built from the title of the topics (short queries) and the title and the description of the topics (long queries), considered as keywords conjunctions.

To estimate the quality of the information retrieval system, two measures are used. The recall is the ratio of relevant documents retrieved to those relevant in the collection, and the precision is the ratio of relevant documents among the documents retrieved. Since the precision at x, denoted Px, which is the ratio of relevant documents in the x first retrieved documents, is easier to estimate, it is usually used to represent the system performance. Precisions at 5, 10, etc. noted P5, P10, are thus computed. MAP is the mean average precision for a set of queries. An average precision of a query is obtained by averaging the precision values computed for each relevant retrieved document of rank x. Exact precision is the mean of R-precision for a set of queries. R-precision of a query is the precision after R documents have been retrieved, where R is the number of known relevant documents in the collection for the query.

Table 1. Precision of the Mercure system

	P5	P10	P15	P20	Exact	MAP
short queries	0.4851	0.3936	0.3319	0.2883	0.4352	0.4622
long queries	0.4936	0.3979	0.3418	0.3064	0.4874	0.5100

Comparison of ranking methods. We will evaluate the ranking method presented in sections 2 w.r.t. the one used in Mercure. To apply these ordered weightings, the vectors containing the weights of each query term in the document are decreasingly ordered. As the queries considered here do not introduce further preference levels, the ordered vectors are then weighted using a kind of *most of*-like operator as in section 2.1, based on Dienes or Gödel implications. This type of operator gives more importance to the highest term weights, minimizing the impact of the lowest ones. The weighting vector is computed according to the query length l, $w_i = 1$ if $i \le l/2$ and a decreasing linear function from 1 to 0 is used when i ranges between $l/2$ and l. Moreover, a threshold of

3 terms is kept with a weight of 1, to avoid too short queries. When two documents have the same relevance value, we compared them using the different lexicographic-based ordering method.

Moreover, the numerical precision of term degrees is not meaningful, since resulting from the normalization, which leads some values to differ only at the fifth decimal. Since the lexicographical comparisons need to decide if values are equal, the relevance degrees used between terms and documents have been rounded. The results depend on this rounding, and several precision levels have been tested to estimate the impact of the rounding on the system performances. We present here only the best results, obtained with one decimal value rounding.

We used 50 queries, using different aggregating and ranking methods, to estimate the document relevance degrees.

Table 2 shows the results of refined methods compared with the classical approach using the *sum*. Values are percentage of improvement.

Table 2. Improvement of multicriteria methods w.r.t the sum (in %)

	Ranking method	P5	P10	MAP
	$LexiSum_R$	0	-3.22663	-3.00736
	$LexiSum$	-0.865801	-2.15955	-3.59152
Short queries	$Leximin + OW_G$	-0.865801	-1.62602	-8.54608
	$Leximin + OW_D$	-0.865801	-2.69309	-9.75768
	$Leximin$	-1.75222	-2.69309	-8.71917
	$LexiSum_R$	**1.72204**	**4.8002**	0.588235
	$LexiSum$	0	0.527771	-1.11765
Long queries	$Leximin + OW_D$	-9.48136	-9.62553	-14.4902
	$Leximin$	-16.3695	-20.3317	-21.1569
	$Leximin + OW_G$	-18.0916	-20.8595	-22.5882

First of all, we notice that most of refined ordering procedures do not bring a significant benefit in terms of performances comparing to the classical *sum*, for both short and long queries, except for $Lexisum_R$ in the case of long queries.

We also clearly notice that both *Lexisum* and $Lexisum_R$ operators behave better than *Leximin* and its variants, specially for long queries. This is not surprising since *Lexim* and its variants perform an *exact matching*, *i.e.* a document is retrieved if and only if it contains all query terms. This is a hard constraint which is not suitable for IR, in particular because of the synonymy problem. Indeed a document could be relevant to a query even though it does not contain a given term of that query. This problem is even much more crucial for long queries. As it can be seen in Table 2, the performances of *Leximin* for long queries decrease up to 20%, which is not surprising since the long queries are more likely to contain terms that are not present in documents.

However, as *LexiSum* operators behaves as a *best matching* procedure they seem to be more suitable for IR. The results of $LexiSum_R$ for long queries are even better than those of the classical approach, improving P10 up to 4.8%. This last result is quite interesting in IR. Indeed as the precision at top documents is improved this implies that our approach is more suitable for high precision evaluation, where good precision at top retrieved documents is desirable. Indeed, it improves the number of relevant documents retrieved in the top of the list, but can miss some relevant documents at a lower rank. This improvement is thus obtained to the expense of the average performance.

As it was mentioned above, the length of queries seems to have different effects depending on the method used, from small improvement to huge deterioration. We recall that short queries are built from the title field only and they have 2.58 terms in average while long queries are built from both the title and the description fields and they have 6 terms in average. We have tried to better investigate this point by evaluating whether adding only spefic terms of the description field to long queries could have any impact. This evaluation is discussed in the next section.

4   Refined Sum by Expanding Queries

We recall that the queries are automatically built by extracting terms from a natural language description of the need, some of these terms can be useful or even necessary, but others can degrade the system, and are just adding noise. Indeed, these terms may to be not relevant for evaluating documents, being meta-descriptive terms that are never in documents, or cannot bring any additional information.

This suggests to build the query only with terms that are discriminant enough, that is terms having non-uniform weights among the retrieved documents. Indeed, terms having quite the same weights in all documents are not useful to discriminate them. This can be seen as a kind of blind relevance feedback, but terms are extracted from the topic description instead of the top retrieved documents themselves, and the terms selection is based on the variability of their weights with respect to possibly relevant documents.

We assume here that terms present in the titles of the topics are more likely relevant than the terms of the description.

The evaluation is done in two steps. First, the queries are built from topic titles only and submitted to the system. The second step identifies terms from the topic description that have non homogeneous weights in the 20 top retrieved documents. The lack of homogeneousness is established by comparing the maximum and the minimum weights of a term in the given documents. If the difference is greater than a chosen threshold, then the term is assumed to be able to discriminate more precisely documents, and its weight is therefore added to the current sum made of the weights of the title term and of the heterogeneous weights of description terms already handled. Documents are then re-ranked.

Figure 1 shows the average length of queries obtained with different values of required heterogeneity. This figure may be compared with Fig. 2, showing the repartition of the term/doc weights in the collection. Since most of the weights are between 0.05 and 0.35, the number of terms added to the queries stabilize for a difference greater than 0.3.

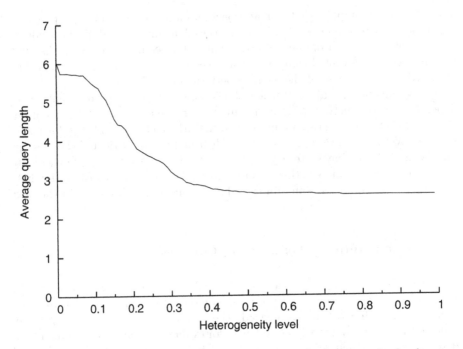

Fig. 1. Average length of queries depending on the heterogeneity level

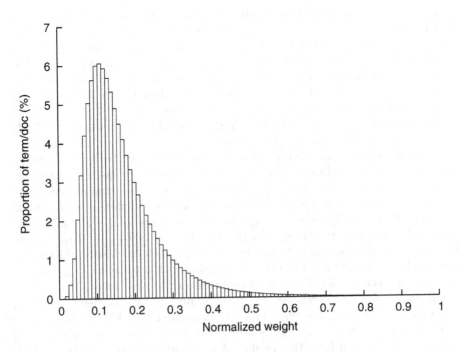

Fig. 2. Repartition of weights in the collection

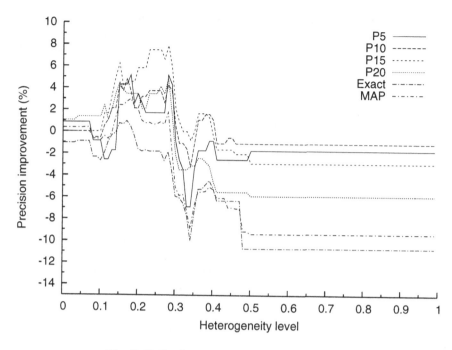

Fig. 3. Refined queries compared to long queries

The same correlation can be observed in Fig. 3. This figure shows the improvement in precisions obtained with the expanded queries compared to queries built using keywords from titles and descriptions, with respect to the heterogeneity level. The maximum of improvement is obtained for an intermediate level. We can deduce that short queries, using only keywords from titles, which are equivalent to an expansion with a level of 1, are not rich enough to retrieve all the relevant documents. On the other hand, adding too much terms from the description leads to consider terms that will not improve the search, such as terms used to describe the need but that cannot be considered as significant keywords, terms that are never in relevant documents, or terms having quite the same weight in all documents, and are therefore not discriminant. By adding these terms, the impact of relevant terms in the final sum used for ranking documents is minimised, leading to performances decreasing. Filtering these terms to keep only those that are susceptible to bring additional information, that is terms having sufficiently different weights among documents, minimise this side effect, and improve greatly the performances. Indeed, as shown in Fig. 3, the intermediate level of 0.28 improve the sum by 7.9% at P15 and by 5.17% at P5.

5   Conclusion

In this paper, we have presented a new approach to rank documents according to their relevance, using flexible aggregation methods and refined vector-based rank ordering methods. This approach was evaluated on a subset of the CLEF2001 collection. We compared the refined rank-ordering approach (possibly using some ordered weighting method) with the classical approach based on relevance scores aggregated by a weighted sum. These experiments suggest the effectiveness of the refined rank-ordering approach, as it outperforms sum aggregation methods to some extent.

We have also refined the sum aggregation by expanding queries only with description terms that are discriminant enough, to avoid the noise induced by having too long queries. This method obtained quite good results.

These first preliminary results indicate that ranking documents can take advantage of the full weights vector, rather than using an aggregated value. In future works, we plan to evaluate the approach on larger collections, such as TREC collections, and secondly to explore other variants of the flexible aggregation/ranking techniques. Indeed, the statistical result of system performance are heavily dependent on the collection. Moreover, the ranking techniques explored, from the decision making field, are only a subset of the one available.

Such a vector-based approach is not restricted to textual IR, but could be applied to any documents retrieval system using several criteria for describing them, such as in picture or audio sources.

References

1. Grossman, D., Frieder, O.: Information Retrieval: Algorithms and Heuristics. Kluwer Academic Publishers, Dordrecht (1998)
2. Salton, G., McGill, M.: Introduction to modern information retrieval. McGraw-Hill, New York (1983)
3. Salton, G., Fox, E., Wu, H.: Extended boolean information retrieval. Communications of the ACM 26, 1022–1036 (1983)
4. Robertson, S.E.: The probability ranking principle. Journal of Documentation 33, 294–304 (1977)
5. Yager, R.: On ordered weighted averaging aggregation operators in multicriteria decision making. IEEE Transactions on Systems, Man and Cybernetics 18, 183–190 (1988)
6. Dubois, D., Prade, H.: A review of fuzzy sets aggregation connectives. Information Sciences 3, 85–121 (1985)
7. Fodor, J., Yager, R., Rybalov, A.: Structure of uni-norms. International Journal of Uncertainty, Fuzzyness and Knowledge Based Systems 5, 411–427 (1997)
8. Schamber, L.: Relevance and information behavior. Annual Review of Information Science and Technology 29, 3–48 (1994)
9. Kraft, D.H., Bordogna, G., Pasi, G.: Fuzzy set techniques in information retrieval. In: Fuzzy Sets in Approximate Reasoning and Information Systems, pp. 469–510. Kluwer Academic Publishers, Dordrecht (1999)
10. Bordogna, G., Pasi, G.: Linguistic aggregation operators of selection criteria in fuzzy information retrieval. Int. J. Intell. Syst. 10, 233–248 (1995)
11. Losada, D., Díaz-Hermida, F., Bugarín, A., Barro, S.: Experiments on using fuzzy quantified sentences in adhoc retrieval. In: Handschuh, H., Hasan, M.A. (eds.) SAC 2004. LNCS, vol. 3357, pp. 1059–1064. Springer, Heidelberg (2004)

12. Boughanem, M., Loiseau, Y., Prade, H.: Improving document ranking in information retrieval using ordered weighted aggregation and leximin refinement. In: 4th Conf. of the European Society for Fuzzy Logic and Technology and 11me Rencontres Francophones sur la Logique Floue et ses Applications, EUSFLAT-LFA 2005, Barcelonnan, Spain pp. 1269–1274 (2005)
13. Peters, C., Braschler, M., Gonzalo, J., Kluck, M. (eds.): Evaluation of Cross-Language Information Retrieval Systems. In: Peters, C., Braschler, M., Gonzalo, J., Kluck, M. (eds.) CLEF 2001. LNCS, vol. 2406, pp. 3–4. Springer, Heidelberg (2002)
14. Dubois, D., Prade, H.: Semantic of quotient operators in fuzzy relational databases. Fuzzy Sets and Systems 78, 89–93 (1996)
15. Dubois, D., Fargier, H., Prade, H.: Beyond min aggregation in multicriteria decision (ordered) weighted min, discri-min, leximin. In: Yager, R., Kacprzyk, J. (eds.) The Ordered Weighted Averaging Operators, pp. 181–192. Kluwer Academic Publishers, Dordrecht (1997)
16. Moulin, H.: Axioms of Cooperative Decision-Making. Cambridge University Press, Cambridge (1988)
17. Dubois, D., Prade, H.: On different ways of ordering conjoint evaluations. In: Proc. of the 25th Linz seminar on Fuzzy Set Theory, Linz, Austria, pp. 42–46 (2004)
18. Boughanem, M., Dkaki, T., Mothe, J., Soule-Dupuy, C.: Mercure at TREC-7. In: Proc. of TREC-7. pp. 135–141 (1998)
19. Robertson, S.E., Walker, S.: Okapi-keenbow at TREC-8. In: Proc. 8th Text Retrieval Conf. TREC-8, pp. 60–67 (1999)
20. Porter, M.: An algorithm for suffix stripping. Program 14, 130–137 (1980)

A Qualitative Bipolar Argumentative View of Trust

Henri Prade

Institut de Recherche en Informatique de Toulouse (IRIT-CNRS)
Université de Toulouse, 118 route de Narbonne
31062 Toulouse Cedex 9, France
prade@irit.fr

Abstract. The paper views trust as a matter of levels ranging from full trust to full distrust on a finite scale. The level of trust of an agent w. r. t. an information source or another agent may not be precisely assessed due to the lack of information. Assessing a level of trust is viewed as a decision problem, which is handled in an argumentative manner. The interest of an argumentation approach is to be able to articulate reasons for supporting trust or distrust. Moreover, the updating trust process takes advantage of the bipolar nature of the representation, and is based on information fusion methods that are able to handle conflicts. The integration of these different features provides a novel view of trust evaluation.

Keywords: Trust; distrust; reputation; argumentation; bipolar information; classification.

1 Introduction

Trust evaluation has become an important issue in computer sciences in different distributed artificial intelligence areas such as Semantic Web (Berners-Lee et al., 2001; Shadbolt et al., 2006), and Multiple Agent Systems (Ramchurn et al., 2004), for seeking to minimize the uncertainty in interactions, in particular for e-commerce applications and security issues (Kagal et al. 2001). A rapidly increasing literature with a variety of representation settings, emphasizing different aspects of trust modeling and management, has been developing in the past five years. See (Sabater and Sierra, 2005) for an introductory survey of this literature in computer sciences.

Castelfranchi and Falcone (1998; 2001) in their cognitive approach to trust modeling advocate that 'only agents with goals and beliefs can trust'. Trust is generally viewed as a mental attitude towards another agent, and is also a matter of deciding to rely or not on some other agent for some particular purpose. Trust is based on the evaluation of past behavior (and possibly on what can be expected).

However, one can distinguish between different types of trust. An agent A may trust B, either i) as a source of information (B is well-informed and does not lie); or ii) for its judgments (the diagnosis, the decisions made by B are generally good); or iii) for its engagements (when B promises to do something, it tries to do it). Depending on which trust bears, the contents of the arguments relevant for trust evaluation will be different. Note also that one may also trust a particular piece of information rather than an information source when the information is asserted by many sources and can be

H. Prade and V.S. Subrahmanian (Eds.): SUM 2007, LNAI 4772, pp. 268–276, 2007.

checked, or trust a particular judgment rather than an agent, independently from its quality of judge, if the judgment is convincingly explained (using correct inference patterns, and trustable pieces of information in the explanation).

There is still a need for more advanced models of trust that go beyond the dynamic assessment of numbers in a numerical scale, and where the reasons of the assessment of a particular level of trust can be laid bare. The paper proposes a qualitative bipolar argumentative modeling of trust. The approach is qualitative since only a finite number of levels is assumed in the trust scale. It is bipolar since trust and distrust can be independently assessed, and trust evaluation may remain imprecise when information is insufficient (Dubois and Prade, 2006). It is argumentative since trust assessment is the result of a decision process, based on arguments in favor or against a classification of the agent or the source to be evaluated, at a particular trust level.

The paper is organized in the following way. Section 2 discusses the representation of trust evaluations using a bipolar univariate scale. Section 3 views trust evaluation as a diagnosis or classification problem, which is handled in Section 4 in an argumentative manner. Section 5 is devoted to a discussion of the updating mechanism for trust when new information becomes available. Section 6 discusses the relations and the differences of the approach with respect to related works.

2 Representing Trust Evaluation

Trust may be just binary, when an agent has to decide if it will trust or not an information source, or another agent for a particular purpose. However, trust may also be graded (rather than binary), if one needs to assess to what extent an agent or a source is trustable, and what can be expected from the agent or the source.

When classifying agents or sources according to their "trustability", a scale with discrete levels is generally enough (except in case where precise statistics are available about the times when the information source was wrong). In the following, we use a bipolar univariate scale, named 'trust scale', of the form

$$S = \{-n, ..., -2, -1, 0, +1, +2, ..., +n\},$$

where $+n$ stands for 'full trust', $-n$ stands for 'full distrust', 0 is neutral (no particular trust or distrust), $-n, ..., -2, -1$ are levels that correspond to "negative trust", while $+1, +2, ..., +n$ are levels of "positive trust". Note that any level $-k$ (with $k > 0$) of negative trust can be turned into a level $+k$ of (positive) *distrust*, while a positive level of trust $+k$ (with $k > 0$) might be viewed as a negative level $-k$ of distrust.

Trust with respect to a source or an agent may be unknown, ill known, or roughly known. In that respect, a particular trust evaluation will be represented in the following as an interval in the scale S, ranging from 'full distrust' $(-n)$ to 'full trust' $(+n)$. Such an interval will be denoted $[t-, t_+]$, where $t- \in S$ and $t_+ \in S$ with the following intended meaning the ill known trust τ is not larger than t_+ ($\tau \leq t_+$) and not smaller than $t-$ ($t- \leq \tau$). Clearly, $t-$ and t_+ are not in general defined from each other, due to incomplete information. The quantity $-t-$ (resp. t_+) may be, somewhat abusively, called "level of distrust" (resp. "level of trust").

Thus, $[t-, t_+] = [+n, +n]$ and $[t-, t_+] = [-n, -n]$ correspond respectively to 'full trust' and to 'full distrust', while $[t-, t_+] = [-n, +n]$ expresses a state of total ignorance about the value of trust τ. This state of total ignorance is not to be confused with 'neutral' that is encoded by [t-, t+] = [0, 0]! More generally, when t-> 0, the trust τ is positive, even if it is imprecisely assessed, while when t+ < 0, the trust τ is negative and thus corresponds to a clear state of distrust. When t- < 0 and t+ > 0, the situation remains ambiguous in the sense that it is not known if the trust τ is positive or negative.

Note that an obvious *consistency* condition should hold between "trust" and "distrust" (using the abusive vocabulary), namely

$$t- \leq t+.$$

In other words, in case one would have t- > t+, it would mean an inconsistent state of information about the actual level of trust.

In this setting, *reputation* will be naturally defined as what is commonly known of the way *other* agents (dis)trust the considered agent/source. Thus reputation Rep(o) of an object o (source or adgent) is represented by a set of intervals of the form

$$\text{Rep}(o) = \{[t-(a_{o(1)}), t+(a_{o(1)})], \ldots, [t-(a_{o(r)}), t+(a_{o(r)})]\},$$

corresponding to r (potentially imprecise) evaluations of the trust in o according to the agents (or sources) $a_{o(j)}$'s. This information can be summarized into a unique interval R(o) by fusing the different intervals in Rep(o), into

- R(o) = $\cap_j [t-(a_{o(j)}), t+(a_{o(i)})]$ provided that R(o) ≠ ∅,

or into

- R(o) = $\cup_j [t-(a_{o(j)}), t+(a_{o(i)})]$ in case of inconsistency.

However, the intersection fusion mode presupposes that the agents $a_{o(j)}$ have partial, but consistent evaluations of the trust in o and are all considered as perfectly reliable. The case where the agents are unequally reliable will be discussed later. In case of inconsistency, the disjunctive fusion is very cautious by taking all the points of view into account, but may lead to a very imprecise evaluation of the reputation.

Lastly, it has been often pointed out that trust may be topic-dependent. A source of information may be reliable on some particular topic and less reliable on some other topic. In such a case, the trust in o, for topic t, of agent or source a, will be denoted $\tau_{(a, t)}(o)$, which will be represented by an interval indexed by t and a.

3 Evaluating Trust: A Diagnostic Point of View

An agent a may evaluate its trust into an object o (a source or another agent) on the basis of two types of information: on the one hand the observed behavior of o, and on the other hand the reputation of o according to the other agents.

Reputation information may be viewed as an input information used by agent a for revising or updating its own trust evaluation based on its perception (this will be the topic of Section 5). Reputation information could also contribute to provide direct arguments in favor or against some trust evaluation, using pieces of knowledge such as "if t-> ρ then o should have a high reputation (all the higher as ρ is high)", or "if if t+ < σ then o should have a poor reputation (all the poorer as σ is small)". However, the only arguments that we shall consider in the paper, for the sake of simplicity, are the ones that can be built from the known behavior of o, and from the knowledge of the expected behavior of an object having its trust level in some area (the argumentation aspect will be discussed in the next section).

Indeed trust evaluation requires having some observed or reported behavior (leaving reputation aside), and the definition of the trust categories in terms of possible behaviors. Let $F(o)$ be the base of behavioral facts regarding o. We assume that $F(o)$ only contains two types of literals, the g_i's pertaining to good points, and the b_j's referring to bad points. The base $F(o)$ is supposed to be given here, but may be itself the result of an inference or learning process. So $F(o)$, which is assumed to be consistent, may include literals of the form g_i, $\neg g_k$, b_j, or $\neg b_h$. In other words, $F(o)$ may report that good points are present (g_i), or are not present ($\neg g_k$), in the behavior of o, and the same for the bad points (b_j, or $\neg b_h$). Moreover, a complete preorder rank-orders the good points (some are more important or better than others), and rank-orders the bad points as well (some are worse than others).

Let K be the knowledge base made of if then rules relating levels of trust to agent/source behaviors. This means that K contains rules expressing that t- is all the higher as no important bad points, or important good points are reported in the behavior of o, and rules expressing that t_+ is all the smaller as no important good points, or important bad points are reported. For instance, one may have rules such that "if it is fully trustable (t-$\geq + n$), what it says is always true" (for a source), or "if it is fully unreliable ($t_+ \leq - n$), there are situations where it did not do at all what he promised"

More precisely, the rules are of one of the forms:

"if t-$\geq \rho$ (where $\rho \leq 0$) then $\neg b_h$" (b_h is all the less bad as ρ is high);
"if t-$\geq \rho$ (where $\rho > 0$) then g_i" (g_i is all the better as ρ is high);
"if $t_+ \leq \sigma$ (where $\sigma \geq 0$) then $\neg g_k$" (g_k is all the less good as σ is small);
"if $t_+ \leq \sigma$ (where $\sigma < 0$) then b_j" (b_j is all the worse as σ is small).

Generally speaking, the idea is that a very trustable source provides very good results, that a reasonably trustable source provides reasonably good results, that a source that is at least moderately trustable does not provide bad results and so on.

Evaluating the trust in o from $F(o)$ and K, amounts to find ρ maximal and σ minimal such as t-$\geq \rho$ and $t_+ \leq \sigma$ are consistent, i.e., such that $\rho \leq \sigma$, and such that

$$t\text{-}\geq \rho, \; t_+ \leq \sigma, \; K \; \vert - F(o)$$

or the weaker requirement

t-$\geq \rho$, $t_+ \leq \sigma$, K and $F(o)$ are consistent together.

These correspond to the logical formulations of a model-based, and consistency-based diagnosis (or classification) respectively, viewing $F(o)$ as the effects and t-$\geq \rho$ and $t_+ \leq \sigma$ as "the causes"; see (Le Berre and Sabbadin, 1997) for the more general case when K may be pervaded with uncertainty, and $F(o)$ is prioritized. It is very close to a decision problem (where a candidate decision would replace t-$\geq \rho$ and $t_+ \leq \sigma$, K would stand for the knowledge about the world, and $F(o)$ for a set of goals.

It is also worth noticing that depending on K and $F(o)$, the result may remain imprecise, namely such that $\rho < \sigma$.

4 Argumentation-Based Evaluation

Then trust evaluation may be easily turned into an argumentation-based evaluation. Generally speaking, an argument in favor of a claim c is a minimal consistent subset of formulas S that logically entail c. In the following, the arguments used have rather an abductive format. Namely, an argument in favor of a trust evaluation te will be of the form $S, te \mid- f$, where f is an observed behavioral fact (where $\mid-$ denotes a consequence relation). There are two kinds of arguments in favor of trusting o to some level, i. e., having $t- \geq \rho$ for some ρ. Namely, the arguments of the form

$$\text{if } t- \geq \rho \text{ then } \neg b_h, t- \geq \rho \mid- \neg b_h \quad \text{where } \neg b_h \in F(o)$$

pointing out that a bad point is avoided and those of the form

$$\text{if } t- \geq \rho \text{ then } g_i, t- \geq \rho \mid- g_i \quad \text{where } g_i \in F(o)$$

pointing out that a good point is reached. The argument is all the stronger as a better point is reached. It tends to increase ρ, since the high values of ρ should be associated by the rules in K with stronger good points. Similarly, there are two kinds of arguments against trusting o to some level, i. e., having $t_+ \leq \sigma$ for some σ. Namely those pointing out that a good point is not reached or that a bad point is satisfied, i. e. arguments of the form

$$\text{if } t_+ \leq \sigma \text{ then } \neg g_k, t_+ \leq \sigma \mid- \neg g_k \quad \text{where } \neg g_k \in F(o);$$
$$\text{if } t_+ \leq \sigma \text{ then } b_j, t_+ \leq \sigma \mid- b_j \text{ where } b_j \in F(o).$$

Arguments against trusting o to some level, i. e., having $t_+ \leq \sigma$ for some σ, tend to decrease σ, since the small values of σ should be associated by the rules in K with stronger bad points.

The above arguments have an abductive form, and correspond to the types of arguments introduced in (Amgoud and Prade, 2006) in favor, or against a potential decision. They also have weak counterparts, corresponding to consistency-based diagnosis, where instead of concluding on a fact f (i. e., $\mid- $ f), one would only conclude to the consistency with f (i. e., $\mid\!\!\not- \neg$f).

The strongest arguments in favor, and against trusting o provide the highest ρ, say $\rho(o)$, and the smallest σ, say $\sigma(o)$. When $\rho(o) \leq \sigma(o)$, we have obtained a trust evaluation under the form of a regular interval $[\rho(o), \sigma(o)]$. Naturally it may happen in practice that $\rho(o) > \sigma(o)$. In such a case, if one wants to be cautious, it seems natural to give priority to $\sigma(o)$ that reflects the negative part of the information (pessimism), and to decrease the value of $\rho(o)$ to $\rho*(o) = \sigma(o)$. This may be also a principle for revising trust information at the light of reputation information, as we are going to see.

5 Revising Trust

Let $[\rho^{TE}(o), \sigma^{TE}(o)]$ be the interval obtained by agent a at the end of the trust evaluation process. Assume that another interval $[\rho^R(o), \sigma^R(o)]$ encodes the result of the reputation assessment (after the fusion step), as described at the end of Section 2.

Then there are basically two possible situations (the two intervals are consistent or not), and several possible attitudes for agent a (be pessimistic, give priority to its own evaluation, ...).

If the two intervals are consistent, one may perform the intersection and obtain the more accurate interval $[\max(\rho^{TE}(o), \rho^{R}(o)), \min(\sigma^{TE}(o), \sigma^{R}(o))]$. In case of inconsistency, being pessimistic, one may prefer the most negative information, namely $[\min(\rho^{TE}(o), \rho^{R}(o)), \min(\sigma^{TE}(o), \sigma^{R}(o))]$. However, in case of inconsistency, agent a may also privilege its own judgment, and keep its own evaluation $[\rho^{TE}(o), \sigma^{TE}(o)]$, even if it is more positive.

These different fusion modes can be generalized to fuzzy evaluations. The fuzzy evaluations may be naturally produced through discounting operations. First, when synthesizing the reputation information $Rep(o) = \{[t\text{-}(a_{o(1)}), t_{+}(a_{o(1)})], ..., [t\text{-}(a_{o(r)}), t_{+}(a_{o(r)})]\}$ in Section 2, by taking the intersection of the intervals (in case of consistency), or the union (in case of inconsistency), the equal reliability of the other agents has been assumed. Let π^{j} denote the characteristic function of the interval $[t\text{-}(a_{o(j)}), t_{+}(a_{o(j)})]$, and let $\theta_{j} \in [0, 1]$ be the reliability level of this information. Assuming the normalization condition $\max_{j} \theta_{j} = 1$, intersection and union are generalized by

$$\pi^{R(o)} = \min_{j} \max(1 - \theta_{j}, \pi^{j}) \quad \text{(intersection)}$$

and by

$$\pi^{R(o)} = \max_{j} \min(\theta_{j}, \pi^{j}) \quad \text{(union)}$$

When all the other agents have equal reliability, i. e., for all i, $\theta_{j} = 1$, we recover the standard intersection and union, as expected, while if the reliability is 0, the information is ignored.

Let π^{TE} be the characteristic function of the interval $[\rho^{TE}(o), \sigma^{TE}(o)]$. If agent a chooses to give priority to its own evaluation, considering the reputation information only if it is consistent, it will use consistency-driven prioritized fusion operators (Dubois, Prade, Yager, 1999) for computing the resulting evaluation, here denoted $\pi^{TE+R(o)}$:

$$\pi^{TE+R(o)} = \min(\pi^{TE}, \max(1 - cons(\pi^{TE}, \pi^{R(o)}), \pi^{R(o)}) \quad \text{(intersection)}$$
$$\pi^{TE+R(o)} = \max(\pi^{TE}, \min(cons(\pi^{TE}, \pi^{R(o)}), \pi^{R(o)}) \quad \text{(union)}$$

where the consistency of π^{TE} and $\pi^{R(o)}$ is evaluated as

$$cons(\pi^{TE}, \pi^{R(o)}) = \max_{t} \min(\pi^{TE}(t), \pi^{R(o)}(t)).$$

Note that when $cons(\pi^{TE}, \pi^{R(o)}) = 1$, one recovers the standard intersection and union, while when $cons(\pi^{TE}, \pi^{R(o)}) = 0$, the information π^{TE} is kept unaltered.

Besides, the pessimistic attitude that privileges the smallest evaluation, would correspond to perform the minimum operation, now extended to general possibility distributions, rather than to intervals. See (Dubois and Prade, 1980) for the definition.

Lastly, another type of revision or updating can take place when the information in $F(o)$ are expanded, modified, or challenged due to the arrival of new pieces of information, leading to revise $[\rho^{TE}(o), \sigma^{TE}(o)]$ in a way or another (making it more precise, or more imprecise, and possibly moving the interval inside S).

6 Related Works

Many models of trust have been already proposed (Sabater and Sierra, 2005). Trust may be a binary notion (an agent trusts or does not trust another agent), a graded notion, generally in a numerical way, or may be even fuzzily graded. There are only a few works that distinguish between trust and distrust, starting with (McKnight and Chervany, 2001). De Cock and Pinheiro da Silva (2006) use both a grade of trust μ and an independent grade of distrust ν. Their model refer to the setting of Atanassov (1986)'s intuitionistic fuzzy sets, where the sum of the degree of membership and the degree of non-membership to an intuitionistic fuzzy set of an element is always less or equal to 1. Indeed they assume $\mu + \nu \leq 1$, with $\mu \in [0, 1]$ and $\nu \in [0, 1]$. However, the pair (μ, ν), can be turned into an interval information $[\mu, 1 - \nu]$ (e.g. Dubois et al., 2005). This interval is somewhat similar to the one used in Section 2 (on another scale!); however, our interval is more the imprecise evaluation of a degree of trust than a pair of independent evaluations propagated separately. Guha et al., (2004) also distinguish between trust and distrust, but aggregate them into one value.

Since human opinions about others are vague, some authors (e. g., Carbo et al., 2003; 2004) value reputation by means of fuzzy terms. Here our fuzzy view of reputation is rather the result of an aggregation process of different opinions having different levels of reliability. Moreover our representation framework could be extended by modeling our evaluation of trust by means of fuzzy intervals extending interval $[t-, t_+]$ by means of membership functions expressing for instance that trust is "rather positive even if it might be slightly negative".

Stranders (2006) seems to be the first to use a form of argumentation for trust evaluation viewed as a decision process, taking inspiration from (Amgoud and Prade, 2004), using fuzzy rules also. Our proposal, which is simpler rather use the different forms of arguments presented in (Amgoud and Prade, 2006).

Other works propose Bayesian network-based trust models (Wang and Vassileva, 2004; Melaye and Demazeau, 2005; Melaye et al., 2006) for modeling social multi-agent processes, where dynamic aspects are handled by a Bayesian Kalman filter. Although, we have indicated some basic mechanisms leading to revision of trust values, the paper has mainly focused on trust evaluation rather than trust dynamics in a multiple-agent world. This latter aspect is left for further research in our approach.

7 Concluding Remarks

The paper has outlined a new approach for trust evaluation. The evaluation is qualitative, thanks to the use of a discrete scale and of qualitative fusion modes. It is bipolar in distinguishing positive and negative features. It leaves room for an imprecise evaluation, when the information that would be necessary for a more precise assessment is missing, or when the opinions of the other agents are conflicting and lead to an inconsistent reputation assessment. The approach accommodates inconsistency by using appropriate fusion modes. Lastly, the evaluation relies on the use of arguments, which make the result of a trust evaluation easier to explain.

Besides, it is worth noticing that the problem of trust evaluation presents some similarities with the problem of experts' calibration and pooling, which has been considered in different uncertainty settings (Cooke, 1991; Sandri et al., 1995). This is a topic for further investigation.

References

Amgoud, L., Prade, H.: Using arguments for making decisions: A possibilistic logic approach. In: Proc. 20th Conf. of Uncertainty in Artificial Inelligence (UAI'04), Banff, Canada, July 7-11, 2004, pp. 7-11. AUAI Press (2004)

Amgoud, L., Prade, H.: Explaining qualitative decision under uncertainty by argumentation. In: Proc. 21st National Conference on Artificial Intelligence, July 16-20, 2006, pp. 219-224. AAAI Press, Boston, Massachusetts, USA (2006)

Atanassov, K.T.: Intuitionistic fuzzy sets. Fuzzy Sets and Systems 20, 87–96 (1986)

Ben-Naim, J., Weydert, E.: Information merging with trust. Extended abstract.In: Workshop on Logics and Collective Decision making (LCD'07), Lille, France (March 13-14, 2007)

Berners-Lee, T., Hendler, J., Lassila, O.: The Semantic Web. A new form of Web content that is meaningful to computers will unleash a revolution of new possibilities. Scientific American (May 2001)

Carbó Rubiera, J.I., Molina, J.M., Dávila Muro, J.: Trust management through fuzzy reputation. Int. J. Cooperative Inf. Syst. 12(1), 135–155 (2003)

Carbó Rubiera, J.I., García, J., Molina, J.M.: Subjective trust inferred by Kalman filtering vs. a fuzzy reputation. In: Wang, S., Tanaka, K., Zhou, S., Ling, T.-W., Guan, J., Yang, D.-q., Grandi, F., Mangina, E.E., Song, I.-Y., Mayr, H.C. (eds.) Conceptual Modeling for Advanced Application Domains. LNCS, vol. 3289, pp. 496–505. Springer, Heidelberg (2004)

Castelfranchi, C., Falcone, R.: Principles of trust for MAS: Cognitive anatomy, social importance, and quantification. In: Demazeau, Y. (ed.) ICMAS 1998, Paris, France, July 3-7, 1998, pp. 72–79. IEEE Computer Society Press, Los Alamitos (1998)

Castelfranchi, C., Falcone, R.: Social trust: A cognitive approach. In: Castelfranchi, C., Tan, Y. (eds.) Trust and Deception in Virtual Societies, pp. 55–90. Kluwer Acad. Publ., Dordrecht (2001)

Castelfranchi, C., Falcone, R., Pezzulo, G.: Trust in information sources as a source for trust: a fuzzy approach. In: AAMAS 2003, Melbourne, Australia, pp. 89–96. ACM, New York (2003)

Cooke, R.: Experts in Uncertainty. Oxford University Press, Oxford (1991)

De Cock, M., da Silva, P.P.: A many valued representation and propagation of trust and distrust. In: Bloch, I., Petrosino, A., Tettamanzi, A.G.B. (eds.) WILF 2005. LNCS (LNAI), vol. 3849, pp. 114–120. Springer, Heidelberg (2006)

Dubois, D., Gottwald, S., Hajek, P., Kacprzyk, J., Prade, H.: Terminological difficulties in fuzzy set theory - The case of Intuitionistic Fuzzy Sets. Fuzzy Sets and Systems 156, 485–491 (2005)

Dubois, D., Prade, H.: Fuzzy Sets & Systems: Theory and Applications. Academic Press, New York (1980)

Dubois, D., Prade, H.: Bipolar representations in reasoning, knowledge extraction and decision. In: Greco, S., Hata, Y., Hirano, S., Inuiguchi, M., Miyamoto, S., Nguyen, H.S., Słowiński, R. (eds.) RSCTC 2006. LNCS (LNAI), vol. 4259, pp. 15–26. Springer, Heidelberg (2006)

Dubois, D., Prade, H., Yager, R.R.: Merging fuzzy information. In: Bezdek, J., Dubois, D., Prade, H. (eds.) Fuzzy Sets in Approximate Reasoning and Information Systems. The Handbooks of Fuzzy Sets Series, pp. 335–401. Kluwer, Boston, Mass (1999)

Guha, R., Kumar, R., Raghavan, P., Tomkins, A.: Propagation of trust and distrust. In: Proc. International World Wide Web Conference (WWW2004), pp. 403–412 (2004)

Kagal, L., Cost, S., Finin, T., Peng, Y.: A framework for distributed trust management. In: Proc. 2nd Workshop on Norms and Institutions in MAS, at the 5th Inter. Conf. on Autonomous Agents, Montreal, May 28-June1 (2001)

Le Berre, D., Sabbadin, R.: Decision-theoretic diagnosis and repair: representational and computational issues. In: Proc. 8th Inter. Workshop on Principles of Diagnosis (DX'97), Le Mont Saint-Michel, France, September 14-18, 1997, pp. 141–145 (1997)

McKnight, D.H., Chervany, N.L.: Trust and distrust definitions: One bite at a time. In: Falcone, R., Singh, M., Tan, Y.-H. (eds.) Trust in Cyber-societies. LNCS (LNAI), vol. 2246, pp. 27–54. Springer, Heidelberg (2001)

Melaye, D., Demazeau, Y.: Bayesian dynamic trust model. In: Pěchouček, M., Petta, P., Varga, L.Z. (eds.) CEEMAS 2005. LNCS (LNAI), vol. 3690, pp. 480–489. Springer, Heidelberg (2005)

Melaye, D., Demazeau, Y., Bouron, T.: Which adequate trust model for trust networks? In: Maglogiannis, I., Karpouzis, K., Bramer, M. (eds.) Artificial Intelligence Applications and Innovations, 3rd IFIP Conference on Artificial Intelligence Applications and Innovations (AIAI 2006), Athens, Greece. IFIP 204, June 7-9, 2006, pp. 236–244. Springer, Heidelberg (2006)

Ramchurn, S.D., Huynh, D., Jennings, N.R.: Trust in multi-agent systems. The Knowledge Engineering Review 19, 1–25 (2004)

Sabater, J., Sierra, C.: Review on computational trust and reputation models. Artif. Intell. Rev. 24(1), 33–60 (2005)

Sandri, S., Dubois, D., Kalfsbeek, H.W.: Elicitation, assessment and pooling of expert judgements using possibility theory. IEEE Trans. on Fuzzy Systems 3, 313–335 (1995)

Shadbolt, N., Berners-Lee, T., Hall, W.: The semantic web revisited. IEEE Intelligent Systems 21(3), 96–101 (2006)

Stranders, R.: Argumentation Based Decision Making for Trust in Multi-Agent Systems. Master's Thesis in Computer Science, Delft University of Technology, p. 138 (June 2006)

Wang, Y., Vassileva, J.: Bayesian Network Trust Model in Peer-to-Peer Networks. In: Moro, G., Sartori, C., Singh, M.P. (eds.) AP2PC 2003. LNCS (LNAI), vol. 2872, pp. 23–34. Springer, Heidelberg (2004)

Author Index

Lecture Notes in Artificial Intelligence (LNAI)

Vol. 4571: P. Perner (Ed.), Machine Learning and Data Mining in Pattern Recognition. XIV, 913 pages. 2007.

Vol. 4570: H.G. Okuno, M. Ali (Eds.), New Trends in Applied Artificial Intelligence. XXI, 1194 pages. 2007.

Vol. 4565: D.D. Schmorrow, L.M. Reeves (Eds.), Foundations of Augmented Cognition. XIX, 450 pages. 2007.

Vol. 4562: D. Harris (Ed.), Engineering Psychology and Cognitive Ergonomics. XXIII, 879 pages. 2007.

Vol. 4548: N. Olivetti (Ed.), Automated Reasoning with Analytic Tableaux and Related Methods. X, 245 pages. 2007.

Vol. 4539: N.H. Bshouty, C. Gentile (Eds.), Learning Theory. XII, 634 pages. 2007.

Vol. 4529: P. Melin, O. Castillo, L.T. Aguilar, J. Kacprzyk, W. Pedrycz (Eds.), Foundations of Fuzzy Logic and Soft Computing. XIX, 830 pages. 2007.

Vol. 4520: M.V. Butz, O. Sigaud, G. Pezzulo, G. Baldassarre (Eds.), Anticipatory Behavior in Adaptive Learning Systems. X, 379 pages. 2007.

Vol. 4511: C. Conati, K. McCoy, G. Paliouras (Eds.), User Modeling 2007. XVI, 487 pages. 2007.

Vol. 4509: Z. Kobti, D. Wu (Eds.), Advances in Artificial Intelligence. XII, 552 pages. 2007.

Vol. 4496: N.T. Nguyen, A. Grzech, R.J. Howlett, L.C. Jain (Eds.), Agent and Multi-Agent Systems: Technologies and Applications. XXI, 1046 pages. 2007.

Vol. 4483: C. Baral, G. Brewka, J. Schlipf (Eds.), Logic Programming and Nonmonotonic Reasoning. IX, 327 pages. 2007.

Vol. 4482: A. An, J. Stefanowski, S. Ramanna, C.J. Butz, W. Pedrycz, G. Wang (Eds.), Rough Sets, Fuzzy Sets, Data Mining and Granular Computing. XIV, 585 pages. 2007.

Vol. 4481: J. Yao, P. Lingras, W.-Z. Wu, M. Szczuka, N.J. Cercone, D. Ślęzak (Eds.), Rough Sets and Knowledge Technology. XIV, 576 pages. 2007.

Vol. 4476: V. Gorodetsky, C. Zhang, V.A. Skormin, L. Cao (Eds.), Autonomous Intelligent Systems: Multi-Agents and Data Mining. XIII, 323 pages. 2007.

Vol. 4457: G.M.P. O'Hare, A. Ricci, M.J. O'Grady, O. Dikenelli (Eds.), Engineering Societies in the Agents World VII. XI, 401 pages. 2007.

Vol. 4456: Y. Wang, Y.-m. Cheung, H. Liu (Eds.), Computational Intelligence and Security. XXIII, 1118 pages. 2007.

Vol. 4455: S. Muggleton, R. Otero, A. Tamaddoni-Nezhad (Eds.), Inductive Logic Programming. XII, 456 pages. 2007.

Vol. 4452: M. Fasli, O. Shehory (Eds.), Agent-Mediated Electronic Commerce. VIII, 249 pages. 2007.

Vol. 4451: T.S. Huang, A. Nijholt, M. Pantic, A. Pentland (Eds.), Artifical Intelligence for Human Computing. XVI, 359 pages. 2007.

Vol. 4441: C. Müller (Ed.), Speaker Classification. X, 309 pages. 2007.

Vol. 4438: L. Maicher, A. Sigel, L.M. Garshol (Eds.), Leveraging the Semantics of Topic Maps. X, 257 pages. 2007.

Vol. 4434: G. Lakemeyer, E. Sklar, D.G. Sorrenti, T. Takahashi (Eds.), RoboCup 2006: Robot Soccer World Cup X. XIII, 566 pages. 2007.

Vol. 4429: R. Lu, J.H. Siekmann, C. Ullrich (Eds.), Cognitive Systems. X, 161 pages. 2007.

Vol. 4428: S. Edelkamp, A. Lomuscio (Eds.), Model Checking and Artificial Intelligence. IX, 185 pages. 2007.

Vol. 4426: Z.-H. Zhou, H. Li, Q. Yang (Eds.), Advances in Knowledge Discovery and Data Mining. XXV, 1161 pages. 2007.

Vol. 4411: R.H. Bordini, M. Dastani, J. Dix, A.E.F. Seghrouchni (Eds.), Programming Multi-Agent Systems. XIV, 249 pages. 2007.

Vol. 4410: A. Branco (Ed.), Anaphora: Analysis, Algorithms and Applications. X, 191 pages. 2007.

Vol. 4399: T. Kovacs, X. Llorà, K. Takadama, P.L. Lanzi, W. Stolzmann, S.W. Wilson (Eds.), Learning Classifier Systems. XII, 345 pages. 2007.

Vol. 4390: S.O. Kuznetsov, S. Schmidt (Eds.), Formal Concept Analysis. X, 329 pages. 2007.

Vol. 4389: D. Weyns, H. Van Dyke Parunak, F. Michel (Eds.), Environments for Multi-Agent Systems III. X, 273 pages. 2007.

Vol. 4386: P. Noriega, J. Vázquez-Salceda, G. Boella, O. Boissier, V. Dignum, N. Fornara, E. Matson (Eds.), Coordination, Organizations, Institutions, and Norms in Agent Systems II. XI, 373 pages. 2007.

Vol. 4384: T. Washio, K. Satoh, H. Takeda, A. Inokuchi (Eds.), New Frontiers in Artificial Intelligence. IX, 401 pages. 2007.

Vol. 4371: K. Inoue, K. Satoh, F. Toni (Eds.), Computational Logic in Multi-Agent Systems. X, 315 pages. 2007.

Vol. 4369: M. Umeda, A. Wolf, O. Bartenstein, U. Geske, D. Seipel, O. Takata (Eds.), Declarative Programming for Knowledge Management. X, 229 pages. 2006.

Vol. 4363: B.D. ten Cate, H.W. Zeevat (Eds.), Logic, Language, and Computation. XII, 281 pages. 2007.

Vol. 4343: C. Müller (Ed.), Speaker Classification I. X, 355 pages. 2007.

Vol. 4342: H. de Swart, E. Orłowska, G. Schmidt, M. Roubens (Eds.), Theory and Applications of Relational Structures as Knowledge Instruments II. X, 373 pages. 2006.

Vol. 4335: S.A. Brueckner, S. Hassas, M. Jelasity, D. Yamins (Eds.), Engineering Self-Organising Systems. XII, 212 pages. 2007.

Vol. 4334: B. Beckert, R. Hähnle, P.H. Schmitt (Eds.), Verification of Object-Oriented Software. XXIX, 658 pages. 2007.

Vol. 4333: U. Reimer, D. Karagiannis (Eds.), Practical Aspects of Knowledge Management. XII, 338 pages. 2006.

Vol. 4327: M. Baldoni, U. Endriss (Eds.), Declarative Agent Languages and Technologies IV. VIII, 257 pages. 2006.